CATCHING LIGHT

CATCHING LIGHT

Looking for God in the Movies

ROY M. ANKER

William B. Eerdmans Publishing Company
Grand Rapids, Michigan / Cambridge, U.K.

Wm. B. Eerdmans Publishing Co.
255 Jefferson Ave. S.E., Grand Rapids, Michigan 49503 /
P.O. Box 163, Cambridge CB3 9PU U.K.
www.eerdmans.com

Printed in the United States of America

09 08 07 06 05 04   7 6 5 4 3 2 1

Library of Congress Cataloging-in-Publication Data

ISBN 0-8028-2795-0

The author and publisher wish to thank the following sources for permission to reprint materal in this volume:

For Emily Dickinson's Poem #315, "He fumbles at your Soul," reprinted by permission of the publishers and the Trustees of Amherst College from THE POEMS OF EMILY DICKINSON, Thomas H. Johnson, ed., Cambridge, Mass.: The Belknap Press of Harvard University Press, Copyright © 1951, 1955, 1979, 1983 by the President and Fellows of Harvard College.

For excerpts from Robert Frost's poem "Birches," in THE POETRY OF ROBERT FROST, ed. Edward Connery Lathem (New York: Holt, 1969). Reprinted by permission.

For excerpts from "The Dry Salvages" in FOUR QUARTETS, copyright 1941 by T. S. Eliot and renewed 1969 by Esme Valerie Eliot, reprinted by permission of Harcourt, Inc., and Faber and Faber Ltd.

For Elizabeth, David, and Christina,
the best of all possible children

Contents

Preface

This book came in stages.

The first stage took place, start to finish, on New Year's Day 1978. My then four-year-old daughter, Elizabeth, her friend Michelle, and I ventured forty-five miles on a bitterly cold Iowa day to take in a matinee of the newly released movie *Superman*. We first waited outside the theater and then waited some more inside an unheated lobby before someone remembered to turn up the heat. Our big day out was not going well, but it seemed to be going markedly less well for a young mother waiting with the many in the lobby. In her late twenties, she seemed harried, downcast, and alone — except for her three kids, two boys and a girl, between the ages of two and five. She was, for who knows what reasons, conspicuously unhappy. Finally the doors opened, and we all slid into the dark to take in the story of Kal-el/Clark Kent/Superman.

Two hours later, we all poured out into the gathering dusk, and there again was the hapless mother; but now she was glowing, exultant, and ever so kind to her children. What happened in that dark theater to effect this? What mood-altering thing happened in that story, or in the manner of its telling, for it was decidedly not a new story? Or did she perhaps simply have a good nap while the kids flew along with Supe? I wanted to ask her, but I decided not to risk breaking the spell. In any case, the itch to know did not go away.

This book started in earnest in 1988, when I began teaching at Calvin College and had to come up with a course for Calvin's January Interim, a three-week, one-course undertaking meant to pique student interest while indulging professors' private passions. So amid the dark, cold, and snow of a Michigan winter, flocks of Calvinist youths, who had been forbidden to watch movies just a few years before, were viewing films by Ingmar Bergman, a Swedish Lutheran of an even darker sentiment, as well as, among others, Steven Spielberg, George Lucas, Sidney Lumet, Woody Allen, Francis Ford Coppola, and even one of their own, Paul Schrader. We saw roughly a movie a day for fifteen days, screening them in the morning and dissecting them, *ad infinitum et nauseam,* in the afternoon. Those many stalwart students helped immeasurably in shaping this book.

That course, then and now called "Finding God in the Movies," has changed shape and substance over the years as filmmakers dropped from the list and others took their place, such as Kieslowski, Duvall, Salles, and Majidi. Always, though, students have been generous with their insights, thoughtfulness, and patience, especially when given the task of reading early drafts of some of the chapters of this book.

The same can be said for those wonderful folks in CALL (Calvin Academy of Lifelong Learning), who viewed films and then generously shared their reactions, life experience, and abundant wisdom. And that is also true of the many in assorted church groups who over the years have freely contributed their enthusiasm and fresh thought.

Colleagues and friends have helped in more ways than I can count or even know. Carl Plantinga and Joan Zwagerman Curbow have read portions of the manuscript; their comments and encouragement have been enormously helpful. And, of course, my ever-gracious editor, Reinder Van Til, has saved the book from much tiresomeness and more than a few inanities.

I am daily grateful to find myself situated among wonderful colleagues in the Calvin College English Department, a place of perpetual kindness, thoughtful support, and high spirits. Calvin College has over the years generously supported the growth of film study with equipment and resources, and has — in the form of Calvin Research Fellowships — supported this project with the best gift of all, time to do the work.

And I wish to thank my wife, Ellen, the best of critics and a proofreader par excellence, who scrupulously read the whole thing and, for one protracted span of time, patiently suffered her spouse's many long solitary mornings in the dark with Juliette Binoche. Last, I want to thank our three splendid children, who just about daily inspired the book, and for whom it was written.

Introduction

"Catching light" is what film does, of course. In the physical chemistry of cinema, light passes through the lens, aperture, and shutter to expose rolling film stock. Light reflected from what lies in front of the lens enters the camera to expose the moving negative, twenty-four frames per second, from which comes the final print that snakes its way through motion picture projectors at the local cineplex. In the digital technology now emerging, photography begins not with film stock but with a photoelectric sensor that initiates the translation of the light into digital code that is eventually transposed to the film print (the 36-millimeter print is also now on its way out, about to be displaced by the digital video disk). No matter what the means are, though, the end result is the same: a prolonged array of visual images — many tens of thousands in a full-length motion picture — that "picture" what the world looks like and feels like as it moves along. Film stock catches light, and a filmic world takes shape and comes to life. If the movie is any good, viewers move as well, plopped in their seats though they be, and very often in more ways than they can comprehend or count.

Catching light is also very much what people wish for deep down. This is true in just about every area of living, whether in bothersome daily decisions of what clothes to buy or food to eat, or in the "really big" life reckonings about marriage and career, or, as this book discusses, in the even larger metaphysical explorations of the possibility of some sort of divine Light — usually called God — that is somehow engaged in human affairs. In any or all of these explorations, a little light helps, and the more the better. On this just about everyone, everywhere has agreed, though they do disagree, sometimes fiercely, about what comprises real or true light.

1

And the quest goes on, fervent and unceasing, no matter how wrong we may have been in the past. One wag has said that 98 percent of all the science ever done has been dead wrong. When scientists find new information that "displaces" previous truth, they do not talk about how wrong they were but about how they made a new discovery — and they keep on looking. Past error stops neither the search nor the elation at coming upon a new sliver of the answer to the puzzles of being alive.

One reason humankind has such high regard for light becomes clear when we look at the wonderful consequences of harnessing it. It happened first when cave dwellers tamed the source of light, fire itself, and by doing so made life fundamentally more congenial. A hostile natural world relented: in the light thrown by fire, darkness abated, warmth flowed, wild beasts retreated, people gathered, food cooked, and through signal fires people even knew where they were in the dark — and where others were. Since then, every civilization has labored to expand the benefits of the simple gift of light, even focusing it in lasers for surgery to improve sight itself. So common is the notion that light is good that almost everyone refers to new knowledge of any kind as shining new light in dark places. Even though human survival does not depend on generating its own light, having light "on call" so fundamentally enriches human life that we can hardly conceive of going without it. Put simply, in light the human creature flourishes, and so it seems reasonable for our species to venerate light.

Light does make a difference, if only because darkness, and all that it implies, is not appealing. Save perhaps for romance or crime or contemplation, people do not much take to the dark. And darkness in various modes is everywhere, though people, especially amid the frantic diversions of American culture, work hard to forget that. The worst of it is moral darkness: the entire living world partakes of this considerable darkness, either as victim or agent — and usually both. All living beings scramble to survive in a habitat that runs on enmity and competition. And the fearsome things that go bump in the night frolic around in broad daylight as well. In what seems a breathtaking perversion of the essential qualities of light, humanity has even managed to turn light into darkness in the creation and use of nuclear — and, more recently, laser — weapons. Whether through the agency of people or nature, calamity happens, constantly and randomly. The good die young, bad people prosper, and the rain falls on the just and the unjust.

It is no wonder, then, that people care profoundly about finding a

"dearer life," as Annie Dillard has described the great human thirst.[1]
And it's no wonder that people struggle for the bright light of day; nor is
it surprising that they tend to define the poles of their experience on
earth in opposing binary images of light and dark, as well as their close
cousins: warmth and cold, dawn and midnight, home fires and exile,
clarity and confusion, to name but a few. These kinds of oppositions have
always suggested the central experiential polarities of human experience.
What's good for people generally ends up identified with light, while images of darkness denote threats to security, health, and personal contentment. It is pretty clear that what the human species most wants is light
of some kind, and then more of the same — light and ever more light.
Over the millennia in the Western world, light has been the signal image
of felicity, and it seems to have lost none of its capacity to define and
speak to the human circumstance. Indeed, of all human symbols for
well-being, light is perhaps the most persistent, universal, and profound.

Light in the Movies

Obviously, cinema also depends on light — in several ways. In filmmaking, catching light is the means of making a story. In theaters, the
finished product depends on physical light to project, or "picture," its
filmic world up onto the screen. The medium's greatest significance and
promise lies in its capacity to "shed light" on the world it portrays, to see
that world for what it is, illumining its perils, sorrows, and delights —
and how all these tangle together. Cinema seems uniquely endowed to
do this: it has long been a wonderfully synergistic medium. Visually, the
medium seems almost omnipresent, a transcendent eye able to go anywhere in an instant, up close or far away, even spanning the globe in the
blink of an eye. At the same time, its capacity for realism has dazzled audiences and bestowed on its storytelling an almost instant authority,
putting viewers "right there" in the action. In the first fabled nickelode-
ons, audiences ducked when waves crashed on the rocks — for fear of
getting wet. There is the audience pleasure of simply seeing up close the
enormous power of theater, the acting out of stories, whether they be
quiet dinner conversations or fierce battles, such as in Spielberg's *Saving
Private Ryan* or Lucas's *Attack of the Clones*. After the early silent films, the
"talking pictures" added not only speech but sound effects and increas-

1. Dillard, *Teaching a Stone to Talk* (New York: Harper, 1982), p. 15.

ingly affecting musical scores. And in many theaters today, one doesn't so much see the picture as one feels it rattling the furniture. Every technical innovation, from the first panning of the camera in *The Great Train Robbery* (1903) to the deep-focus photography of *Citizen Kane* (1941) to the current visual wizardry of the Harry Potter films, has extended the transfixing marvels of the medium. Such are its powers of inclusion and inspection that movies often seem to see the world as only the omniscient God sees it.

And, of course, there is the story itself, displayed huge on the screen in microscopic detail, visually and aurally. No matter what the genre — from romance to science-fiction horror movie — the product is the same: a vast prolonged array of images and sounds that conjure up a vision of what a world looks and feels like as it moves along. Most moviemakers set out to convince viewers that the stories they etch with light "show" in some way what the world is, or what it could or should be. People have always been hungry for this sort of thing, because there is a voracious human appetite for story, a craving as old as tales told around campfires or paintings on cave walls, as Madeleine L'Engle has put it.[2]

For some inexplicable reason, the human creature, even though now sophisticated and rational, loves stories, no matter what medium, whether they are delivered in opera, reality television, or rock video. For some reason we relish the sensation of "losing ourselves" in a tale, of being seduced into another sense of reality, at least for a time. This can be pure escapist diversion, something everybody likes from time to time; but movies can also sometimes offer a way of exploring life's larger riddles and testing out possible solutions to those riddles. Storytelling of all kinds, cinematic and otherwise, stimulates people with the vital questions of what the world is like, what is likely to happen next, and why what happens does happen. Everyone wants to know the answers to those questions, from prime ministers to streetsweepers. A good story told well — or, in the case of film, "shown" well — can envelop, surprise, and transfix its audience as it reveals something about life.

The truth is that every film, whether a Bergman or a fairy tale, has its own version of the way the world is: garden or jungle, friendly or hostile, party or wake, full of delight or full of sadness, and so on. In traditional terms, the conflict between these binary pairs is called drama, and

2. L'Engle, *Walking on Water: Reflections on Faith and Art* (Wheaton, IL: Shaw, 1980). p. 13.

the contest usually involves mine or yours, love or hate, clarity or confusion, ad infinitum. From its very beginnings, not much more than a hundred years ago, one of cinema's great appeals has been its regular, and often compelling, attempt to throw some light on those "big questions" about the way the world is. Synergistic medium that it is, cinema can do this with fullness, immediacy, and even dazzle.

The particular kind of light I wish to examine in this book is the attempt of cinematic light to catch Light — with a capital "L" — specifically the display of divine Light. This is not as unlikely a subject for film as it may first seem. From the beginning, filmmakers have regularly tried to put some overt display of Light on the screen. Hollywood's first full-blown, feature-length spectacle, David Wark Griffith's infamous racist film *The Birth of a Nation* (1915), ends with a portrait of its white protagonists ensconced in a resplendently white heaven. In Griffith's even bigger spectacle, *Intolerance* (1916), a film meant to repair his reputation, he went so far as to bring in Jesus himself and a host of what he thought to be "flashes" of Light. Then and now, even though the makers of movies have usually taken up residence in a pretty thoroughly secular universe, a whole host of films, past and present, have tried to illuminate the inescapable big questions about the possibility of Light. And one does not have to go very far back to find numerous starkly realistic wrestlings with those same big riddles of recent vintage: Robert Zemeckis's *Contact* (1997), Robert Duvall's *The Apostle* (1997), and M. Night Shyamalan's *Wide Awake* (1998) and *Signs* (2002). In addition to those are the fabulously successful mythmakers who push the same "Light" question: Lucas's *Star Wars* saga (1977-2005), Peter Jackson's *Lord of the Rings* trilogy (2001-2003), and even the Wachowski brothers' *Matrix* trilogy (1999-2003).

In short, despite its reputation as a mindless, soul-less diversion, even cinema regularly wrestles with the central deep mysteries about origins, meaning, purpose, intimacy, destiny, morality, and the possibility of God — those domains of human inquiry to which philosophy, theology, and the arts have traditionally devoted themselves. On occasion, films have attended to these riddles directly. That engagement with the possibility of Light, or its absence, and the means by which Light shows itself has resulted in an array of compelling, provocative, and affecting films, including some of the best and most popular ever made. Improbable as it may seem, light as Light does end up on our movie screens.

Catching Light, though, is in many ways a tricky business. Unfortunately, those most earnest about putting Light (or God) up there on the screen for all to see are very often the ones who fail most miserably. Fervor does little to win either credulity or understanding from audiences, and that is especially true when it comes to art: good intentions simply do not get the would-be artist very far. The truth of that is readily apparent in the checkered history of movies that chronicle the life of Jesus, Moses, or even saints such as St. Francis of Assisi or Joan of Arc, two who have repeatedly received film treatments. Literal transcriptions of Scripture or holy legend usually have a hard time being inspired or believable to filmgoers.

Another difficulty of catching Light in cinema lies in the nature of Light itself. In ordinary human circumstances, people do not see even the physical light emitted by the sun; they see what it illuminates, but the light itself is invisible to the human eye. But, even though they do not see light itself, they readily believe it is real because they see what it illuminates. That is greatly compounded when it comes to seeing or creating divine Light, the transcendent entity that in most religious traditions — Eastern and Western alike — proclaims its very hiddenness, invisibility, and inaccessibility to human perception, no matter how much people yearn for clear indications of divine presence.

Thus the question for filmmakers is how to make the Invisible visible, the Transcendent immanent, the Impalpable manifest. Needless to say, questions about who or what Light (or God) is and how far that Light is removed from ordinary mundane experience have hounded humans through the millennia. When people look for tangible proof, divine mystery usually remains mysterious, shadowy, and distant, and we see at best "through a glass, darkly," as the Apostle Paul famously put it in his first letter to the fractious church in Corinth (1 Cor. 13:12, KJV).

Catching Light — or Why It Is So Hard to See Light

Now and then, in some way or another, Light does flash inexplicably, sometimes blazing, as in Moses' burning bush, or "like shining from shook foil" (G. M. Hopkins). Most of the time, though, Light comes in flashes near the edges of vision, in a faint gleam, or in a tremor of color. Most often Light comes not as people would like — such as pure light spread sky-wide in bright neon dazzle — but refracted through an altogether different prism, one simultaneously more ambiguous and more personal, by means of touch or embrace, image or sign, glimpse or gaze, sound or music, beauty or horror, words or song, meeting or coincidence, forgiveness or blessing. The means are endless and always as new and unique as people themselves. In other words, when the divine does appear, it proves endlessly inventive and astonishing in the instruments of its showing. It is certain only that, by stealth and surprise, the entity people label "divine" or "Light" or "God" tips its hand, manifesting in untold ways a holy presence among people. The stubbornly opaque "dark glass" through which people strain to spy God goes translucent, and the Other becomes more clear, like a crash or a whisper, or a crash within a whisper, the "still small voice" in the self, or even, in rare instances, something startling and undeniable, like that burning bush in the wilderness.[3]

In short, the forms of disclosure are countless, unfathomable, and almost always unexpected. Then and maybe ever thereafter, in some measure at least, because of the "showing" of the divine that has transpired — the academic term for this is *hierophany* — people of all kinds come to see and act differently. Transcending mundane limits and perception, either briefly or lastingly, the soul itself encounters and is often infused, engulfed, or cheered by a presence from beyond human agency, and the Invisible becomes known. A transcendent Other imparts to individual people, and sometimes whole communities, the light they require to travel their arduous path of love, fortitude, and even — amid the most dire circumstances — exultant gladness. Generally, though, when people think they've got that holiness cased, contained, and controlled, they've very likely lost it.

Those artists, especially visual artists such as filmmakers, who venture to dramatize religious encounters or any other means by which God, or Light, manifests its presence, face a formidable challenge, namely, how to refract that invisible Light, as through a prism, to make some portion of it perceptible. How, in other words, can one show on a screen or canvas some glint of Light, how render the Invisible visible? In the Western world it is not a new problem, but part of the inviolable nature of the divine: in the major Western traditions, Light/God is essentially of a wholly different or "transcendent" nature and by its very nature plainly invisible and "unsayable," at least in human terms. Strands of thought within both Judaism and Islam consider God so far above humans and so

3. Jesuit poet Gerard Manley Hopkins is something of a rarity in this regard. He finds God's presence immediate and resplendent, and he sees divine light, "God's Grandeur," infusing the natural world, making it "charged," as with electricity, that on blessed occasions flames forth like that "shining from shook foil," fully blinding the whole self with its radiance.

INTRODUCTION

impenetrable that they have historically proscribed any attempt to make an image of God, resulting in the practice of iconoclasm. French intellectual historian Alain Bescanon summarizes this in *The Forbidden Image*: "For Islam, it is God's insurmountable distance that renders impossible the fabrication of an image worthy of its object; for Judaism, it is God's intimate familiarity."[4] Whatever the case, it is the extreme brightness of the Light, near or far, that results in prohibitions of even trying to glean a part of God's being within some human form of expression. Within these iconoclastic traditions, words — but no pictures or sounds — seem to thrive.

Nor is this recognition of the incommensurability between the human and the divine anything new to poets. American poet Emily Dickinson concluded that in telling the truth, given its brightness, we must "tell it slant" lest everyone "be blind" (#1129). Pulitzer prizewinner Annie Dillard does the same in her account of Moses' reluctant recognition of the fearsomeness of the majesty of God. God refuses Moses' request to see God because one glimpse would kill him. Instead, God places Moses between two boulders and covers him with his hand as he passes by. God allows Moses to glimpse the hem of God's raiment; any more and he's dead.[5] Still, trying to capture or refract somehow the brightness of this Light is much of what the long history of art has been about, from Rembrandt, Goya, Bach, and Mozart to Monet, Messiaen, and U2. But the fact that there is a large measure of transcendent holiness and sublimity surrounding the divine Holy One that dwarfs human comprehension has not deterred hordes from talking, drawing, singing, dancing, miming, and so on — all in the wild hope of making known some small sliver of the radiant mystery. And not a few moviemakers have also chased that divine fox.

Still another factor that greatly complicates attempts to portray the divine-human encounter is the sad shortfall in humanity's own expressive capacities. The apprehension of Light is a task for which the human species does not seem well suited, in part because of the blinding radiance of the brightness and in part because of ordinary human finitude. This is the human "downside" of divine transcendence: people are all too human, carnal, earthbound, and otherwise limited. Which is another way of saying that, for the most part, humans do not prove up to the task of comprehending or recapitulating either the cognitive or affective di-

4. Bescanon, *The Forbidden Image* (Chicago: University of Chicago Press, 2001), p. 2.
5. Dillard, *Pilgrim at Tinker Creek* (New York: Harper, 1974), pp. 204-5.

mensions of what sense of the divine they have achieved. Artists and mystics wish to limn the illimitable being of God with human tools, but most often they end up complaining, with T. S. Eliot, the great modern poet of the divine, of the "intolerable wrestle with words and meanings" in the desperate

> Raid on the inarticulate
> With shabby equipment always deteriorating
> In the general mess of imprecision of feeling,
> Undisciplined squads of emotion.[6]

At his or her best, the poet or filmmaker can only approximate what Eliot himself called the "distraction fit," that "still point" of the "intersection of the timeless with time" when the divine approaches.[7] Whatever transpires when mere mortals encounter the sacred, it is not easily transmuted or translated into ordinary human experience. Acknowledging these limits up front and trying only "to tell it slant" is not much help: finding that appropriate and winsome angle of approach proves elusive. How can one explain red to those who only know and understand gray? Nor does the mere intensity or sincerity go far in conveying the disclosure of Light, the epiphany or hierophany, the "transcendent experience" — or whatever term one chooses to label the Light that makes itself known in some way. There are, to be sure, rare artistic achievements that transport viewers into whatever the artist glimpsed, or heard, or felt — what God was and what it was like to find God up close — and sometimes those pieces of art are movies.

So, rendering the divine in art is difficult to pull off, due both to the nature of the divine and the limits of the human apparatus in apprehending the divine. How, then, can we show it? That is the great artistic challenge: conveying whatever the artist has caught of the divine in fetching and believable terms, the full-blown burst of light that imparts clarity, certitude, and joy. The "dark glass" inevitably intrudes, though it is not a marble barrier. Rather, all kinds of people receive "hints and guesses," again as Eliot put it, that help un-puzzle the riddles of being alive, and these tokens come in all shapes and measures, including music, laughing children, and even "the stillness between two waves of the sea."[8] Despite

---

6. T. S. Eliot, *The Complete Poems and Plays, 1909-1950* (New York: Harcourt, 1962), p. 128.

7. Eliot, pp. 136, 119.

8. Eliot, pp. 136, 145.

the apparent parsimony in revelation, and though ardent materialists of all kinds dismiss it as a dangerous delusion at worst and a childish kind of "wishful thinking" at best, the depthless human craving for Light shows no sign of abating.

Such insistent recurrence of the "God wish" in so stalwartly secular an age as ours argues that at least the thirst for, if not the reality of, Light simply does not subside, no matter how much the head announces the silliness of the soul's hungers. Perhaps the single most unexpected place where this appetite for Light appears is among a group of contemporary novelists, poets, and even filmmakers who contend that the human species is instinctually and irrevocably hungry for Light, hard-wired in heart, soul, and head with this craving for God — or at least for divine Light. If one listens to these artists, the human species still scrambles around looking for something to satisfy its pressing need for Light.

Refracting Light for the Screen

One of the more surprising turns in the contemporary cinema of North America and Europe has been the regularity and maturity with which it has cast cinematic light on those "animating mysteries of the world," as Clarissa Vaughn in Michael Cunningham's novel *The Hours* (1998) puts it.[9] Like other characters in that novel, Clarissa ponders the origin and significance of the majesty she feels all around her: the possibility that ordinary physical light in fact emanates from Light, that ours is a radiant world made so by a Love that transfigures the material into resplendent glory. And this large question focuses other questions that many contemporary films often consider: What constitutes Light? What is it like to encounter it? What validates its reality? And where and how does Light make itself known within the often tragic depths of human life? Because films habitually attend closely to making individual lived experience seem real for the viewer, they tend to wrestle most often with questions concerning the difference an encounter with Light makes in the understanding of one's own life. The responses to these encounters are usually labeled "religious" or "spiritual," nebulous terms that lack very specific meaning today because they are overused.

"Religious" here does not mean doctrinaire or sectarian, a connotation that often leaps to the minds of many who encounter the term. This

---

9. Cunningham, *The Hours* (New York: Farrar, 1998), p. 35.

is true largely because the films asking these questions investigate the broadest theological questions and not the doctrinal particularities of who's right or wrong, in or out. Overall, they seem far more interested in chronicling how the encounter with God or grace occurs in an individual human's experience than in dramatizing or proof-texting any particular creedal or ideological perspective. In other words, these "religious" stories are in just about every way theologically "minimalist," no matter how many religious people subsequently put the stories to their own uses. As a group, they chronicle something else altogether, namely, recognizing the actuality of a loving divine presence that aids people in peril, confusion, and general lostness.

The same is true of the traditional name for what these films are dealing with — *God.* The word "God" is no longer particularly evocative, having accrued mountains of negative associations, especially for moviegoers. Nor is the term any longer — in the polymorphic culture in which we live — particularly precise, having long since become the great cosmic catchall for anything slightly strange, repressive, or, for that matter, unjust — either in politics or personal life. This is at least part of the reason that many of the films discussed here are very cautious about using the word "God" to identify the remarkable events in them. Appropriately, they are more about *showing* than *naming.* And that approach is fitting not only in light of the medium, but also — for Jewish and Christian viewers — in view of the biblical caution about trying to contain the Limitless within a single term, particularly in a term that has become so multivalent and depleted as "God."

There is also the sad historical truth that humans' tools of apprehension and naming have proved to be inept. The certainty is that people keep trying, as well they should, to put up a verbal fence around the Transcendent or the divine Light, the holy, the wholly Other, or even "the Force." Whatever the label, words and images abound, and they proliferate still, as they always will. The histories of religion and also of the arts often seem but records of humanity's everlasting desire to get some fix on a Reality that is in very large part unfathomable.

For these reasons, this book suggests a rather broad definition of what constitutes a religious response to living. The films discussed here almost always focus on a personal apprehension of the divine, even when they simultaneously — such as in Michael Cimino's *The Deer Hunter* and David's Puttnam's *The Mission* — have enormous social and cultural import. William James's very helpful definition of religion, from his classic *Varieties of Religious Experience* (first published in 1902), delineates the sort of highly individualized subject matter that filmmakers treat over and over again: "the feelings, acts, and experiences of individual men [and women] in their solitude, so far as they apprehend themselves to stand in relation to whatever they may consider divine."[10] This critical emphasis gels with a phenomenological approach to religious experience insofar as this strand of phenomenology highlights personal "lived experience," as Alan Hodder puts it in *Thoreau's Ecstatic Witness* (2001). It entails close attention to "the forms and phenomena of experience" and implies that the interpreter work "wherever possible to coordinate these descriptions according to some larger classificatory scheme." Further, this approach strives to let the subjects — in this case characters and filmmakers — speak for themselves in order to determine "the nature of these experiences and meaning for the subjects under consideration."[11]

What is important in this approach is that experience in the film is understood, so to speak, from the inside out, in its own terms rather than preemptively bringing to bear external categories with which to analyze the story, whether those categories be sociological, political, or religious. The goal is to understand the "text" of the film experience itself as fully as possible, and then, after the fact, to discover with what religious categories that "lived experience" might fit. That, of course, is more easily said than done, and the strategy may sound remarkably naïve to many in this postmodern critical era. My preference here is to investigate what the film text might "show" of individual lives, the usual subject of film stories, as they try to catch some measure of Light or — as is more typically the case — Light catches them. Thus a phenomenological approach comports well with the dominant narrative focus in films that give us even a small glimpse of religious experience.

In contemporary cinema, most encounters with Light happen to quite ordinary people who seem to stray into its path, and Light, literally or metaphorically, encompasses them, usually much to their surprise. That is not to say that they walk away blind or dumb, as was the case with St. Paul or the father of John the Baptist. It is not news to anyone that there are very rare instances of breathtaking displays, at least in Western culture, when God has made God's presence known — has shown up and shown off, as it were — conspicuously and undeniably: in

10. James, *Varieties of Religious Experience* (Cambridge: Harvard University Press, 1985), p. 34.

11. Hodder, *Thoreau's Ecstatic Witness* (New Haven: Yale University Press, 2001), p. 24.

floods and rainbows, in burning bushes and plagues, in wine from water and healings aplenty. Yet, instead of trying to catch the miraculous and unmediated Light for the screen, filmmakers have for the most part taken a different approach, one more complex, demanding, and cogent. In short, instead of big displays, filmmakers have largely focused on chronicling and analyzing the encounter of ordinary people with the divine. The filmmakers' gaze fixes on how God comes and how the divine presence affects those it strikes. Very often it is only by tracking the response of recipients of that presence that the reality and nature of God is made clear. In the depiction of human behavior, the filmmaker and audience detect the presence of the divine by witnessing some event, such as in Spielberg's *Close Encounters of the Third Kind,* or by deducing its nature from the kind of response God evokes. This is the drama of the apprehension of God, the reaction of people as they run into the different displays of the Holy in innumerable ways. In other words, Light refracts through a human prism, and the filmmaker refracts that light through the lens.

Light works its way through to recognition, and audiences see Light as the characters themselves come, by some means or another, to see or sense Light (or it may be in sound, as in Krzysztof Kieslowski's *Three Colors: Blue* [1993] or David Puttnam's *The Mission* [1986]). The camera makes known the reality of God by trying to portray what the character perceives and by tracking the visible consequences as the characters wrestle with it in mind, heart, and soul, that subjective domain "where the meanings are," as Emily Dickinson put it. That is a demanding venture because the camera cannot see very far into personal interior realities; as witness and narrator, the best the camera can do is suggest the tangled psychic realities that contend and roil within mind and soul. But astonishment, anguish, tears, and especially laughter can show a great deal about the nature of the God who has variously whispered, sung, blinded, warmed, or rescued ordinary people as they've traveled their way. The human response functions as a kind of photographic plate, hazy and distorted though it may be, on which light has registered. Indeed, people themselves are far from ideal receptors, because they are vain, overeager, expropriating, tough-skinned, thick-headed, or, as is sometimes the case, all of the above.

Furthermore, there is the problem of the chariness of God: as we have seen, God showed Moses but the hem of his raiment — for reasons of safety. Or God speaks in the still small voice that is barely distinguishable from the thousand other mutterings of the noisy self. In Christianity, for example, Jesus' miracles tended to be small-scale and personal, and Jesus went out of his way to keep them quiet, studiously avoiding the melodramatic poses of Moses in Egypt or on Sinai. Quiet revelations often make a profound difference in the recipient's experience of life itself. Many of the world's religions argue that when this Light comes, even in quiet inward measures, it fully overtakes the self, clearing the mind, warming the heart, exulting the soul, and, in the process, fundamentally reorienting the self toward hopefulness, love, and ecstasy.

Even so, religious fear and trembling or ecstasy in union with God do not usually look plausible on the screen. Words in screenplays go a ways to dissipate the divine improbability or the soul's opacity; but many words in movies soon overwhelm or violate the medium, quickly turning it into a stage play or a novel, and viewers usually complain about it. In filling this expressive "void," cinema as an art form features other avenues of conveyance: events and images carry the burden of telling the tale (this does not mean that filmgoers are particularly patient with a film's absence of verbal explanation either). Acting helps as well, giving credibility to the playing of Light in the self. And the language of the medium itself carries the rest: production design, setting, costuming, music, lighting, and a host of camera strategies — all helping to make visible those interior apprehensions that the camera cannot record. No matter how much viewers want movies to both show and tell, that is, using sufficient words to make everything clear (as if words alone can do that), it is important to allow filmmakers to tell their stories as they wish, giving the benefit of the doubt long enough for a particular manner of cinematic "speech," or what is often called "style," to work its way with the viewer. Needless to say, storytelling strategies differ greatly from film crew to film crew, sometimes resulting in legendary fights and firings.

The same is true for the differences between writers and directors (though many of the filmmakers whose works I discuss here are "auteurs," those who take on both tasks of writing and directing). Even though they may share thematic similarities, filmmakers with common interests can differ greatly in subject matter and cinematic style, as is the case with, say, Spielberg and Lawrence Kasdan. Film is an expansive and plastic medium, and thus it is able to flex and stretch, potentially at least, to as many different "takes" on human experience as there are writers and directors. In this regard — again, as many of the films treated here suggest — the medium is very much in its infancy, exploring and innovating the formal capacities of cinematic storytelling in sometimes astonishing ways. The best filmmakers show wonderful adventurousness in the stories they try to tell and in the means they improvise to make their stories enticing and affecting.

Usually when Light does show, the display tends toward the fleeting, subtle, and elusive, so much so that many characters wrestle with the authenticity of their own experience, and what largely ends up on the screen is a filmmaker's impression of individual apprehension and pursuit of the divine. Fortunately, despite its limitations, film has at its disposal virtually all the resources of all the fine arts: storytelling, drama, the visual arts in form and color, and music — all brewed together in one aesthetic kettle. As a highly collaborative enterprise, filmmaking marshals a startling variety of the traditional arts in limning humanity's multitudinous engagements with Light and uses them within the seemingly limitless capacities of modern technology. So the art piece becomes a tool of analysis, of reflection and understanding, going as far as possible with available representational or logical tools to comprehend the mystery. Artists seem to have the special impulse to recapture or represent Light itself as fully as possible — or at least the experience of being enveloped by Light, which is above and beyond the ordinary. Re-creating that experience allows them and their audiences to hang onto something of the original glowing ember.

Bearings

The subtitle of this book emphasizes the common appetite for God of just about everyone — filmmakers, characters, and viewers. Whether conscious of it or otherwise, almost everyone instinctively thirsts to find light of some kind that will clarify and improve significant portions of their lives. Like it or not, that simply is the way the "normal" human psyche is structured. We look — and we hope — for the best possible thing going, no matter if we are theists or avowed secularists. And sometimes we get it fabulously wrong. The incomprehensibly bloody last century featured secular messianic movements, replete with their own rationalized metaphysical views of history, which promised to imbue all aspects of life with great waves of light, a kind of kingdom of God on earth without God, or at least without a God recognizable to traditional religions. By and large, these movements proved even less successful — calamitously so, in fact — than traditional religions in constructing heaven on earth. Still, the appetite for all manner of light does not fade.

The subtitle of this book, "looking for God," emphasizes looking as opposed to actually finding. My conscious choice here, first of all, is to avoid any note of the triumphalism that so often colors discussions of religion and film; popular religious critics often love a film simply because it supports a particular religious or moral point of view. Second, the term "looking" also disputes the notion that, once "found," God becomes something one thereafter "has," much as a found coin belongs to the finder entirely and permanently. That claim of certitude does not in general fit with religious experience, neither in the films examined nor, for that matter, in the main currents of the Judeo-Christian tradition, the context in which all these films occur. The entire biblical record teems with all sorts of characters, from Abraham and David to Peter and the early church, who often get central notions all wrong, and then Light comes along in surprising and unexpected ways to adjust the wrong-headed thinking of those who are certain.

Further, "looking" suggests the necessity of some skepticism about claims of complete religious clarity and certainty. Sometimes there is religious clarity, to be sure, and legitimately so, but it does not seem by and large to be the case in the films treated here. For most people, the dark glass that St. Paul evokes remains shadowy and opaque. A different set of films from those treated here might merit the conclusion that characters have definitively found God; but for the most part, the stories I discuss here show people who, to their immense good fortune, come upon an unexpected burst or refraction of Light within the encompassing tragic mystery of existence, and although they arrive at an immensely different place because of the numinous realities they've encountered, they thereafter seem reluctant to avow dazzling certainties. My posture is to err on the side of epistemological caution, knowing that humans are wont to misperceive and misappropriate even the clearest of divine promptings. The realism of the traditional Calvinism that broadly informs the critical perspective of this book emphasizes the brightness of God, on the one hand, and the darkness of the human creature on the other, taking full account of the inveterate human penchant for egregious self-aggrandizement. Finally, the notion of "looking" for Light perhaps captures what viewers do when they head to the movie theater, whether it's for airy diversion or Shakespeare.

One point, the necessity of cognitive caution, does deserve elaboration. Few people seem to know anything but a small portion of what is called — to use traditional language — "the counsel of God." The finite does not readily encompass the Infinite, and most of the time we perceive but a small slice of an infinitely complex and layered world within "our little corner of cognition," as novelist William Dean Howells put it.[12] Most people are skeptical about the divine, usually for good reason; and so while they do "progress," they usually end up with no more than, in a phrase from John Updike, "a handhold on sheer surfaces."[13] The film stories recounted here suggest that, when it does show up, grace befalls unlikely and unsuspecting people in surprising and unforeseeable ways that are quite beyond human prediction, conception, or charting. The ones usually most surprised by the "preposterousness" of this drama, to use Frederick Buechner's word, are those who claim privileged knowledge of the mind of God, and that is breathtaking spiritual presumption, to say the least.[14]

This is to opt for an expansive rendition of Light or, again in traditional terms, of "grace," that is, the disclosure of the love of God. Part of this derives from the simple Christian declaration in the Gospel of John that "God so loved the world . . ." (3:16). Another way of saying the same, amply supported by the Christian Bible, is that God bathes this world in love and that love goes everywhere, even into the damnedest places. An eloquent expression of this notion comes near the end of John Updike's novel *The Centaur*, when the main character, George Caldwell, a self-doubting school teacher wrestling with imminent death, recalls the words of his Lutheran minister father as they pass a bar that pours out a torrent of "cruelty and blasphemy." "All joy belongs to the Lord," says the Reverend Caldwell. In this the young son finds reassurance: "Wherever in filth and confusion and misery, a soul felt joy, there the Lord came and claimed it as his own; into barrooms and brothels and classrooms and alleys slippery with spittle, no matter how dark and scabbed and remote, in China or Africa or Brazil, wherever a moment of joy was felt, there the Lord stole and added to His enduring domain."[15]

From film to film, the apprehension of Light by characters differs markedly, and the films examined here effectively catalogue a broad swath of contemporary religious experience. It is not the whole spectrum, to be sure, for there are a number of films that feature recognitions that fall under the heading of New Age religion, such as John Travolta's *Phenomenon* (1996). The films treated here fit more or less comfortably within the confines of traditional Jewish and Christian thought and ex-

12. Howells, *The Shadow of a Dream* (New York, 1890), p. 109.
13. Updike, *The Centaur* (New York: Knopf, 1963), p. 63.
14. Buechner, *Telling the Truth: The Gospel as Tragedy, Comedy, and Fairy-Tale* (San Francisco: Harper, 1977).
15. Updike, p. 296.

perience, though another set of interpretive goggles might view some differently. Even those films that explore unremitting darkness, namely *The Godfather* saga and *Chinatown*, do so with understandings of evil that are distinctively Judeo-Christian. Similarly, the substance of the Light that opposes this darkness seems to flow from traditional Jewish and Christian understandings of the nature of God, best understood as limitless love for the well-being of this world, commonly denoted today by the concept within the Hebrew word *shalom*. The idea is that God cares lavishly about human flourishing and that the created world was made for just that. The Genesis creation accounts picture a gorgeous pacific world of harmony, intimacy, and beauty for the delight of all living things. In the Genesis narrative, the created world is first a garden and then an animal park and then a festival of beauty where predation and death are unknown. It is the intention of God to restore this realm of felicity to a badly broken world.

A Map

There are many ways to approach and understand this cinematic search for Light and its struggle for the means to show the Invisible. To a large extent, these are shaped by the current array of academic disciplines, all of which try to understand causative factors in the human mystery, ranging from the sociological and psychological to the theological and biblical. The approach in this book is useful for talking about the way Light does — and does not — strike and refract in the human circumstance. It conflates literary and theological frames of reference, emphasizing the literary and theological meaning of the modes and shapes of the stories. Its chief virtue is that it provides for a reasonable and crisp discussion of the kinds of film that contribute to questions about the nature of Light and how it comes. This architecture separates these Light-bound stories into four kinds. The primary inspiration for this perspective comes from Frederick Buechner's wonderful little book on Christian religious understanding, *Telling the Truth: The Gospel as Tragedy, Comedy, and Fairy-Tale* (originally written as the Beecher Lectures on Preaching at Yale University in 1973). My book adapts Buechner's three categories and adds another to delineate films that emphasize religious search.

PART ONE

DARKNESS VISIBLE

This first section examines tales of darkness, films that depict a thirsting world that craves the breaking of Light. If one is looking for God in the movies, these three films go to where God is not, and two of them stay there, the third finding Light after a long stretch in dire hell. For the most part, though, these films travel a spiritual and moral landscape emptied of any shred of the divine, where God is absconditus, absentia, gone, dead, whatever. One question Frederick Buechner asks is more than appropriate: where in hell is God "because Hell is where the action is, where I am and the cross is"?[1] Buechner argues that for people in general, and certainly in a Judeo-Christian view of things, "the news . . . is bad before it is good."[2] The first section analyzes three films that present the "bad news" in incisive haunting clarity.

The refrain in these stories is that the natural human condition is darkness, a state in which people are beset by evil inside and out, and cannot find their way to any slight portion of Light, whether as rescue, safety, or love. On the one hand, that notion restates the Christian doctrine of the Fall — that humankind is born into a perilous life that itself ends in death, is disposed to do evil, and throughout is pretty thoroughly lost. Even though people may want a better world, they not only lack sufficient sense or virtue to find or forge a path to that destination, but their best efforts to get there will more than likely only aggravate their already grievous fix. In short, like it or not, humankind dwells in darkness. Evil

1. Frederick Buechner, *Telling the Truth: The Gospel as Tragedy, Comedy, and Fairy-Tale* (San Francisco: Harper, 1977), p. 39.
2. Buechner, p. 33.

is all about, no matter how bright or privileged the place we live. It encompasses and pervades, and from it there is no protection.

Theologically, the world is a dark place. The Gospel of John announces, even proclaims that as the basic datum of human life: Light shines, only shines, and the rest is darkness that has not yet "overcome" the Light, although the language deployed by John makes the struggle sound like a close call. In literary terms, this is tragedy, and it is to that fate that people seem naturally bent. The supreme examples of this lay in Greek tragedy, particularly Sophocles, and in the tragedy of Shakespeare and, say, Arthur Miller. This section on "Darkness Visible" explores this place of lostness, examining three already classic films from the 1970s that expose different locales or domains of human experience in which evil romps. Taken together, these films display the way in which evil devises avenues of destruction by personal, social, and cultural means. The habit of the Church to see evil as primarily a personal domain is disputed by the last two films in this group. They certainly bring to mind St. Paul's warning about the "principalities and powers" that rule the world (Romans 8).

Darkness may be an odd place to start in a book about Light. It is unavoidable for two reasons. Historically, religious films have, surprisingly, shied from realistic portrayals of evil, largely for moralistic reasons. They have chosen instead to emphasize, though not very convincingly, redemption and the triumph of finding Light. That squeamishness has not, among other problems, helped their work either as proselytizing or as art. As film critic Eric Metaxas has put it, "In order to be redemptive, art has to convince us there is something real from which we need redeeming."[3] The mincing of evil adds nothing to the case for the cogency of redemption.

That is not, however, the best reason for fixing on films that make plain the evil of evil. The examination of darkness is strategically useful because it is by arriving at a clear purchase on what afflicts the human creature that people have some hope of understanding the Light or "good" that might dispel evil's distortion and malice. In other words, in delineating darkness filmmakers suggest what sort of Light is necessary to defeat its sway. These are included here because they work to define the utter darkness of "not God," absence of hope and love, the nullity of self, the defeat of self and Light. What they have arrived at instead of

3. Eric Metaxas, "To End All Christian Films," *Books and Culture,* July-August 2002, p. 6.

Film as Visual Medium

To a large extent, the marriage of film to the visible world results from the very nature of the medium: it can only record what it sees; it cannot "see" into thoughts or feelings. Only the most venturesome and inventive of filmmakers have even tried to get behind these physical screens between the "insides" and the viewer. From its origins, then, film has always dealt with "externalities," those surfaces of experience that are easily recordable and have readily enticed viewers. The first films astounded audiences with the sheer realism of their record of ordinary events such as passing trains and waves crashing on a beach (viewers ducked for fear of getting wet). "Seeing is believing" and — in terms of creating the illusion of reality — "a picture is worth a thousand words," or more, for that matter. Indeed, audiences have always seemed to give film fictions, even the most fantastic and clumsy of stories, more than the benefit of the doubt simply because they represent the physical world and its events in a believable form. If it "looks" real, well then, the rest of it is real, too, including whatever preposterous events or people come along.

A savvy lot, filmmakers have preempted audience skepticism by making their worlds look "real"; indeed, audiences historically have suspended their disbelief rather too readily, have lent credulity too eagerly to movies just because they look real and seem plausible, as in the case of Oliver Stone's fanciful version of the Kennedy assassination, *JFK*. Nonetheless, in the cogency of its illusion lies this medium's extraordinary popularity and power. In contrast to its close cousin, the stage or dramatic theater, film as a medium is virtually mute, eschewing the use of many words for the attractiveness of images. Indeed, one of the worst indictments of a film would be that it is "talky," or too much "like a play." One of the chief attractions of cinema historically has been that it *shows* the world rather than talks about it, as theater does (usually endlessly, many students complain, in Shakespeare's or Arthur Miller's plays, for example). More recently, especially with younger, MTV-saturated audiences, the complaint is that many films are too slow, not having enough images coming fast enough to sustain the interest of video-age viewers.

God or any sort of goodness is the devouring anti-life that is evil. Of that the last century knew plenty, especially as it came masked in the guise of progress, namely Fascism and in different Marxist experiments.

The Godfather saga (1972-90) examines in harrowing moral precision the descent from idealism into ruthless personal evil. Young Michael Corleone (Al Pacino) deemed himself morally distinct from his family and wanted no part of the "family business." Events push him to "join up," at least for the moment of crisis. Thereafter, however, he becomes ever more embroiled in its darkness. Ultimately, Michael embraces a measure of ruthlessness that exceeds the restraint his venerable father Vito (Marlon Brando) practiced. By the end of the first film (1972) Michael has triumphed but lost a vital dimension of his integrity. As director Francis Ford Coppola makes clear, Michael himself has become evil, and he comes to resemble in his brutality and even his appearance the very Prince of Darkness himself. Matters only darken in *The Godfather: Part II* in which Michael, for little good reason, becomes a fratricide. In the last installment, an aging and ill Michael, sensing his own great personal evil, undertakes a search for redemption that comes to naught when "events" once again demand that he strike his enemies. And upon that, once again in his sorrowful life, incalculable loss follows.

Chinatown (1974) tours a landscape of social evil that unblinkingly devours innocence of any and every sort. Set in 1930s Los Angeles amid a severe drought, Robert Towne's story, loosely based on local history, spins a noirish tale of labyrinthine social evil, whose darkness and complexity surprises even this savviest of private eyes who thinks he has seen it all. P.I. Jake Gittes (Jack Nicholson) undertakes "domestic surveillance" on the LA water commissioner only to find himself set up and embarrassed. And then things go from bad to worse, including murder, massive political fraud, and then, in a possibility never contemplated, the vilest of crimes about which he can do nothing at all. The evil he finally grasps and confronts unashamedly deceives in order to subvert and then destroy, whether it is the public trust or girlish innocence. Director Roman Polanski changed the end of the film to have his likeable do-gooder hero lose against the iniquity he finally discovers. The final suggestion is that while God perhaps died in Western culture in the twentieth century, evil thrives as never before. It is a bleak tale whose pessimism reflected the 1970s but now, again, in the years after September 11, 2001, seems all too timely. Evil pervades the social structure, itself becoming an agent of subversion, and there is not much any single individual can do about it.

The evil depicted in *The Deer Hunter* (1978) goes even further. In *Chinatown* the protagonist and the society as a whole still harbor sensible notions of morality and social well-being. In *The Deer Hunter,* this broadly embraced social ideal itself becomes the agent of evil. Writer-director Michael Cimino details the way in which a frontier creed of macho individualism enamored of coercive violence destroys people and communities. The film follows that journey of three young men from a small steel mill town in Pennsylvania to the battlefields of Vietnam and, all now severely maimed to varying degrees in body or soul, back home again. The toll of a cultural ideology that venerates violent coercion as an expression of masculinity, of which the Vietnam war was itself an instance, is dire and catastrophic. Because the story's protagonist, the deer hunter for whom the film is named, ends up recoiling from all he had previously celebrated, the film suggests that Light might indeed break even into the meanest places of earth. As such, it provides a fitting bridge to the next section, films in which Light breaks full and clear, at least for a time.

These films from the 70s suggest humankind's worst fears about the hegemony of evil are amply warranted. The wolf medieval poet Dante inserts into the opening sections of his *Divine Comedy* trenchantly symbolizes the reign of rapacious, devouring, and perhaps untamable evil: "She tracks down all, kills all, and knows no glut,/but, feeding, she grows hungrier than she was."[4] From this darkness, in search of the safety of love and light, everyone flees.

4. Dante, *Inferno*, trans. John Ciardi, in *Norton Anthology of World Masterpieces*, Fifth Continental Edition, ed. Maynard Mack et al. (New York: Norton, 1987), p. 769.

23

CHAPTER 1

UTTERLY LOST

Michael Corleone's Descent in *The Godfather* Saga

At the very end of *The Godfather: Part II* (1974), Michael Corleone (Al Pacino) sits by himself on the lawn of his large Lake Tahoe estate. It is late fall, and the low sun sheds no warmth and color on his face or the leaf-blown landscape behind. He is bundled in a bulky black sweater, as if trying to shelter himself from the cold. The camera slowly approaches to the point where his face, the right half shadowed in darkness, fills nearly half of the widescreen. His hand is at his chin, an intent, almost quizzical expression on his face. The scene in effect continues the previous one, in which Michael, alone in his dark cavernous house, sits slumped in a large chair while he recalls in lengthy detail the moment when he, then but a college student, announced his intention to depart from the violent paths of his notorious crime family. The implication is that Michael now wonders, given the Cain he has become, at the strange route that has brought him from selflessness — enlisting in the Marines in World War II — to this dire fate of venomous brutality and complete personal isolation. And well he might, for in this transit, to his surprise and the viewer's, Michael has become darkness itself (to underscore this fact, most of Michael's story in *Part II* is filmed in very low light and shadow). Indeed, it is not too much to say that Michael has become, as the details of the shot make painfully clear, evil incarnate: predatory, ruthless, and completely stone-hearted. As such, this exquisitely wrought closing view of Michael seems a fitting closing to his story, and it comprises what is at once the scariest and saddest scene in a generation of American film that is noted for its tragic realism. (Usually "scary" and "sad" do not go together in the movies.)

The scary essence of this scene derives from the crime Michael has

Michael (Al Pacino) sits alone pondering his life in the last frames of
The Godfather: Part II.

commanded. Only a few hundred yards from where Michael stands at a
window, his older brother, Fredo (John Cazale), while fishing and reciting the Hail Mary (for luck), has taken a bullet in the back of his head
from Al Neri (Richard Bright), his present fishing companion and Michael's loyal henchman. Clearly, Fredo has not died by Michael's own
hand, as Abel did by Cain's; but insofar as Michael has decreed the execution, he has become as much the murderer as if he had actually pulled
the trigger himself. Indeed, he has become the full-blown moral horror
his estranged wife has come to "dread," as Kay (Diane Keaton) will tell
him years later. Michael has here repeated the primal arch-crime, brother
killing brother, and he has done so — much as the first Cain did — out of
rank pride and revenge. For all his intelligence, power, wealth, and
aplomb, Michael is still at heart a fratricide and, worse still, a serial
killer, as the first two *Godfather* films make clear. Debonair, well-dressed,
articulate, and remarkably successful, he is a far cry from his father's en-
forcer, the barely verbal Luca Brazzi (Lenny Montana); but he is a serial
killer nonetheless. Simply put, in the words of writer-director Francis
Ford Coppola, Michael Corleone has become a "monster," lost and
"damned" in a "hell he [has] created for himself."[1]

1. Audio Commentary, *The Godfather DVD Collection*, dir. Francis Ford Coppola, Paramount DVD, 2001.

With this abomination also comes deep sadness, even lament, for the terrible place to which the once-idealistic Michael has come. In this final murderous deed, all the ambiguity about Michael's moral status and motives, which was murky for some in the original *Godfather,* disappears. And with this closing shot, etched in light and shadow, director Coppola evokes Michael's great inner wreckage of wrenching isolation and crushing guilt. The moment of his greatest power and triumph, when he has vanquished all his enemies, is also the moment of his greatest desolation. After all, Michael has gone up against forces of an unbridled malevolence and has triumphed; ironically, he has done so by marshalling all of his own malevolence. By conventional American cultural standards, he has achieved unparalleled success: his foes are defeated, the "family business" is almost legitimate, and he is on the way to a vast financial empire (twenty years later, at the beginning of *The Godfather: Part III,* Michael is worth billions, which becomes obvious when he thinks little of giving one hundred million dollars to the Vatican). At the same time, though, he has lost everything, particularly his family, the very thing which he was supposedly laboring to protect and nourish. And he has become an even darker version of the family violence that he so steadfastly opposed in his youthful idealism. As Parts II and III of *The Godfather* make clear, the primary victims of Michael's ruthlessness are members of his own family, and then any others who might try to diminish Michael's sway in any way. Irony piles on irony, and Michael's history soon ripens into a contemporary version of the stone-hearted protagonists of nineteenth-century American storyteller Nathaniel Hawthorne, whose dark tales typically delineate the courses by which good turns to evil. Over and over again, these self-consumed idealists — whether Ethan Brand or Rappaccini — become monsters by virtue of a cloaked self-concern that destroys those around them. The horror is unspeakable, and as Michael himself seems to glimpse in his closing reverie, he himself is horror (a conclusion that forecasts Kurtz's recognition at the end of Coppola's *Apocalypse Now* [1979]).

That is a difficult prospect to absorb, particularly coming from a preeminently American medium that invariably makes its handsome male protagonists into heroes. Once, at the very beginning of the saga, there was a young and idealistic Michael: handsome, urbane, and moral, a Dartmouth graduate who against family wishes enlisted in World War II and returned a much-decorated hero. From the start, he seems a worthy candidate for heroism, especially in his resolve to distance himself from the criminality of his Mafia family; and even after circumstances propel him into the family, he does accomplish much, particularly protecting his family from the designs of other mobsters who seem to lack any semblance of conscience. Young Michael does desperately want to break free from every aspect of the "family business," and particularly from the vision for his future cultivated by his mob-boss father, Vito Corleone (Marlon Brando). Vito had hoped that Michael's brains and charisma would blaze the path toward both legal and social respectability for the large Corleone mob family. Oddly, Vito's own youthful self was not so different from the willful Michael's sense of himself.

Father and son both want something "different" for Michael, but he is determined to find his own future. This becomes apparent when, at the very beginning of the saga, he shows up at his sister Connie's wedding reception with a decidedly blonde girlfriend, Kay Adams (his eventual wife), a story-book incarnation of full-blown American WASPishness (as her name suggests, Kay is from old New England stock, and her father is a Protestant minister and scholar). It is in the midst of this very personal family gathering that Michael proclaims to Kay his own "differentness." Whatever his family is, he says, "it is not me." But not many years later, by the time of that closing shot at Lake Tahoe, the terrible, searing irony is that Michael, in trying to protect and save his family, has actually defeated them in that he has lost them all — either by death or estrangement. He has won the mortal stakes of mob control, but he has lost everything of value — everything — though he is loath to admit it to himself or anyone else.

The hard truth Michael reluctantly ponders at the end of *Part II*, one that greatly darkens and complicates Coppola's tale, is that he himself, just as in *Part I*, bears the blame for the destruction of his family. The first two *Godfather* films are, to put it in the starkest terms, stories of personal evil and damnation. No other terms begin to suggest the depth of Michael's culpability for the destruction that has followed in the wake of his supposed good intentions. For all his brains and passion, Michael himself is the cause of his losses; he has, by himself, thoroughly destroyed most of what he values in life. To be sure, he continually faces wily fearsome enemies, and he defeats them. But what he has lost — wife, children, sister, and only surviving brother — he has lost by himself, and he has lost it all in the midst of thinking that he was protecting the family.

The great achievement of *The Godfather* saga, Hawthornian in stature, is that screenwriters Mario Puzo and Francis Coppola track the complex process of self-deception by which Michael Corleone — in his con-

The Godfather (1972)

Studio:	Paramount
Screenwriters:	Mario Puzo, Francis Ford Coppola
Director:	Francis Ford Coppola
Cinematographer:	Gordon Willis
Production Designer:	Dean Tavoularis
Composer:	Nina Rota

Cast

Marlon Brando	Don Vito Corleone
Al Pacino	Michael Corleone
James Caan	Sonny Corleone
Robert Duvall	Tom Hagen
John Cazale	Fredo Corleone
Diane Keaton	Kay Adams
Talia Shire	Connie Corleone
Richard S. Castellano	Peter Clemenza
Abe Vigoda	Sal Tessio
Sterling Hayden	Captain McCluskey
John Marley	Jack Woltz
Richard Conte	Barzini

Academy Awards

Best Picture	
Best Actor:	Marlon Brando
Best Adapted Screenplay:	Mario Puzo, Francis Ford Coppola

Additional Academy Award Nominations:

Supporting Actor:	Al Pacino
Supporting Actor:	James Caan
Supporting Actor:	Robert Duvall
Director:	Francis Ford Coppola
Sound:	Bud Grenzbach, Richard Portman, Christopher Newman
Costume Design:	Anna Hill Johnstone
Film Editing:	William Reynolds, Peter Zinner

science and soul — makes fatal errors of sympathy and judgment that decimate the family he desperately wants to save. And thus at the end of the second *Godfather* film, Michael sits utterly alone, Job-like, on the posh ash-heap of his own malice. The crucial difference between Job and Michael is that Michael's life has not become a shambles as a result of some wild divine wager in which he has been played a pawn for testing. Rather, Michael has made his own fate, done it all himself, executed his own conscience and soul — all in the name of what he deems to be virtue. How that magnitude of blindness and descent can actually transpire comprises the central riddle explored in *The Godfather* saga. Much of the great power of the long saga, almost nine hours of screen time, comes from this soul-haunting mystery, one of the world's great perplexities, what the Old Testament aptly calls "the mystery of iniquity." There are no tidy answers to the harrowing enigma of how evil comes about, though Michael's history is not uncommon. As scholars love to speculate, contemporary political history, from Nixon to Clinton, is replete with Michael Corleones among leaders and other public figures. The only certain conclusion in Michael's darkness is the cry, a desperate hope — first from the film's viewers, and then, in *Part III*, from Michael himself — for some exit from the encompassing darkness toward a dawning, however small, of light and redemption.

In the toughest irony of all, the second somber reality of Michael's experience is not that he has failed in some way, which happens often enough to everyone, but the terrible depth of failure to which he descends: despite his initial desire to reject the ruthless criminality his family represents, Michael ends up many times the villain his father ever was. From a high plane of moral aspiration, Michael descends to a nadir of ruthlessness and vengeance that contrasts with his father Vito's pragmatic but humane moral vision and practice, which the latter sustained even while running a large crime family. For all his love and regard for his father, especially his father's devotion to family, Michael does not finally "get it": he does not begin to understand the old man's expansive and complex embrace of mutuality, obligation, justice, respect, forgiveness, and honor as fundamental moral obligations. *The Godfather* renders Vito's approach to the enigmatic questions of power and human tragedy with exquisite narrative and cinematic force, just as it also charts the origins and first steps of Michael's fall. *The Godfather: Part II* alternately looks backward at what in Vito's past made him what he is and forward to Michael's attempt to legitimate his family by moving its enterprise and people to Nevada and into gambling. Through all of this, Michael deceives himself much as the flawed heroes of Greek tragedy did, and his blindness, akin to that of Oedipus, results in a malignity that elicits from Kay, many years after their divorce, that reaction of deep visceral "dread."

In *The Godfather*'s searching exploration of Michael's personal embrace of evil and the toll it takes lies the saga's lasting brilliance and power. No American film, except perhaps for *Citizen Kane*, has offered such a compelling depth of insight into the abiding and complex mystery of how personal evil happens. So incisive and penetrating is the portrait of Michael Corleone delivered by Puzo, Coppola, and Pacino that the character joins a distinguished company of American literary evildoers, ranging from Hawthorne's malefactors and Melville's Ahab to Faulkner's Snopes family and Updike's Harry Angstrom: all are characters who have done evil and should have known better in the midst of doing what they thought was the good or the necessary. For all the sensation in *The Godfather* trilogy, a world dense with conflict and violence, the long saga is at its heart an old-fashioned morality tale that features the question of how the individual soul comes to embrace a darkness so devouring that it withers the heart and conscience. In that fatal journey lies its real and lasting terror.

The accomplishment of *The Godfather* is to show that evil is real, mysterious, deceptive, and lethal, despite the elaborate prettifying and apologizing that cloak its operations. Coppola does this in multiple ways, including especially his approach to cinematic violence, which he treats as a violation of the deepest purposes of human life and divine creation. The full horror of Michael's slow slide into an abyss comes clear only when we compare his history to his father's moral accomplishment, the very mode of living Michael initially rejects. Father and son inhabit the same darkly tangled world, as Michael belatedly realizes; but Michael's course through it departs sharply from his father's vision and practice. Ironically, and despite his fearsome reputation, Father Vito has in fact used his considerable power, albeit improbably, to achieve a humane communitarian ideal for a broad "family" that survives by interdependence within a relentlessly cruel and lawless world. As the close of *Part I* makes amply clear, son Michael has succumbed to the mobster's code of ruthless domination, an amoral code his father had warred against through his many years as a Mob boss. So thoroughly lost is Michael that, as the imagery of the film repeatedly emphasizes, he has come to embody and personify evil itself, its inmost destructive core, embracing power in order to dominate, coerce, and get even with any who would slight or oppose him — even his own brother.

30

"The Old Man"

In the beginning, so to speak, there was *The Godfather* (1972), one of the greatest of all American movies. The three-hour film tells the story of the Corleone mob family in the years immediately following World War II. Much confronts the family as the "business" of the underworld goes through dramatic change, specifically the "opportunities" to move into illicit drugs and Nevada gambling. Despite its conspicuously sordid subject matter, at its narrative core the story engages the viewer with fairytale simplicity and directness: "Once upon a time, there was a wise old king who had three sons. . . ." The eldest and heir apparent, Santino, or "Sonny" (James Caan), is hot-tempered, vindictive, and violent — and thus ill-suited for leadership, as his father himself concedes. He eventually dies a violent death, the direct result of his own volatility. The second son, Fredo (John Cazale), is oversensitive, uncertain, and a bit dim, and thus never a real candidate for succession. Michael, the third son, Dartmouth graduate and war hero, swears never to have anything to do with the "family business" ("That's my family . . . not me"). And yet it is Michael who ascends to the position of Don and preserves the family and its underworld hegemony as they face the sustained assault of rival Mafia families. On the surface at least, this seems like it may be the ideal solution to the long travail of the family: Michael is savvy, educated, urbane, and most of all — as his initial distance from the family would suggest — moral. Or so it seems at the beginning. By the end of the film, however, Coppola has constructed a moral universe whose complexity thoroughly undercuts the audience's appetite for triumphant, identifiable, feel-good heroes and clear moral resolution. Michael does win, to be sure: he has conquered his likely enemies and won the fealty of his mob subordinates. But not everything is as it seems, and Michael's moral fate in particular poses tough questions.

The primary obstacle to an assessment of Michael as the hero of the family and the story is the moral history and status of the *pater familias*, Vito Corleone, marvelously played by Marlon Brando (a role that won him the Best Actor Academy Award). The character of Vito is usually defined and remembered by his famous dictum, "I'll make him an offer he can't refuse," a euphemism for physical threat and moral coercion. Slowly and surely, however, Coppola offers narrative and especially visual information that not only counters the ominousness of Vito but exalts him to a high plane of moral discrimination and rectitude. Some of the strongest evidence in this apologia for Vito comes in his first appearance in the story.

His reception of supplicants at his daughter's wedding shows that, for reasons explained at some length in *Part II*, Vito is a man who has sought to do a measure of good in a brutish world that bluntly ignores the constraints of any external moral guide, such as Christianity, as a future pope will point out to the aging Michael in *The Godfather: Part III*. The problem is that this amorality does not flourish only in the underworld of mob competition; the same predatory barbarism pervades business, government, and law as well, and these institutions are not trustworthy protectors from injustice. In Sicily there is no law but that of the Mafia clans; in the United States (to which these Sicilians have immigrated) police, judges, and politicians are also corrupt, for sale to the highest bidder. In Vito's early days, the police simply seem to consign Little Italy to its own devices. In any case, what ultimately runs both of these worlds — the respectable legal one and the "underworld" — is the quest for power, relentless and amoral, and neither realm provides hope for the powerless, no matter how just their cause. In response to the cruelty of this Darwinian world, young Vito sets out, as *The Godfather: Part II* makes clear, to establish an alternative, extralegal moral universe that is informed by a quasi-feudal ethos of mutuality, respect, and interdependence. Within this ethos Vito tries to do justice, always using as little violence as possible in accomplishing what he must to defend and protect the weak and maltreated.

This is not to say that Vito Corleone is in any way a saint. On two occasions he personally murders opponents, both grievous criminals who have prospered because of the indifference of law enforcement. The pompous Fanucci tyrannizes the Little Italy neighborhood in New York, extorting bribes from the community and robbing young Vito of his ability to support his family; and in Sicily the Mafia lord Don Ciccio has capriciously murdered Vito's father and then, in fear of revenge, has killed Vito's mother and brother and attempted to kill the eight-year-old Vito as well (shown at the beginning of *Part II*). Even after he has given up the practice of homicide, Vito freely uses physical threat and coercion to get the results he wants. Nonetheless, especially by the time we see him as head of the Corleone family in *The Godfather*, Vito has come to regard murder as a last recourse. Indeed, it is his deep aversion to violence that brings him to bother with "making an offer." Even when the well-being of his family is at stake, he wields his very considerable power with restraint, and he seeks, as much as possible, to do justice and shore up the bonds of peace within his own family and between the underworld families. This is always the note struck by the "old man." Repeatedly, he uses his power for people, almost in the manner of public service. The Don wishes to fashion an old-world peasant ethos of interdependence and mutuality, a code founded on respect and reciprocal obligation, an ethic that manifests itself in the dignity and gentleness with which he treats the lowliest of his supplicants, no matter how burdensome he personally finds the necessity of meeting with them. Needless to say, this posture is a demanding goal to sustain in the midst of a bustling individualistic capitalism — inside and outside the family.

The prime example of this view of his work and "family" comes in the film's long opening conversation between Vito and Bonasera, the undertaker who has come to ask the Don to kill the men who raped and maimed his daughter when she resisted their sexual advances. His haunting opening words, "I believe in America," push the very point: as the Don gently points out to him, this moderately prosperous immigrant funeral director has put his trust in his new land, and in the most vital matter of his life, the brutal rape of his daughter, the country has failed him. The courts have sent the assailants home free men, smirking as they left; now the undertaker comes to Vito "for justice." The tuxedoed Don listens to this long complaint quietly and patiently, benignly stroking a family cat that rolls in his lap. Before he responds to Bonasera, he slowly scratches his head and chin, a characteristic gesture that gives him time to arrive at a just response; when he does speak, it is quietly and with measured politeness and eloquence (he typically inverts the syntax of his sentences and uses an elevated vocabulary to give his words *gravitas*). He asks not about the details of the crime but only why Bonasera first went to the police and not to him, making it clear that what most concerns him is the fabric of cohesion and interdependence that lies at the center of his vision of human relations and "family."

Vito pursues the question of why Bonasera visits him only now, though they have known each other for years and his wife is godmother to their child. The Don responds with sympathy and understanding to the predicament of the upstanding immigrant, but he talks mostly about friendship, respect, indebtedness, service, and obligation — strange words indeed to be coming from the mouth of a notorious criminal. When Bonasera finally offers to pay the Don to kill the rapists, Vito responds with measured indignation, putting the cat aside, slowly rising from his chair, and asking why Bonasera treats him "so disrespectfully." Still Vito remains moderate in tone, no doubt considering this a teachable moment: "You come to me and you say, 'Don Corleone, give me justice.' But you don't ask with respect. You don't offer friendship. You don't even think to call me Godfather. Instead, you come into my house

The Success of *The Godfather* Movies

Preparation for making *The Godfather* actually began before Mario Puzo's novel had reached super bestseller status. When Paramount bought the film rights and committed to making the picture, they had in mind a B-grade gangster flick that would cost about $2.5 million (the final production costs were in the neighborhood of $6 million). By the time the film was released in 1972 (Puzo and Coppola collaborated on the script), Puzo's 1969 novel had sold 1 million copies in hardback, 12 million in paper, and had spent sixty-seven weeks on the *New York Times* bestseller list. The novel had become so prominent a property, in fact, that Coppola contends that, had Paramount waited much longer to begin production, he probably would not have been chosen as director. According to Peter Biskind, the thirty-two-year-old Coppola was the studio's thirteenth choice for director.

The success of *The Godfather* was phenomenal, especially for a film that the director feared, right up to opening day, would be an abysmal failure. It opened on March 15, 1972, and was an overnight sensation; filmgoers waited in lines for hours to get tickets. The film grossed an average of $1 million a day for its first twenty-six days, setting a new record. By the end of its first year, it had become the all-time box-office leader, displacing *Gone with the Wind*. And it was a huge success in Europe as well. Perhaps the best indication of its popularity is that, by 1975, 132 million people had seen the film. *The Godfather* made Coppola a rich man. Badly in need of money when he began work on the movie, Coppola had agreed to a small payment for di-

on the day my daughter is to be married, and you ask me to do murder for money." The difference between American commercial individualism, where cash buys just about anything, and the Don's communitarian ethos of mutual obligation could not be more sharply drawn. Rather than this for-hire arrangement, the Don points out that, if they had been friends, then the "scum" who had injured his daughter would already be suffering and, because of their bond of friendship, people would "fear you," an obscure immigrant mortician. Nonetheless, justice is the gift the Don will give on the day of his daughter's wedding. He instructs consigliare Tom Hagen (Robert Duvall) to entrust the retribution to responsible men who will "not get carried away," for "we are not murderers, in spite of what this undertaker thinks."

rection but a 6 percent cut of the net rentals. The first two *Godfather* films made him well over $7 million; he had refused one of the studio's offers for less up-front salary in exchange for a 10 percent cut, and that choice ultimately cost him $4 million. Coppola also received over a half million dollars for editing and introducing the film for television (his intro is part of the archival material in the new DVD collection of the three films; see DVD sidebar). NBC paid $10 million for rights, about fifteen times the going rate for successful films. *The Godfather* was televised in November 1974, a month before the release of *The Godfather: Part II*. Ninety million people, or 38 percent of all households with television sets, watched the film over two nights.

For *The Godfather: Part II*, Coppola was paid $1 million up front for writing, directing, and producing, plus 13 percent of the distributors' gross, which amounted to another $3-4 million. The film opened in mid-December 1974, and it finished fifth in box-office numbers for the year 1975, behind such blockbuster movies as *Jaws* and *The Towering Inferno*. The reviews were mixed: some critics dismissed the film, while others proclaimed that it surpassed the first film in quality.

Perhaps the greatest indication of the lasting stature of *The Godfather* is that, after three decades, it stands out on just about every "great movies" list as the most popular film ever made.

[The information included here is taken from Peter Biskind's *The Godfather Companion* (1990).]

It is a gripping scene, delicately orchestrated and shot, and it displays the complex, finely tuned moral code of the mob boss. His treatment of Bonasera is intended to induct this undertaker into the pragmatic extralegal world of mutual help and obligation. In one of American film's great acting performances, Brando imbues the Don with gravity, wisdom, and genteel fatherly restraint. It is there in the raspy voice, the puffed jowls, and especially the dramatic pacing and repeated gestures of thoughtful deliberation before he says anything whatsoever — gestures that persist throughout the film. The Don wears his power with great care and restraint, and the visual atmosphere of the room emphasizes the same point. In the opening full-screen close-up of the film, a harsh light at once shadows and glares off the cheeks and brow of bald

Bonasera, who stands in the mostly dark room; in contrast, the Don always seems to be in the center of an island of soft golden light in the room, especially when he rises to talk to Bonasera (this same effect virtually transfigures him in the meeting of the mob families). The lighting scheme itself suggests the ambiguous mottled ethical realities of the dark, hard world in which Bonasera and the Don must necessarily live: mostly dark, but within this room — representing the Don's office and person — is light that is an inviting haven from the shadows. Coppola and cinematographer Gordon Willis go so far as to have the Don emanate this warm light by making it almost an aura that follows him around. Later, when Michael visits the hospital room of his critically wounded father, he walks from a corridor that is gray, drab, and forbidding into a room bathed in a warm, softly golden light.

More notable still is the contrast in lighting between Vito and Michael, and it says much about the filmmakers' judgment of father and son. In effect, the inviting warm light seems to die with Vito — not to be carried on with Michael. This is especially clear in the baptism of Connie's child: the numerous close-ups of Michael, who stands as godfather to his sister's baby, are consistently lit with key lights, an intense narrow beam of white light that shines on his face and produces glare and shadow, giving the character a harsh and haunted look. Here the lighting (and Michael's unshaven face) tells us all we need to know of his insincerity in repeating his baptismal vows. Furthermore, the church where the baptism is celebrated is more like a tomb — empty, dark, and hard. The same scheme is carried into *Part II*, a film that is devoid of any kind of visual warmth. In interior shots, for example, Michael is often barely visible in the shadows that envelop him. His world has become so dark that he seems swallowed up by and lost in the dark recesses of the stony family compound in Lake Tahoe, which he has bought, ironically, in order to legitimate the family business and sanitize its moral status.

In contrast — and in straightforward representation of an old cliché — Coppola means to show the light Don Vito reflects as coming from who he is, a would-be humane man caught in a brutish and amoral world, and much of what he does throughout the film supports this judgment. After finishing with Bonasera on that wedding day, he goes on to treat a baker with dignity and generosity, as he does his enormous, servile henchman Luca Brazzi (former World Wrestling Federation champion Lenny Montana, six feet six and 300 pounds), who wishes to thank him for the kindness of an invitation to the wedding. The most

The always deliberate Don Vito Corleone (Marlon Brando) scratches his head as he ponders how to handle "justice" for the rape of Bonasera's daughter.

problematic of Vito's supplicants is his godson, singer-actor Johnny Fontane (Al Martino), loosely patterned after crooner Frank Sinatra, who has come from Hollywood for the wedding. Vito is gushingly pleased by this visit, even though his lawyer, Tom Hagen, ventures that Fontane is probably in trouble again and has come, after a two-year absence, only because he needs Vito's help. When Fontane whimpers about his new problems, the Don turns tough, enjoining him to act manly and responsibly by taking care of his health and his family, which is what men are called to do. It was Fontane's early career crisis that prompted Vito's "unrefusable offer" to a bandleader, the story that Michael tells Kay as they sit together a few feet away at the outdoor wedding reception. It is Fontane's current plight, a sagging career and a withheld movie part that might revive it, that prompts the infamous — and masterfully effective — horse's head incident. While sensational, the deed is actually one of restraint on the part of Don Vito, since he forgoes violence against Woltz himself. The death of the animal, regrettable as it is, effectively addresses the smarmy producer's pride and pocketbook — not his life. The Don shows the same forbearance to his children that he does to Johnny Fontane, treating them with respect but also letting them know his disapproval, especially of Sonny's anger and his extramarital appetites. Perhaps remembering his own life, he gives his children time to grow up — especially Michael.

To help make their case still more emphatic, the screenwriters strategically provide foils to the Godfather that make him look remarkably appealing ethically. The most conspicuous example is that of Woltz, who is vain, domineering, bigoted, crass, sexually predatory, and power-hungry. In Tom Hagen's initial meeting with him, he blusters and fumes, managing to insult in the length of one sentence just about every known ethnic group in North America. When he finds out that Hagen works for the Corleone family, he turns servile, at least until he realizes that Hagen will not relent on the Fontane issue. He launches into a tirade that exposes the source of his indignation, his sexual vanity: Johnny Fontane will not get the role he covets because he has wooed from Woltz a young woman with star potential but who was "the greatest piece of ass I've ever had, and I had them all over the world." It is clear that Woltz is a raging and vile materialist, defining himself only by what he owns and controls; his character has no inkling of kindness, respect, or love. He deserves what he gets; in contrast, the Don seems to be a well of human kindness. The Don is also elevated by the contrast between the way he and the other families "do business." He treats Sollozzo respectfully in their meeting, but then Sollozzo proceeds by stealth, deception, and ruthless violence. Luca Brazzi suffers a needlessly horrific death, his executioners seemingly enjoying their task, and the Don is pulverized in front of his son. It is difficult to imagine the Don engaging in such tactics, even when he finds himself with his back against the wall. Put in the company of those he must do business with, including the legitimate successes of American culture such as Woltz, Don Vito stands out for his understanding, civility, and self-restrained fairness.

Vito's humanity and wisdom appear most fully when it would be easiest to act vindictively, occasions that abound in *The Godfather*. He does not seem to like the "work" he has to do. After Tom Hagen reports the successful "punishment" of Woltz, Vito ponders, raises his eyebrows in a gesture of self-inquiry, and finally simply shrugs, a gesture of regret and resignation, as if to say that sometimes deeds like this cannot be avoided, given the way the world is (film scholar Peter Cowie, the best reader of Coppola, interprets the gist of Brando's portraiture in much the same way).[2] When a rival family wants the Corleones to become partners in the hard drug business, a bold departure from the traditional mob enterprises of prostitution and gambling, Vito straightforwardly demurs, noting the great difference between drugs and those irrepressible

2. Peter Cowie, *The Godfather Book* (London: Faber, 1997), pp. 183-84.

vices that harm no one in particular ("victimless crimes," as sociologists now refer to them). The Don delivers this refusal in his usual courtly manner; but it leads directly to an attempt on his life as he, in a habit that seems to reveal the man, lingers to buy fruit from a street vendor outside his Genco Import Company.

The uniqueness of the Don's moral posture is made all the clearer by what follows. After the Don is critically wounded, Sonny takes over and, predictably, strikes back, initiating gangland war. As matters escalate, Michael is drawn into the war and himself becomes a murderer, making it necessary for him to go into hiding from both the police and other mob families. Shortly after the Don comes home to convalesce, Sonny himself is set up and brutally murdered. Instead of retaliating, the frail and grieving father tells Tom Hagen that he wants "no acts of vengeance," for "this war stops now." Further, it is he who calls a meeting of the heads of the families to "make the peace"; Vito promises that he will not be the one to break it — that is, unless something violent happens to his exiled son, Michael. Again, lighting emphasizes this point: as the Don rises to speak to the assembled family heads, the small lights of a faux candelabra on the wall rest, luminous and halo-like, on his head, clearly bestowing a mantle of peacemaker.

It is that pledge that Godfather Michael, haunted and dark, breaks in his "baptismal" massacre of the family heads. Michael's course is one that Vito would never have contemplated because of his nonaggression pledge; it is outlandish in its violence and treachery, and it is a blasphemous hypocrisy because of Michael's simultaneous embrace of the church in his role of a "holy" godfather.[3] To cap matters, shortly after the baptism, Michael coldly watches the garroting of his godchild's father, which he allows to take place within the family compound. Son Michael is not like father Vito. While the father humanely does what he can to temper the coercion that is sometimes necessary to make the world run with a modicum of fairness, the son avenges earlier deaths and preemptively murders all who have crossed him and — worse still — those who simply might stand in his way. The father's apparent credo of "live and let live" seems to have little, if any, appeal for the son. The temperamen-

---

3. The above DVD edition of *The Godfather* includes a compendium of deleted scenes. One shows Michael telling his father that he intends to wipe out the heads of the rival families, a prospect to which Vito seems to consent, telling Michael that they'll have time to talk later about it. That scene seems to have been supplanted by the long conversation in which Vito gives his apologia, a scene that was written by script doctor Robert Towne.

tal individualism of Michael seems to make him reject the cooperation or trust his father has fostered among enemies.

Near the end of the first film, and shortly before his death from a heart attack, the aging Vito offers an explanation of a life for which he does not apologize. He tells Michael that at one point he had to make a choice of whether to be a puppet controlled by powerful others or to assert himself (the line drawing of a marionette on strings is the logo for the whole *Godfather* series). Simply put, powerlessness risks the welfare of too many, particularly of those dependent on his strength. His rationale is made clear in *Part II*. That film begins in Sicily with the funeral of Vito's father, who was murdered for slighting the local Mafia boss, Don Francesco Ciccio. In fear of retaliation, Ciccio then hunts down and murders Paolo, Vito's older brother; when the mother begs for the life of her younger son, who is all of eight years old, the boss's henchmen murder her — though the boy manages to escape to a family that smuggles him out of the country to America.

Nor is Vito's life in the New World much better. As a young man (played by Robert De Niro), married and a father, he works for a neighborhood grocer in New York's Hell's Kitchen. One day the flamboyant, power-hungry local mob boss, Fanucci, who rules by terror and prospers by extortion, comes to the grocer to insist that the grocer hire Fanucci's nephew. To make room for the nephew, the grocer is forced to let Vito go, which he greatly regrets. Vito has again run into the inordinate cruelty of unchecked power. With no job, Vito falls in with young Clemenza's life of petty crime, which then turns large-scale. Fanucci, extravagantly bedecked in a white suit and wearing his overcoat like a cape, takes a cut from every business in the community and thus demands part of the action. After Fanucci has ostentatiously given money at a religious street festival, a huge statue of Christ dominating the procession, Vito murders Fanucci as he enters his apartment. The crime seems necessary for personal and family survival, neighborhood well-being, and even justice, although viewers might wonder if a more mature Vito might have first made "an offer he couldn't refuse."

Lest the rising young Vito look like another Fanucci in the making, the last segment on Vito's early life shows him intervening, at his wife's insistence, in behalf of a widow whose landlord wants to evict her. Aware of his power, he wears it lightly, even deferentially. Vito Corleone is clearly no Robin Hood, although there are echoes of that legend, and Puzo-Coppola do not sentimentalize him into an unlikely paragon of selfless virtue (Peter Cowie argues for a strong connection between

Robin Hood and Vito as Coppola's means of rhetorical justification for Vito's deeds).[4] Nonetheless, his moral accomplishment is not inconsiderable. An orphan in the New World, without family or friends, he has had no recourse but himself. Because of prejudice, indifference, and Mob control in the early twentieth century of New York's Italian community, the police and courts offer no correction to crime and injustice, a situation that does not change for decades, as the beginning of *The Godfather* emphasizes. Rather, the filmmakers portray Vito as a decent, even humane man caught in terribly thorny circumstances. His choices are stark: either he becomes a puppet of local extortionists, or asserts control himself to protect his family and community. The travail and losses of his childhood have made him a wily survivor, and the ease of attaining power quite surprises him.

Without this careful portrait of Don Vito, the trilogy's meditation on the significance of son Michael's actions and the descent they indicate would be far less clear and affecting. The moral benchmark provided by Vito allows for insight, understanding, and judgment: Michael has suffered a terrible fall from the high standard set by his father. Audiences are often reluctant to recognize the discomforting truth of Michael's damnation because he looks and acts like a hero; he is commanding, he does win, and he does "save" the family. Unfortunately, that alone seems to suffice for many viewers who naively equate winning with heroism and goodness, a posture that blithely ignores the frequently dire moral costs of triumph. For a host of reasons, some temperamental and some situational, Michael becomes the kind of man his father labored to avoid, becoming ruthless, cold, unjust, deceitful, vengeful, murderous, and merciless. Michael either does not understand or too readily discards his father's finely wrought moral perception, particularly Vito's sense of interdependence and responsibility not only for his family but also for his larger "family" of mutual obligation. Vito's work has never been "just business," as his sons seem to think; it is informed by a tragic sense of the fragility of life and the necessity of mutual care. In contrast, Michael's goal throughout the three films is to recast his father's enterprise into the mold of modern American entrepreneurial individualism. In effect, Michael wishes to discard his "father's way of doing things," which he thinks is defunct, as he tells Kay, in order to "legitimize" the family business within the often dubious legalities of American free enterprise. What he will find out — though it takes him decades to realize it fully —

4. Cowie, p. 183.

is that the world of supposed moral and legal purity is not only darker than he ever imagined but darker far than the expedient but humane criminality of his father. Michael soon discovers that a brutal world requires brutal action, but he does not learn until too late the basic lessons of the heart: that the powerful must both modulate power and, with Solomon-like wisdom, learn to forgive and to nurture mutuality and love — the kind of wisdom his father carried in his bones. Michael's world is a darker place, both outside and in.

Crossing Over

The single continuous mystery through the three films of *The Godfather* saga is the moral-spiritual fate of Michael, and a long, tortured journey it is. That Michael does indeed fall, even to the point of becoming darkness himself, is difficult for viewers to swallow, especially for Americans habituated to handsome young males always playing the good guys. By the end, inescapably, there comes the sudden jolting recognition that evil goes everywhere and that no one is immune, which is part of what makes evil evil. Somehow the handsome boy in the white hat — or in Michael's case the dashing uniform — embraces malice and turns foul. It is Michael who starts out as the paragon of virtue, the stalwart and emphatic dissenter from his father's mores and "business"; in the early scenes the young fresh-faced war hero looks very much like the shining light who just might rescue his family from its now inveterate criminality. As Coppola himself put it, Michael "started as a good man and ended up as a bad man."[5]

The opening scenes make that criminality more than clear, just as they emphasize Michael's dissent and conscious distance from the family. He arrives late at Connie's wedding reception — it appears that Michael has not even bothered to attend the ceremony — in uniform and with that conspicuously WASP woman on his arm, blonde, brightly dressed, and sporting a flamboyant straw hat. By the enthusiastic way he is greeted by his brothers, it is clear that he has not seen any of the family in a long while. His blunt telling of the "offer he can't refuse" legend and his overt "not me" rejection of his family displays his resolute departure from everything the family represents. Throughout the long celebration, Michael shows no inclination to join the merry-making by either dancing or drink-

5. Audio Commentary, *The Godfather DVD Collection*.

ing. Nor is there any indication of any sort of simmering anger, resentment, or contempt, as is often the case with youthful rebels. Instead,
there seems to be in his declaration of separateness a note of sadness or
resignation, an awareness of his essential aloneness and "differentness"
in relation to his family. Furthermore, those early scenes show a marked
contrast between Michael's apparent uprightness and the behavior of the
other Corleone sons: Fredo is very drunk, and Sonny is generally out of
control, first taking his rage out on some FBI photographers and then, in
the middle of the reception, having frantic sex in an upstairs bathroom of
the family home with one of his sister's bridesmaids. Only Tom Hagen,
the adopted Irish son and confidant of Vito, seems reasonably normal and
moral, although he is clearly the middle-man agent of Vito's criminality.
In this crowd, Michael looks virtuous and admirable.

However complicated Michael's relations with his family, they become immensely more complex when his father is critically wounded in
the assassination attempt. His distance from his family is again emphasized when Michael learns of the murder attempt from a newsstand
headline as he and Kay walk a Manhattan street. Meanwhile, the family
has no idea of Michael's whereabouts. As much for his own safety during
the gangland war that might follow as for any close attachment to the
family, Michael takes refuge in the family compound in New Jersey. Then
suddenly, and very unexpectedly, a visit to his hospitalized father
changes matters drastically for Michael — and for everybody else — and
viewers see an entirely different side of the stand-offish son. Arriving at
the dreary hospital, he finds it empty of almost everyone, including,
alarmingly, Vito's bodyguards. When a nurse tells him that the police
had just ordered everybody out, Michael instantly grasps that the police
order is part of the plot to kill his father. He calls Sonny to sound the
warning, and Sonny hysterically commands Michael to keep cool until
reinforcements arrive; it is, in fact, Michael who is perfectly calm while
Sonny flusters and rants on the other end of the line. Michael effects his
father's rescue, first, by coolly convincing the nurse to hide Vito in another room and, second, by posing as a guard, though unarmed, outside
the hospital. That bit of imposture manages to deter a carload of thugs.

These actions speak clearly not only of Michael's strategic savvy and
poise under fire but also, more importantly, of his real attachment to the
family and to his father in particular. To be sure, almost any son would do
the same, whether he had a rift with his father or not. But then, in a moment that is revealing for the audience and very likely for Michael as well,
he unexpectedly and perhaps inexplicably returns to the world and de-

43

mands of his family, discarding his separateness and his idealism. The decisive moment comes after Michael has moved his father to another room: he returns to his bedside, kisses his critically wounded father's hand, and says to him with tender passion, "I'm with you now, Pop." Now completely immobile, the old man smiles, and a tear runs from his eye. Again, Coppola takes great care with lighting to emphasize the solemnity and meaning of the moment. In the course of this arresting sequence, Michael moves from the grim, gray hallways of the hospital — and, by implication, of the world in general — into the soft radiant warmth and love of his father's person. Here, as always, Vito is bathed in — even seems to emanate — transfiguring warm light, which Coppola signals almost as blatantly as on a neon billboard (actually the "glow" that surrounds Vito is a product of both background palette and lighting). So it is that Michael in a moment of dire crisis finds his way back into the family and, however briefly, into a depth of love that the light around his father signifies. In *The Godfather: Part III*, Michael will try to explain to Kay this turn in his life by citing the necessity to protect his family, just as he would, later in *Part II*, act to protect Kay and his children. However, a good deal more seems to be going on in his expression of devotion and fealty to his father's world than reactive protection. Nor does the apologia he offers to Kay explain the lethal turn his actions take and his own moral descent in conducting that defense. Decades pass before he grasps the truth and magnitude of the darkness that begins to burgeon within.

The full measure of Michael's seriousness in this crossing over becomes amply clear soon after when the family leaders — Sonny, Hagen, and the capos — meet to determine how to fend off the insurgent boss, Sollozzo, whose plan for takeover depends on the death of Don Vito. The camera observes the group in the Don's large study, where Michael sits quietly in a chair on the periphery of the group and the frame, and the camera attends to the two main participants in the discussion, Hagen and Sonny. Off to the side, observer more than member, Michael finally interrupts, at which time from across the room the camera fixes on Michael, tilts downward to put the sitting Michael in the center of the frame, and then slowly approaches as he, in his "nice Ivy League suit," as Sonny will tease him, lays out his plan for winning the gang war that has erupted following the attempt to murder the Don. That is a rare gesture in Coppola's cinematic world where the camera only very carefully moves to embrace a character. Speaking through his newly broken jaw, an apt symbol of his entrance into and sacrifice for the family, Michael calmly proposes that he personally assassinate Sollozzo (Al

Littieri) and McCluskey (Sterling Hayden), the corrupt police captain who protects Sollozzo. By the end of Michael's speech, his sitting figure, relaxed and confident, has come to fill the frame. This wordless cinematic effect neatly dramatizes the shift in power in the family. If the direction of the family in crisis was until now uncertain — as the rambling discussion and camera movement suggest — by the time Michael finishes laying out and defending his plan, his intelligence and resolve have in effect become the new strategic center on which the fate of the family rests. Indeed, Michael is now "with" the family, though there seems to be little choice for him. The tangled necessities of circumstance have hauled him into the illegal and morally ambiguous realm of family survival: his father's life and the well-being of the whole family is at stake. Intelligent fellow that he is, he also knows well enough what this choice entails for his own future: the killing will make him a major criminal figure, push him into years of hiding from the revenge of the police and the other families, very likely end his relationship with Kay Adams, and compromise his heretofore "pure" sense of himself.

Mindful of all that, he nonetheless does the deed, and his baptism by blood-letting into the family and its business is complete. Still, his exact motives are not altogether clear. Perhaps he realizes, as he did when he saved his father at the hospital, that his leadership offers the only hope for the family: only he has sufficient wit and calm to pull off the rescues of his father and the family. Choice here is inescapable, and neither option agrees with conscience or necessity. To some extent, Michael's choices in this circumstance resemble those his father faced as a young man (as told in *The Godfather: Part II*): watch the injury of one's family or embrace criminal behavior in order to fend off the devouring forces. These are questions of what deeds are either necessary or just in a morally ambiguous world. And there is, too, in the faint bravado of his declaration — "then I'll kill them both" — a note of the pleasure of revenge and getting even for their offense against the family and Michael himself in the reality of his broken jaw, and it is perhaps Michael's willingness to do so that signals his future course in life. In any case, a good part of the status of *The Godfather* saga as a cinematic classic derives from the careful construction of its realistically complex moral universe.

Michael does indeed pay a high price. His terror at the prospect of killing Sollozzo and McCluskey is marvelously rendered in the restaurant assassination scene. The camera watches Michael's eyes flit and dart in his hollow, darkened face (he'll have much the same look and lighting at the baptism of Connie's baby), and the roar of a passing elevated train provides a deafening aural corollary to the roar of distress and turmoil in his mind and soul. Only after long uncertainty does he finally retrieve the gun from the restaurant's bathroom and return to the table, pointedly ignoring Clemenza's instructions to come out shooting. Instead, Michael dawdles in conversation, his eyes flitting in anxiety, and as the roar in his head crescendos, he finally shoots the pair point blank and flees the scene. As usual, the camera lingers on the carnage, making sure that the audience reckons its cost, even of miscreants like these two. For safety Michael flees to Sicily where he marries a charming young local girl, Apollonia, whether out of loneliness or as a further "joining" of his family and its culture. In the midst of his new happiness, his new wife dies in a botched assassination attempt on Michael by Michael's own traitorous bodyguard (in the novel and in the film's outtakes, Michael does not forget; though it takes years, the killer is tracked down and murdered).

The next view of Michael comes years later, and it could hardly be a more startling indication of change. Kay has not seen or heard from Michael since his exile, and she has since become a solitary New England elementary school teacher (in the novel she has returned home to live with her parents in a small town where her father is a Congregational minister). As she shepherds a class along an idyllic leaf-covered street, she looks up to see Michael standing next to a large black automobile. Michael himself now seems enveloped in darkness — or is at least very ominously dressed in black: he wears a long, bulky black overcoat, a black suit, a shiny black-and-white striped tie riding high up his neck, and a large black fedora that rests well down his head, merging with his long dark sideburns. As he and Kay walk the street in the pastoral beauty of the New England fall, Michael's chauffeured black car creeps behind at a few paces, it and Michael looking very much like a dark stain on the natural splendor that surrounds them. Much of the impact of this elegant scene lies in its simple visual elements. Whatever reluctance Michael felt when he first crossed over, his attire suggests that he has now thoroughly abandoned his distance and idealism, and he now dresses more like the stereotypical mobster than even brother Sonny, the one who loved the rough-and-tumble of the Mob life. He is clearly a long way from either war hero or fresh-faced, corduroy-suited Ivy League "college boy." Nor does he dress like his father, who always diverged from the "mobster style" by wearing old-world tweeds and earth-tones, another indication of his essential humanity.

"I work for my father now," he tells Kay, and he tries to convince her that his father is no different from other men who wield great power, such as senators or presidents. When Kay objects that he is naive in thinking that national leaders kill their rivals, Michael in turn accuses her of naivete (for this claim Puzo and Coppola have the warrant of the then-rumored — and since confirmed — reports that the Kennedy administration hired the Mob to kill Fidel Castro, or of the pattern of assassination supposedly undertaken by the American military in Vietnam). Kay wishes to know why he has come back, churning up a passion that had gone dormant. Michael's motives in pleading that Kay return to his life are not entirely clear; and whatever he says is belied, at least potentially, by his new mode of dress and that ominous black car that haunts the pair even now. What is clear, though, is the urgency of Michael's petitions. They will have children together, he urges, and he concludes, "I need you." Altogether, the speech — or is it a proposal? — is an odd mix of emotional vulnerability, suggesting loneliness and hunger, and old-world Sicilian values, invoking children and the necessity of marriage. Strangely, the word "love" is never spoken. But at this stage the question of who Michael has become and what he thinks still hangs in the air — idealistic college boy or smooth-talking Mafia hood, as Kay will call him in *Part III*.

The answer to the question of Michael's character and motivation comes clear in the last section of *The Godfather*, which leaps forward years into the marriage and parenthood of Kay and Michael. That conclusion centers on several contrasting events: the passing of the old world as seen in the death and funeral of Vito, the possibility of new life seen in the baptism of sister Connie's first child, and the preparation of Michael, now the official leader of the family, to move the family business to Las Vegas. Whatever uncertainty or ambiguity there is about Michael's moral status disappears in these events, though after the film's release Coppola feared that many viewers missed the dire import of Michael's choices — simply because Michael defeats his enemies. The gist of the matter and a prediction of the future appears in the visual foreboding of Michael's new Mob attire as he proposes to Kay. The gangster "look" broadcasts the fact that Michael has embraced a part of the underworld that his father always eschewed.

After Sonny's death, Don Vito makes peace with the other families and arranges for Michael's return from exile in Sicily, thus handing over power to his returned son. Michael begins his lifelong quest to "legitimize that family business," particularly by entering the world of legalized gambling in Las Vegas. But father and son both fear another attack on their preeminence by the other Mob families. The father counsels a defensive position, but after his death Michael wages a preemptive strike that kills the heads of all the rival families, therein breaking the peace that his father had sworn to keep. To emphasize the depth of Michael's descent, the screenwriters locate his savage vendetta during the baptism of Connie's child. The baptism gives Michael the perfect alibi for any direct participation in the murders, and it provides a setting that magnifies the depth of his inner corruption. While Michael swears his vows as godfather — gaunt, unshaven, and shadowed, as he was when he killed Sollozzo and McCluskey — the camera cuts between shots of his sacramental denials of fealty to evil and his henchmen's murderous rampage. At the very instant in the baptismal ritual that Michael forswears Satan and all his "pomps," the baby (Sofia Coppola) — innocence itself — begins to cry, and Michael's henchmen begin to slay his foes. As Peter Cowie points out, the brilliant editing of the montage "supplies a heavy, inexorable rhythm, like the tolling of bells," even as the organ music slowly loudens and turns ominous.[6] It is a stunning sequence of extraordinary power, ranking as one of the most brilliant montage constructions in American film history. It is here that Michael's status not as Christian godfather but as the Prince of Darkness is made emphatically clear. He looks it, he acts it, and later the same day he removes all doubt as to the depths of his descent. At the family compound, Michael tricks Connie's husband, Carlo, into confessing his role in the murder of Sonny, telling Carlo that nothing terrible will happen if only he admits to the betrayal. Once he has made his confession, of course, Carlo is garroted in the backyard, Michael (and the camera) coolly observing his death throes as Carlo's feet kick through the windshield of the car in which he dies. The deed itself, as well as its location, is a desecration of the sacred space of the family, and Vito would never have approved either (nor does Michael, or so one suspects, given the way he shuffles off toward the house hunched over and grim). Michael proceeds to lie about the murder to his sister and then, climactically, to his own wife. In the last shot of *The Godfather*, Kay, his last tie to a traditional moral sensibility, is quite literally shut out of Michael's world as his henchmen kiss his hand in a gesture of loyalty.

On the day of baptism, the symbolic initiation of souls into the church's new life of love, forgiveness, and trust, Michael embraces its very opposite — treachery and serial murder — as he sets out to "settle all the scores" in the family, wiping out all those who have already crossed him or may at some future time conflict with his wishes. Coppola's bril-

6. Cowie, p. 202.

liant cross-cutting between the murderous rampage and the baptism amounts to, as critic John May has put it, the "most stunning instance of the use of Catholic ritual for ironic purpose in any Hollywood film."[7] Lest we doubt the power of evil, the idealistic college boy who wanted no part of the family business has, for whatever dark reasons, outstripped everyone in heartless cruelty and murderous rage. Michael has won, but in the most important ways, he has lost profoundly, killing not only his foes but his own conscience and, as the next two films make clear, his soul.

This same vindictiveness dominates *The Godfather: Part II* (1974), where Michael again sets out to kill all those who offend or threaten him. Coppola decided to make *Part II* because he feared that too many American filmgoers did not get the message of the first film: namely, that Michael Corleone was not the prototypical individualistic hero, like some Western gunfighter who wins simply by virtue of defeating his conspicuous enemies. Rather, as Coppola makes clear during the baptismal sequence, Michael personifies evil itself — cold, dark, haunted, deceptive, traitorous, and predatory. If there was any doubt about this in the first film in the trilogy, the second film drives home the wrenching truth of Michael's mounting vengefulness. At one point in the second film (set in 1958-59), stepbrother/assistant Tom Hagen, reacting to Michael's plans for widespread retribution, asks him if he intends to kill everyone. "Only my enemies," Michael responds, and it is apparent that he has a sweeping, broadly inclusive definition of "enemy."

Along the way Michael has but slight doubt about either the rightness or necessity of his intentions, although at one point he asks his mother if it is possible to lose one's family while trying to save it (the question echoes a frequent complaint about American military strategy in the Vietnam war then raging: whether it was necessary to destroy the country in order to save it). By the end, Michael again has won the game of power and control both outside and inside his family — or what's left of it; but the cost is mortifying, for he has lost everything of value, although it takes him years to comprehend fully the toll of his misdeeds. He has cast away and banned his wife after she confesses to having had an abortion — of a son — in order to stop the insidious corruption and murder that falls to the males in the family line. To his children he is cold, unapproachable, or distant. He has once again dealt with all his enemies by

7. John R. May, "The Godfather Films: Birth of a Don, Death of a Family," in *Image and Likeness: Religious Visions in American Film Classics,* ed. John R. May (New York: Paulist, 1991), p. 68.

49

murdering them, and the story line of *Part II* concludes with the murder of his needy quisling brother Fredo who has out of jealousy betrayed his brother. His father would never have contemplated the murder of a family member but would have turned the offense into an occasion for strengthening the bonds of family and mutual obligation. Cinematically, as suggested earlier, the second film is shot with Michael quite literally in the dark much of the time, often barely visible as he haunts the spaces of his Lake Tahoe estate, and those last shots show a starkly isolated figure on an empty, dark, and windblown estate. So much for family values.

Why Michael ultimately takes this turn toward evil remains a mystery, and the most Coppola does is suggest different possibilities for his motivation. The most likely — and sympathetic — possibility argues that a long series of tragic misfortunes, beginning with the attack on his father, inevitably exacted a terrible toll on both his spirit and his moral sense. Whatever he was at the beginning of the saga, the assassination attempt on his father, the death in Sicily of his first wife, the brutal murder of Sonny, repeated betrayals by trusted subordinates, including his brother-in-law Carlo and his own brother — all of these profoundly subvert Michael's sense of the trustworthiness and rationality of the world. Going to war to fight off foreign madmen is one thing, but confronting the same savagery as an immediate peril to and by one's own family is quite another. Michael is thus scared into doing whatever he feels he must to increase the safety of his family. Indeed, the prospect of a constant threat seems to foster a posture of suspicion, hyper-vigilance, anger, and, in behavioral terms, outright ruthlessness. Knowing the darkness of the world, Michael chooses to beat the devil at his own dark game, thinking that his high motives of protection, as opposed to other mobsters' lust for money or power, will ensure his essential innocence, or at least redeem what guilt he incurs. As long as his intentions are good, he seems to think no real damage will come to him or his essential purity. He fails to contemplate the possibility that one actually becomes, to some extent at least, what one does, and good intentions do not excuse treachery and barbarism.

Unlike his father, Michael chooses to best his enemies at their own game by moving from a collaborative and essentially defensive posture to a lethally aggressive one. In *The Godfather: Part II*, Michael's preemptive ruthlessness, what he deems necessary to protect his family, turns to paranoia and rage when foes attempt to assassinate him while he is inside the supposedly safe confines of his Nevada estate (there is some irony in this invasion after his ordered assassination of Carlo within the walls of the New Jersey compound). This explanation for Michael's turn

toward evil says that circumstance invariably affects Michael's fundamental perception of the world — turning it dark and reactive — and the
measure to which anything in it, especially people, can be trusted. Thus,
he has to defeat the devouring darkness before it gets him or those he
loves. In short, Michael is just plain scared into perdition.

Another possible reading is that Michael was from the beginning —
and all along — the person who surfaces in the course of his reign as the
Don: a prima donna of self-concern and control, and a vengeful one at
that. Or perhaps, as Coppola suggests in his DVD commentary, there was
always "a kind of thug lurking in Michael," though Michael does not seem
by any means comfortable in that role. Certainly some of his actions as a
young man suggest that Michael always was a law unto himself, standing
apart from the norm, self-righteously justifying his independence and autonomy from the family. In his self-involvement Michael fails to understand the ethos or purposes of his father's rule, even though he is both
smarter and closer than any of his siblings to the old man. Nor does Michael ever seem to trust anyone, not even the long-suffering Kay or the
always-competent Tom Hagen, both of them loyal to a fault. Even worse,
for someone who deems himself ethically — even spiritually — superior
to his family, Michael is blind to the moral import of his actions, never
quite catching the consequences for those he most loves. For example, he
cannot comprehend Kay's reasons for coming to loathe the Corleone code
of manhood and his own role in the ongoing strife with his siblings — the
wastrel Connie and the ever-so-incompetent Fredo, who, as is clear to everyone but Michael, is profoundly wounded by his younger brother's attitude of superiority. This is the view embraced by Peter Cowie, who argues
that Michael changes profoundly the moment he is first struck by
McCluskey and is soon thereafter "deluded by power" into a kind of
megalomania.[8] Thereafter he records every offense to his power, no matter how slight, and responds sooner or later with furious retribution. For
Michael, ultimately, everything is personal, despite the family dictum of
keeping a clear line between business and the personal feelings that are
likely to cloud one's judgment.[9]

8. Cowie, p. 186.

9. "A Look Inside," the documentary on the making of *The Godfather,* included in
the DVD boxed set, contains an alternative to the scene in which Michael offers to kill
McCluskey and Sollozzo. That scene has Michael asserting that ultimately everything is
personal and not business. Needless to say, it is an interesting variant that would entirely change the portraiture and meaning of Michael's character for the whole of the
saga.

The Godfather on DVD

The three films in *The Godfather* saga are a major cinematic accomplishment, and the best way to digest it — for they require large swallows — is with *The Godfather DVD Collection,* which appeared in October 2001. The widescreen video image is crystalline, displaying Gordon Willis's lovely burnished cinematography. In Dolby digital 5.1 Surround Sound, or for that matter, ordinary stereo, the soundtrack is very clear, so that one does not miss any of Brando's mutterings or Nina Rota's spare but elegant score. The three films appear as they did in their theatrical release. Over the years, different editions of *The Godfather* have come along. One edition integrated scenes deleted during editing, and another one, a made-for-television version, rearranged the entire three-volume story to tell it in chronological fashion. A VHS release of the trilogy is also available, but with notably diminished video quality and none of the wonderful supplemental material attached to the DVD collection.

The best part of the DVD collection is the inclusion of those extra goodies. Chief of these is Francis Coppola's commentary over the length of the three films, a discussion that becomes more interesting as the story progresses. Coppola's comments on the original film focus on difficulties in production: why he got the job, his fears of being fired in the early weeks of shooting, obstacles in casting (the studio wanted neither Brando nor Pacino), struggles over editing, and so on. There is nary a comment on the significance or meaning of the film. The second disk is largely the same, although there Coppola becomes more forthright in stating his views on his characters and the film's meaning. By the third film, Coppola spends much of his time talking about the shortcomings of Michael, specifically Coppola's own sense that, up to this point in his life, Michael had not suffered enough for his crimes.

There is a very packed bonus disk, over three hours of material that contains an array of entertaining and revealing materials. An audio tape of the

The riddle of Michael's iniquity becomes the central question in *Part III,* where he very belatedly (twenty years later) confronts a considerable gnawing guilt for his many past crimes (especially the murder of Fredo), as well as the present discord in his own immediate family — his children and Kay, now his ex-wife. Michael's acute diabetes, which has rehearsal of the scene where Michael volunteers to kill Sollozzo features an expanded version of the script where Michael argues that everything is in fact not just business but very, very personal. A host of deleted scenes show Michael as vengeful from the very start. One scene shows him announcing his plans to "break the peace" to his father. The inclusion of this material (not used in the final version) would have greatly changed the gist of the story and character of Michael.

In addition, there are a number of wonderful short featurettes. Production designer Dean Tavoularis conducts a tour of the three streets on the Lower East Side of Manhattan that were transformed for the three films. The featurette on the music includes an audio tape of Coppola's meeting with Italian composer Nina Rota during which Rota plays piano renditions of the music for different scenes in the original film as those scenes play. The music featurette concludes with glimpses of Carmine Coppola, the director's father, conducting and recording the film's music. A third featurette has cinematographer Gordon Willis explaining his celebrated lighting design. Perhaps the most interesting is Coppola's display of the enormous notebook of the novel that he constructed for the writing and shooting of *The Godfather.* The vignette on the role of storyboards suggests the meticulous preparation that motion pictures usually require.

Shot mostly during preparation and production for *The Godfather: Part III,* a seventy-five-minute documentary, *A Look Inside,* surveys the history of the saga, featuring most of the principal actors and Coppola recalling the production and, in the case of Al Pacino, some rumination on Michael Corleone. The film is especially notable for its inclusion of archival material, such as screen tests of Al Pacino, Martin Sheen, and Robert De Niro for the role of Michael. Long sections of this documentary show Coppola and Puzo working on the script and Coppola directing Pacino during Michael's casket-side vigil. For *The Godfather* devotee, the abundant supplemental materials in this documentary offer a cinematic feast.

ravaged his health, is a physical manifestation of the profound dis-ease that pervades his soul. Coppola's commentary makes the point amply well: "his face is a mirror of his soul; [the soul is] ravaged and sickly and very, very heart-broken because what he values the most he has lost." That is the core of Archbishop Lamberto's observation that "The mind suffers and the body cries out," and Pacino not only looks physically ravaged but acts the part of a man ill from the inside out. Indeed, the aging Michael as portrayed by Pacino suggests the affliction of a man on the rack of his own guilt.

At a critical point in *The Godfather: Part III* (Coppola wanted to call it "The Death of Michael Corleone"), in one of the most powerful sequences in contemporary film, carried by Pacino's remarkable acting, Michael confesses his avalanche of crime to an Italian cardinal, the man who will become Pope John Paul I. Michael has gone to the Archbishop who will soon head the Roman Catholic Church for advice on how to respond to the Vatican bank. Soon after they begin their chat in the courtyard garden of the Archbishop's villa, Michael falls into diabetic distress simultaneously with the Archbishop's repetition of the name Christ as he indicts the historic corruption of Europe: "for centuries men in Europe have been surrounded by Christianity, but Christ has not penetrated. Christ doesn't live within them." The repetition of the name, emphasized nicely in the acting, falls on Michael as lightning or exorcism, and he sinks to a nearby bench amid, as he calls it, "stress." When asked if he wishes to make confession, Michael says his sins are too many, for it has been thirty years since his last, and furthermore, he is "beyond redemption." And, as Michael points out, "What is the point of confessing if I don't repent?" After the Archbishop suggests Michael has nothing to lose, Michael quietly begins, first with the fact that he "betrayed" his wife and also himself and that he "killed men and I ordered men to be killed. . . . I ordered the death of my brother. He injured me. I killed my mother's son. I killed my father's son." By the time he arrives at Fredo he has begun to weep, and as the enormity of his crime repeats in his words, the weeping turns to sobbing. Meanwhile, amid the garden roses, birds sing and a bell twice sounds, as if heaven itself takes note of the pleas of even the likes of Michael. When he finishes the Archbishop tells him he will be redeemed, though Michael himself does not believe it, and pronounces absolution. As Michael wipes his tears and regains his composure, a look of relief upon his face, the tolling bell peals continually as the scene segues, in dissolve and a lovely sound bridge, to the Vatican in Rome. Thereafter Michael, largely because of the candor and compassion of the future pope, turns toward Catholicism and its promise of forgiveness and release from guilt. As Cowie observes, as the film progresses Michael increasingly "assumes the role of penitent."[10]

---

10. Cowie, p. 204.

That continues in the questions he poses to himself as he sits through the night beside the casket of Don Tommasino, his murdered Italian host, the same who had once protected him during his youthful exile, who has again welcomed him in his return to Sicily for the operatic debut of his son, Anthony. Grieved by this murder of his friend and protector, pressed by the full-blown assault on his business interests, and contending still with his guilt and new hope for redemption, Michael reels in self-doubt as he ponders the course and consequence of his own days. During his long vigil, which is as much for his own dead soul as it is for the dead Tommasino, he wonders why Tommasino was so loved as a Don and that he himself was "so feared." Confronting the stark reality of this question for the first time, he asks, "Was it my mind or my heart that failed me?" Without answering the question, he prays for another opportunity to set things aright, pledging that given a chance at redemption he "will sin no more." Here the perplexity that lay on the face of Michael at the end of *Part II* pointedly surfaces decades later in his contemplation of the source of his profound and bloody personal failure. In that query lies the mystery of iniquity. What is sure here, and what Michael at last realizes, is that what devours him and all those he loves emanates as much from himself as from any external threat to anyone's life and happiness. It is this inescapably dire reality that will haunt Michael for the rest of his days — from the moment of Mary's death, shot in the heart on the steps of the opera house in Palermo to the dust of the obscure Sicilian courtyard into which an aged Michael, alone and morose, falls and dies.

Violence and the Soul

One prominent indication of the depth of Coppola's brilliance and vision is that he shows what is at stake in such questions. Evil is not only an exterior, ominous threat that simply endangers physical well-being, as portrayed in most films, where the more-or-less virtuous hero must protect himself and those he loves. To be sure, throughout *The Godfather* saga, evil is very much out there, seeking to devour the Corleones; but Coppola's portrait is far more complex and full because of the truth that evil abides everywhere, even — perhaps especially — in those selves seeking refuge from the external evil that seeks to despoil their world. As the trilogy makes clear, the evil Michael should fear most, and does not, hides in himself: ultimately, he is the one who savages whatever goodness and happiness the Corleones have known. Indeed, except perhaps for Vito, evil happens from the inside out in this family, as was the case with vengeful Sonny and the jealous Fredo. *The Godfather*'s source of dramatic power is the constant tension Coppola sustains between the sources of peril and evil, inward and external alike, making for a rich portraiture of the human condition. He sets these dark predilections and conflicts, however, within the larger framework of value that shows how the world should be. What makes evil evil is that it destroys the ideal of personal, social, and even natural well-being, the goodness for which people and the whole creation were made.

Much of the power and meaning of the film derives from the care Coppola takes to establish a rich, exquisitely textured realm of value, whose destruction the audience fears and ultimately laments. Throughout *The Godfather* saga, in subtle and eloquent ways, Coppola constantly asserts the essential beauty of being alive: the simple, basic goodness found in love, family, kindness, and pleasures as quiet and unexceptional as silence, bird song, autumn trees, growing vegetables, and the joy of grandchildren playing among the tomato plants. The director's exaltation of such a world emerges most conspicuously in three different aspects of the film, two of which come early and establish an overt frame of reference for all that follows, and a third that comes with Coppola's stylized treatment of violence throughout the film.

The most obvious assertion of the goodness of life comes in Coppola's careful construction of the character of Vito. The whole purpose of his enterprise, Vito says again and again, is the preservation of family — his own immediate family and his wider kinship family of mutual respect and obligation. All this is done to fashion a space for imbibing the ordinary goodness of life, which assumes its greatest intensity in all the pleasures and affections of family life. He chastises his son Sonny and godson Johnny Fontane for their irresponsibility about family, and late in life he is solicitous of the well-being of Michael's family. Since he lost his entire family as a boy, nothing is more important to him as an adult than preserving family bonds. Tough-minded gangster realist that he is, he nonetheless feels acutely the toll of violence and the sorrow it yields. The business he conducts in his study on the day of his daughter's wedding repeatedly emphasizes that.

The wedding that begins *Part I* of *The Godfather,* as with the religious celebrations that begin *Part II* and *Part III,* offers glimpses of the way human life should be all the time — festive, hopeful, harmonious, and full of relish. But while all this flourishes briefly during the wedding, the "real" world presses in, both in the "business" being conducted in the Godfather's study and in the FBI taking photos of guests and recording license numbers outside the gates of the estate. The outside world of "reality" remains: it is real and it is very ominous. The dark world of illegal business in the Don's dimly lit study, in which he attempts to correct wrongs, abides in simultaneous, uneasy relationship with the festive brightness of the outdoor reception.

The same can be said of the religious ceremonies that begin the other two films, although each of those is increasingly clouded by Michael's declining moral stature. In *Part II* the audience eventually concludes that Anthony's first communion celebration is mostly about getting access to the Nevada senator who controls the state's gaming licenses. When the senator proves recalcitrant, Michael's decision to frame and blackmail him with the murder of an innocent prostitute is, once again, a strategy that his father would never have countenanced. The ceremony at the beginning of *Part III*, Michael's receiving a medal from the Vatican for charitable work, is especially morally ambiguous and ironic: it is a plum that acknowledges his donations as a bribe of the Vatican for business favors. Unlike the first two, this last ceremony takes place indoors — in Michael's lavish Manhattan apartment — suggesting not only how closeted and darkened Michael's doings have become but also his own desperate thirst for the full light of day on his crimes. The story returns outdoors only after Michael confesses his sins and begins to seek personal redemption and reconciliation within his family, particularly with his embittered ex-wife, Kay.

Coppola's most effective assertion of the intrinsic goodness of life emerges most clearly and forcefully — and unexpectedly — in his treatment of the abundant graphic violence in the films, especially in the initial one. That, of course, became quite controversial, but Coppola himself tells the story of studio heads who, viewing the dailies of *The Godfather*, initially objected to the lack of violence in the film. So Coppola supplied what the studio wanted — a lot of violence — but presented it in a way that would counter the studio heads' appetite for lurid titillation: he subverted their purposes by making every instance of violence play both as an expression of character and as a profound violation of the ordinary goodness of life, beginning each violent incident with the tranquility it violates and following each one with a long look at its toll. The result is that, in sequence after sequence of *The Godfather*, violence not only looks horrific but feels horrific, displaying with jolting force its true nature: rather than being exciting or heroic, it is obscene and blasphemous. As Christian theology puts it, death itself is the enemy, especially violent death, and that is exactly how Coppola deploys violence throughout the trilogy.

To make this weighty thematic point, Coppola forged a determinedly aggressive cinematic strategy whose intent was to help viewers see violence for what it is — a violation that is never justified or regenerative — and to recoil from it. Coppola stubbornly stuck to this cinematic practice through all three films of the trilogy. Virtually every instance of violence begins with a lengthy prelude of calm, usually a quiet interlude in the narrative that precedes the actual eruption of violence. The first film contains five conspicuous instances. The first, and perhaps most infamous, involves the movie producer Woltz and his discovery as he awakens in his bed of the severed head of his prize racehorse, Khartoum. From the dinner, where Woltz has loudly and obscenely fulminated at Tom Hagen, the scene shifts to the quiet sound of crickets and a long distance shot of Woltz's mansion with the roseate dawn lighting the sky. Through a series of dissolves, dollies, and tilts, taking a full twenty-five seconds, the camera slowly approaches and finally enters Woltz's bedroom, where the producer sleeps on gold satin sheets. Another forty seconds transpire as Woltz slowly awakens. The approach is about as peaceful a sequence of shots as there is in the whole saga, but we know by the mounting plaintive horn music that some horror awaits. Then Woltz awakens, mysteriously covered with blood, to discover the horse's head in bed with him, and his wail of terror remains loud and constant as the camera slowly retreats through a series of dissolves in the same manner that it approached. The horror comes when it least should, in the freshness of the new morning; and the severed head of the magnificent animal, an emblem of Woltz's own rapine, mars and disfigures what is good and fine in life (the novel and outtakes from the film make Woltz more odious still, displaying his appetite for pubescent "starlets").

This is also the case in the assassination attempt on Don Vito. The old man leisurely shops for fruit in the open market outside his Genco Import Company in Little Italy, a placid act of relish and domestic care. Then come the hurried footsteps that suddenly violate this pastoral domain, and then the many gunshots that riddle the body of the crumbling Don. The camera watches from above as the Don is repeatedly wounded and slowly crumples to the ground. The sequence protracts, and it feels as if it is filmed in slow motion though it is not. In a third instance, Luca Brazzi dies after his long slow walk to the hotel bar and his deal with Sollozzo; after the offer of a drink, relaxed and trusting, comes the ice pick through the hand and the wire around the neck. The fourth instance is the murder of Sonny on his way to help his sister after she has suffered another beating by her low-life, traitorous husband. A long shot of a full twenty seconds simply watches the approach of Sonny's car to the solitary tollbooth on the empty New Jersey flatland. The wind blows, the sun shines, and birds sing. Like Sonny, the audience has no idea of what "massacre," as Vito will call it, awaits the volatile young Don; again, the violence plays as a violation of a serene setting that should bode no ill or harbor any calamity.

Fifth and last is Michael's preemptive vengeance while he stands in church as godfather at the baptism of his sister's child. The prelude — a church setting, organ music, and the Latin of the sacrament — comes in the usual way. Here, though, Coppola supplies a vital addition that significantly deepens its impact. He intercuts the stages of the sacrament with scenes of Michael's horrific vendetta. The cross-cutting between the hands of the priest preparing the elements of baptism, the work of life, to the hands of Michael's henchmen as they ready the instruments of death offers as blunt a visual counterpoint between life/love and death/hatred as is found in cinema. This juxtaposition between a central Christian ritual of blessing and murderous evil, the deepest possible violation of the gifts of creation, repeats insistently throughout this film trilogy.

The only notable exception to Coppola's vivid use of sudden and extreme violence preceded by tranquil moments of goodness and beauty is Michael's murder of Sollozzo and McCluskey. There, instead of setting up a placid prologue, Coppola stokes the suspense to heighten and highlight Michael's considerable fear and what we conclude is his inner moral conflict about crossing the line into the family's full-blown criminality. The intent and effect are the same, though the means differ. What is most distinctive about Coppola's actual filming of the violence itself is that he almost always keeps the camera back at least at middle distance, putting viewers in the position of neutral bystanders, allowing them to take it all in, startling them first that the violent eruption is happening at all and then appalling them with its extremity. The audience sees the whole event at some distance to afford a better chance of absorbing its totality. Only on a couple of occasions does Coppola close in to show the ugliness of the acts themselves, especially the terrible cruelty in garroting or mutilation that reflects an extremity of hate and violation. And it makes little difference who does what to whom. Coppola refuses to zoom in on the faces of villains or victims (except perhaps to show the surprise and alarm of the victim) in order to elicit emotion from the viewer; the distance ensures that the viewer does not take sides, which increases the likelihood that he or she will arrive at some sort of moral recoil. The violence's ample measures of deceit, surprise, ferocity, and viciousness speak for themselves.

After the violent eruption comes the aftermath, which is an equally distinctive aspect of Coppola's staging of violence. This always amounts to a kind of parting meditation — ranging from a few seconds to, in the instance of Sonny's murder, a full thirty seconds — that broods on the carnage to emphasize the real human toll of the violence. This is in contrast to the usual Hollywood style, which immediately cuts away from the wounded and dead to move to more mayhem, supposing that violence and more violence is a film's greatest "sell" point. Instead, Coppola's brooding camera allows the horrific cost of violence to seep into every violence-hungry viewer. This is occasionally aided by a chilling audio effect, such as Woltz's scream (*Part I*) and the concluding agonizing silent scream of Michael as, in a reverse Pieta, he reacts to his daughter's death (*Part III*). The camera lingers on Fredo weeping over his father, wounded and crumpled on the street. Sonny dies pulverized and alone amid the quiet emptiness of New Jersey, and the camera simply observes him lying dead for a long twenty-five seconds. Fredo slumps forward in death in a rowboat in the twilight on picturesque Lake Tahoe as a gull screeches overhead. And when Mary falls dead to the steps of the opera house, Michael screams and screams. Indeed, the body count runs high, and the wreckage is very great — even for those who survive. In his insistent habit of bothering to observe the aftermath of carnage, Coppola leaves no doubt whatsoever that Mob life carries an inestimably high price, and in its moral gamesmanship there are no winners or heroes.

The tripartite structure of Coppola's stylization of violence makes clear that all violence invariably and essentially opposes the goodness of life. To make his point still more pointed and emphatic, he regularly situates that violence within the context of Christian imagery and ritual. Not only does violence disrupt the natural goodness of life, but it specifically transgresses the core theological and moral values of the Western world's major religious tradition. A strong case can be made from the opening chapters of Genesis that the sin the Jewish-Christian God most hates is violence, and that stance is a constant refrain throughout the Old and New Testaments. The most conspicuous instance of Coppola's use of Christian ritual comes in the "baptism/slaughter" montage of the initial film. In *Part II*, Coppola goes out of his way to situate most of the

violence in the context of religious rituals: that movie begins and ends
with funerals, and in between there is more violence and murder closer
to home. In Sicily, Paolo, the young Vito's older brother, is killed while
trying to attend his father's funeral (the father was killed for insulting
the local Don); and their mother is killed while begging the same Don
for mercy for the younger boy, Vito. Again, violence intrudes on the quiet
and the sacred, and this double violation now becomes a regular ingredient in Coppola's construction of the prelude. Vito's murder of the tyrannical street boss Fanucci takes place during a festival street procession
that features a huge figure of a compassionate Christ (the camera cuts to
the image repeatedly). Explosive noises in the religious celebration on
the street outside help cover the sounds of Vito's gunshots in the apartment house. This foreshadows Michael's use of religion to cloak his preemptive rampage at the end of the first film. In both instances Christianity serves simultaneously as camouflage for doing evil and as judgment
on the evil deed. In Part III, Connie, Vinnie, and Al Neri plot the murder
of Joey Zasa in the hospital chapel beneath a looming crucifix, and a
smiling Virgin dominates the street while Vinnie murders Joey Zasa. A
large crucifix also appears on the stage during Anthony's opera debut,
again in counterpoint both to the preemptive assassinations that are taking place with Michael's consent and to the assassins lurking about in an
attempt to kill Michael. The way the world should be opposes the way
the world is. Compassion and love oppose hatred and violence. That is
also the thematic gist of the opera in which Anthony sings. This is a particularly ominous motif, which on the one hand elicits instinctive visceral recoil and, on the other, features the sacred confronting the demonic and losing. The Virgin's looming face of love argues that life is not
meant for the deeds of Fanucci, Vito Corleone, or his son Michael. The
only recourse is lament, for which there is plenty of cause by the end of
Part III, to which is sometimes added the subtitle "The Death of Michael
Corleone." Of course, the most conspicuous instance of the counterpoint between the sacred and profane appears in the murder of Fredo on
a quiet lake while he recites the "Hail Mary." How bad things have gotten is shown in the fact that Michael gives the order for Fredo's murder
within the context of his mother's funeral. The family devours itself.

Ultimately, Coppola's eruptions of violence oppose and desecrate
both a benign natural order and the redemptive purposes of Christian
ritual. The suddenness and extremity of violence devours life itself: in a
recurrent and telling image of the film, the simple loveliness of fruit is
overcome by death (somehow perhaps echoing the eating of the apple,

the first violation of the creational goodness that was meant to pervade the entirety of life). Second, violation is writ especially large in Coppola's constant use of pointedly Christian religious imagery, especially of benign images of life and loving: weddings, baptisms, confirmations, confessions/repentance, festivals, and funerals. In the first film, instead of baptism's newness of life there is the embrace of evil in Michael's rampage of death. One can hardly imagine a starker contrast between religious ideal and moral reality.

More than anything, the display of violence emphasizes the extremity of Michael's fallenness. The violence always plays as violation of a benign natural order, but in Michael's baptismal slaughter sequence, the violence he perpetrates assumes a darker, more thoroughly malignant character. In its utter totality — wiping out everybody — it introduces a new measure of ruthlessness, and worse still, it breaks Vito's promise not to break the peace. When juxtaposed with the baptismal ceremony, Michael's rampage becomes defilement, desecration, and straight-out blasphemy of the innocence and festivity God intended for human life. Critic Peter Cowie ventures further than most critics in pointing to the enormous contrast between Michael's father and Michael: the old Don "spent a lifetime acquiring friends and dependants," but in his brief career "Michael acquires none but enemies, and believes that only by eliminating those foes can his power survive."[11] Especially telling is Michael's "inner ruthlessness . . . diamond-hard and unforgiving, more devious, less personable," far different from his father's ethic and much like the amorality of the real-life gangland of contemporary New York.[12]

Finale

Michael does eventually grasp that in deceit and murderousness he himself, possessed by fear and rage, has become darkness and hell, lethal not only to others but to himself. Michael does not renounce Satan but becomes Satan, the Prince of Darkness, and, as Coppola himself has explained, *The Godfather: Part II* was produced to make sure we all get the point. As such, *The Godfather* films constitute a sustained lament for the soul of Michael Corleone, swallowed and consumed by the eternal darkness. That is made amply clear in *Part III* in which Michael Corleone actu-

11. Cowie, p. 174.
12. Cowie, p. 173.

ally comes to repent of his life of destruction, although in the end it proves too little and too late to stave off final disaster.

To a large extent the last film in the trilogy takes its lead from the very end of *Part II* where Michael sits on the lawn of the Lake Tahoe estate pondering all that has happened (the first frames of the film brood on that now abandoned estate, directly linking its history to *Part III*, and Michael also recalls the murder, although nearly twenty years ago, as he receives the papal medal). Michael has become enormously successful, living a posh life in an enormous New York City apartment and dispensing $100 million to Vatican charity for the restoration of Sicily (the gift is also a bribe to win the support of the Vatican bank for the deal that will finally legitimize the family business). However, all is not what it seems, for in the hour of Michael's apparent triumph enemies gather their strength to foil him. He is almost assassinated, and gang war breaks out, only on an international scale ("Just when I thought that I was out they pull me back in"). And part of the problem is, as might be expected, Michael himself, whose conspicuously frail health is as much psychological as physical. Michael seems on the verge of dying from guilt. The plot, especially the business dealings, is convoluted and difficult to follow, and in a way these events are irrelevant to the internal drama taking place in Michael's "soul," which seems the only term to describe the depth of turmoil that rages within. As recounted earlier, the decisive moment in the film comes when Michael goes to Cardinal Lamberto (Raf Vallone), an actual historical figure who becomes the short-lived John Paul I, for counsel on working with the Vatican and ends up, to his own astonishment, wracked with grief, confessing his staggering load of guilt for his murderous career, especially the slaying of brother Fredo. In the best acting of his career, Pacino makes the implausible substance of the scene wholly compelling.

From that point on Michael seems to set upon another path. He tells sister Connie that he had made his confession, although she sees no reason why, still insisting that Fredo died in a boating accident. And when ex-spouse Kay arrives in Sicily for son Anthony's operatic debut, Michael welcomes her warmly, despite her announced "dread" of him, and forthwith humbly seeks her forgiveness "for everything." His initial justification of his actions — the necessity to protect first his father and then her and the children — seems uncomfortably glib to her and the audience. What follows though begins to locate the source of his errors with greater precision — not with circumstance but himself: "every night in Sicily," he tells Kay, "I dream of how I lost my wife and my children." And then there is the vigil by the casket of the slain Don Tommasino that completes Michael's journey to moral-spiritual self-recognition. Wrestling aloud and, yes, praying, he wonders pointedly why Tommasino was so loved and he, Michael, "so feared . . . I wanted to do good. What betrayed me, my mind or my heart?" He ends his soliloquy, seemingly on the verge of emotional collapse, in fervent petition: "I swear on the lives of my children, give me a chance to redeem myself and I," eyes turning upward, "will sin no more." That oath soon proves costly for Michael, for one more time, the family's back again against the wall, Michael consents, under the prodding of young Vincent, to wiping out his enemies, although this time, tragically, they are a half-step ahead of him.

For the wrenching climax of the story Coppola again deploys his signature construction of violence. As the family gathers on the steps of the Palermo opera house after Anthony's triumphant debut, a lone assassin fires from the shadows, wounding Michael in the arm, but an errant shot strikes daughter Mary (Sofia Coppola) in the center of the chest. Once again tranquility is shattered by the eruption of violence. Mary spies the wound, sinks to her knees, says a last petition to her father, "Dad," and falls dead to the stone stairs. Needless to say, Michael is horrified, all the more so because Mary is the prize of his life (at the very beginning of the film in a letter to his children, he writes "The only wealth in this world is children — more than all the money, power on the earth," and he tells Mary at one point, "I would burn in hell to keep you safe"). He frantically tries to shake her back to life, in the process staining himself, appropriately, with her blood and yelling "Oh God, no" repeatedly. As the distraught Kay gathers the body of her dead daughter in her lap, the camera looks straight at Michael in close up as head back and eyes turned heavenward, he begins to scream, first silently and then from the depths of his soul. Finally the camera pulls back to catch the last tableau of death; for another twenty-five seconds the camera simply gazes at the remnants of the Corleone family as they once again try to comprehend what they have yet again lost.

That scene dissolves into images of Michael dancing with the three women whose lives he has blighted: first, Mary, from the celebration at the beginning of *Part III;* Apollonia after their wedding in Sicily; and finally Kay at the celebration of Anthony's confirmation. The last image dissolves to a close-up of a markedly older Michael, eyes closed, and it is clear that the scenes of dancing are his recollections. He haltingly restores his sunglasses to his face, so decrepit is he now, and the camera

The camera dwells on Michael Corleone as he, upon the steps of the opera house in Palermo, screams and screams following the murder of daughter Mary.

pulls back to see him sitting alone on a folding chair in the dusty court-yard of a villa that is no doubt somewhere in Sicily. Michael slowly slumps forward and then crumples from his chair. He dies alone in the dust with only a dog in attendance. The end is abrupt and unexpected, but eerily emblematic. His last thoughts are for the incalculable wrongs he has waged. He has indeed lost just about all he has ever cared for, and those by his own hand. So great is the cost of vindictiveness, no matter if it comes from heart or mind. Nor does his one-time hope of redemption offer consolation.

So radical has been Michael's fall, and so fierce his misdeeds, that the story as a whole argues for the potency, pervasiveness, and mastery of evil that suggests a mournful metaphysical possibility: God may not exist, but Evil certainly does as it labors to massacre all light and good-ness. The trilogy may not make the viewer believe in God or Goodness, but it certainly scares one into believing in the reality and mystery of a consuming evil that plunders and savages all in its path. Darkness can swallow light.

Coppola Filmography

Films Written and/or Directed by Francis Ford Coppola
The Rainmaker (1997)
Jack (1996)
Making Bram Stoker's Dracula (1992) (TV)
Dracula (1992)
The Godfather: Part III (1990)
New York Stories (1989)
Tucker: The Man and His Dream (1988)
Gardens of Stone (1987)
Peggy Sue Got Married (1986)
Captain Eo (1986)
The Cotton Club (1984)
Rumble Fish (1983)
The Outsiders (1983)
One from the Heart (1982)
Apocalypse Now (1979)
The Godfather: Part II (1974)
The Conversation (1974)
The Godfather (1972)
The Rain People (1969)
Finian's Rainbow (1968)
You're a Big Boy Now (1966)

Coppola received his first Oscar for co-writing *Patton* (1970).

CHAPTER 2

"THE DESIGN OF DARKNESS TO APPALL"

Metaphysical Evil in *Chinatown*

Director Roman Polanski's 1974 film *Chinatown* garnered heaps of critical praise and fistfuls of nominations and awards, and more than a quarter century later it has lost none of its power to jolt and haunt with its stark portraiture of an evil that is smart enough to win out in the end. Polanski was able to pull off so dire a theme — not one to entice filmgoers habituated to happy endings — because it is in large part a wonderfully made film, with superb acting, lush production design, spare but evocative music, elegant lighting, and deft camera work. These elements together create a rare measure of atmosphere, one that is, in Kenneth Turan's words, "at once elegant and elegiac"[1] and, according to Jay Cocks, "cunning and exotic."[2] Most of all, though, the success of the film derives from the power of the story that these cinematic elements combine to tell extraordinarily well: a tangled, demanding, and ever-darkening tale, written by veteran screenwriter Robert Towne, with the conclusion redone and darkened by director Roman Polanski. That ending goes where very few films go, even the bleakest of noir pictures, such as *Double Indemnity*. Usually even the most dire portraits of evil hold out the hope that, at its worst, evil is still somehow detectable, tamable, preventable, or that it gets its just deserts by being simply so clumsy that it does itself in by the weight of its own venality. Of this cheery prospect, Polanski will have no part.

The truth lies in the riddle of the tale, specifically in *Chinatown*'s journey, surprising and deft throughout, to very dark conclusions about

1. Kenneth Turan, "In Chandler Country," *The Progressive* (September 1974): 54.
2. Jay Cocks, "Lost Angelenos," *Time* (July 1, 1974): 42.

the depth and pervasiveness of rank evil. Even though the filmmaker supplies plenty of hints along the way, the film's "triumph of evil" denouement, against which the forces of light are powerless, comes as an abrupt, gut-turning shock. Polanski utters an emphatic "no" to silly hopes that good at last wins out. Those who think so have not attended to a modern history whose barbarities hide behind a smiling face (as a boy in Poland, Jewish Polanski survived the Holocaust by taking refuge among Catholics in the countryside). So it is that *Chinatown* out-glooms all those earlier noir flicks by suggesting a nature and depth to evil about which its own hard-boiled private detective, Jake Gittes (Jack Nicholson), taken straight from a long noir tradition, seems entirely clueless. A hip 1930s private eye, whose "metier," as he calls it, is the relatively tame work of domestic surveillance, ends up staring, stunned and incredulous, at an appalling evil that first beguiles and then destroys — and is something he can do nothing about. What makes this all so troubling for the viewers, as we travel with our protagonist into this heart of darkness, is that in this *Chinatown* world the operations of the worst evil are not hidden and tidy but shameless and all-devouring. By the end of the story, the moral, if not physical, locale of *Chinatown* plays as an apt metaphor for hell itself. Making matters worse is the fact that in *Chinatown*, as in actual human history, people are an easy mark because of their relentless capacity for naiveté, especially those who believe they are savvy. The voraciousness of evil and the invincible naive hopefulness of people do not make for a happy outcome.

Throughout the film Towne and Polanski continually emphasize this disparity between Jake Gittes's naiveté and the incipient destruction that awaits. The story as a whole largely consists of the street-wise P.I. Gittes running into ever-darker depths in an investigation of what initially seems a rather ordinary case of infidelity in 1930s Los Angeles. This fast turns into a matter of public scandal, and then land fraud, followed by murder and finally one of the vilest of human distortions. All along, Gittes keeps thinking he has the mystery all figured out, only to discover that he is stone-cold ignorant and that the next truth is bigger, deeper, and scarier than the last. The central structural motif is the reiteration — five times in all — of new surmises that subsequent events then prod Gittes to reject, sending him to search harder and look deeper till he reaches the horrific bottom of a well of evil that on its deceptive surface seemed ordinary, innocuous, and even conspicuously respectable. Eventually, largely by coincidence or pure luck, he does get to the bottom of it all. Robert Towne's original screenplay had Gittes winning in the end, just barely; Polanski's rewrite flipped that victory on its head. Darkness wins, and all Gittes can do is go home and pour himself another drink. While Gittes does finally come to "know it all," acquiring the status of the person he likes to think he is, the story suggests that knowledge is not only not power but, more than that, is not necessarily worth having. Furthermore, it can sometimes prove lethal, especially to the innocent and helpless. As he makes wrong turn after wrong turn, Gittes takes a long time to arrive at the full picture of a supremely dark evil that flourishes in sunlit, "proper" Los Angeles. Here, in spite of the full light of day, nothing is as it seems and darkness runs wild, hand in hand with respectability and success — "a moral midnight in the solar glare of Los Angeles," in Paul Zimmerman's compact phrase.[3] The term most often used to describe the gist of the conclusion of *Chinatown* is nihilism.

Indeed, all this happens — and this is the brilliant twist in *Chinatown* — because the face of the evil it depicts is not at all obvious or conspicuously scary but is, rather, respectable and very disarming. This is the harrowing truth, the burden of the film's meaning: that the supposedly worldly-wise P.I. of *Chinatown* has yet to learn the truth of what he should have long since grasped by this time in his life. He is an ex-cop and now a private detective, and Jake Gittes should know better, a lot better, as should every other half-sensible adult. Throughout the story, Gittes must constantly revise, and darken, what he thinks he knows — right up to the very end, when, in Donald Lyons's wonderful phrase, a "lubricious malevolence" smiles in Gittes's face and he arrives at the final horrific truth.[4] But he is no different in that regard from most moderns, who have been largely forgetful of the monstrous political and military horrors that have romped through the last century and begun this one.

In what seems to be an almost methodical manner, as if setting forth a primer on the mystery of evil, *Chinatown* scores successive points that culminate in a chilling proposition about the nature and means of darkness, and viewers glimpse these as Gittes reckons with their reality. Gittes's experience is key: there are no scenes without Gittes in them, functioning as the filtering consciousness for the audience. Of necessity he constantly revises what he thought he knew for sure. These revisions suggest an inveterate naiveté, the tendency to underestimate or even ignore the measure of guile — the character of evil, so to speak. Gittes repeatedly

---

3. Paul D. Zimmerman, "Blood and Water," *Newsweek* (July 1, 1974): 74.

4. Donald Lyons, "Flaws in the Iris: The Private Eye in the Seventies," *Film Comment* (July-August 1993): 52.

69

misjudges what he might be dealing with. Simply put, he is not suspicious enough, especially given all that time as a beat cop in Chinatown, where the tangled mess of this world plays out its nasty complex web. Gittes presumes that significant evil always signals its presence and intentions, and thus he neglects the ancient counsel of Homer and the Old Testament prophets about human gullibility in the face of guile and treachery. After all, part of what makes evil what it is, is that it usually doesn't look dangerous. In *Chinatown*, as the viewers learn along with Gittes, evil wears a smiling face, full of charm and respectability, beguiling and seducing in order to trap and rape. In this regard, in history's oldest lesson, evil initially looks pretty and pleasureful, but ultimately it destroys those it seduces.

Perhaps, though, one can hardly blame detective Gittes or the host of other naifs, including the audience, for not knowing better, for not guessing or wanting to know how pervasive evil can become. No sane soul wants to know the gut-turning nastiness of this sort of thing. By the end of *Chinatown*, however, it has fully revealed itself, has taken off the mask, showing its power and all its narcissistic relish in destroying innocence and light. The reality of such complete enmity toward human well-being delivers a crushing blow to the soul and, worse still, raises the grim thought that evil, made all the more insidious for its seeming benignity, does indeed run the world. This revelation eerily recalls Robert Frost's portrait of dissembling evil in his poem "Design," in which a snow-white spider on the white heal-all flower beguiles the innocent white moth to its destruction. In this beautiful setting, where the innocent glory of the creation seems to flourish, Frost conjures up the ultimate desecration, which catches the full predatory character of a starkly Darwinian universe that obliterates humankind's fond hopes for things to ultimately prove otherwise. Frost concludes by questioning what economy of evil has wrought this carnage: what "steered the white moth thither in the night?/What but design of darkness to appall?"[5]

The Sap in the Setup

To emphasize just how much the story of *Chinatown*, as with all noir detective stories, depends on "what ya know," the film begins with a ruse, a setup, that blinkers Gittes into a first — and sensational — wrong guess about what's really going on in an infidelity case. Gittes is hired by a

5. *The Poetry of Robert Frost* (New York: Holt, 1975), p. 302.

Chinatown (1974)

Studio:	Paramount
Producers:	Robert Evans, C. O. Erickson
Screenwriter:	Robert Towne
Director:	Roman Polanski
Cinematographer:	John A. Alonzo
Production Designer:	Richard Sylbert
Editor:	Sam O'Steen

Cast

Jack Nicholson	J. J. (Jake) Gittes
Faye Dunaway	Evelyn Cross Mulwray
John Huston	Noah Cross
Perry Lopez	Lt. Lou Escobar
John Hillerman	Russ Yelburton
Darrell Zwerling	Hollis I. Mulwray
Diane Ladd	Ida Sessions
Roy Jenson	Claude Mulvihill
Roman Polanski	Man with knife

Academy Award

Best Original Screenplay:	Robert Towne

Additional Academy Award Nominations

Picture	
Director:	Roman Polanski
Actor:	Jack Nicholson
Actress:	Faye Dunaway
Art Direction:	Richard Sylbert
Cinematography:	John A. Alonzo
Costume Design:	Anthea Sylbert
Editing:	Sam O'Steen
Original Dramatic Score:	Jerry Goldsmith
Sound:	Charles Grenzbach, Larry Jost

It is interesting to note that *Chinatown* won all the major awards (picture, direction, and acting) at the Foreign Press Association's Golden Globe awards ceremony, as well as at the British Film Academy awards.

vampish blonde (Diane Ladd) to investigate the private life of her husband, Hollis Mulwray (Darrell Zwerling), water commissioner of Los Angeles, who she suspects is having an affair. Gittes promptly begins snooping around, putting his two "associates" on the case while he himself trails Mulwray. We see Gittes at a city council meeting observing Mulwray, a bespectacled and bookish man, vehemently protesting city plans to construct a huge new dam, which he deems unsafe and flatly refuses to build. The issue is eminently serious because Los Angeles is in the middle of a lengthy drought, and the dam promises to capture runoff water from distant mountains (see sidebar for historical backdrop to *Chinatown*). Gittes trails Mulwray from the council meeting to a dry riverbed and then to a large ocean-front storm drain, where Mulwray waits through the night. He has, as Gittes concludes, "water on his brain," implying that he does not seem to be the sort of person who is susceptible to illicit passion. On another occasion Gittes's associates report that they have seen Mulwray in a furious argument with an elderly man over an "apple core"; but what all this has to do with anything extramarital seems cryptic indeed. But finally Gittes is able to get a photograph of Mulwray with a young woman in a rowboat in Echo Park — a girl, really, who is twenty years his junior. This is a bit strange, certainly, but it seems to be unsurprising and run-of-the-mill philandering to Gittes, whose specialty is "matrimonial work."

The next thing Gittes knows, much to his chagrin, his picture and name appear on the front pages of Los Angeles newspapers below headlines about the water commissioner's "love nest." Worse still, in a wonderfully comic sequence at the expense of Gittes, he returns to his office to encounter another Mrs. Hollis Mulwray (Faye Dunaway), this time the real one, with her lawyer in tow. She announces that, since she does not know Gittes, nor he her, she clearly did not hire him and will therefore sue Gittes for defamation. Needless to say, Gittes is not pleased, and his reaction reveals a good deal about him. His back is against the wall, publicly and legally, because his pride and profession are what he has to protect. After all, his posture is that of the hardened ex-cop who has seen it all and is supposed to know how the world works — that is, how rotten people can be and how shabbily they can treat one another. Indeed, though he prides himself on recognizing chicanery of all kinds, he has just been publicly duped, and he doesn't like it a bit. More than that, though, it slowly becomes clear that Gittes does not like being baffled. For all the devil-may-care aplomb that he works so hard to convey, Gittes in fact cares: he cares not only about his stature and his "role" but also, though he would think it corny, about people, truth, and rightness.

Chinatown and Water

A water scandal may seem an improbable context for a murder mystery; but the fact is that the story in *Chinatown* closely resembles major events in the history of Los Angeles. The city of Angels is, after all, built in a desert. By 1904, with a population of 175,000, Los Angeles had a demand for water that far outstripped the water supplied by the Los Angeles River. The only recourse seemed to be importing water from the Owens Valley, the recipient of the spring runoff of the Sierra Nevada Mountains, but 250 miles from Los Angeles. Under dubious pretexts, Fred Eaton, a former mayor of Los Angeles, managed to secure the land rights for an aqueduct (he had implied he was an agent for the Federal Land Reclamation Service), and he later sold the rights to the city. Instead of getting water for irrigating their crops, the farmers of the Owens Valley lost all their water to the city. To this plan there was both armed resistance and sabotage. Completed in 1913 after five years of construction, the aqueduct now delivers water to Los Angeles at the rate of 27 million gallons an hour.

In order to store the water, the city constructed a number of reservoirs by means of dams. The St. Francis dam became the most famous of these when, in the middle of the night of March 12, 1928, the newly constructed dam, 600 feet long and 180 feet high, burst and sent a gigantic wall of water through small farming towns as it made its way to the ocean 45 miles away. When it was over, 500 people had died, and parts of Ventura County were buried in 70 feet of mud and debris. William Mulholland, the architect of the dam, took full responsibility, and the public judged him guilty of malfeasance. He withdrew from public life and died five years later. Recent studies suggest that with the geological science available in the 1920s, Mulholland could not have known of the features that made the site unsuitable for a dam.

In *Chinatown*, Water Commissioner Hollis Mulwray makes reference to the St. Francis dam, saying he will not construct another like it. The more specific reason for the scandal in the film is Noah Cross's plot to buy up much of the parched San Fernando Valley. He has managed to keep the valley from getting water, thereby forcing its farmers to sell their land; once he owns the land, Cross hopes to escalate land prices by annexing the valley to Los Angeles and getting the city to supply the valley with an abundance of water. That parallels the history of Los Angeles, which did annex the valley and then sent water from the Owens Valley. While nothing like the murder in *Chinatown* seems to have happened, financial stakes were very high indeed.

He is so bothered by these personal and moral matters, in fact, that he seeks out Hollis Mulwray, first at his city hall office and, when he is not there, at his home, a large, elegant villa-like estate that overlooks the ocean. There he speaks with Evelyn Mulwray again, and she promptly volunteers, to Gittes's surprise, to drop the lawsuit. But Gittes also has a surprise for her: even with this incubus removed, he doesn't walk away but persists in wanting to see her husband. He explains that, while he does not like his status as a "local joke" and for reasons of professional pride wants to find out who hired "that phony broad," his real motivation stems from his perception that someone is clearly out to get Hollis Mulwray: "If I can see him, I can help him." This display of the "real" Gittes convinces Evelyn Mulwray of his fundamental integrity, and she informs him where her husband is: out walking a city reservoir.

This sequence shows a moral depth to Gittes that we did not expect. The man we see here is different from the Gittes we have seen at the film's beginning, again suggesting that, in the Los Angeles of the 1930s, not all is as it seems. That first scene shows Gittes in his well-appointed office playing cool with a client who has just received the bad news that his wife has been cheating on him. Gittes wears a natty white suit — Donald Lyons calls him a "fastidious dandy" and a "stylist" — and while it is clear that he is no white knight, neither is he a court jester or a phony who is rotten to the core.[6] He offers the shaken fellow a stiff drink from his elegant liquor cabinet and tells him not to worry too much about the bill. Peel away the tough P.I. exterior, and he seems to be all right, a rather genial though blustery mix of common traits — cynicism, bravado, and decency. This becomes even clearer when he is personally tainted by scandal. On the one hand, the public embarrassment is not good for either his image or business, and he is indignant at being set up and played the fool; after all, he's supposed to be the smart guy, not the sap. On the other hand, in the middle of his public pickle he wants to help Mulwray out of whatever trouble he's fallen into. So we get glimpses of Gittes's tenacity in defending others early on, and we see the first traces of his relentless passion in tracking down the plain truth of things, regardless of danger to himself. He cares enough to try to see truth; but at the moment, he doesn't have a clue about the extreme difficulty he will face in discerning and then reckoning with that truth.

Gittes's task is immeasurably complicated by the starkly confusing, even contradictory, realities of his world. These paradoxes appear in both

6. Lyons, p. 52.

His "associates" in the background, the very dapper Jake Gittes (Jack Nicholson), fastidiously attired in cream suit and vest, meets the "real" Mrs. Evelyn Mulwray.

the plot and in the look of the world he inhabits, both of which quietly deepen his befuddlement. In one of the many ironies that give the story its power, this film noir journey into metaphysical darkness mostly takes place amid the dry hard light of drought-stricken Los Angeles: the film as a whole is shot in a kind of parched sepia, a brown-and-white where the sunlight always seems hot and over-bright, inhospitable to life in general and people in particular. The suggestion is that this evil is ubiquitous, does not contain itself to the night, and has parched the land both ecologically and spiritually, like the valley of dry bones in Ezekiel 37. Many contradictions and ironies surface in the story itself. Water Commissioner Mulwray, whom Gittes is tracking, dies an accidental death before long, apparently by drowning while trying to find out who stole the water he himself once owned but gave away to the city. Of course, from the beginning there was enough water around in this drought-stricken city to get the water czar in "hot water" and even to kill him, an appropriate fate for a man with "water on his brain." In this city, in a reversal of traditional expectations, as with light and darkness, water itself seems more lethal than life-giving.

So devastating is the drought that is laying siege to the city that the one man designated to defeat it dies in the battle, which is the first of *Chinatown*'s many unsettling variations on the Oedipus story. And the villain in this tale about water, in an irony both funny and dead serious, has the first name of Noah (and aptly so because his rottenness is of biblical proportions), and he knows all too well the value of water. Screenwriter Towne emphasizes this wealthy and respectable old fellow's moral status even further by giving him the last name Cross: on the most literal level this refers to his penchant for a double-crossing deception but, more significantly, the extent to which he is at cross-purposes with any notion of goodness. Most of all, with heavy narrative irony, the surname — especially when coupled with the biblical import of his first name — suggests the extent to which Noah Cross represents an inversion of everything suggested by the cross in Christian theology and symbolism, namely any disposition toward love, self-sacrifice, or hope. In his review of *Chinatown*, Colin Westerbeck caught the perceptual and moral flavor of its fictional world exactly right: a "mélange of double-talk, double-crosses, double dealing and double trouble."[7]

In keeping with the shifting perceptual anomalies, and the nature of the evil it depicts, the story in *Chinatown* is long and convoluted, even more than the one in the *Godfather* trilogy, and viewers sometimes complain — particularly younger ones raised on adventure melodramas — about its complexity and leisurely pace. But this labyrinthine intricacy, far from showing ineptness, makes the major thematic point that is at the very core of the story, the very thing Gittes himself must comprehend and confront: the most insidious evil usually comes not from conspicuous external threats, the unambiguous transparent enemy, but almost imperceptibly appears from within the supposed safety of the familiar and "normal." This is evil that fundamentally revises almost everything we think we know about the way the world is. It has no patience for sentiment and scary monsters, for these comprise the sheerest nonsense.

Drowning in a Drought

The film suggests that much of Gittes's post-police career as a P.I. has been an effort to forget the deep-down meanness of the world, the harsh realities he ran into trying to help people when he walked a beat in Los Angeles's Chinatown. The second stage in Gittes's re-education in the ways of evil follows on his conclusion that someone is out to humiliate Water Commissioner Mulwray; but because Gittes, typically, underestimates the sway of evil, he has no idea of just how much help Mulwray really needs, or that he might even be too late to give it. Following

---

7. Colin Westerbeck, "The Small Sleep," *Commonweal* (July 26, 1974): 405.

Evelyn's suggestion that her husband often walks a particular reservoir, Gittes drives there and finds a police barricade and Lou Escobar (Perry Lopez), his old partner from their beat-cop days in Chinatown, now a detective lieutenant. At the instant that Escobar tells Gittes that he has indeed seen Hollis Mulwray, the camera cuts to a lengthy gruesome shot of policemen dragging Mulwray's corpse — to Jake's great surprise — up one of the reservoir spillways. Needless to say, the timing of Mulwray's sudden demise confuses matters greatly: amid scandal and drought, the water commissioner dies mysteriously, and no one knows whether its cause was accident, murder, or suicide. While it is now too late to aid Mulwray, Gittes's natural curiosity sends him deeper into the increasingly tangled question of just what is going on. By now chastened and wary, Gittes thinks he has one thing clear: the setup of the sex scandal points to someone's major effort, for reasons not yet apparent, to discredit Mulwray. And Mulwray's death in the aftermath of that fuss suggests that something ominous is afoot, and more is at stake than the politics of getting water to the city.

In surprising ways, Gittes's pursuit of the who, how, and why of this tawdry sex scandal about a water engineer fast turns into a much darker mystery, and while Gittes's gut suspects that possibility, he does not begin to guess at what horror will eventually confront him. For their part, the police dismiss Mulwray's death as an accident: the release of water in a spillway knocked him unconscious and swept him into the reservoir. No longer willing to accept anything at face value, Gittes follows a hunch fueled by the offhand comment of the county coroner, an old friend of his, about a tramp found dead — he "drowned too" — under a river bridge. Gittes is incredulous, arguing that L.A.'s rivers are bone dry, and it is hard to drown in a damp river bed no matter how soused one is. The next scene finds Gittes examining large puddles under the bridge and talking to a young Hispanic boy on horseback, a lad to whom Mulwray, as Gittes had observed during his surveillance, had earlier talked. Gittes learns that at night someone regularly dumps huge quantities of water in "different parts of the river, every night a different part."

Perplexed, Gittes makes a night visit to the reservoir where Mulwray's body has been found. After he has scaled a high chain-link fence, gunshots make him dive for cover in a spillway. Seconds later a rush of water bounces Gittes down the watercourse, a tumbling from which he barely rescues himself. As he tries to hurry out of the place, drenched and cursing the loss of a fancy shoe, he is accosted by Claude Mulvihill (Roy Jenson), a very large ex-cop who now works, Gittes notes,

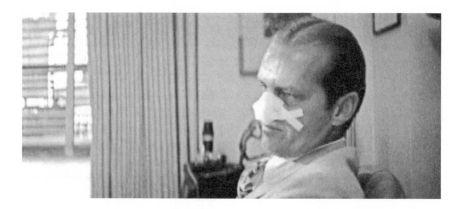

Gittes must endure even further humiliation after his encounter with the "midget" who dislikes nosy people.

for the water department. With him is a well-dressed short fellow, clearly Mulvihill's boss, who yells at Gittes in a clipped accent, "Hold it there, kitty-cat," an epithet to which the irrepressible wise guy Gittes immediately responds by dubbing him "the midget" (director Roman Polanski in a cameo appearance). The jumpy "midget" hauls out a huge switchblade, all the while badgering Gittes: "You're a very nosy fella, kitty-cat, huh?" He proceeds to place the tip of his knife in Gittes's left nostril and then slices through it, spouting blood all over and telling Gittes that nosy people, those too know-sy, "lose their noses," threatening that the next time they cross paths the nosy Gittes will lose his whole nose. With wonderfully suggestive symbolism, the scene ends with Gittes, the professional nose-around, covered in blood and painfully groveling in the dirt. So much for curiosity, passion for the truth, and knowing what's going on. Indeed, untold dark forces do hide and stalk in the night.

Exactly how malignant all this will prove, everyone must wait to discover. That last shot of Gittes, once hip and dapper in his white suit but now bleeding in the dirt, signals both the thematic gist of the story and the way *Chinatown* differs from almost every other noir detective flick. Not often do presumed heroes end up, even briefly, in such ignominious straits; in this case, the utter brutality of the crime and Gittes's loss of control and finesse suggest how formidable the foe is. Sometimes, no matter what kind of bravado the best and brightest muster, this world can inflict deep wounds and bring all to grovel in the dirt in pain. With Mulvihill and the "midget," specters of heedless cruelty, Gittes has run into an eruptive power to which he must succumb. The nose-slicing proves profoundly humiliating to Jake, as did his earlier exposure in the newspaper: the next shot shows him with a huge bandage covering his damaged nose, and the episode becomes a very public declaration that Gittes is not savvy enough to control his world or protect his dapper image, the part of his reputation he no doubt cares most about. Nor could he protect Mulwray, the man he set out to help. And despite the ferocity of the evil he has just encountered, the know-it-all P.I. still doesn't get it; he does not begin to guess the nature or enormity of what he is pursuing. He thinks he now knows what is going on. The next day he tells his "associates," Walsh and Duffy, that the dumping of water and the violence stem from big-time political graft that will allow politicians and contractors to get rich on kickbacks in the construction of the new dam. The whole thing, he figures, is just old-style greed and graft that got out of hand. Still indignant, though, he persists in wanting to get the "big boys making the payoffs." Events will prove him grievously naive.

The Widow and the Old Man

Again, as was the case with the threat to Hollis Mulwray, Gittes is not wrong about this, but he is very far from getting the whole picture. Indeed, from the perspective of what Gittes will come to learn at the film's conclusion, his present certainty about venality and graft seem laughable, though these vices do prove to be a part of the motivation for much of the evil in the film. Events again subvert his conclusions, as they do throughout the movie; each time Gittes thinks he knows what is going on, he is proven wrong, and each time he must revise his calculations, his estimate of the forces driving this world grows darker. His next guess comes not from his own clever figuring but from a confession prompted by another's remorse. Out of nowhere — by pure luck, it seems — the woman who posed as Mrs. Mulwray in the first scene phones Gittes to apologize for her role in the Mulwray "affair." Ida Sessions first asserts that she never thought anything bad would come from the ruse, and she then volunteers that the answers to the death of Mulwray can be found in the morning's newspaper obituaries, which Gittes peruses as he awaits the arrival of his lunch date, Evelyn Mulwray. The latter has frequently changed her mind about hiring him, and this puzzles Gittes; he is convinced, as he tells her over lunch, that she is "hiding something." His suspicion deepens when she admits that she was glad that her husband was having an affair, because his philandering has removed the moral incubus from her own promiscuous habits, in which she doesn't "see anyone very long." Her nervousness throughout this confession convinces Gittes that more can be told; to pry it out of her, he tells her that her husband was murdered because he discovered that "somebody's been dumping thousands of tons of water from the city's reservoirs." And he tells her in his best wise-guy fashion that, while no one in the city seems to care about the lost water, the price for him has been high, insofar as "I goddamn near lost my nose, and I like it, I like breathing through it," and he for one will not be deterred from finding the evildoers.

At the water department to visit the new chief, Russ Yelburton (John Hillerman), who is already having his name painted on Mulwray's office door, Gittes learns from the department secretary the significance of the pictures on the office walls: namely, that Hollis Mulwray and a man named Noah Cross once "owned" the water department and that they sold it to the city on Mulwray's insistence that the public should own the water. In short, Mulwray saved the water for the city. At the sight of Gittes's nose, the new chief smirks, but Gittes fires back accusations that the chief is the one who "hired that chippie to hire me" and that he also knows about the diversion of water, a claim that Gittes is willing to bring to the newspapers. This alarms the new water boss, and, eager to head off Gittes's suspicions, he concedes that the department has diverted some water to help desperate fruit farmers in the northwest valley, a practice whose runoff has the appearance of the "water-dumping" suspected by Mulwray and Gittes. Unconvinced, Gittes offers him a way out ("I don't wanna nail you") in exchange for those who put him up to it, telling him, "Call me; I can help."

When Gittes returns to his office, Evelyn Mulwray is there to hire him to find out who was involved in her husband's death, dangling in front of him a five-thousand-dollar bonus if he gets answers. With his new knowledge of the history of the water department, Gittes now probes the connection between Evelyn, whose maiden name he knows to be Cross, and the Noah Cross of the water department. In response to these questions, Mrs. Mulwray becomes visibly upset, lighting a second cigarette while the first one still burns and stammering badly when she repeats her maiden name or says the word "father." Indeed, Noah Cross is her father. She ascribes her distress to the uneasy relationship between her husband and her father over the building of a huge dam years earlier, a dam whose collapse killed hundreds of people. The two never

Evelyn Mulwray (Faye Dunaway) tries to respond to Gittes's questions about the relationship between her late husband and her father, Noah Cross.

talked, she says; but Gittes doubts this because he has surveillance photos showing Mulwray and Cross arguing violently outside a restaurant over an apple core.

Following a hunch, Gittes arranges for lunch with Noah Cross (played with malicious delight by veteran director John Huston) at Cross's Albacore Yacht Club, of which the latter seems to be the sole member (the phrase "apple core" is but a slight variation on albacore, especially when heard from across a street filled with traffic, which is how Gittes's associates heard it). An ingratiating elderly man, Cross flatters "Mr. Gits" (his repeated intentional mispronunciation of Jake's name) for his "nasty reputation" as a tough P.I. Over an elaborate fish luncheon, they talk of the mysterious death of Mulwray, with Cross asking "Gits" why he thinks Mulwray was murdered and why, then, the police persist in labeling the death an accident. Gittes reassures him that the investigation is in the good hands of his old partner from Chinatown, Lou Escobar, who is honest "as far as it goes" because he has to "swim in the same water we all do." The talk then takes a bizarre turn as Cross asks "Gits" if in his work for Evelyn he is "taking my daughter for a ride, figuratively speaking, of course" — by any standard a lurid inquiry by a father to a stranger. Jake brushes off Cross's tasteless remark, but the old man asks point-blank if he is "sleeping with her," prodding him with, "Come, come, Mr. Gits, you don't have to think about a thing like that." Offended by the foul voyeuristic turn of the talk, Jake rises to leave in mid-meal, telling Cross that if he really wants to know the answer to that question, he'd be happy to put one of his men on the case.

Over lunch at the Albacore Club, Noah Cross (John Huston) explains to Gittes that he has no idea of what he is getting into in his investigation of Mulwray's death.

Sensing Gittes's sober resolve, Cross tries to deter Gittes by warning him directly, in one of the film's two pivotal lines: "You may think you know what you're dealing with, but, believe me, you don't." Gittes's reply is ominous, given the film's title: "That's what the district attorney used to tell me in Chinatown," a neighborhood whose hauntingly dark shadow always looms, it has become increasingly clear, over Gittes's life and soul. Seeing that Jake remains unafraid, Cross offers to pay him twice his daughter's offer to find Hollis Mulwray's disappearing girl-friend; Cross says she is probably the last one to see him alive. Cross evades Gittes's inquiry about when he last saw Mulwray; but when Jake indicates that he has photos of their argument, Cross suggests that they were indeed fighting about his "daughter," an answer whose horrible meaning does not become clear until the last minutes of the film.

From this point on, the story moves with some speed, for all the principal players, particularly Cross, have now made their appearances. From the Albacore Club, Gittes drives to the Hall of Records to confirm his hunch that in the last few months most of the valley farmland has been bought and sold; and while he's there, he manages to sneak out a list of purchasers. Then he travels to the orange groves of the northwest valley, the location to which the new water commissioner says the city is diverting water. There Gittes is surrounded and beaten unconscious by orchard farmers who mistake him for someone from the water department. They hold the department and Hollis Mulwray responsible for poisoning their water supply and blowing up their wells, which has forced farmer after farmer to sell desiccated land for next to nothing, a truth that is directly opposite the water commissioner's claim. This time the re-injured Gittes is retrieved by Evelyn Mulwray, whose card the farmers have found in his wallet. On their drive back to the city, Gittes puts some of the pieces of the puzzle together, explaining that "that dam is a con job": "Someone's conning L.A. into building it, but the water's not going to L.A., it's coming right here. Do you have any idea what this land would be worth with a steady water supply?"

As Evelyn drives, Gittes reads off names from his pilfered list of new landowners in the valley. The name of Jackson Lamar Crabbe rings a bell, because the name appears not only there but also in the obituary column to which the fake Mrs. Mulwray pointed Gittes. The coincidence seems not all that unusual to Evelyn until Jake explains, again in his splendid wise-guy fashion, that J. L. Crabbe "passed away two weeks ago and one week ago he bought the land; that's unusual." Spurred on by Jake's discovery, the pair connive their way into the late Mr. Crabbe's residence, the Bar Vista Rest Home, an expensive retirement home that houses "every name" of the buyers of the parched land in the valley. Of these purchases — which make each one very wealthy — the home residents know nothing. It is with some surprise that Gittes learns that a chief sponsor of the retirement home is, yes, the Albacore Yacht Club. Before long, the manager becomes suspicious of the snooping pair and summons the "midget" and Claude Mulvihill. Gittes has to fight his way past them, and in the end he is rescued only through the help of Evelyn in her speeding car.

Love, Sex, and Doom

A lot happens in the final fast-moving section, and once again Gittes thinks he understands everything. No sooner has he grasped the tie between the land scheme, the retirees, and Mulwray's death than he reaches for Evelyn Mulwray herself, as if the resolved circumstance now permits seduction, and the romantic possibility that has hung over the film from the start finally comes to realization. Evelyn tends to Gittes's injured snout at her home, and she asks when he has last had a day like this. Gittes answers "Chinatown," where everyone on the police force, in accord with the district attorney's instructions, did "as little as possible." After they make love, Gittes further explains, somewhat cryptically, that he left the police force because working in Chinatown "bothers everybody who works there." Chinatown is a place, it seems, where "you can't always tell what's going on," language that hearkens back to Noah Cross's warning that Jake doesn't know what he's getting into. Gittes paid a heavy price in his Chinatown days, he tells Evelyn, when he tried "to keep someone from being hurt, and . . . ended up making sure that she was hurt," an ominous recollection that, in this case, also forecasts the future. By this point, for sure, the audience has come to grasp the ominous character of Chinatown, a place that has become, as one critic put it, "a metaphor for the impenetrable nature of that morass into which its private-detective hero finds himself sinking."[8]

Their soiree is interrupted by a phone call that prompts the suddenly panicked Evelyn to break off their evening. As she is virtually running from the house, her parting words inform Jake that her father owns the Albacore Yacht Club, which he already knows. Gittes's revelation that he has met her father elicits her usual tongue-tied stammer, and she tries to impress on Gittes the reality of her father's malevolence, which Gittes is still only slightly aware of. "I want you to listen to me," she says. "My father is very dangerous; you don't know how dangerous; you don't know how crazy." Indeed, when Jake finally does confront the full magnitude of Cross's evil, he will for once in his life not have a wisecrack but fall into stunned silence. At this point, still suspecting that Evelyn has not told him everything about the death of her husband, Gittes follows her as she drives into the night.

The real surprises of the story soon begin to come in rapid succession, just when Gittes thought he had it figured out once and for all. At a respectable middle-class house, he peaks through a window to see Evelyn talking earnestly to her dead husband's distraught girlfriend. When Evelyn leaves, Gittes waits in her car; there she explains that she is simply trying to help the girl because Hollis was very fond of her. Gittes again suspects deceit: "It looks like she knows more than you want her to tell" — specifically, who murdered Hollis Mulwray. When Gittes inquires about the girl's identity, Evelyn replies, again getting the words out only with laborious difficulty, that the girl is "my sister." Evelyn has not opposed her husband's liaison, she says, because Hollis was the "most gentle, decent man imaginable. He put up with more from me than you'll ever know."

Unconvinced and irritated at Evelyn's long trail of deceit — and

8. William S. Pechter, "Everyman in Chinatown," *Commentary* (September 1974): 73.

still thinking that there is far more to know — Gittes refuses Evelyn's invitation to return to her house and bids "Mrs. Mulwray," as he once again calls her, a good night. Literally and figuratively in the dark, and again entangled in a riddle, and now half-asleep, Gittes is lured by a pre-dawn phone call to the home of Ida Sessions, the impostor Mrs. Mulwray. He finds her body there on the kitchen floor, and Escobar and the cops waiting to find out why his phone number was on her wall. They especially want to know the connection between her murder and Mulwray's, which they have now concluded was homicide because of a new revelation: the autopsy has found salt water in Mulwray's lungs and not the fresh water stored in the reservoir where his body was recovered. Escobar threatens Jake with arrest if he does not find Evelyn Mulwray, whom Escobar suspects of killing her husband — and Jake now does as well.

When Gittes goes to the Mulwray home to locate Evelyn, he finds the furniture covered and Evelyn gone. In the back yard the Mulwrays' Chinese gardener complains, as he tears up the sod next to a large fish pond, that "salt water [is] bad for [the] grass." Suddenly Gittes realizes that the pond is supplied with salt water from the ocean below, and with that recognition he believes he has found the murder scene. This suspicion is confirmed when he spies a shiny object on the bottom of the pond, a pair of bifocal eyeglasses that, Gittes concludes, belonged to Hollis Mulwray. Finally, oddly, with the aid of someone else's broken eyeglasses, Gittes thinks he now sees the truth fully. The fact that Mulwray was murdered in his own back yard again points to Evelyn Mulwray as the perpetrator, and her hurried, unannounced departure makes her look all the guiltier. To reach her before she escapes, Gittes speeds to Evelyn's "safe house," where she keeps her sister, or Hollis's girlfriend — or whoever she may be.

Gittes barges into the house and finds suitcases packed in the living room. He asks Evelyn if she is "going some place" and if she knows "any good criminal lawyers." After calling Escobar to notify him, he shows Evelyn the eyeglasses and angrily tells her that they mean she killed her husband; he demands the full truth before the police arrive, accuse him of collusion in the murder, and he loses his P.I. license. He then asks her who "the girl" really is. When Evelyn remains silent, Gittes begins, in one of the more wrenching scenes in contemporary film, to slap Evelyn over and over as she repeats, now weeping, that the girl is her sister *and* her daughter. Slowly the reality of incest dawns on Gittes, as Evelyn says, "My father and I . . . understand? Or is it too tough for you?" She tells him now that when she ran from the horror back then — at fifteen years old, hysterical, and pregnant with her daughter-sister — "Hollis came and took care of me." That kindness is exactly what Mulwray was trying to accomplish once again, this time for his step-daughter, and that got him killed — the price of running afoul of Noah Cross's deepest affections. And for once Gittes, the street-savvy, know-it-all smart-talker, the one who thought he had seen the worst distortions the world had to offer during his Chinatown days, is chastened and silent. Indeed, as Noah Cross had warned him, "You may think you know what you're getting into, but believe me, you don't." The horror of it is beyond anything Gittes has imagined; his nosiness has led him to a wound that will last much longer than the one to his nose. But now, abruptly stunned into sympathy, he becomes Evelyn's protector and tells her to leave before the police arrive. He arranges to meet her at her butler's house — ominously, in Chinatown. But before she leaves, Evelyn tells Jake that the eyeglasses could not have been her husband's because he did not wear bifocals. Gittes quickly manages to elude the police and to arrange for Evelyn and her daughter to escape by boat to Mexico.

To Chinatown

The end begins with Gittes arranging to meet the real culprit, Noah Cross, whom he lures to the Mulwray estate with the promise that he has "the girl." When Cross arrives, Gittes lets him know that he finally knows everything when he tells him that the girl is with her mother. And when Cross can't focus on the small print of the obituary column Gittes hands him — a listing that Gittes contends reveals who killed Hollis Mulwray — Gittes knows that Cross drowned Mulwray in the backyard pond and lost his bifocals in the process. As is his wont when confronted with unpleasant realities, Cross ignores Gittes's claim and begins to muse about Mulwray's love of tidepools — because life comes from them. More than that, he says, Hollis Mulwray "made this city" and made Cross a rich man. When Gittes questions Cross about the water scam, the latter explains it: "If you can't bring the water to the valley, you bring the valley to the water" by annexing it into the city.

Perplexed by the magnitude of Cross's greed, Gittes asks him about the size of his fortune, at which the former laughs, admitting that he really doesn't know how much he has but that he is surely worth more than $10 million. Why more, asks Gittes: "How much better can you eat?

What can you buy that you can't already afford?" Cross's reply is ecstatic and cryptic at the same time: "The future, Mr. Gits, the future" — surely a statement of megalomania for an elderly man to make. For now, though, he confesses bathetically that he simply wants the "only daughter I got left," since "Evelyn was lost to me a long time ago." When Gittes asks whose fault that might be, Cross offers an apologia, in effect, for everything he has done: "I don't blame myself. You see, Mr. Gits, most people never have to face the fact that in the right time and the right place, they're capable of anything." After this declaration of zestful narcissism, Cross instructs his thug, Claude Mulvihill, who has been hiding in the darkness, to take the incriminating eyeglasses from Gittes; then, with Mulvihill's gun in Gittes's ear, Cross demands to know the whereabouts of "the girl," who is both his daughter and granddaughter at the same time.

The last scene takes place, appropriately, in Chinatown, where Evelyn is hiding with her sister-daughter. In a brief montage, the camera becomes aimless and kaleidoscopic, and the musical score jumps from the sultriness of its recurrent saxophone to a jarring, ominous percussion that emphasizes discord and chaos. To his immense relief, Gittes finds not only the two women waiting where he has told them to meet him but also the cop Escobar, to whom Jake announces that Cross is "the bird you're after . . . I can explain everything . . . just give me five minutes . . . that's all I need." When Escobar ignores Gittes's petition, the desperate P.I. implores him further, explaining that Cross is "rich, do you understand? He gets away with anything." More and more flustered, Escobar tells Gittes to keep quiet. Escobar clearly knows the person he is contending with here; but he doesn't want the truth to come out because he wants to keep his job. After all, the horror, once it is objectified in words, made plain and public, loses its deniability, and then everyone has to contend with the stark inescapability of a heretofore hidden, because unspoken, reality that devours everything in its path.

Gittes will not relent, insisting that Cross is "crazy" and is behind everything. To prove his point cinematically, Polanski suddenly has Cross look aside to something outside the frame, and the camera shifts to Cross's point of view, a shot of Evelyn and daughter-sister Catherine fleeing to the nearby convertible. The old man approaches, and in a demeanor that is both simpering and leering, begs Evelyn to "please, please, be reasonable" because — parading his bathetic self-pity — he says that he has only a few years left and "she's mine, too." Horrified by Cross's bald-faced admission that he intends to repeat his crimes, Evelyn says, "She's never going to know that." When she pulls a gun, Gittes screams that the police will take care of Cross. But Evelyn answers that her father "owns the police," something that is clear to everyone but Gittes, lingering as he does in his naiveté. When Cross approaches, Evelyn shoots him in the arm, hops in the convertible, and drives off. Escobar and his sergeant draw their guns, and while Gittes spoils the aim of one of them, the other fires repeatedly. The camera lingers on the escaping car: as it rolls to a stop, with its horn wailing, a woman's scream reaches back; dashing to the car, they find Evelyn Mulwray dead from a head wound. The camera now assumes Jake's point of view as he looks down on the body of the dead mother-sister and then up to see Cross sheltering the horrified Catherine, repeating over and over, in a voice sopping with falsity, "Oh Lord, oh Lord."

When the camera at length cuts back to Gittes, he mutters "as little as possible," a phrase he has earlier used to describe the district attorney's directions for law enforcement in Chinatown. The fate of Evelyn Mulwray repeats the earlier one of someone Gittes tried to help in Chinatown, showing how the best intentions of those who confront gargantuan evil can go awry. In trying to help another love, Gittes has inadvertently made her death a certainty. Seeing his despair, Escobar tells Jake's partners to take him home. "Just get him the hell out of here. Go home, Jake; I'm doing you a big favor." Stunned and defeated, Gittes gazes, stupefied, at the debris of all his efforts. His partner then reminds him, "It's Chinatown, Jake, it's Chinatown," a simple, haunting declaration that distills the utter futility of human efforts to fend off, let alone defeat, the kind of systemic evil that Noah Cross represents and of which Chinatown is the most conspicuous display. Again the camera says it all: in the last lengthy take, the camera slowly rises from street level to brood on the sight of Gittes's partners taking him off through the small crowd of bystanders and down the long street behind them. It lingers there long after the viewer has lost sight of Jake Gittes and while the credits roll. And again the music plays, mournful and loud, like the stuff of life itself.

The Design of Darkness to Appall

What Gittes thought he knew, he did not — over and over again. Even for one so savvy, even jaded, one who thought he knew the depth and ways of evil, to him has come a final dark and inescapable surprise. This man, Noah Cross, so fundamentally at cross-purposes with the universe and the warm hopes of a weary, beleaguered humanity, smiles on all around him only to disarm and then devour them. His voracity is made all the more insidious by his respectability and apparent kindliness. A quiet and leisurely noir mystery, *Chinatown* soberly, even reluctantly, gives its protagonist — and the viewers along with him — the profound noetic shock that it's possible that this insatiable malice actually runs the world, and that even the smart and well-intentioned are powerless against it. The truth beneath the veneer that inclines the protagonist and the viewers to extend their trust is that evil abounds where it is least expected.

Chinatown's remarkable achievement lies in this portrayal of humanity's worst nightmares about evil: at work here is no middling sort of petty chicanery, though that's how the film starts out, but an obdurate enmity that thrives at the heart of a community's affairs. That anything of this kind can exist is occasion for despair, which is the mournful, necessary lament to which Towne and Polanski bring their viewers. For Polanski in particular, given his history as a child and as a husband (Polanski's pregnant wife, actress Sharon Tate, was murdered by the Charles Manson gang), the world is, as Donald Lyons has deftly argued, "Chinatown — an arena of random, meaningless, and omnipotent malevolence where the worst that can conceivably occur will. It was Polanski who . . . insisted that Evelyn perish and Noah survive."[9] And this is a major theme in Western literature, one that resounds in Sophocles, Shakespeare, Dostoevsky, Hawthorne, Melville, Frost, and many more of history's great writers: the possibility that the final triumph of history belongs to evil and that there is little that human beings can do to defeat it, simply because of its very nature. It is subtle and deceptive, usually presenting to its prey a benign face instead of the sentimental caricature of evil broadcasting its presence, like a clumsy ogre that brandishes teeth and claws and slavers in its victim's face, as does the cannibal Cyclops in Homer's *Odyssey*. Rather, the evil depicted in *Chinatown* is far more fearsome and ominous because of its capacity for disguise and treachery. Like Homer's seductive goddess Circe in *The Odyssey*, evil comes in a "chill sweet song" that steals the soul before the self even begins to detect its loss. Behind a benign countenance flourishes an unforeseen evil that is no less voracious than Dante's she-wolf, who "tracks down all, kills all, and knows no glut, but, feeding, she grows hungrier than she was."

9. Lyons, p. 53.

Chinatown Filmography

Films Directed by Roman Polanski

The Pianist (2002)

The Ninth Gate (1999)

Death and the Maiden (1994)

Bitter Moon (1992)

Frantic (1988)

Pirates (1986)

Tess (1979)

The Tenant (1976)

Chinatown (1974)

What? (1972)

The Tragedy of Macbeth (1971)

Rosemary's Baby (1968)

The Fearless Vampire Killers (1967)

Cul-de-sac (1966)

Repulsion (1965)

Knife in the Water (1963)

This is what ultimately gives *Chinatown* its religious pertinence and gives shape to its withering irony: behind a smiling face lurks a ferocity that will, by whatever means it can, consume whatever it can, body or soul, and it is all the more dangerous because its malice goes incognito. In the late nineteenth-century, novelist Joseph Conrad went to the remote, humid jungles of Africa to find the heart of darkness; in *Chinatown*, a tale for our time, we find it in an arid, drought-stricken Los Angeles. So great is its force and guile, as Frost's poem reminds the cheerful and sentimental, that its very design, once seen clear and full, suffices to prompt terror in any sensible heart. Evil wins.

Films Written by Robert Towne
Mission: Impossible II (2000)
Without Limits (1998)
Mission: Impossible (1996)
Love Affair (1994)
The Firm (1993)
The Two Jakes (1990)
Days of Thunder (1990)
Tequila Sunrise (1988)
Greystoke: The Legend of Tarzan, Lord of the Apes (1984) (as P. H. Vazak)
Personal Best (1982)
The Yakuza (1975)
Shampoo (1975)
Chinatown (1974)
The Last Detail (1973)
Villa Rides (1968)
My Daddy Can Lick Your Daddy (1962)
Last Woman on Earth (1960)

Towne has worked on innumerable other films as a consultant or script doctor, for which he has not received credit. The chief instance of this is Coppola's *The Godfather,* for which he wrote the long exchange between Michael and his aging father just before Vito's death.

CHAPTER 3

"JUST COME HOME"

Violence and Redemption in *The Deer Hunter*

The story falls neatly into two parts, a before and an after, divided by the film's pivotal event, a mysterious life-turning of enormous import. Throughout the film — at its very center — is the intrepid Michael (Robert De Niro), a small-town steelworker who goes off to fight in Vietnam, a would-be John Wayne who wants to go "where the bullets are flying," as one of his buddies puts it. Instead of finding thrills and glory, he has experiences there that shake him to the core of his being. On the one hand, he returns from Vietnam the genuine warrior hero he wanted to be, having escaped — with two fellow hometown enlistees — from the Vietcong. But his homecoming makes clear, on the other hand, that new uncertainties roil within his heretofore cocksure self. The wound that has afforded him recuperation leave is physical; but there is another wound, one that is entirely and deeply spiritual, inflicted by the horror and caprice of real violence in real war — a necessary wound in his case.

That is deeply understandable, because Michael and his friends have suffered violence as sport, in ways beyond imagining, done to them for the amusement and diversion of those with power. In only a few hours, in a grass shack on a river, everything is changed, utterly changed, in the incinerating reality of a rapaciousness that delights in the terror of its playthings. All three friends survive that horror, though not in one piece; but in the aftermath, Michael's world is no longer as he thought it was. What he must now make of life — particularly of power and sport, his life passions — is no small matter.

Michael himself undergoes a change, a "turning" that is decisive and profound, which reverses the course of his own life and alters the many lives around him as well. That turning happens about halfway through *The Deer Hunter,* and, as befits such an occasion, it happens when Michael is alone on a mountaintop in the course of a deer hunt (to which the title refers), which for Michael, and for director Michael Cimino, is a potent symbol that defines how one approaches the purposes and meaning of living in general. While home on medical leave, Michael goes to the mountains with three pals who did not go off to war (the two from the original group who went to Vietnam have been swallowed up by the war, one a triple amputee and the other mysteriously AWOL in Saigon). This hunt reprises an earlier hunt, a long sequence in which Michael fully exhibits not only his mastery in the hunt but his macho credo that a deer "has to be taken in one shot." If a hunter cannot do that, he falls short, both as a stalker of deer and as a marksman.

Michael traverses the rugged rock ridges under an expansive blue sky, with a surging Russian Orthodox choral refrain overlaying his search for prey. Two minutes elapse before he spies a magnificent buck with a full rack (it is really a full-grown male elk that the filmmakers have sneaked in to give the prey magnificence and the scene *gravitas*). The creature stands stock still on the ridge, oddly unperturbed, looking at Michael as he approaches and aims. This is a once-in-a-lifetime perfect shot at the perfect buck. But Michael hesitates as he looks down the barrel of his rifle, and in the instant that he fires, he pulls up, intentionally missing. Instead of immediately springing off at the loud report of the rifle, as deer invariably do, the animal remains stationary; it looks straight at Michael and then, calmly and slowly, walks away. Stranger still is Michael's response: in the very next scene, he stands by an enormous mountain waterfall and shouts into the expanse of mountain, water, and sky a very loud "okay," an assent to preserving life that then echoes back from the rugged landscape over and over.

With this exchange between him and the mountains, Michael has made some kind of compact: it is a wordless, visually stunning sequence that receives no verbal comment or interpretation whatsoever from Cimino in the remainder of the film. What is clear, though, is that the Michael who leaves the hunt and then returns to the smoky mill town, the place where he and his friends grew up and call home, is very different from the Michael who went looking for deer to shoot before his Vietnam experience. Understanding the depth of what happened during the hunt, the center and pivot of the tale, demands a close look at Michael's own history and deepest self, at what we might most meaningfully best call his soul. After all, whatever it is that sounds back "okay" suffices to turn him from the "killing fields," here and in Vietnam, to revere all the

The Deer Hunter (1978)

Director:	Michael Cimino
Story:	Michael Cimino, Deric Washburn, Louis Garfinkle, Quinn K. Redeker
Screenplay:	Deric Washburn
Cinematography:	Vilmos Zsigmond
Editing:	Peter Zinner
Art Direction:	Ron Hobbs, Kim Swados

Cast

Robert De Niro	Michael Vronsky
John Cazale	Stanley ("Stosh")
John Savage	Steven
Christopher Walken	Nick
Meryl Streep	Linda
George Dzundza	John
Chuck Aspegren	Axel

Academy Awards

Best Picture	
Best Director:	Michael Cimino
Best Supporting Actor:	Christopher Walken
Editing:	Peter Zinner
Sound:	Richard Portman, William L. McCaughey, Aaron Rochin, C. Darin Knight

Additional Academy Award Nominations

Actor:	Robert De Niro
Supporting Actress:	Meryl Streep
Cinematography:	Vilmos Zsigmond
Original Screenplay:	Michael Cimino, Deric Washburn, Louis Garfinkle, Quinn K. Redeker

best of what is meant by home and community. It is a radical, mysterious, and completely unexpected turnabout in which Michael sheds his central conception of life to embrace one that is wholly opposite. It is to embrace a world he had always held at arm's length, a world that was best managed with "one shot," a credo derived from the heart of American myths about the frontier, violence, and triumph.

"One Shot"

The small, very dingy Pennsylvania steel town ironically named Clairton (clear town) is not a picture of American civic health. All the buildings are grimy and shabby, except for the imposing Russian Orthodox Church; the sky is permanently hazed over by the chemical smoke and pollution of the mill. The townspeople are notably depressed: the men seem dependent on alcohol, and the women, at least the older ones, on the Russian Orthodox faith, whose stately church seems to dominate the town (the actual church in the film is St. Theodosius Russian Orthodox Church in Cleveland). The opening shots display the setting in emphatic terms: a place sodden with a soot-gray sky and buildings, a landscape where semis laden with freight hurtle ominously through the center of the town. The interior of the steel mill, a workplace full of flame and smoke and ghostly figures, looks a lot like the hell portrayed by artists, or at least like the death-in-life creatures that inhabit the ash heaps in F. Scott Fitzgerald's *The Great Gatsby*. Even going to war seems like a better idea than staying in this cheerless place, at least in the minds of the story's young — and very naive — protagonists. The story begins with three local high school friends finishing their last night shift at the mill before they are to leave for the Army and what is likely to be a combat tour in Vietnam. And a long last day it will be after they have joined their three other friends: breakfast and beer at a local bar, a wedding and reception later in the evening, and then an all-night trip to the mountains and deer hunting. This is a hardscrabble world of grungy physical and emotional realities that some — at least these young men — are lucky enough to temporarily escape through booze and hijinks.

The young men are all in their twenties (except for John [George Dzundza], the kindly barkeep, probably in his thirties), old friends from high school who stayed in Clairton to work in the mill. They now hang around together, not because they all like each other particularly, but for lack of anything better to do. The strongest personality in this ragtag crew of six young men is Michael, the deer hunter. Then there is Axel (Chuck Aspegren), a once promising football player who ruined his knees; Stanley (John Cazale), a wannabe tough guy and ladies' man; Steve (John Savage), whose wedding to a notably older — and pregnant — bride they'll all attend that evening; and Nick (Christopher Walken), the sweet, sensitive roommate and best friend of the manly Michael. Although Michael has about him a kind of natural authority, he dodges any kind of leadership role within the group because his stalwart individualism keeps him from caring enough to bother to lead anyone anywhere. And Michael is indeed a distinctive personality: he is independent and idealistic, resolute and disciplined, though his animating vision is at best sorely constricted and, at worst, wholly distorted, admirable in one small way but essentially quite destructive, as he himself will come to discover.

The problem is that Michael venerates a particular brand of individualism that celebrates a nostalgic myth of frontier self-sufficiency and control over whatever is untamed, whether it be self, society, or environment. For Michael, the real consummation of this ideal of mastery lies in the achievement of the perfect hunt and of "one shot" in particular: "A deer," he tells his friend Nick, "has to be taken in one shot." Hunting is one thing, but for Michael "one shot" occupies an exalted, even sacred domain all its own. And Michael uses the term frequently, applying it in cryptic manner to domains of life where it has no pertinence or value whatsoever. "One shot" somehow defines his deepest sense of self and of what is worthy in human achievement, and Michael embraces it with an intense, religious zeal; but the phrase ramifies to his own horror, tragically and ironically, throughout the course of the story. Far more is involved than mere marksmanship, the art of being a good shot. "One shot" entails an elaborate code of values, a whole way of living, about the preparation and conduct of the hunt and, for that matter, life in general.

Michael takes it very seriously, but it ill equips him for the central and vital activities of life, such as friendship, love, or worship. Instead, Michael's notion of the triumphal self venerates the capacity to subdue an unwieldy world by guile or plain physical force, to bring everything under one's will. The self is thus autonomous but at the same time dangerously unmoored, its only reference point being its own independent rule and thirst for control. And it is reckless because everything is subject to this thirst for domination and mastery, and in the wake of its coercive will to power lies all manner of human wreckage. In fact, as Cimino makes clear by the somber end of the film, in "one shot" lies both the rationalization and the recipe for the romance of being predatory; and it is all sanctioned by the wild-west myth of the challenge and necessity of rugged individual triumph.

This is apparent from the very first scenes. When the group of friends leaves the mill, Michael walks in front, slightly apart from the others, a composition Cimino follows throughout the movie. And when Steve points out strange shapes made by the sun, Michael promptly identifies these as "sun dogs" and interprets them, according to Native American lore, as an omen of blessing on the hunt sent by the gods. Astounded and half embarrassed by Michael's reference, Stanley then discourses on Michael's weirdness: "There's times that nobody but a doctor can understand you." And while the others make bawdy jokes about Steve's wedding night, Michael remains silent and apart, ignoring the banter as if romance and sex were trivial pursuits, especially compared to the challenges and glories of the hunt. His distinctiveness is again emphasized by his flashy choice of a car: an enormous white 1959 Cadillac coupe with monster fins. It is, for that time and place, perhaps the closest he can come to a proud and flashing "mount," a variation on the Lone Ranger's celebrated white horse Silver of frontier lore. Its significance is made clear when Michael, on a bet, matches the car with great aplomb against an eighteen-wheeler, passing it on the inside, budging it over, and then doing a daring 180-degree turn right in front of the roaring truck and finally bringing his car to a perfect parking position next to the curb of Welsh's bar. Nor does Michael take the money he has just won on the bet off his buddies. Here is a fellow who is bold, brave, and adept — a very cool head indeed.

That Michael sees himself as separate — and also superior — is evident in a pre-wedding conversation with his trailer roommate, Nick. It is here that Michael confesses his veneration of the creed of "one shot," telling Nick that he's the only guy he'll go hunting with. All the other friends are "great guys" all right, but when it comes to hunting and life in general, they're also "assholes," lacking any measure of seriousness and resolve about anything in general. Nick, it's clear, once shared Michael's passion for "one shot." But frankly now, he admits, he doesn't "think much about 'one shot' anymore," meaning the poetics or skill of the hunt; what appeals to him now is simply "the trees," though he is shy about admitting it. "I like the trees," he confesses as his voice tapers off, both in embarrassment and inability to articulate exactly what it is he likes about the trees. Michael, though, does not relent, meticulously preparing for the hunt and for the wedding. He even chastises Nick for not having his wedding tuxedo pants pressed ahead of time, to which Nick rejoins, aptly, that Michael is a "control freak."

The extremity and centrality of that impulse toward "control" dominates the sequence immediately before Michael's first deer "kill." The six hunters have traveled in Michael's car through the night to their deer-hunting location in the mountains. When they finally pile out of the car, Michael is dressed and ready to go in stocking cap, boots, and vest, and while he sits waiting on the hood of the car, checking his rifle, the others, still dressed in their formal wedding garb, search through the trunk for their hunting gear, slowly change clothes, clown around, and snack. Through all of this Michael is impatient, but the mood suddenly changes to outright conflict when Stanley can't find his boots and asks super-prepared Michael if he can borrow his extra pair (the control freak apparently brings two of everything). Michael refuses because Stan has a long history of being ill-prepared, always forgetting some part of his hunting gear. For Michael that is not only irresponsible, but when it comes to the sacred call of the hunt, it approaches sacrilege. As the argument begins to erupt, Cimino again poses Michael apart from the others, sitting alone and proud on the front of his big white car, rifle at the ready, with the forest and the mountain in the background. His separateness becomes more pronounced when Stanley gets abusive. Even when Axel encourages Michael to loan the boots, Michael simply digs in, indignant and adamant, reciting Stan's history of flakiness. Finally, in a cryptic diatribe, angrily holding up a rifle shell, Michael declaims: "See this: this is this. This ain't something else, this is this." It is a revealing and somehow ominous gesture, suggesting the kind of ultimacy that Michael bestows on control, domination, and coercive violence. The bullet, or what it symbolizes, counts for all and is all that counts. Just how much it does count is made clear in the remainder of the film, for that exaltation of the shell as somehow the final locus of reality repeats throughout the film — to the lasting horror of everyone. Those after-echoes, Cimino makes clear as the movie develops, define the inmost demonic character of "one shot."

The dialogue at the car disintegrates further. John gives Stan the boots; but Michael again refuses, after which Stan turns sulky and insulting, calling attention to Michael's lack of interest in women as evidence that he is a "faggot," which in this blue-collar macho world is the worst of all accusations. John pouts, threatening to go home if these boys don't stop bickering. Only the intervention of Nick resolves the issue, as he hands the boots to Stan and then says to Michael, "What's the matter with you?" Michael desists, but he gives his gun the final word as he defiantly fires into the sky, startling everyone with the loud report of the

In response to the hapless Stanley's request to borrow Michael's extra pair of boots, Michael (Robert De Niro) angrily brandishes a bullet that symbolizes his creed of one-shot, the ultimacy of power and coercion, proclaiming, enigmatically, "This is this. This ain't something else, this is this."

shot. Like his words, this gesture is also cryptic, suggesting at least the vehemence of Michael's veneration of the mystique of physical force as the final arbiter of power. The hunting trip ends with Michael and Nick hunting together along rugged mountain ridges amid the clouds, with the sound of Russian Orthodox liturgical music — appropriately sacral — in the background. Michael stalks a deer and finally gets a clear shot. After he fires, the deer staggers away and eventually falls, and when the camera cuts to it in close-up, the deer looks straight into the camera, its eyes wide open and full of terror. Vietnam will turn these hunters into similar prey, and their own eyes will become empty and glazed in response to what faces them.

A fitting end to the hunt and the whole long first Clairton portion of the film comes in the group's late-night return to Welsh's Lounge in town. Quite drunk and spraying beer at one another, they raucously sing "Drop Kick Jesus Through the Goalposts of Life" — that is, until John Welsh begins playing, on the barroom piano, Chopin's "Nocturne No. 6 in G minor," a piece that is at once delicate and brooding. They all fall into a pensive reflection, no doubt contemplating the uncertain realities that lie ahead. The camera moves from face to face as each man rather suddenly sobers up about the impending contingencies of life. The scene not only marks the end of this long hometown sequence but effectively summarizes much of what Cimino has been trying to show through the long wedding sequence and also the deer hunt: that is, the essential hu-

manity of these young men, in spite of their tough beginnings, their conflicts, and their carousing. Contrary to Pauline Kael's view of it, this portrait by no means idealizes either these very flawed, even pathetic,
characters or the dingy town of Clairton; nor does it cast them as blue-
collar miscreants or the crypto-fascist warmongers that the haters of this
film have found.[1]

Rather, this is a typical motley American community, filled with a
host of imperfect people, and none of them have life or its meaning close to
right, especially at the beginning of the story. Here drunken fathers beat
their daughters, brides dress alone for their weddings, and young men
numb the meaninglessness of their days in the mills with much booze,
dreams of sex, and fantasies of violence. Still, all these characters seem to
know that, no matter what may be said about this town, it is where they
are from and where they have found whatever identity, worth, and love
that life has so far offered. For all its abundant flaws, Clairton is still home,
the only home they have. The smart and sensitive one, Nick, is ahead of
the others in knowing this, when he tells Michael, in what Cimino intends
as a stark contrast to Michael's exaltation of the rifle shell, "You know, the
whole thing, it's right here [in this town]. I love this fucking place." It is
one lesson, among many, that Michael discovers all too belatedly.

Hell

In the silence that follows John's playing of Chopin comes the faint
"whop" of helicopter rotor blades as the scene shifts to a Vietnamese village that has been set aflame by American rockets. On the ground lies an
unconscious Michael, now an Army Green Beret. He awakens to find a
single North Vietnamese soldier who has gone through the village killing
civilians; as this enemy soldier is about to shoot a woman, Michael attacks him with the closest available weapon, setting him on fire with a
flame-thrower. U.S. troop helicopters land to drive off the invading
North Vietnamese, and among these soldiers are Nick and Steve who, to
their amazement, encounter the still dazed Michael.

The scene then quickly shifts to a wide and fast-flowing river; in the

---

1. Kael's lengthy and very negative review of the film, entitled "The God-Bless-
America Symphony," appeared in *The New Yorker*, December 18, 1978. It also appears in
Kael's collection of selected reviews from the length of her remarkable career, *For Keeps:
30 Years at the Movies* (New York: Penguin, 1994), pp. 800-807.

distance sits a small bamboo hut. The camera approaches slowly, gradually revealing that below this river hut is a small prison for captured South Vietnamese and American soldiers — among them the three soldiers from Clairton. More prisoners struggle in cages far out in the river, their heads barely above the water; but most prisoners stand hip-deep in the river below the building. Of the three Americans whose fate we have been following, Steve is rattled to the point of complete emotional disintegration, and Nick is clearly spooked. The reasons for this soon become abundantly clear. The captives are being forced to play Russian roulette for the amusement of their Vietcong captors, who put down wagers on each pull of the trigger. With each pull, whether it results in the click of an empty chamber or a bullet through the temple, Steve sobs and quakes in ever deeper terror. Michael, the calm and composed one of the trio, does his best to comfort and reassure Steve, but there is no slowing the mounting dread as their moment as game bait approaches.

The sequence goes on and on, relentless and graphic, fully displaying the horror of these shots in the head. The comprehensive frightfulness of this sequence comprises what is perhaps the most excruciating violence ever put on film, mainly because Cimino goes up close and inward to display the profound terror of the roulette "players." Almost all of the terror portrayed onscreen is psychological rather than the usual Hollywood recipe of violence and gore, though there is quite enough of that as well. None of this graphic display of power and violence is the least bit appealing or titillating to the viewer; as in the real world, violence is very messy and exacts a terrible human toll on body and soul. It would be another twenty years before an American movie (the opening moments of *Saving Private Ryan* [1998]) approached the same measure of realism about the violence of war, and then only the lovable reputation and cinematic skill of Steven Spielberg could actually pull it off. Two other recent films have tried, *Black Hawk Down* (2001) and *When We Were Soldiers* (2002), but neither one comes close, because neither registers the human toll with the precision and fullness of *The Deer Hunter*.

When Steve is made to play the deadly roulette game against Michael, he pulls the revolver away from his temple at the instant he pulls the trigger, and though the gun fires, the bullet merely creases his skull. For this violation of the rules of the "game," his captors throw him into the rat-infested river cage where, now virtually catatonic, he is expected to drown as soon as he tires of the effort to keep his head above water. Only Michael remains calm and even defiant throughout, urging Steve to have "balls" and Nick to pull the trigger no matter what the conse-

101

quences might be. Michael convinces Nick of his plot to provoke their captors into putting three bullets in the gun so they might have a chance to overpower them. They accomplish this, but not before terror vanquishes Nick's very soul, if not quite his sanity. After they shoot their way out of their watery prison, starting with the three bullets in the "roulette" gun, the three float down the river on a log and eventually are spotted by an American helicopter. They manage to load the wounded Nick onto the hovering craft; but when enemy fire comes from the jungle, Steve and Michael have to hang onto the runners as the copter heads off down the river. When Steve drops into the river, Michael lets go as well and plunges down into the river to help his friend — which is good, because Steve lands on rocks in a shallow spot, breaking both legs and an arm. Once they are ashore, Michael hoists Steve onto his shoulders and eventually joins a convoy of refugees, where a South Vietnamese officer puts Steve on the hood of his jeep to carry him to a hospital.

While the three young men escape the Vietcong and are rescued, they do not — after experiencing horror akin to hell — by any means find release or relief, as the two remaining sequences of the middle section of the film very pointedly dramatize. The first focuses on the haunting of Nick, who seems swallowed up by the very horror of his experiences. We first see him at the end of the camera's long brooding tour of a crowded and disordered military hospital in Saigon: the survey slowly and painstakingly emphasizes the carnage war has wrought on its soldiers. Just before coming to Nick, the camera lingers on a black soldier who has lost his limbs and his sight. A few feet from the man's bed, Nick sits in a window looking down on a courtyard that serves as a staging area for the transport of dead soldiers' bodies back to the United States. Row upon neat row of body bags await transfer into metal coffins. Death is the order of the day, and here, just as on the river, Nick is caught up with the encroaching, and what will prove for him inescapable, reality of it. When a doctor approaches and asks him simple questions, such as his name, Nick seems hardly able to speak: he returns reluctant, short answers, and he keeps glancing down at the courtyard, as if wondering whether one of his friends is in one of the body bags. When the doctor asks if Nick's nametag is indeed his, Nick nods toward the armless soldier and says, "It's his." Then he descends into a sobbing, fathomless sorrow that lies beyond words. When words don't come, he gestures and fumbles, nodding again toward the armless man, unable to express the sorrow that lies within him. To this the doctor simply says, "We're gonna have to get him out of here."

102

Released from the hospital, Nick tries to call his girlfriend, Linda (Meryl Streep), back in Clairton; but, looking at her picture while waiting for the call to connect, he tells the operator to forget the call. From there he jostles his way through the jammed nighttime streets of Saigon's bar-infested red-light district. He is immediately approached by a prostitute in a bar, and when he agrees, they retreat to her room upstairs. But Nick abruptly leaves when the woman's two-year-old begins to cry. Wandering empty back alleys alone, Nick follows the sound of a pistol shot, and then another, until he comes upon two men depositing a body on top of other bodies in the alley — all shot in the head.

Nearby, smoking quietly in an elegant old sports car, is an aging Frenchman, a Mephisthophelean character who procures for the roulette betting parlors of the Saigon underground. He offers Nick champagne, and when Nick refuses, he remarks that those who refuse champagne are in effect "saying no to life." The pile of bodies speaks for itself, and to the fellow's inquiry Nick confesses that he has played the game "up north." Sensing that he has before him a new player, the Frenchman urges Nick inside, while Nick somewhat lamely insists that he's not interested. Inside, two men with red cloths around their heads sit at a small table in the center of the room. Between them stands a Vietnamese man, a combination referee and emcee who brandishes a single bullet and a pistol before the raucous bettors who hold up cash and yell out their bets on favorites. With great ceremony and formality, the referee displays the bullet, inserts it into one of the chambers, spins the cylinder, and hands the gun to one of the "contestants," who holds it to his head and pulls the trigger. Nick watches all of this intently; but so does Michael, who, unbeknownst to Nick, sits in the back of the room observing, though he is not wagering any money. After the gun clicks on an empty chamber, Nick rushes forward, grabs the gun, spins the cylinder, holds it to the contestant's head, and pulls the trigger. When the hammer clicks on an empty chamber again, he puts it to his own head and fires — and then runs out of the place when the gun does not go off. Michael pursues him, but Nick is picked up by the Frenchman in the sports car, who tells him that he is lucky and could make a lot of money risking his life in the "game." Although Nick sees Michael running behind the car, calling his name, he ignores him and throws the money he has just won into the air.

This is the third scene in *The Deer Hunter* in which a bullet is held up and celebrated as having some sort of ultimate meaning. It also happened in the first Russian roulette scene in the hut on the river "up north." But the gesture first appeared back in Pennsylvania, when Michael, sitting on

103

the hood of his Cadillac, angrily proclaimed about his rifle shell, "This is this." For Cimino, the exaltation of power and the ability to kill is part of a malignancy that inexorably culminates in the carnage of soul and body symbolized by the "recreational" roulette of this war-devastated country's river camps and betting parlors. It is a fitting metaphor for a country and a people who are at the end of their desperate rope. In the precise repetition of the "one shot" gesture used by Michael on the hunt and the Vietcong captors in the river hut, Cimino clearly suggests that Michael's passion for hunting deer lies on a moral continuum at whose far end lies the roulette game that coerces beaten people to kill themselves for the amusement and profit of others. In each instance, the sponsor becomes the agent of death who is seduced into its evil either by the rush of power that resides in ultimate control or by the potential for easy wealth. Hell is thus brought above ground for pleasure and profit, and the violence demolishes the goodness that can be found in human life, which is discernible even in towns as grimy as Clairton and especially in the magnificent setting of the deer hunt. At its core, violence is violation, the demonic incarnation of blasphemy insofar as it voids for both its perpetrators and victims the possibility of life and goodness.

Nick's psyche and soul are blasted, and in despair over the extreme evil people can do to one another, the worst of which he has suffered, he succumbs to the mysteriously compelling power of death. It is within this context that Cimino casts the whole American venture in Vietnam as an Anglo-European variation on this Vietnamese practice of roulette. Cimino's invention of the "game" is pure historical fiction: nothing like this practice ever took place in Vietnam, despite the very specific geopolitical setting in which Cimino situates it. Since he invented this fantasy of the Russian roulette game, Cimino no doubt had a very specific purpose for using it as a metaphor. But he does not use it to indict the Vietnamese, as many have read the film, but to show the logical fruition of the sort of coercive domination manifested by a long history of Western imperialism. If the Vietnamese play roulette for fun and profit, American powers-that-be undertake for profit their own version of roulette in which the ordinary combat soldier is made to play the deadly game.

In the American context, it is seen in the exaltation of the myth of frontier individualism, an ideal that is distilled in the cowboy-settler's domination of the non-European. In *The Deer Hunter*, there is self-righteous pleasure in the notion that American firepower should "civilize" any who oppose it or whomever they deem to be miscreants or villains. The motif of the exalted bullet, a uniquely American kind of eucharistic "exalted host" of power and transformation, emphasizes the continuity between Michael's naive frontier romanticism and the games of Vietnam. Morally, they are parallel insofar as both thrive on the pleasure of domination and death. Most of all, at the heart of both enterprises — the roulette game and the American venture in Vietnam — is the thirst for wealth. In both, the ordinary "grunt" soldier, naive and powerless in the hands of such forces, is made to play a game of life and death for the pleasure and profit of others. (As the film emphasizes, this was America's first "live" television war.) In the American context, that "service for country" is in fact for the "masters of war," those who, in the words of Bob Dylan's memorable 1960s protest song, "build to destroy." Nick, Steve, and Michael all fall victim to the shabbiness of the motives of the American war effort, a vast kingdom in which young soldiers were sent to horror and death for tawdry political and economic motives.

Cimino's view of the war is quite clear early in the film when, during the long wedding reception, a passing Green Beret stops by the legion hall for a drink. The three future soldiers greet the man with amazement bordering on veneration, but when they try to toast the man and the war, his sole, twice-repeated response is "Fuck it," an obscenity for an obscenity — a term whose connotation of indictment was far more extreme in 1978 than it is today. Both regular citizens and soldiers are duped by the patriotic rhetoric that cloaks the crass motives behind the war. They are disposed to be credulous because of the conditioning provided by the grand cultural mythos of "domination by force," which lies at the very center of traditional notions of American maleness. Michael derives his entire sense of self from the myth of the solitary hero who proves his worth by his capacity to hunt and destroy. Nor is Michael's code far from Stanley's, the obnoxious character who more conspicuously threatens or uses violence to shore up his flimsy sense of manhood, be it with women or with friends.

The underside of Michael's code is laid bare in Stanley and, needless to say, in the Russian roulette game played in Vietnam, especially in the soul-rending experience of the Clairton soldiers. For these young men, violent ritual does not baptize them into a triumphant manhood of violent mastery, but into hell itself. For those unfortunates who find themselves at the wrong end of a gun, the world fast fills with terror, as it did for the deer Michael shot. For the hunter who becomes the prey, the world changes abruptly and completely, the light turning into the darkness that erupts when people suffer violence for the purposes of amusement and profit. In the Jewish-Christian ethic, such violence violates the deepest intentions of the created world.

Home

From Nick's descent into the Saigon underground of death, with Michael in hot pursuit, the story goes back to Pennsylvania and jumps forward to Michael's homecoming. Expecting him to arrive at a particular time, his friends prepare a "welcome home" party. But as he approaches in a cab, he tells the driver to drive by, and we next see him in a cheap motel room across the river. In a long silent sequence, save for delicate, intense guitar music, we see him first on the bed and then on his haunches leaning against the wall churning through deep emotions of some kind, head propped in his hands, as if he is trying to bear up amid great pain or distress. Near the end of the scene, he takes Linda's picture from his wallet and stares at it, softly stroking her face. The next morning Michael walks to the double-trailer he and Nick once shared — and where Linda has now moved to free herself from her alcoholic father. About to leave for her job at the grocery store, she is surprised to see him, particularly after the previous evening's disappointment, and they stumble through feeble attempts at conversation. She immediately confesses that she was hoping Michael would have Nick with him, because the latter has been reported AWOL in Saigon and has never written or called her.

Linda is clearly happy to see Michael, as he is to see her, but their attempts at communication are bumbling. She tries to see whether a sweater she has knitted for Nick will fit him; she concludes that it's too big but can be altered to fit Michael, an apt metaphor for her adapting her affection to Michael. In confusion and longing, muttering "O Christ" — and he looking a bit like a pop-art portrait of Jesus — she embraces him yet again. They walk to the grocery store, and Michael is greeted warmly by townspeople along the way and by the workers at the store. He stops by the plant to greet Axel and Stanley as they leave work. To keep the theme of the gun prominent, Axel mentions that Stanley has a new little handgun that he carries with him all the time. At John Welsh's bar, they retreat to the back room, where John brings out "Nostrovia," his best vodka, to toast Michael's return and, as always, life itself.

Michael learns from these old friends that Steve is back in the States but that no one knows where he is because his wife, Angela, won't tell. Michael immediately goes to see Angela, who is in bed deeply depressed, almost catatonic. A two-year old in a playpen plays at firing a toy gun at him when he walks in. Unable to speak, she finally writes a phone number on a slip of paper and hands it to Michael. That night he begins to call the number from a phone booth, but then inexplicably hangs up — just as Nick did when trying to call Linda from the hospital in Vietnam. Later, Michael is packing some of his belongings in the trailer when Linda arrives. He is in a hurry to be off, but Linda begs him to stay, suggesting that they go to bed together just to "comfort" one another. Feeling claustrophobic, no doubt from this close association again with all these people from whom he had always kept himself apart and who know nothing about his life-changing war experience, Michael is eager to bolt. He tells Linda that he feels "a lot of distance." But as he starts his car, Linda dashes after him, and the next scene shows her in a motel bathroom with a towel wrapped around her. When she goes into the darkened bedroom, however, she finds Michael in his uniform asleep on top of the bedspread. As a train slowly rumbles by just beyond the walls, the camera pans the room and then watches Linda crawl in beside the sleeping soldier, though it is clear that she will find neither hope nor comfort with this confused, conflicted, and insulated war vet.

Nor does the next phase of Michael's homecoming go well: he ends up deer hunting with John, but also with Axel and Stanley, the two friends least likely to understand either his serious view of the hunt or the life-altering circumstances he has survived. The sequence opens with a long shot that lasts more than a minute, in which Michael emerges from the cabin and walks the rocky ridges against a blue sky of white clouds. Sober but quietly ethereal choral music, again decidedly Russian Orthodox, layers the scene, giving Michael's solitary wilderness walk a kind of numinous fore-sounding of what will soon transpire. In contrast, the three others yell and holler, shooting wildly as they chase after deer. Their understanding of the hunt, as their inane and noisy disruption declares, could not be further from Michael's quasi-sacred quest. It culminates in desecration when Stan tries to drown a deer he has shot in the pond in front of the cabin, while Axel and John look on, laughing uproariously.

Meanwhile, Michael is on his mountaintop seeking and finding that perfect deer, which he then cannot bring himself to shoot. As the sun and the music pour down on him, he jerks the gun barrel skyward as he fires; and the creature looks back, regal and undisturbed, a mysterious uncanny presence that is both beyond Michael's comprehension and an answer to his increasing unrest about his place and purpose in this world. Whatever this is, he assents to its veneration of life, shouting his "okay" to the universe, which then offers its approving "okay" back to him; he thus makes a new kind of contract with the world. Hardly any turning could be more sudden, stark, and extreme: from being a devotee of "one shot," Michael now forswears his personal — and national — mythos of coercion, domination, and death to embrace a wholly different vision of the worth and purposes of human existence. For Michael, everything has suddenly been utterly transformed. In the starkest of terms, he moves from individualism to care, from domination to servanthood, and from predation to nurture.

That something profound has transpired in this mountaintop transaction is immediately apparent on his return to the cabin. In another of his endless infantile arguments with Axel, Stanley is threatening him with the .38 revolver he carries, pointing and cocking it when the latter makes a vulgar insult about one of Stanley's girlfriends. When Michael enters, he angrily wrests the gun from Stan, who protests that the gun isn't loaded. Michael checks the cylinder, closes it and fires into the ceiling, indicating that it is indeed loaded, and he then empties the remaining five bullets. Putting one bullet back into the cylinder, he spins it just as the Russian roulette "referees" did, and puts the gun against Stanley's forehead, crying out whether Stanley now sees "how it feels" to be on the other end of a gun barrel. In his rage he pulls the trigger, and the hammer clicks on an empty chamber. As utterly violent and unreasonable as Michael's action seems, it does show that he now fully understands and abhors the "fucking games," as he puts it, that boys play with violent mastery, the very games with which he himself was once so enchanted. Michael stalks out of the cabin and throws the gun into the pond where Stan had tried to drown the deer that morning. The others do not, needless to say, understand the background or meaning of Michael's behavior, but they do return to Clairton duly chastened and sober.

For Michael, though, everything seems to have changed after this second "hunt," and evidence of that comes in quick succession. He goes first to the grocery store, where he finds Linda in the back quietly crying as she stamps prices on cans. Now, however, comes a very different Michael from the "distant" fellow who runs, insulates himself, or sleeps because he cannot confront his own passionate internal life or clarify it. Here he exudes persistent gentle concern. When Linda does not respond to him right away, he waits in his car outside the grocery store in the dark until she gets off work. When she gets into the car, she asks Michael, "Did you ever think life would turn out this way?" He responds to her with a simple "no." His confession of the absence of control over life's directions not only acknowledges the reality of an obstreperous and indomitable tragedy that ridicules human efforts at control but also the capacity of that same tragedy to change those who suffer its blows. It has surely changed Nick and now, finally, Michael, whose deepest beliefs about the heroism of violence have been cast aside for a loving vision of human relationships. The next scene gives a brief glimpse of Linda and Michael in the dark making love. Indeed, the heretofore chaste Michael, the man who had poured all his virility into the ideal of the hunt and death, now partakes of life, willing at last — to borrow a slogan from the sixties — to "make love, not war."

From this conspicuous indication of a new emotional and moral openness, Michael moves immediately to contact his friend Steve, who is now a triple amputee hiding in a V.A. hospital, refusing to return to his former hometown because he is "a freak." He speaks to Steve on the phone and then shows up unannounced at the hospital to take him "home," the same thing he will urge on Nick when he returns to Saigon. While Michael is at the hospital, Steve shows him the contents of the locked drawer of his bed table, which is full of hundred-dollar bills that arrive anonymously in envelopes from Saigon. Michael concludes that the money is coming from Nick, which would indicate that he is still alive and making large sums of money from his deranged career in roulette.

Recalling that he promised Nick on the night of the wedding — their last night in Clairton — not to leave him "over there," Michael journeys back to Saigon during the very last chaotic days of the war and the American presence there. The city swarms with refugees seeking a way out of the collapsing nation and away from the vengeance of the North Vietnamese. This mass exodus of refugees recalls Michael's earlier heroic rescue of Steve from the roulette hut and the river, his delivery of Steve's almost lifeless body to an ARVN jeep in the midst of another mass evacuation. As people jam into this last refuge in the war, even jumping into the canals to try to escape by water, Michael traverses the dark, fire-pocked back alleys and canals of Saigon trying to locate betting parlors. Scene after scene resembles the dark and labyrinthine chaos of Dante's *Inferno*, replete with suffering and confusion, water, mobs, and fires. In his search for Nick, Michael encounters this story's Mephistopheles, the French "death pimp," as he might be called. He bribes the man to arrange a game with "the American"; once they have found the game, which has become very secretive and "very dangerous," as the Frenchman says, Michael pays $1500 just to get into the parlor. Ironically, his supply of cash appears to be from the money Nick has sent to Steve at the veterans' hospital.

Waiting for Nick to show up, wincing and shuddering, he watches a

109

Vietnamese pair play roulette; the pained expression on his face is in marked contrast to the intent fascination he showed when he was a spectator at his first Saigon game of roulette. Now, in this second visit to the spectacle, he is utterly repulsed when a live round discharges into one player's brain. This feeling multiplies when he intercepts Nick on his way to "perform" in the night's entertainment; but Nick, lost in a psycho-spiritual catatonia resembling nothing akin to an actual human condition of insanity or perdition, fails to recognize him. Nick's existential state is, within the film's terms, pure metaphor for what it means to be ensnared by and swallowed up in the powers of death. His condition is pure anti-life, the furthest pole from what he most valued before he ran head-on into the blasphemy of war and Russian roulette. Michael pleads with Nick to recognize him: "Nicky, I love you, you're my friend, what are you doin'?" Nick responds by spitting in Michael's face. Now desperate, Michael tries to buy his way into the game, giving up all his remaining money (even cajoling the Frenchman, who perhaps feels a twinge of guilt, to contribute to the cause). This is a high-stakes gamble for the Vietnamese "sponsors" of the game, because Nick, the blond-headed American who has so far been lucky playing roulette, is apparently a profitable attraction for them.

Sitting at the dueling table across from Nick, Michael again pleads for Nick not to pull the trigger; when Nick does so and again survives, and it is Michael's turn, Michael asks simply and quietly, "Is this what you want?" With the gun at his temple, hammer cocked, Michael declares simply to Nick again, "I love you, Nick," and pulls the trigger, after which he exhales in relief at still having the gift of his life. This is no longer a test of macho self-sufficiency and defiance, as it was in the hunt in the Pennsylvania mountains and in the hut on the river; rather, it is a gesture of radical love, as well as a ringing pronouncement of the full measure of Michael's radical change. Indeed, it is a gesture that embodies Jesus' words, "Greater love has no man than this, that a man lay down his life for his friends" (John 15:13). For whatever mysterious reason, Michael's gesture of willing self-sacrifice seems to summon some lost part of Nick, perhaps harking back to the river hut, where Michael first held the gun to his head and where Nick fell sway to the power and allure of death. Some faint glint of recognition comes across Nick's face, and he tries to speak as Michael gently implores him to "come home, just come home. Home." Michael asks Nick to "remember the trees . . . and the mountains." Nick in turn responds with the earlier pivotal phrase, "one shot," to which Michael assents, nodding his head and repeating "one shot, one shot," glad that Nick has finally responded. Nick himself then laughs, repeats "one shot," puts the gun to his head, and pulls the trigger. This time it fires and spews Nick's blood all over. Michael grabs Nick's bloody head in his hands, the blood drenching him while he shakes Nick's head, screaming his name for an agonizing twenty seconds of film time. Indeed, "one shot" ends here, from the deer hunt to the river hut and at last to this unfathomable madness and sadness, the inevitable terminus of demonic fulfillment. It is a wrenching sequence, one that Francis Coppola borrows for Michael Corleone's reaction to the death of his daughter, Mary, at the very end of *The Godfather* saga.

In effect, Michael has killed Nick; more accurately, the macho persona Michael aspired to has killed the more sensitive and vulnerable Nick. Cimino draws a clear line from Michael's first exaltation of the bullet at the beginning of the first deer hunt — with the host of attitudes it conjures up about domination and death — to Nick's recollection of "one shot," laced as it is with despair and defiance, which prompts him to yank from Michael his scarred arm (from numerous suicide attempts, for Nick has not been lucky enough to die) to put the gun to his head one more time. The scars on his arm reflect the scars on his soul, a soul that has been blasted and swallowed up by the ultimate evil, death itself. In this regard, Nick's demented courtship of death is but a stage beyond Steve's retreat from life, in which the latter has ample cause to recoil from the coercive violence that is the handmaid of the final enemy. For Steve, as for Nick, overwhelmed in body and soul, the notion of "home" has lost all meaning, though Michael is the one who now feels and understands the concept for the first time — ironically and too late. The profound malignancy depicted in *The Deer Hunter* becomes clear in that irony: Michael renounces his sanctified cultural ideal of "one shot" to embrace, finally, all that is meant by home, the irreplaceable gift of life and other people. He comes to realize, but only after his close encounter with the horrific nature of death in war, the thorough evil of the ideal he had celebrated.

Michael finally comes to realize, in the suffering of his friends and also through the attraction and welcome of Linda, that life is a rich and unfathomable gift, and when love dwells at its center, a gift fully worthy of veneration. This is what Nick always represented and lived, everything that had stood apart from Michael's posture of aloof superiority: loving the trees instead of the hunt, the hometown Clairton instead of the warrior dream, and always playing the peacemaker amid the petty testiness of his friends.

Lament

Few films have endings as controversial — and as misinterpreted — as *The Deer Hunter*'s. The ending can be misinterpreted if the viewer misses, as many have, the transformation Michael has undergone. The script does not spell that transformation out, nor does it lavish many words on it; instead, it trusts events and images, themselves mute but palpable, to convey that transformation to viewers. This places a burden on viewers, some of whom, like Pauline Kael, are not happy unless a screenplay verbally codifies everything the images suggest. This attitude in itself betrays an elitist bias that confines significant cinema to stories about characters who are capable of verbally defining their own experience; in this view, unless they speak paragraphs about the meaning and significance of their experience, they are uninteresting. For Kael, it means that significant cinema is largely confined to depicting the lives of well-spoken, well-educated, and well-shrunk New Yorkers or people very much like them. The blue-collar people in *The Deer Hunter* are steelworkers and grocery-store clerks who have barely finished high school and are not articulate: if they did much self-interpretive talk, the audience would soon doubt their authenticity. This does not mean that these characters cannot feel deeply; in fact, some intuit wisely, but they do not have the cultural resources or habits of probing their inmost thoughts and motives to articulate their deepest hungers and groanings. Nonetheless, they, too, are human beings with the same capacities that all people have for spiritual wonder at both the splendor and inscrutability of human experience; perhaps, unjaded as they are, they have more wonder. And certainly they are no more enclosed in a particular ideological "map of the world" than are Manhattanites, with their manifest pretensions to cultural sophistication, though their two worlds are very different. (See sidebar for more on the critical reaction to *The Deer Hunter*.) The closing sequence of *The Deer Hunter* is almost entirely without verbal exposition, and what words are in it come mostly in the hymnal prayer of "God Bless America," whose inclusion in the film ignited vehement protests from critics that the film was therefore unabashedly patriotic and pro-war. But, to the contrary, the ending plays, in event and tone, as a lament on the toll of the war and the American culture of "one shot": the enshrined American veneration for competitive individualism and domination, relentless even unto death.

After Nick's death in Saigon, the scene shifts to the Orthodox church in Clairton (recalling the early wedding scene), from which

Nick's friends carry his body in a black casket to a waiting hearse. In one arresting shot, Michael, dressed in his Green Beret uniform, looks in on the casket through the hearse's rear door, as the camera looks back from inside and reflects and superimposes his image on the shiny lid of the casket. The image suggests one final time the intimate bond between these two and, simultaneously, Michael's responsibility for Nick's death. A scene in the cemetery shows the consignment of his body to the earth; from the beginning of this sequence, Orthodox choral music, at once sober and exultant, plays a quiet counterpoint to the grimness of the occasion. Afterward, at Welsh's bar for a late-morning breakfast, the mourners fumble around a long table to prepare it for their meal, all awkward and somber, at a loss for words or gestures that might express or mitigate their collective grief. John retreats to the kitchen to make scrambled eggs. As he works, fighting convulsive sobs, he starts to hum the tune of "God Bless America." As Russian Orthodox people, enclosed in their own ethnic enclave, they would not know mainstream Protestant or Catholic hymnody, and thus John sings the one hymn, simultaneously religious and civil, that resonates deep within himself and among Nick's friends. When John emerges with the eggs and stops his mix of humming and singing, Linda picks up the lyric, singing the words clearly and firmly; as the rest join in one by one, it is immediately clear that no one there sings this hymn as jingoistic vindication of the war or American righteousness. Rather, they sing the hymn as a memorial and benediction to Nick, and also as a prayer for themselves, making it appropriate for their sorrow and their circumstance. Indeed, the hymn petitions blessing for the land, the people, and Nick: "God bless America, land that I love, stand beside her and guide her, through the night with Light from above." Even beyond that, the hymn is quite appropriate thematically, for these people have known the loneliness of the darkest night, the eruption of the vilest evil, and have confronted the enemy — death — as in a game. God knows they need light and guidance. As drama, the hymn plays out as petition and gratitude for the restoration and perseverance of what community they do have, having just barely survived the worst that evil from within and without can do to them.

The second stanza shifts to recognize their mutual rootedness in this small town and the preciousness of their connection to one another. And that, too, seems to be a tribute to Nick, for he was the peacemaker and the one who grasped and relished the preciousness of the intense bond that held all these people together, no matter how infantile or fractious some of the group behaved. The last words of the verse speak

113

Critical Reaction to *The Deer Hunter*

There's little doubt now about Kenneth Turan's early judgment of *The Deer Hunter* as "one of the most grueling, forceful war films ever made" (*The Progressive*, March 1979: 52). All the more reason, then, for the controversy that swirled around the film. In fact, few films in American cinema have occasioned so much passionate controversy — from the political left and right alike. Reviews ranged the whole spectrum from embracing the film to denouncing it; and then came a small afterwave of reviews reviewing the reviews and the controversy. Looking at the broad national fuss over the movie, one critic suggested that the film "hit a nerve, becoming overnight the object of the most bitter controversy, dividing critical opinion almost as sharply as the Vietnam war . . ." (Richard Grenier, *Commentary*, April 1979: 78). *The Deer Hunter* was, after all, one of the first post-Vietnam War films to examine that enormously controversial war. It was released in the same year as was *Coming Home*, a film whose antiwar views were as clear as could be, and it preceded the long-awaited *Apocalypse Now* (1979). It is fair to say that a large part of the controversy over *The Deer Hunter* resulted from the fact that the filmmakers' views on the war were not all that obvious, and thus reviewers were more than a little inclined to let the film provide an occasion to express their own deeply held views of the legitimacy of the war.

One focus of the debate was the film's use of graphic violence, specifically the depiction of the fictional game of Russian roulette. More than a few critics thought this exploitative, intended to achieve some quick notoriety for the film. Others acknowledged the power of those sequences. Frank Rich thought them "excruciatingly violent" (*Time*, December 18, 1979: 86). Kenneth Turan caught the curious ambivalence of the viewer response to the roulette sequences for which the viewer was ill-prepared: "Horribly shocking but absolutely riveting" (in the aforementioned *Progressive* review). Jack Kroll in *Newsweek* thought the roulette on the river made for "one of the most frightening, unbearably tense sequences ever filmed and the most violent excoriation of violence in screen history" (December 11, 1978: 113). The film's violence did not pander to but seemed to oppose violence. The gist of the comments implied that such sustained violence (more psychological than physical) would have been unacceptable were it not for the seemingly high purposes of the film. A dissenter on that score was Gloria Emerson, an antiwar journalist, who said that the violence did not "examine cruelty" but exploited it (*The Nation*, May 12, 1979: 541).

The context of the violence, meaning the practice of Russian roulette in war, drew vehement protests from a broad array of the critics in journalism and politics. Simply put, there is no evidence that any such practice ever took place anywhere, at any time in Vietnam. John Simon, writing in the conservative *National Review*, complained that "this supposedly realistic film" lacked a "shred of historical, logical, chronological, or psychological credibility" (February 16, 1979: 248). Journalist Peter Arnett was even more vehement: "The central metaphor of the film is a bloody lie" (quoted in Emerson). For many, the fact that Cimino and the screenwriters made up the practice vitiated any value the film may have had.

And then there was the perceived racism. Writing in *The Nation*, Robert Hatch complained that "without exception, the Vietcong and the citizens of Saigon are pictured as creatures debased almost below recognition as human beings," making them seem "an inferior and deplorable race" (February 24, 1979: 220). Several months later, in the same magazine, Gloria Emerson indicted this "sick and manipulative" film as "the most racist I have ever seen" (May 12, 1979: 540). Even those who liked the film, such as Kenneth Turan, objected to the film's "xenophobic tone, the paintings of evil Orientals as the prime villains of the war." For critic Colin Westerbeck, writing in the Roman Catholic periodical *Commonweal*, the portrait of the Vietnamese was simply one part of the movie that was eager to "indulge in every kind of self-delusion to ease the pain of our having lost 50,000 dead and hundreds of thousands more wounded in either mind or body" (March 2, 1979: 115).

Last — and part and parcel of the above — was the film's closing sequence, the singing of "God Bless America" by the assembled friends of Nick. That was the last straw for many critics, a wildly incongruous gesture that exonerated America of guilt in the war. Robert Hatch confessed to being "really shocked" by the scene, concluding that it makes the survivors, "despite all they have seen and suffered . . . true believers, good patriots." Ultimately, he thinks "the picture may go far to ease the American guilt over Vietnam" (220). On the other hand, conservatives such as Richard Grenier (in *Commentary*) said that the film as a whole signaled the resurgence of "even a florid patriotism" (*Commentary*, April 1979: 81).

clearly enough: "To the mountains, to the prairies, to the oceans white with foam, God bless America, my home, sweet home, God bless America, my home, sweet home." Home was the inducement Michael extended to his fellow travelers to hell, to Steve in the V.A. hospital and to Nick in the Saigon betting parlor: "Just come home. Home."

That this hymn is most of all a tribute to Nick is made fully clear when, at the end of the song, Michael raises a toast, "To Nick," and all of them, quiet smiles of pleasure and recollection on their faces, raise their glasses in appreciation for what he knew and what they have also now come to know — however belatedly. The closing shot of the friends together — limited, maimed, and spiritually as well as physically wounded, and now frozen in a freeze-frame tableau that ends the film — offers the final wordless suggestion that they all now share, even Stanley perhaps, an appreciation of the value and gift of individual life and the bonds of mutuality that so profoundly enrich life. Their solicitude for one another makes that clear. The unusual credit sequence reiterates this point: as each character's name comes up, so also does an image from the film that catches the person exuberant and glad — except perhaps for Stan, who seems terminally lost in fretful machismo dreams. Such is the splendor of individual people, no matter who they are and where they live; they seem made for life and one another. And so the film seems to say: "Home — rejoice and be glad."

Conclusion

The Deer Hunter indicts the hegemonic sway of notions of machismo and "one shot" that prevail in much of American culture. While the film acknowledges the value of stalwart individualism and the "toughness" of the warrior ideal, at the same time it fiercely impugns the veneration of force, domination, and death as moral and spiritual aspirations. Despite their demonic destructiveness, these are enchanting and pervasively powerful attractions for young men, as the film shows. But the exaltation of the capacity for destruction as a measure of human worth runs directly contrary to the core of the Christian tradition, in which death is the ultimate enemy, seductive and voracious, the antithesis of all the loving intentions of the Creation.

Cimino portrays the inmost character of the "one-shot" credo in the Russian roulette "games" of Saigon, but these are contiguous with the individualistic macho values and aspirations of not only Michael but

3

3

2

2

also of blowhard Stanley, and as such they are indeed "hell above ground," as the regular visual references to darkness and fire display. For this celebration of coercion and killing, Michael was for a time both agent and pimp, no less so than the French provocateur of the purgatorial back-alleys of Saigon who panders domination, whether sexual or physical. The great personal tragedy in the film — for everybody — is that Nick is blighted and then ensnared by the all-devouring but penultimate power of the enemy Death. The great national tragedy is that all of this horror and sorrow derives from the thirst for amusement and profit. This fictional practice of Russian roulette used by director Cimino exposes the moral charade of war profiteering, whether Vietnamese or American.

Against this stark intensification of evil — the "blackness of darkness," as Melville described the thematic core of Hawthorne's short stories — *The Deer Hunter* posits the radical affirmation of the incalculable goodness of life individually and communally. As earnest a devotee of "one shot" as he is, Michael recants after his firsthand encounter with the blasphemy of domination, terror, and death. The mystery of the majesty of the world, from friends to deer — all of them fragile, mortal, and resplendent — which resounds in the film's music, "call" to him there on the mountain during his rare opportunity for the perfect "one shot" at the perfect deer, a fit emblem of a pacific God himself. To this radical call to revere life and all its richness, Michael relents from the hunt to proffer his loud "okay," the full-blown conversion from consorting with death to assenting to Being and its undiscriminating love for the world. After that, Michael himself finds new emotional and personal wholeness and labors valiantly to restore the world broken by the domination of violence he had venerated before. The simple facts and conditions of life assume new and wondrous value in the aftermath of the desecration that is torture and death. "Home," not "one shot," now constitutes his locus of value and meaning. His petition to Nick — "just come home" — is as much confession and petition to himself as it to his lost friend, the lover of trees. The last wrenching funeral sequence culminates in recollection, lament, gratitude, and prayer for what was, might have been, and perhaps will be, and at the center of it is a radically revised and luminous apprehension, at once sober and exultant, of the immense value and fragility of the exquisite gift of life, friendship, and love, gifts imparted by that mysterious Other whom Michael has belatedly encountered in the high sacred mountains of God.

PART TWO

LIGHT SHINES IN THE DARKNESS

The title for this section comes straight from the opening section of the New Testament Gospel of John (1:5). The four films in this section are all very specifically Christian in their understanding of the necessity of Light for human well-being and understanding of life's mysteries. Light does indeed come to shine amid thick darkness. This Buechner calls "the Gospel as Comedy" (in Greek, the literal meaning of "gospel" is good news or glad tidings). In literary and biblical terms "comedy" does not primarily mean material that is funny, although it often is. Rather, comedy denotes a story in which initial dark and tangled circumstances get untangled and events and characters end well, although "well" may be a long way from what American culture has come to define as "happy." Each of the four films here, all from the mid-1980s, dramatizes the emergence or shining, against very dark odds, of a redemptive loving Light amid human affairs. These films eschew the path of De Mille in which God shows up forthright and bold. While unambiguous in their religious claims, they are neither pollyannish nor triumphalist, as the evangelical Christian community tends to like their film stories. Rather, the films here are notable for their sensitive, complex, even sober probing of the lure and reality of Christian grace. Buechner himself is starkly realistic about the conditions to which Light comes: while the tragic is inevitable, "the comic is the unforeseeable," the Light happens in a darkness "that only just barely fails to swallow it up."[1]

These are all very different stories set in obscure times and places, and they are all splendid cinematic art. For the most part they view the

---

1. Buechner *Telling the Truth: The Gospels as Tragedy, Comedy, and Fairy-Tale* (San Francisco: Harper, 1977), pp. 57, 58.

religious realities they display rather matter-of-factly, if not incidentally, simply assuming that Love is the sensible, common, and ordinary bed- rock of being. All these films follow rather ordinary lives amid the perils and ambiguities of ordinary life. While quiet, the stories in these films are clear and forceful, and most of all, unpredictable, serving to disman- tle worn notions of how both the world and God in it work. In none of the four films in this section, or in any of those in the book, are the cen- tral characters engaged at the outset in any special kind of God search, though most do believe at least in some nominal way. They do reside in earnest but sorely flawed Christian cultures, and these they variously embrace or chafe against. Still, relentlessly, in spite of the tangled world in which they dwell, Light comes, and by no particular merit of their own, they are, even the devout, newly inducted into a fresh warm prov- ince of love and hope. Their surroundings remain the same, but their sense of the world is infused with meaning, hope, and love that dispel the darkness and loss that has previously beset them. And despite the sadness in which some of these films end, the Light they have come across remains clear and decisive.

Screenwriter Horton Foote's *Tender Mercies* (1983) focuses on the slow process by which a washed-up alcoholic Country Western singer- songwriter, one Mac Sledge (Robert Duvall), finds a new life in the Texas outback. Alcoholic, violent, and broke, he washes up at a two-pump mo- tel run by a youngish Vietnam War widow whose "tender mercies" in- duce Sledge to give up drinking and turn his life around. He marries the widow and inches his way toward his old career when his life once again goes to smash. In the end, in delicate but rapturous fashion he finds himself sustained in his travail by the promise of the "wings of the dove," as a song he sang to his daughter from his first marriage, has it. Here Light comes incrementally, mediated by small gestures of human kindness and affection, till those who have put themselves in its way can exult together in the mutuality of love and the goodness of life.

Writer-director Robert Benton's *Places in the Heart* (1984) examines the possibility of redemptive Love amid multiple personal and social tragedies in Depression-era Texas. Edna Spalding (Sally Field), the plucky young housewife, struggles to keep her family together after the accidental death of her husband, the town sheriff. An African-American hobo (Danny Glover) helps her plant cotton on her unused farmland. Through thick and thin a new family emerges — the widow, her blind boarder, her farm hand, and her two needy children — and neither torna- does nor the economy stands in their way. When all seems like it will end

God on the Screen

Filmmakers who want to display on that big screen a real shaft of Light, or merely someone's glimpse thereof, do not have an easy task before them. The dominant tradition in the United States has been to catch God with historical spectacle: filmmakers have often imagined they could do that simply by filming the most conspicuous showings of the divine in biblical history. Cecil De Mille took this route with the Moses story in two different films entitled *The Ten Commandments* (1923 and 1956) and then again with *Samson and Delilah* (1949) and with the Jesus story in *King of Kings* (1927). De Mille being De Mille, these biblical epics emphasized God the spectacular as a means of eliciting at least a reverential gasp or two from his mostly pious audiences. But the clouds thundering at Moses (Charlton Heston) and then Heston thundering at the Israelites certainly did not do much for most people, save as kitsch, though it was very profitable kitsch for Hollywood.

The notion behind most of these extravaganzas was that by merely filming the conspicuously sacred on a huge scale — the subject matter that just about everyone agrees is to some degree holy — and by shooting it in due splendor, the film would inevitably bear Light of some kind. De Mille clearly hoped that his second try at Moses would evoke Light by virtue of the special effects of celestial fireworks (all that thunder), a windy recitation of the "mighty acts of God" in plagues and miracles, and a general posture of reverence (nearly four hours worth). In supplying the fireworks and the plagues and miracles, De Mille was trying to approximate on film as best he could the *mysterium tremendum,* the full-blown majesty and roar of God himself. If God is mighty and big — and nothing is mightier and bigger than God — then make the movie as large and majestic a Hollywood big-budget spectacle as possible, big enough and flashy enough to trick God into showing up. But all that overblown gimmickry presumes that God is understood quantitatively; it is a strategy for catching Light that yields an aesthetic mistaking Light for how big a shadow it casts. There is plenty of reason for fear and trembling when one encounters the God of the Old Testament, that fearsome *mysterium;* but De Mille simply turns the divine into a cosmic Rocky, the fellow who can outbox the pharaoh. A similar intention to see God directly informed pictures such as *The Robe* (1953) and *Ben-Hur* (again starring Heston, this time as a heroic charioteer convert [1959]), which emphasized the heroism of Jesus' followers.

The innumerable cinematic lives of Jesus have not fared much better, ranging from De Mille's 1927 potboiler to Martin Scorsese's *The Last Temptation of Christ* (1988). In between came the minimalist realpolitik of Pasolini's *Gospel According to St. Matthew* (1964), Nicholas Ray's melodramatic *The King of Kings* (1961), George Stevens's milky *The Greatest Story Ever Told* (1965), and Franco Zeffirelli's ornate television miniseries *Jesus of Nazareth* (1977). Nor does Hollywood seem to have given up on its attempt to picture divinity straight-on. In 1999, CBS television produced yet another Jesus miniseries, this time rendering the Messiah as the archetypal sensitive New Age guy.

One problem with trying to make an interesting Jesus film is that the Jesus story lacks the spectacular melodrama of the Moses story: there are no plagues, social rebellions, fearsome rods to cast down, mass exoduses, and so on. In contrast, the life of Jesus has some rather quiet miracles, lots of talk, a few friends, and a rather unsuccessful end. The substance of the life seems inherently "anti-spectacular," to borrow Lloyd Baugh's term in his 1997 book *Imaging the Divine: Jesus and Christ-Figures in Film* (p. 89). Given this, filmmaking strategy seems to bet that if viewers can just get close enough to the person of Jesus for long enough, then Light is bound to emanate. This is the route of the direct slow gaze. In some ways this task is more difficult — even perilous — compared to movies about Moses and Sinai. After all, a Jesus picture demands that the filmmaker "characterize" Jesus, the most recognized, celebrated, and imagined figure in Western cultural history; and virtually any characterization is likely to strike large groups of people as hugely wrong, hokey, or plainly heretical (as was the case in the enormous outcry against *The Last Temptation of Christ*). Because of the great variety of clearly and deeply held notions of who Jesus was, what he probably looked like, and how he comported himself, just about any attempt to portray Jesus is fraught with great difficulties. One film tried to avoid this pitfall by using first-person narration with Jesus as the camera: the audience never actually saw Jesus but saw his world as he, supposedly, saw it.

Films of Jesus seem torn between this understandable caution and De Mille-like grandiosity. In the early 1960s, director George Stevens, a devout Roman Catholic who had made the celebrated western *Shane* (1953), produced and directed his own Jesus epic, *The Greatest Story Ever Told*. The film starred a blue-eyed, blond-haired Jesus, played by an innocuous young Max von Sydow, Swedish accent and all, and was set in Monument Valley so as to add pictorial sublimity to holy history, as if the scenery could make up for the blandness of this Jesus. The effect was a kind of faux portentousness that never got halfway close to any facsimile of *mysterium* or messiah-hood. Neither cinematic fireworks nor a meek and mild master framed by majesty does a deity make. Oddly, the best of the Jesus filmmakers, Pasolini and Zeffirelli, have been those who have eschewed spectacle, bluster, sentiment, and trendiness, those usual strategies for making God visible, impressive, and godly.

in Hollywood happiness, evil erupts but again, shattering the new makeshift family that has labored so hard to find a path toward security and love. To this Benton appends one of the most remarkable, and profound, endings in the history of American cinema. That conclusion stands out as a most poignant, even iconic portrait of what Christian theology means by reconciliation.

David Puttnam's production of *The Mission* (1986) transpires amid the imperial geo-politics of mid-eighteenth-century South America. A fratricidal mercenary and slave-trader (Robert De Niro) joins the Jesuits and ends up struggling to protect indigenous people from the voracious appetites of European powers, including the Vatican. It is a harrowing, exultant, and ultimately sober tale about the possibilities of radical grace and the rapaciousness of power unrestrained by any sense of morality or God. No other film so fathoms the startling wildness with which divine love sometimes erupts, even in the darkest of places.

And last, in a long meditation on the relationship of art to Christian grace, the Danish *Babette's Feast* (1987), based on a short story by famed writer Isak Dinesen *(Out of Africa)*, tracks the fate of three single women as they live their days in a tiny seaside fishing village in Jutland. While the site is geographically obscure and remote, remarkable events nonetheless take place, illumining the divine surprise that confounds conventional expectations of how and where the divine might appear. It is a quietly rapturous tale of the manner in which the divine transfigures the ordinary into a stage on which beauty and love display the reality of God. Along the way the story meditates on the manner in which art and divine grace must rely on one another to realize the fullness of divine love.

CHAPTER 4

"THE WINGS OF A DOVE"

The Search for Home in *Tender Mercies*

A few minutes into *Tender Mercies,* director Bruce Beresford provides a good long look at the drunken brawler whose fight over a bottle begins the film. The washed-up, alcoholic country singer-songwriter stands in the gravel parking lot of a two-pump west Texas gas station-cum-motel. In that empty driveway Mac Sledge (Robert Duvall) looks around, not quite sure of where in Texas he is; and we soon sense that he is even less sure about where he is in any larger sense — that is, in life. Marooned and dead broke, run up on the shoals of booze and self-loathing, he stands there alone on the vast wind-blown flatlands that stretch out to the horizon of a huge featureless blue sky. It is an arresting shot in a film where images reveal the deepest core of the story: at the center of the frame, a small figure stands dwarfed by an immense nothing. Similar shots recur throughout, always emphasizing Sledge's plight as the quintessential hard-luck Everyman, lost and alone amid a great emptiness that pointedly reflects the condition of his own soul.

Before long, we get the gist: Sledge is in many ways the archetypal Cain figure, especially because of his habits of anger and violence that viewers will witness. In fact, at this stage of his life, he resembles Cain quite a bit: condemned to the fruits of the violent man he has been, he's a solitary wanderer whose world has enigmatically turned empty, inscrutable, and, for all intents and purposes, as indifferent and hard as rock. Indeed, the portrait of Sledge against the sky is, first and last, the defining shot of *Tender Mercies.* Because it is a matter of desperate urgency, Sledge spends a good deal of screen time at the beginning — and regularly throughout the film — trying to read meaning of some sort in the blankness of that inscrutable sky. He does this on his own behalf and for all the other lives that transpire beneath that sky. It matters little whether he has brought his present tough circumstances on himself or if fate has done it to him. He's there and he's stuck, wracked by booze and his own unkempt soul.

Director Bruce Beresford makes his point visually, quietly, and without giving it any extra thump of obviousness or melodrama. His opening shots show Sledge's essential smallness and lostness in a landscape that dwarfs him, just as life seems to have diminished him; but, as telling and poignant as these plains landscapes are in catching the real state of this messed-up cowboy-singer's soul and psyche, they are by no means the whole or final story. What does count in *Tender Mercies* is where Sledge ends under that sky: his world and self are still sorrowful, but they are also enormously changed, even transformed. The great surprise and lasting accomplishment of *Tender Mercies* lies in what Beresford and writer Horton Foote provide for Sledge as he lives his days below that empty expanse of sky. Nothing exceptional or climactic happens: no murders or affairs, no flashbacks of dying husbands or wife-beatings, no sensation or sentiment. But by the end of the movie, everything in Sledge's world has changed profoundly. By that time, that empty land and blank sky no longer define Sledge's world, though he lives still within their lasting inscrutability. The great surprise is that Sledge, this self-medicating Cain-on-the-run, has found unexpected "tender mercies" of refuge, welcome, and ultimately homecoming. With spare, searching imagery and action, *Tender Mercies* displays those salient moments in the progress of lives from pain-ridden enigma toward intimacy, trust, and some measure of understanding of life.

Amid this, the big surprise is not that a "good woman" tames Sledge, which is usually the theme in syrupy country-and-western lyrics. The surprise is that this one, the widowed keeper of a small outback motel, is very much woman-wife and — without the least stretch or sentimentality — also the vessel for mercies that seem to flow straight from the tender heart of God. Much of the story, imagery, and music make clear that Rosa Lee (Tess Harper) becomes for Sledge the "heavenly dove" of whom he sings at one point, and whose "pure, sweet love" comprises a sure "sign from above." Her patient ministrations offer protection, on the one hand, as they fend off the dark of abandonment, and, on the other hand, they entice Sledge away from the abyss of self-destruction toward the consummate goodness of an ordinary life in love, marriage, family, and work — seen in deeds as simple as picking up the trash, which we see Sledge doing at both the opening and close of the film. The grace comes quietly to Sledge, and by surprise and stealth, seeping down deep to shelter and then transform the violent "man who was once Mac Sledge," as the movie puts it. Ultimately, Sledge finds not blankness but love, itself mysterious and inscrutable, a reality that counters the emptiness he has known. Only a few films have managed to capture the gentle quiet splendor by which love, against big odds in this dark world, makes itself known.

Finding Home

The story itself is simple enough, rather too simple for some critics situated in the land east of the Hudson. Sledge hits bottom at that outback motel, and for no apparent reason a kindly young Baptist widow "takes pity" on him, as he puts it near the end of the film. She gives him work (at two dollars an hour), lodging, and meals at the motel — and specifies no drinking. Within a mere ten more minutes of film time, they are married. During that ten minutes come brief wordless scenes of Sledge doing chores around the place, usually under that limitless sky and always in the constant wind: fixing doors, pumping gas, and, at the very beginning, picking up trash by the roadside — the symbolic gesture repeated at the end of the movie. The drunk and the widow stumble and lurch toward each other, watching television and rather stiffly trying to talk. There is one scene of them in a Baptist church, with Rosa Lee singing in the choir as the congregation, Sledge included, belts out "Jesus Saves." Then, surprisingly, while they are working together in the wind-blown back garden, which is as close as they will get to Eden in hardscrabble west Texas, Sledge observes that he has given up drinking and wonders aloud, given his feelings for Rosa Lee, which "even a blind man could see," whether she would "think about marrying" him. She responds with a simple "Yeah, I will," and they both go on working. No hugs, no music, no passion; only sober reflection beneath the prairie sky, as if they both know that, amid the hard conditions of living in general, such caution is the sensible way to conduct matters of the heart. This scene surely ranks as one of the most laconic proposals in film history. We have little idea of how many months have gone by since Sledge first showed up at the motel, since the film is set in a sort of perennial leaflessness, though the garden does grow. (The film was actually shot in eight weeks during the late fall of 1981; the garden plants were brought inside at night to keep them from freezing.)

The two "orphans" in the film, Mac (Robert Duvall) and Sonny (Allan Hubbard), ponder their troubles as the motel, its wings open, looms in the background.

The rest of the story is episodic and elliptical, leaping to various telling moments of small and big trouble in the progress of the marriage and the life of the newly blended family of Mac Sledge, Rosa Lee Wadsworth, and her eight-year-old son, Sonny. In keeping with the film's sober emotional realism, not all is smooth going. Marriage and a new family mark a beginning that will be followed by bumps and valleys aplenty. "Happily ever after" is often a difficult place to find, and in these lives it proves elusive and distant. That is especially true for the boy Sonny, Mac's stepson, whose father died in Vietnam when he was a baby. Like his new stepfather, Sonny has also been abandoned and is trying hard to find a path to respect and maturity. That Beresford sees Sledge and Sonny in much the same way is emphasized by the visual link he repeatedly draws between the two. When Mac first asks Rosa Lee about staying on to work off his room bill, the voices of the conversation are offscreen, and the camera fixes on Sonny as he plays with his toys on the ground. Not long after that, Sonny comes upon Mac sitting alone on a log on the empty prairie, far from the white motel, which sits on the horizon in the background. Sonny asks Mac what he's doing, to which Mac replies, "Thinkin'," a response that fits both well enough, since they both have had their share of woe and loss, and both have brooded on, in their separate ways, life's harder questions and how they got to their present predicaments, as well as the direction and meaning of their lives.

127

Tender Mercies (1983)

Director:	Bruce Beresford
Screenwriter:	Horton Foote
Cinematographer:	Russell Boyd
Editor:	William M. Anderson
Production Designer:	Jeannine Claudia Oppewall

Cast

Robert Duvall	Mac Sledge
Tess Harper	Rosa Lee
Betty Buckley	Dixie
Wilford Brimley	Harry
Ellen Barkin	Sue Anne
Allan Hubbard	Sonny

Academy Awards

Best Actor:	Robert Duvall
Best Original Screenplay:	Horton Foote

Additional Academy Award Nominations

Director:	Bruce Beresford
Music:	Austin Roberts, Bobby Hart
Picture:	Philip Hobel

Sonny is especially hard-pressed because he wonders both about this new man in his house and about what kind of man the father he never knew was, the young newlywed soldier who was shot by a sniper in the war. His small-town, macho schoolmates challenge him about his fatherless past, and about the respectability of this new man living at his mother's place. Throughout the movie Mac and Sonny clumsily grope toward the friendship and familial wholeness for which they both hunger. Scenes regularly alternate between the travail and slow progress of each, and their parallel struggles echo one another to clarify their mutual search for identity and an abiding family of acceptance and trust. Orphans and exiles both, they slowly make their way toward each other and toward wholeness, as the rhapsodic closing scene of the film celebrates.

Sledge has a more difficult time finding his way within the constricting confines of marriage, fatherhood, and personal contentment. The extent of his struggle becomes clearer as the audience learns more, bit by bit, about his personal history and the painful reality of the numerous dark reflexes in his emotional makeup. We learn early that, in addition to once being a violent drunk, Sledge enjoyed considerable fame and wealth as a successful singer-songwriter in Nashville; he then lost all of it, as he tells Sonny, to "too much applejack." Still, the viewer is shocked to learn midway through the film that once, in a drunken rage, he tried to kill his wife at the time, Dixie Scott (Betty Buckley), who made her fame singing Sledge's songs. Unlike her ex-husband, Dixie has managed to retain her star power in country music over the decades. In contrast, Sledge begins the movie with a drunken brawl and periodically thereafter seems on the verge of either erupting or running.

Early in the movie, in his first days pumping gas for Rosa Lee, Sledge appears restless, fingering cash and itching to be on the road again, to carouse again. As the many shots of the road emphasize, this remains a constant temptation for him. Well into his new marriage, despite the balm Rosa Lee affords his wounded soul, Sledge remains jumpy and volatile, though he slowly improves at keeping his impatience and anger at bay. When an entertainment reporter shows up at the desolate West Texas motel to do a story on Sledge's past and present, the latter goes mute, gives the reporter the cold shoulder, hauls Sonny into the house, and then goes out back by himself to gaze at the prairie and brood. In the old days, we sense, Sledge would have cussed the fellow off the property or just outright decked him.

One thing he does learn from the reporter is that Dixie Scott, with his estranged daughter in tow, will soon appear in Austin. Sledge journeys to the concert in an attempt, first, to see the daughter he has not seen for eight years, and second, to interest Dixie or her manager, Harry Silver (Wilfred Brimley), in a song he has written. The venture falls apart when Dixie and Mac begin nasty bickering immediately after encountering each other, just as in the old days — like two-year-olds in a sandbox. Another marital spat follows when Mac refuses to tell Rosa Lee, who is jealous that he went off to hear his famous ex-wife, why he went to see her. He assures her that it was not out of affection since she is "absolutely poison"; but he nonetheless refuses to reveal either of his motives, perhaps out of fear of losing standing in the family. When Rosa Lee pushes him, he gets angry and swears at her, though he soon apologizes. The speed and ferocity of Sledge's quarrel with Dixie and his volatility with Rosa Lee suggest that a psychic cauldron still boils under his placid demeanor.

The fragility of Sledge's self-control becomes clear when Harry Silver shows up to return his song. Silver throws it down on a tree stump out back, announcing that it "ain't no good," that Dixie wouldn't sing it even if it were, and that she wants nothing to do with him. Afterward, feeling dejected and angry, Sledge confesses to Rosa Lee that he went to Austin to sell the song; and he abruptly condemns himself for even trying to do something with the music he says he no longer cares about. Rosa Lee once again tries to take him in hand and offer emotional shelter, recalling her love for him and confessing, as she strokes his face, "Every night when I say my prayers and I thank the Lord for his blessings and tender mercies to me, you and Sonny head the list." She asks him to sing the song his ex-wife and her agent have rejected. Halfway through his voice falters, and he storms out of the house, hops into the pickup, and tears off down the road, this time yielding to the temptations of liberation and forgetting.

How wrong that choice is receives humorous underscoring in a series of admonitory signs as he leaves. As he strides past the Coke machine on the porch of Rosa Lee's little motel office, its ad slogan advises "Here's the real thing" — as opposed to whatever he is looking for down the road or at the bottom of a bottle. As his pickup roars down the expressway entrance ramp, a large billboard in the background proclaims "Prayer Stop." And even inside the tavern, where Sledge stops to drown his sorrows and perhaps get into a fight, a foreground sign on the swinging door that keeps patrons from behind the bar proclaims "Keep Out." Clearly, despite the softening of his character in his new relationship, Sledge has by no means been tamed, and he needs a litany of advice along the way.

The next scenes trace Sledge's feints toward self-destruction: after his stop at the bar, he drives wildly down a tangle of different roads, each one presenting a stark choice about what to do with his life. The film then takes us back to Rosa Lee, who is anxiously waiting into the night: she watches and listens, diverts herself with television, spats with her son and apologizes, and looks at her first husband's picture — no doubt wondering how she has gotten herself into this particular mess. (She first married at sixteen, gave birth at seventeen, and was widowed at eighteen). Finally she climbs into bed and recites Psalm 25 as a prayer for guidance: "Show me thy ways, O LORD; teach me thy paths. Lead me in thy truth, and teach me: for thou art the God of my salvation; on thee do I wait all the day."

Eventually the sounds of a car outside and someone entering the house interrupt her prayer. Mac comes into the bedroom, smiling and proud, confessing that he did buy a bottle but poured it out. He admits to taking off for different places, such as Austin, Dallas, and San Antonio, but that he "kept coming back," even riding by the motel seven times before finally pulling in. While Rosa Lee warms a bowl of soup for the prodigal, a gesture that is as symbolic as it is homey, she offers a confession of her own: she has given a copy of the rejected song — thinking it "real pretty" but, as an old song, probably unimportant — to a local band that worships Sledge, a group of young men who stopped by to drop off posters for their next gig. Mac tells her that it is, in fact, a new song, written only last week; that's why Harry Silver's rejection so angered him (his new stuff is "no good," as Silver put it). Furthermore, he has been writing songs all along because he misses the music. At this moment, pulled back home, welcomed and forgiven, Mac does sing the song for Rosa Lee, because the song is an homage to her, the one whose patience and affirmation have beckoned him from his quite literal wandering in the dark night. The song conveys in its country music idiom the full measure of Sledge's indebtedness and his new hopefulness:

> Baby, you're the only dream I have ever had that's come true.
> If you'll just hold the ladder, baby, I'll climb to the top.

This song displaces the "it hurts so much to face reality" refrain that has cycled as background music throughout the story until now. That deep cold fear about what reality and the future hold will recur in the film only once more. For now, though, the gist of the sequence — and the pivot point in the story — is that the running is over for Mac, for he has found a place of love and trust, a new reality of homecoming. For the first time in his restless roaming for God knows what, he has finally found calm and is married, in the best sense of the word, to a place and a person.

Emblems

Much of the story of *Tender Mercies*, as well as its thematic and emotional power, come from its finely conceived and composed visual images, the figures and shapes on the screen that notably reduce the film's reliance on verbal text and action to establish dramatic interest and meaning. Director Beresford uses a series of potent visual emblems — four in the body of the film and two more at the end — that mark the different stages of Mac's progress toward some wholeness and simultaneously evoke the inner reality of the driving forces in his life. Two are there from the start, almost as antipodes, and they play off each other and gather meaning and emotional heft as the story unfolds. The first, and perhaps most memorable, is Mac himself against that vast sky. (According to production designer Jeannine Claudia Oppewall, Beresford's sole specification for the location of the flatland motel was that no other buildings or physical structures could be visible from it.) The obvious purpose was to emphasize both the emptiness of the land and the stark isolation and solitariness of Sledge — not to mention Rosa Lee and Sonny. On fifteen different occasions the two principal male characters, but mostly Sledge alone, are dwarfed by that vast sky and the broad empty land. The chilling point gets across, and the viewers derive a visceral sense of Mac's plight: the setting, and the repeated inclusion of those two characters in it, elicits a lasting sense of emptiness, insignificance, and isolation, all of which define not only Mac's physical circumstance but, more importantly, the substance of his emotional and spiritual condition as lost, dwarfed, and baffled.

The second emblem, also there from the beginning, is the motel itself, which functions as a counterpoint to the sky. The actual physical layout of the small motel suggests a possibility about the nature and purposes of human life quite different from Sledge's aloneness and perplexity. Seen from a distance, as it often is, the motel seems wedged between forbidding empty sky and limitless land, a thin white wafer of shelter and welcome. Up close, the Mariposa Motel, its central building perpendicular to the road, with two arms or wings extending diagonally toward the road, entices and invites, making it an apt visual corollary for its proprietress. It is here that Sledge awakens from his violent binge to stand within its wings, blinded by light; and here he is allowed to stay on — against all good sense. Early in the film, Sonny and Mac appear in a shot far out on the prairie; the motel hovers in the background, enclosing them even when they are distant from it. It is, especially in its close identification with Rosa Lee, both a refuge and a wellspring of love for both of the forlorn males in this movie. This is fitting because Rosa Lee is the one who brings them together in the first place and sustains them until they can form their own bond. Later, when Mac meets with his grown daughter for the first time in eight years, Rosa Lee and Sonny are seen with that emblem of welcome far behind them. Meanwhile, inside the motel, Mac receives his daughter with the same gentleness that welcomed him. And it is these ever-so-humble physical and symbolic arms, in sharp contrast to the empty sky, the roads to nowhere, and the angry prosperity of Dixie Scott, to which Mac always gladly returns.

Production designer Oppewall deviated from conventions of 1940s and '50s motel design to come up with the singular shape that evokes the tender mercy found within. In addition, she gave the motel its Spanish name, Mariposa, which means butterfly, itself a symbol of the resurrection that Mac receives while in its arms. And Mac is not the only one to absorb its character of refuge and welcome; it is where his own daughter stops for money and succor when she elopes. At its most literal level of a building and a business, it provides shelter and sustenance for the three people living under the vast impersonal sky. In short, it is home. Beresford emphasizes Rosa Lee's identification with this place and all that it and she represent by keeping her firmly rooted and connected to the motel, this place of resurrection. For one thing, she never appears alone in front of the vast impenetrable sky, as Mac and Sonny both do, though she does journey with them below that sky on a couple of occasions. More than that, Rosa Lee's hospitable character finds physical representation in the very shape of the shelter she runs and from which she derives her living.

The tension between sky and shelter, representing the conflict of metaphysical forces, never disappears from the story. But within that tension, Mac Sledge does move toward an embrace of shelter as life's defining hope, and it is within this movement of his character that Beresford situates a third telling visual symbol. A decisive moment in Sledge's progress arrives when the daughter he has not seen in eight years, Sue Anne (Ellen Barkin), now eighteen, appears out of nowhere. Having had no contact since a divorce court gave sole custody of Sue Anne to Dixie Scott, they have a reunion that is, understandably, tentative and shy, halting and muted, so quiet it is almost wordless. But together they gently inch their way toward each other, slowly negotiating the many reasons for her distrust of him — especially his drunken assaults on her mother and his long absence from her life (a circumstance engineered by her mother). Near the end of their talk, daughter asks father if he remembers singing to her long ago, when she was a little girl, a song about a dove and a "pure something love." Enigmatically, Mac denies the memory, but as Sue Anne drives away in her car shortly thereafter, he watches through the window and sings straight through the song he has just claimed he'd forgotten, "The Wings of a Dove" (written by

133

Bob Ferguson and made popular by Ferlin Husky). Why Mac doesn't acknowledge that he knows the song to his daughter is not clear; perhaps the recollection is too dense with personal history and emotion to tackle in this first meeting. Or maybe his Texas-bred reticence has taken over, and he fears the uncharted emotion that may follow. In any case, we should not forget that this is a man who is still relearning how to sing, especially a song of such bursting splendor.

The most likely reason that he cannot acknowledge it to Sue Anne, though, is that the song penetrates to very near the core of her own life and, significantly, to his own very recent experience, catching up in its words all the mysterious things that have lately befallen the hapless, drunken wanderer. This is indicated by the quiet intensity with which Sledge sings the words to himself, more as a confession and recognition than as a simple song. On the chorus, with the perspective of the camera watching from behind him, Mac's solitary body begins to move with the words, as if they well up from the soles of his feet:

> On the wings of a snow white dove,
> He sends his pure sweet love,
> Sign from above, on the wings of a dove.

As he finishes, he sighs a deep exhalation of remorse, hope, and longing, his whole life seemingly distilled in one breath. That Mac has found a full measure of "pure sweet love" is, for him, a "sign from above" of the surprising reality of love in what was heretofore a derelict life, a dark and violent world. In this telling and fetching single take, a very long one, Sledge again stands alone, but this time it is not under the inscrutable sky but from within shelter, from within "pure sweet love" that has become real and palpable, and has retrieved even the likes of him. Instead of wordless perplexity, he sings the song's assent to the reality of solace and hope. As the camera portrays so well, Sledge himself becomes a sign, as he stands — now at last sheltered — gazing after his long-lost daughter, singing a song of love and blessing.

After this moment, Sledge's life seems to turn notably for the better. He has passed the inevitable crisis of rejecting booze as a sop for disappointment; a new family has grown up, and his estranged daughter has again entered his life; and most of all, summarizing these other events, a new reality of love has, as "The Wings of a Dove" suggests, brought him to other recognitions. Shortly after Sue Anne's visit and Mac's assent to the claim of her love, both he and Sonny are baptized in

Back home after his daughter's funeral, and agonizing about the inscrutable, unfair ways of Providence, Mac explains to Rosa Lee that he "doesn't trust happiness" or, for that matter, God.

the Baptist church, a sequence that Beresford plays out at some length, showing first Sonny and then Mac immersed and dripping. Like much of the other imagery in this film, it comes unanticipated and stark: Mac stands in the baptismal tank — soaked, sheepish, and glad — and Rosa Lee smiles proudly, knowing more than he the full meaning of everything the sacrament represents, especially for someone with a history like his. Symbolically, the immersion of Mac's body into the water reiterates the immersion of his inmost being into the "wings of a dove" when he watched his daughter drive off. From the troubled waters of alcoholism that have threatened to swallow him up, Beresford suggests, he lives now in the "living water" of new life. The baptism is the fruition of a saving process that asserts that divine love, manifest here in redemptive human love, does have some sway in the world after all. To emphasize his point, screenwriter Horton Foote poses the hard question, asked by Sonny as they ride home from church: Does baptism affect how people look or how they feel? Mac laughingly replies that he can't tell any difference, but the truth of the matter is starkly obvious: such turnings have their consequence on the inside, where "the meanings are," as Emily Dickinson wrote. With the image of Mac's baptism, cleansed and pretty whole, Beresford's visual imagination posits an emblem that measures how far Mac has journeyed.

135

Trials

Even though the baptism is a culmination of a long slow turning in Sledge's understanding of the nature of human life, it seems but a beginning. The baptism is the signal event that initiates an unexpected interlude of well-being in his life. For one thing, his music gets a boost. The local band that took his "old" song wants him to perform and record it with them. With growing confidence and pleasure, the Sledge who thinks himself a failure sings his song to Rosa Lee before a large crowd in a local dance hall. Because of her, the song proclaims, the world is open again, full of hope and possibility: "There's so much to reach for thanks to you." And the hopeful chorus argues for the potential of new life:

> And now I'll be everything this man can be,
> If you'll just hold the ladder, baby, I'll climb to the top.

The family quietly exults in his success, however modest. Afterward Mac dances off with his wife, and proud as punch of his dashing new father, young Sonny finally achieves some respect among his peers.

Everything seems notably better for Sledge, and it very much looks as though *Tender Mercies* is headed toward a typical Hollywood happy ending or one of the jejune Christian stories where faith proves a good-luck charm or a rabbit's foot in "victorious Christian living." Still, while everything in Sledge's life seems to be turning toward living happily ever after, tragedy gathers in the wings, unrelenting, more than ready to despoil renewal and hope, testing the measure of Mac's newfound belief. The first shadow looms when Sue Anne elopes with the thrice-married drummer in her mother's band, a person Dixie abhors. The hard irony of life again rears its ugly head on the very morning that Mac's new single record, his song to Rosa Lee recorded with the local band, plays on the radio. Mac and Rosa Lee are about to climb into the pickup to go off and celebrate with the boys in the band when Mac returns to the motel to answer a ringing phone. Just as Rosa Lee finds the song on the radio, Mac's hand reaches into the pickup and turns off the music, that song of new life and possibility. The camera pulls back as Mac closes the door of the pickup and slowly returns to the porch and sinks into a chair. When Rosa Lee approaches to find out what is wrong, he tells her that Harry Silver has called to inform him that his runaway daughter was "killed in an automobile accident somewhere in northern Louisiana." Again, in that medium distance shot, the sky looms, quietly asserting the insignificance of the human scene that transpires beneath it. The next shots show Mac in Nashville for the funeral, and then as he goes to Dixie's mansion to visit the sealed casket and a hysterical Dixie. All the narcissist Dixie can think about is, "Why has God done this to me?"

As bracing a picture as *Tender Mercies* is in its moral and psychological honesty about Sledge's struggles and in its hopefulness about the power of love, its strength as a story and a film comes in its closing minutes, where Foote and Beresford etch a spare, tough-minded appraisal of religious faith, the reality of evil, and the nature of religious hope. As at the beginning, random evil again smacks the characters and the viewers in the very soul. The entirety of the film thus far has dealt with the toughest moral and spiritual challenges of a person's life: the reality and difficulty of how to conquer inner beasts; in response, the story details a cogent portrait of the means necessary to overcome the human penchant, for whatever reasons, toward self-destruction. With the death of Sue Anne, the story confronts the darkness of an arbitrary evil that, for no good reason — through accident and disease, for example — kills children, virtuous and wayward alike. The theme has hovered in the background throughout. After all, war killed Rosa Lee's first husband, Sonny's father, when he was not even old enough to vote or drink. In Sue Anne's death, the man she eloped with was drunk, and the accident was entirely his fault; ironically, he will be the one to survive. Clearly, the line between personal, inner evil and impersonal, external destruction quickly blurs to a muddle and stays that way.

The first phase of the conclusion poses the riddle of evil, which in this case is ascribed to the nature of the universe itself. The camera cuts from Dixie's hysterical grief to Mac back at home: in another memorable image, he fervently hoes away in the back garden, again blown by the prairie wind and dwarfed by that huge empty sky. Rosa Lee comes to ask how he is doing, and the usually laconic Mac launches into his longest speech in the film, a detailed lament on the unfairness and mystery of human life. He recalls that he barely survived an auto accident of his own; drunk and alone, he rolled the car four times but survived. Now he prays to know "why I lived and she died," but he gets "no answer." He doesn't know the why of anything, either the good or the bad: why he ended up at Rosa Lee's motel and she "took pity" on him and helped him "straighten up," or why Sonny's father died in the war, or why his daughter died in an auto accident. Why, why? He despairs, concluding that he does not "know the answer to nothing, not a blessed thing"; he "can't trust happiness, never did and never will." Wisely, Rosa Lee offers noth-

Horton Foote and Robert Duvall

Horton Foote, the screenwriter of *Tender Mercies* and of roughly sixty other plays and screenplays, and Robert Duvall, winner of the Academy Award for best actor for his portrayal of Mac Sledge, have had a long and remarkable association that dates back to the earliest days of their careers.

At age seventeen, Horton Foote left the small Texas town of Wharton to enroll in drama school at the famed Pasadena Playhouse. After limited success as an actor in New York, Foote realized that his theater gifts were in writing. One-act plays led to work in the illustrious early days of television, off-Broadway productions, and eventually screenwriting. Foote was established in the New York theater world when a young Robert Duvall landed a role in Foote's "The Midnight Caller." Duvall (b. 1931) had earned a drama degree at Principia College in Illinois, joined the army for two years, and then in 1955 headed off to acting school in New York at the renowned Neighborhood Playhouse. Five years after he first met Horton Foote, Duvall was recommended by the playwright/screenwriter for the role of Boo Radley in Foote's Academy Award-winning screenplay of Harper Lee's best-selling novel *To Kill a Mockingbird* (1962). From that screen debut, Duvall's career prospered, as did Foote's (see sidebar for a list of Foote's screenplays).

ing in response, none of the cliches or nostrums that pious people are wont to mouth. She simply walks away to leave Mac prodding the garden dirt, as if he can beat the very soil into giving up an answer to the human condition — what novelist William Dean Howells, over a century ago, called "the riddle of the painful earth." Or it might as well be the soil of his own heart that Mac pounds, working out in that way his own anger and grief, as Joan Zwagerman Curbow has suggested.[1]

To be sure, as Mac's new life attests, there is still a garden here of sorts, but clearly it is also sorely fallen. No doubt Rosa Lee herself has asked these questions, since her young husband was killed mysteriously. Perhaps the inscrutable, indifferent sky wins; perhaps love does not emerge after all from the horror and mystery. This grim absence of conclusion on the import of tragedy is modulated by the largely visual em-

1. Joan Zwagerman Curbow, "Silence in the Movies," *Perspectives: A Journal of Reformed Thought* (January 2001): 15.

Duvall next encountered Foote material in Lillian Hellman's film adaptation of Foote's novel *The Chase* (1966), an escaped convict story directed by Arthur Penn and starring Marlon Brando, Jane Fonda, and Robert Redford. In 1972, Duvall starred in Foote's adaptation of William Faulkner's "Tomorrow," giving a performance that many consider to be his best. In that same year, Duvall received an Academy Award nomination for best supporting actor as Tom Hagen in Francis Ford Coppola's *The Godfather*.

In 1983 Foote wrote *Tender Mercies* specifically for Duvall, and the film won Oscars for both Foote and Duvall. Foote was again nominated for an Oscar in 1985 for his screen adaptation of his celebrated play *A Trip to Bountiful*. A last collaboration came in 1990, with Duvall and James Earl Jones starring in another screen adaptation of a Foote play, *Convicts*.

Over the years, Duvall has regarded Foote as a mentor and a confidant. Their work has emphasized the life of ordinary people in such ordinary places as the Texas countryside. Foote's collection of plays has detailed the life of the fictional small town of Harrison, Texas, modeled on his own hometown of Wharton. The same milieu was dramatized in *Tender Mercies*, and by Duvall in *The Apostle* (1997). Another commonality of the two is a strong interest in Christian Science.

blems that close the film, the last in Beresford's splendid gallery of images. Sonny arrives home from school to ask questions about the death of his father, who, his mother reminds him, was "just a boy, but he was a good boy." Taking things in the long view, she adds, "I think he would have been a fine man." The arbitrariness of death pertains in his death as it does in Sue Anne's, and again the film asserts the essential sameness in the respective plights of Mac and Sonny, decades apart in age but both trying to find their way toward understanding.

The overriding enigma of evil and human meaning sets the intellectual context for two remarkable sequences that end the story. When Sonny emerges from the building with the new football Mac has brought home for him, the audience hears Sledge's voice quietly singing "The Wings of a Dove." The camera then cuts to Sledge, who is off in the distance, at the side of the road picking up trash, just as he was at the beginning of the film. As Sonny approaches, Mac's singing continues, strong and quietly hopeful, if not exultant. The exact significance of his singing that song, the one he sang to his young daughter, is not altogether clear, except that it captures well his experience in the film. Here Foote and Beresford provide no explanatory film conversation; there is only his singing, the only thing juxtaposed to the dire gist of the talk he has recently had with Rosa Lee in the garden. The image of the solitary Mac still singing as he attends to the menial chore of picking up the trash by the roadside suggests that, while there is plenty of heartrending darkness in the world, there is also the inescapable reality of Love, the "sign from above" — living water, light, human warmth, renewal, and hope. Somehow, mysteriously, these together suffice to stave off despair.

This last note prevails as the camera fixes on Mac and Sonny playing football together, first playing catch and then, laughingly, trying to tackle each other. Here the camera again is deftly articulate, tying together the dominant thematic images of the film. Periodically it pulls back to see the pair within that broad horizon and blue sky cavorting within the open arms of the motel and the woman inside. The point is made more emphatic when the camera cuts to the motel porch, where Rosa Lee watches, pensive and approving, absorbing the wonder of what she sees: the miracle of the two lost males in her life laughing and playing together, home at last, despite the woe that has assailed them. The last glimpse of Rosa Lee is through the screen door as she looks again at their play before she returns to her chores. The parting glance is there to relish the moment that has taken so long to get to. But her willingness to work again, amid this time of crisis, suggests her sense that now, at last, all will be well with those she loves.

The makers of *Tender Mercies* wrestle with crushing personal tragedies and treat them with precision, delicacy, and honesty. A good deal of the film's considerable power derives from their refusal, first to last, to contrive sentiment or easy answers to the difficult riddles it poses. In fact, the filmmakers seem to go out of their way to respect these characters who have, to say the least, suffered their fair share of hard knocks. Sledge especially is beset by demons; but against all odds, against everything he has come to expect of life, against the emptiness of darkness, he comes upon the waters of tender mercy. On the vast empty plains of Texas, that small white motel of open arms, a pinpoint of light and warmth, shelters the wanderer. What Sledge does find, as much as this earth allows, is consummate Love itself, embraced as he is by the "wings of a dove." Sledge finds not only respite from the storm but a welcome of sufficient kindness that he again finds music in his weary, booze-sodden soul. There love happens, all the more convincingly for its apparent slowness — enfolding, consoling, approving, and repairing.

Just as the opening shots of Sledge alone under that blank sky convey almost perfectly Sledge's literal circumstance and its metaphoric existential import, so the film as a whole — narratively, visually, and aurally — almost perfectly realizes his subsequent course. There is throughout the movie a lovely and potent consonance between image and theme, each perfectly representing and catching up the other. His effort, and ours, to know and understand drives the film from beginning to end and explains its starkly elliptical narrative. The storytelling leaves out many of the usual features of Hollywood stories in order to attend to more pressing matters, an approach that drove a number of critics to distraction. But in their own odd way, Foote's story and Beresford's direction make for a measure of visual clarity and expressiveness that is rare in cinema, even though film is, obviously enough, a visual medium in which the image itself provides the simplest and most basic element.

Tender Mercies Filmography

Screenplays by Horton Foote
Of Mice and Men (1992)
Convicts (1990) (also play)
Courtship (1987) (also play)
On Valentine's Day (1986) (also play)
1918 (1985) (also play)
A Trip to Bountiful (1985) (also play)
Tender Mercies (1983)
Hurry Sundown (1967)
The Chase (1966)
Baby, the Rain Must Fall (1965) (also play, entitled *The Traveling Lady*)
To Kill a Mockingbird (1962)
Storm Fear (1956)

Notable Films Directed by Bruce Beresford
Evelyn (2002)
Paradise Road (1997)
A Good Man in Africa (1994)
Black Robe (1991)
Mister Johnson (1990)
Driving Miss Daisy (1989)
Crimes of the Heart (1986)
Tender Mercies (1983)
"Breaker" Morant (1980)

CHAPTER 5

THE PLACE BEYOND WORDS

Image and Meaning in *Places in the Heart*

In many ways, prospects for the success of *Places in the Heart* (1984) were not encouraging, either at the box office or as high art. The story of a nearly destitute young widow and her two children trying to survive on a farm in rural Texas during the Depression does not sound like the stuff of high drama, comedy, or adventure. Besides, that year was filled with hard-pressed farmer movies, such as *The River* and *Country,* and the year before had seen *Tender Mercies.* Not even the presence of esteemed writer-director Robert Benton (*Bonnie and Clyde* and *Kramer vs. Kramer,* among others) was enough to attract sufficient financing to make the movie. Not until the much-loved actress Sally Field signed on to play the lead did a studio agree to bankroll the film. That signing made for commercial appeal, certainly, but it did not excite critics, who anticipated a heavy dose of Fieldian sappiness and pluck in what seemed sure to be a reprise of the indomitable Norma Rae in the film of the same name, the role for which Field had won an Academy Award in 1979. Nonetheless, *Places in the Heart* was a huge commercial success and won a quiverful of awards, including the Academy Award for best actress for Sally Field and for best original screenplay for Robert Benton, who was also nominated for best director.

Even so, *Places in the Heart* mystified many audiences, and movie critics in particular howled about its melodrama and sentiment (John Simon thought it full of "sentimental dishonesty," brought to a "new height of soft-core non-pornography").[1] And just about everyone found the ending unconventional and confusing. To some extent, those charges

---

1. "Herstories," *National Review* 14 (December 1984): 49.

143

have merit, for at its core *Places in the Heart* seems at odds with itself. The bulk of its long middle section does play as pure melodrama, but that development is perhaps, for several reasons, not without warrant. Admittedly, the story of a young widow struggling to keep her farm during the Depression after her husband's untimely death may seem contrived. On the other hand, the story is set in an era before the days of social safety nets, and untimely death is part of life during very hard times. So what looks like melodrama today may, in fact, have considerable historical truth; after all, the Depression hit Texas hard, as do its frequent tornadoes. Furthermore, Robert Benton, a writer not much given to sentiment, grew up in Waxahachie in the 1930s and very likely knows of what he writes.

The melodrama of the long middle section is pointedly framed by a stark realism that unflinchingly portrays an aggressive evil that is neither tame nor tractable, and whose effects are fatal and lasting. Evil in this film, extreme and dark, is simply not susceptible to quick fixes and tidy resolutions. The sentiment and melodrama that do show up soon run into harsh, intractable realities of that very palpable evil, which the film does not try to dilute. The truth is that Benton seems to go out of his way first to develop and then subvert all the expectations of melodrama: the film begins and ends with lasting deep tragedy, lacks very much real suspense, eschews romance (except incidentally in a smarmy subplot), and has nothing to do with a tidy happy ending that sets hearts aglow. Moreover, it repeatedly refuses opportunities to pander to emotion and bathos. Instead, its consolations and hopefulness are at best bittersweet and provisional, and they are achieved only by means of an extraordinary leap to an abruptly surprising and, many critics complained, farfetched kind of metaphysical hopefulness.

Largely, though, critics have failed to recognize how much of what they label "melodrama" contributes to the film's thematic coherence and especially to the expansive metaphysical vision that closes the film. What melodrama there is serves a higher purpose; *Places in the Heart* uses those conventions in order ultimately to transform and transcend them. It does not stop with emotion for emotion's sake or excitement and suspense for their own sake, but pushes beyond conventions to surprising, soul-shaking places — the very places, cited in the title, that make up the deepest terrain of the human heart. Benton first gives a glimpse of what seems to be Eden itself, bucolic small-town Texas in the mid-1930s; but then he shatters it with a display of the cosmic brokenness that afflicts all people and makes them into exiles, orphans, and wanderers. From that tragic given in the human circumstance, Benton places at the center of the story the deep human longing for the repair of what afflicts humankind, specifically for deliverance from the suffering and estrangement that all people contend with everywhere.

The central datum of *Places in the Heart,* shown repeatedly in the film, is that people are beset, inside and out, by an enmity that wrecks people, families, societies, cultures, and nature itself — the physical and metaphysical landscape in which humanity has its being. People's deepest hope, then, is that somehow the human penchant for destruction might disappear so that the world might mend and heal. In quiet and profound ways, Benton dramatizes the desire of all people for a realm of trust, harmony, and intimacy where, at the very least, violence and discord are no more. The Jewish-Christian understanding of human history sees this as the pervasive thirst for the return to the state of being and relationship of the biblical Eden, a place for delighting in the loveliness of the creation and the lovingkindness of the Creator. *Places in the Heart's* great accomplishment is that it moves audiences both backward and forward to an entirely different, and stunning, destination. To the utter perplexity of most critics, tone-deaf to their marrow, *Places in the Heart* ends with nothing less than an exultant vision of the reconciliation and restoration that is the healing of the world.

It is with this kind of world — a place that looks and feels a lot like Eden — that Robert Benton opens *Places in the Heart.* The film begins with a lengthy lyrical display of an idyllic rural landscape and village beneath the credits. Far longer and more substantial than the usual establishing sequence, lasting some two minutes and consisting of eighteen widely varied shots of a town and its people, this locational montage gives the film as a whole both a mood and expectation of tranquility and harmony. The opening shot looks on a small town surrounded by sun-drenched prairie grass; after that comes a stately Romanesque courthouse and then, since it's Sunday, a crowd leaving a small pink stucco church; a couple sits in a restaurant and prays over their meal, as an evicted elderly woman who lives in her car begs for food; on a back-porch stairs a homeless black man prays over his hand-out. Always the camera returns to the larger setting itself: an abandoned rural house among tall cottonwoods, fairgrounds, country dirt roads, and a field of blue flowers. In shot after shot, Néstor Almendros's muted but warm cinematography transfigures the landscape and people with a precision and delicacy that avoids the florid and rhapsodic. This is all reverential, but it's neither sentimental nor bathetic. If the visual treatment does not quite celebrate the town

145

Places in the Heart (1984)

Director:	Robert Benton
Screenplay:	Robert Benton
Cinematographer:	Néstor Almendros
Editing:	Carol Littleton
Production Design:	Gene Callahan

Cast

Sally Field	Edna Spalding
Lindsay Crouse	Margaret Lomax
Ed Harris	Wayne Lomax
Amy Madigan	Viola Kelsey
John Malkovich	Mr. Will
Danny Glover	Moze
Yankton Hatten	Frank Spalding
Gennie James	Possum Spalding
Lane Smith	Albert Denby

Academy Awards

Best Actress:	Sally Field
Best Original Screenplay:	Robert Benton

Additional Academy Award Nominations

Best Picture

Director:	Robert Benton
Supporting Actor:	John Malkovich
Supporting Actress:	Lindsay Crouse
Costume Design:	Ann Roth

and its encompassing landscape, it does affirm, quietly and with sober lyricism, the essential goodness of ordinary life.

The mood of the visual meditation is reinforced by the music that plays over the montage from the beginning, though it is somewhat odd within the conventions of Hollywood scoring. An unseen, full-throated church choir clanks through the old evangelical Protestant hymn "Blessed Assurance":

Blessed assurance, Jesus is mine!
O what a foretaste of glory divine!
Heir of salvation, purchase of God,
Born of His Spirit, washed in His blood.

This is my story, this is my song,
Praising my Savior all the day long;
This is my story, this is my song,
Praising my Savior all the day long.

The music effectively clarifies the cultural setting; but, more than that, the words of the hymn interpret what we see on the screen and anticipate much of what will transpire in the course of the story. The montage emphasizes the landscape's quiet visual splendor, human devotion, and the simple habit of gratitude for the goodness of life — all suggesting both a sense of divine care and a "foretaste of glory divine." What Benton lays out is a large part of what is commonly meant by goodness. At the same time, though, the montage and what soon follows look like a sentimental evocation of a bygone Norman Rockwellish America of happy faith and social warmth; and for the time being at least, Benton is out to create just that impression. The opening minutes encourage expectations of optimism and happy endings. Very soon, however, *Places in the Heart* undercuts any optimism whatsoever about the necessary goodness of American life and, for that matter, of human life in general, about whose safety there seems to be little assurance of any kind. In doing so, Benton insistently puts assertions about goodness and divine care for the world to the harshest tests.

Eden Lost

The intention to test that optimism becomes clear in the first segment after the montage of town and countryside, a sequence that poses the riddle that informs and shapes everything that follows. The opening montage ends, and the story proper begins as the camera settles on a white frame house, picket fence and all, on the edge of town. Inside, a handsome young father prays gratefully and at length for a blessing on Sunday dinner and on others less fortunate. It ranks as one of the more sincere and articulate prayers in Hollywood film history. At the table are the two cutest possible kids, a boy and a girl, and the adorable Edna

(Sally Field), wife of the man praying, Royce (Ray Baker). Everything about the scene still looks about as close to heaven as one could imagine, except for the distant gunshots that sound at the margins and suggest that trouble and woe are never far away, even in so perfect a world. While Royce prays, and in the small talk that follows, the parents exchange anxious glances; we soon learn that Royce is the town sheriff when he is beckoned by his deputy to deal with "a drunk Negro down in the train yard." Royce grabs his sidearm from the front closet, and as he departs, he sweetly tells his wife, "I won't be gone long."

In the train yard a falling-down-drunk but genial black teenager gleefully fires an old revolver at cans he throws in the air. Royce keeps his distance, trying to humor the amiable Wiley (De'voreaux White), who looks eminently unthreatening, into giving up the gun. Wiley apparently empties the gun first, because his last shot clicks on an empty chamber. He then turns toward the sheriff and pulls the trigger. The gun fires, a bullet that was not supposed to be in the gun hits the sheriff square in the chest, and he flops backward dead on the ground. Needless to say, this sudden, accidental death surprises and wrenches the viewers, for nothing thus far has prepared them for this eruption of random violence, even though it was completely inadvertent. If anything, in the film's portrait of bucolic splendor up to this point, and in the conventional expectation that the handsome young sheriff will take care of this small business, Benton seems to go out of his way to suggest that nothing of this kind could possibly happen in so idyllic a world.

Royce's wife, Edna, has no sooner finished clearing the dishes, but for a heaping dinner plate awaiting the absent Royce, than her husband's body returns home to be laid out on the table where he had prayed a half hour before. The sequence plays all the more effectively for its understatement: instead of hysterics, Field, with Benton's direction, shows enough shock and horror but refrains from paroxysms of grief. Tragedy speaks for itself, and matters are clearly bad enough without mushing them up further. The camera watches Edna's speechless horror for five long seconds and then finds her in the backyard as she summons her children to tell them of their father's death. Again, Benton refuses to milk any of this for emotion: Edna gets no further than "something's happened to your pa" before the scene ends. And this is not the only scene in which Benton uses emotional restraint. Throughout *Places in the Heart*, virtually all the principal characters respond to the onslaught of tragedy with stoic calm, acutely aware of the inevitability of "trouble" in this life. When Benton does dwell on pure emotion, it is for a special purpose.

And then, almost immediately after the utter calamity of Royce's death, comes another tragedy, for which we are no more prepared than the first. Two truckloads of horn-blowing local Klan members, not even bothering with hoods, arrive at Edna's house. Between the vehicles, bound and tethered to the rear of the lead pickup, dragged on the ground, dust-covered, and dead lies young Wiley, whom the Klansmen have promptly executed for killing the white sheriff, even though it was accidental. Only when Edna's sister Margaret (Lindsay Crouse) arrives and rebukes the vigilantes do they leave. The whole sequence lasts only one minute, with the camera pausing to brood on Wiley's body for four long seconds. Benton's treatment here is again quick, but he does not soften or dilute the horror of the torture and murder of Wiley. The realism is forthright and spare, all rather matter-of-factly presented. The toll of evil is real and biting, and Benton's one-two punch of cosmic harm and brokenness speaks for itself.

To show that evil is not simply "out there" somewhere, distant and alien, Benton provides a moderately prominent subplot that brings evil up close and personal. Margaret's husband, Wayne (Ed Harris), is having an affair with Viola (Amy Madigan), a local schoolteacher and the wife of his best friend. The affair is anguished and mired in guilt, especially on her part; but Wayne, handsome and mild-mannered, hardly the sort to seduce and lie, persists in his advances and his deceit. The consequences of this are also dire, for apart from their own wrestling with personal guilt, late in the film Margaret detects the infidelity. Again there is breakage and sorrow.

The tone throughout these stories is more akin to sober lament than shock or rage at the horror of this world. Benton chooses to trust his audience to make sense of what they see and to get the point of how bad the news of this earth can be. Without sensation or melodrama, and with deft efficiency, he provides just enough information to allow audiences to identify with his characters' experience of loss and confusion. He treats the sudden death of the sheriff matter-of-factly, as if these kinds of things happen all the time, and the brutal killing of Wiley happens offscreen. The point is clear enough, though: very often, even in a world as lovely as the one displayed in the opening montage, evil still reigns and is always a lurking presence, full of malice and peril, regularly making known its persistence with swift clarity.

Exiles

Most of the remainder of *Places in the Heart* chronicles the efforts of the widow Edna to keep her shattered life from disintegrating any further. She must now struggle to hang on to her farm and her family, for she has little money, no means of making a living, and a bank that is eager to foreclose on the mortgage. The screenplay quietly makes the point that, in American society in the 1930s, women were trained only to be wives and mothers. The practical daily world of writing checks and taking care of household finances were entirely in the realm of men. Royce's death has left Edna without any resources, as her visit to an insistently greedy banker and then to her sister makes clear. The polite but wolfish banker tells her that there is not nearly enough in her savings account to pay the mortgage and that she might as well sell the farm to the bank (cheap) and send her kids off to live with relatives. So much for a community's kindness to widows and orphans. From there Edna turns to her sister Margaret, who runs a beauty shop out of her home but hardly brings in enough to support herself and her shiftless, cheating husband. Edna's idea of opening a gift shop in her home is as feasible as turning straw into gold. On the day after her husband's funeral, she finds that her predicament is very dire.

It is here that Benton for the second time turns his story in a sharply different direction, shifting from despair to a modest hopefulness. The first stage of this reversal happens on the evening of Edna's husband's funeral. A black hobo (Danny Glover), the same man we saw praying over his hand-out in the opening montage, begs a meal at her back door. Edna fixes him a plate of leftovers, and then Margaret, who has stayed to help with the dishes from the wake, shoos the man away. Nonetheless, the next morning, after spending the night in her rocking chair, Edna awakens to the sound of chopping wood. The same black man is splitting firewood in the back yard, and he volunteers to do more chores around the place. Edna tells him that she will give him breakfast but then he must move on. The genial fellow tells her that, first, "there ain't no such thing as a job nowadays" and, second, she ought to plant cotton on the farm's uncultivated ten acres, a suggestion she regards as preposterous. But this conversation takes place on the morning before Edna has her dispiriting encounter with financial reality. After that, Edna will try anything, and that is exactly what she does.

Late that spring evening, the deputy sheriff rings her doorbell with the morning's hobo in tow. He was caught at the train yard with a pocketful of silverware, which he had grabbed from Edna's table when she wasn't looking. In his defense, the suspect has pleaded that he was working for Edna. To his surprise, the deputy's, and ours, Edna responds that the man is indeed working for her, even though it is clear that she doesn't even know his name. Still skeptical, the deputy reluctantly frees the man and leaves. Immediately, Edna quizzes Moze Hudnut on how much money she could make if they planted cotton and whether he could pull it off. Moze explains that he "knows everything there is to plantin' cotton," which prompts the widow to hire him, telling him he can stay in the barn. When he thanks her for getting rid of the sheriff, Edna declares that if he ever steals anything from her again, she'll shoot him herself. Neither Edna nor we the viewers have any idea exactly how valuable Moze will come to be.

That will also prove true for the second surprise in the reversal of Edna's fortune, the arrival of the blind war veteran, Mr. Will (John Malkovich), who rents a room and boards in Edna's house. Soon after Edna launches her cotton-growing scheme, Mr. Denby (Lane Smith), the greedy banker, shows up at her house with his brother-in-law, Will, who has stayed with the banker and his wife for the last year — since his mother died. Now, eager to be rid of him, Denby suggests that, as his gesture of Christian charity to help out the widow, he'd be happy to entrust Will to Edna's home and care. It is clear that the sullen Will wants no part of it, and neither does Edna. When she informs the banker of her refusal, he resorts to coercion, noting that the bank would look favorably on her efforts to raise money to keep her farm. "When would you like him to move in?" asks Edna, and the banker replies that Will's belongings are in the car.

Will is not a vagabond and a thief like Moze, but that doesn't make him a desirable house guest. He is surly and self-pitying, and he bluntly informs Edna in their first conversation that he does not wish to be in her home any more than she wants him there. Will wants only to be left alone to weave baskets, listen to his beloved phonograph records, and spew bile. This demeanor continues until one evening he discovers that Edna's children have invaded his prized record collection and scratched one of his treasures. He storms into the kitchen and berates their mother about the terrible "vandalizing" by her "hooligan" children, proclaiming that, if he had any other place to go, he would. The scene simultaneously plays seriously and humorously because, unbeknownst to the unseeing Will, Edna listens to his rant while bathing in her portable bathtub in the middle of the kitchen. Will's umbrage relents when by chance he realizes the grievous offense to manners and hospitality that he has just committed. Completely chagrined by his oafish invasion of the privacy of a lady in her bath, Will is unable to recall the way out of the room, and Edna kindly directs him toward the door.

The beginnings for this motley hard-luck group are not auspicious; they are full of trouble and uncertainty, as might be expected. Events have thrown them together, and if they wish to survive, they have little choice but to work together. Despite their widely divergent histories, they do share the fact that they have each been "done unto" by life, having suffered the knife edge of tragedy — Moze by race, Will by war, and Edna and her children by a random, pitiless accident. Against all odds, they slowly move toward one another. A good fellow from the start, the kindly Moze fills something of the hole left by the dead father. When the local cotton mill owner tries to bilk Edna with inferior seed, Moze tells her about the scam, at the risk of offending the racist power structure of which the mill owner is a conspicuous part. After his humiliation of disturbing Edna's bath, and the kindly way she has responded, even Mr. Will begins to mellow. In one mildly comic scene, the two men and the little girl Possum all commiserate when the single mother must assume the burdens of disciplining Frank for smoking at school. The sequence borders on corny, but it does effectively illustrate the distance this unlikely bunch has traveled toward becoming a cohesive interdependent group.

Exactly how much they have melded becomes clear midway through the film, when a tornado approaches. On one level, this long sequence unfolds like the usual Hollywood close-call melodrama that is meant to show the resourcefulness and pluck of the widow and her new compatriots. But more to the point — and the purpose — of the whole sequence are the images Benton puts on the screen, images that disclose the emergence of a new relational reality among them, a foreshadowing of the startling close of the film. While caning the chairs he makes for a living, Will hears the approaching storm, and instead of heading straight for the storm cellar in the back yard, he gropes and stumbles his way up to the attic, where Possum is blithely playing with her dolls. After he leads the terrified girl down the stairs, Edna grabs his hand to lead him and the little girl through the storm to shelter. Meanwhile, Moze lurches through the wind and dust to rescue a dim shape whose cries for help he has just barely heard; it turns out to be Frank, who has run home from school to help his family in peril. They all make it to the shelter, finally together and safe from the battering wind. When it's clear that they will

In one of the film's more arresting tableaus, the new, makeshift family of the widow, the outcast, and the blind huddle together in the Spalding storm cellar as a tornado, both literal and figurative, passes over them.

survive, and the excitement is over, the film should move on. But instead of hastening on, Benton abruptly slows the pace of the film to a virtual standstill, complete stasis, simply to observe this ragtag crew as they huddle for dear life in the shelter. The camera first dwells on each individually, noting their fear as the storm rages above, and then the camera pulls back to frame the whole group within the golden light of a lantern. Necessity has fused them into a makeshift but nonetheless very real working unit; the shot perfectly distills the newfound interdependence that will allow them to harvest the first bale of cotton to win the prize and allow them to keep the farm.

Benton's choice to slow down the movement and make this shelter gathering into a tableau-for-the-watching suggests that he wants to do more than serve narrative suspense about whether the widow will keep her farm and family. In fact, the tableau goes far beyond that, seeming to leap out of its own literalness to speak of an altogether different kind of success that has already happened, which the participants themselves no doubt but faintly grasp. The point is this: against all odds, especially for this cluster of losers, those who have lost much and who have themselves been lost by their society, an unlikely new family has come into being. As improbable as it seems, they have found one another. It is certainly a makeshift, odds-and-ends kind of family; but that's the very

153

point Benton emphasizes with a visual emblem that precisely and movingly distills the central human craving for the connectedness and intimacy that family represents. All dispossessed in their own ways, and all exiles from Eden — the widow, the fatherless, the blind, and the vagabond — they shelter and cling to one another amid the storms of life's tragedies. We don't doubt this new family's depth of mutuality and care, which is perfectly distilled by this image of them in the shelter.

Furthermore, as becomes clear within the story, this group portrait in the shelter bears striking resemblance to the sorts of people to whom Jesus, in his inaugural sermon, promises to bring the good news of deliverance from bondage.

> He has sent me to announce good news to the poor,
> to proclaim release for prisoners
> and recovery of sight for the blind;
> to let the broken victims go free,
> to proclaim the year of the Lord's favor.
>
> (Luke 4:18-19, REB)

These are the very kinds of "broken victims" who are to compose the new community of love, modeled by divine love, that the New Testament so emphatically forecasts. These random people have stumbled into, or simply been given, a radical sort of lovingkindness. This is the surprise of the promise of good news: in undetectable, unfathomable ways, the exiles and forlorn come to meet; and while the consequences of their individual misfortunes and tragedies have not been reversed, the dire breakage they have known is to some extent soothed or repaired, and in this they have found unforeseeable joy of another kind. This refuge inside the shelter provides an image of what goodness can transpire despite the worst a heart-wrenching world can offer. On the one hand, it is lovely and dearly loved, as the opening montage suggests, and on the other, it devours what is loved most dearly. These people have found, amidst hard and painful reality, shelter in one another from the relentless destruction of caprice and malice; the momentary equilibrium featured in this visual stasis prepares and forecasts the full repair of brokenness portrayed in the surreal conclusion of the movie, where Benton leaps beyond time to make clear the radical gist of Christian historical expectation.

This long meditative pause midway through the story displays, then, the new relational reality that has grown up in this unlikely place

among these disparate and desperate people. It derives from — and precisely captures — the shape and substance of the improbable good news
of relief to captives, widows, orphans, and the infirm. That Benton intends all this is clear from the Edenic portrait in the opening sequence,
which suggests the world these people have lost, and, even more, from
the radical surprise of the closing sequence.

Travail

With the accomplishment of this improbable melding, the actual success
of planting, growing, harvesting, and baling the cotton crop seems almost anticlimactic, though Benton does his level best to stoke the challenge with melodrama. Edna meets and defeats a host of adversities
along the way, such as falling cotton prices, physical exhaustion, and a
go-for-broke financial risk. The remarkable fiery determination of the little lady rings loud and clear. When Moze explains at length that it will be
impossible for the new family to bring in the first bale of cotton, the diminutive widow replies that she would rather die trying than give up,
and if Moze and Will do not want to try along with her, they "can go
straight to hell" — an uncommon way for a southern 1930s church lady
to talk. Everybody does help, even Will, who has become cook and angel:
he rigs a clothesline between the house and the workers in the field so
that he can find his way to the workers to bring food and encouragement.
To the music from Will's phonograph (now he gladly lends it to the
group), they work by lantern light until dawn, and succeed they do.

Edna and Moze deliver the first bale to the mill, and by plying the
odious mill-owner's pride, Edna manages to extract an above-market
price for her crop. So great is the widow's renewed capacity for hope that
she immediately thinks of what she would have earned if she had
planted all her land instead of just the ten acres. Moze dismisses her enthusiasm, joking that harvesting another ten acres would have killed
them all. Nonetheless, when Edna mentions the possibility of buying a
tractor, Moze readily embraces her plans for the future.

Within Hollywood formulas, *Places in the Heart* should conclude on
this practical triumph, accompanied by sunlight, celebration, and a
swelling score rolling over the credits. Instead, Benton not only resists
the trite ending but works hard to subvert all the usual expectations
about the triumph of virtue and the happy life ever after. Just when the
conventions of melodrama dictate that everyone be home free, evil again

erupts to destroy their hard-won good and gladness. And Benton records this with the same sober, patient realism with which he depicted the death of the sheriff and young Wiley. While Edna and the kids attend a harvest dance, Will and Moze chat on the back porch — until Will hears noises. Moze goes to investigate and is abruptly surrounded by five hooded Klansmen who have come to even the score with the uppity black farmer who has bested them all. Their sense of race, caste, and gender will not permit them to suffer defeat by either a black man or a woman, both of which happened when Moze and Edna won the harvest prize. Meanwhile, hearing the disturbance, Will grasps the cause of it and grabs the sheriff's sidearm from the closet; by firing at the sound of the voices, he manages to stop their beating of Moze. When the Klansmen effectively disarm him by diverting his fire, Will again stops their deeds by identifying all of them by the sound of their voices, which he knows well from having sold them his wares for years. While the invaders have eagerly beaten a black man, they dare not harm a blind war veteran; so they reluctantly leave, but not without first warning Moze that they will return to finish him off. Again, as he did in the storm cellar, Benton slows the story to let the camera simply watch people; but this time he contemplates the direct opposite of the miracle of the new community. On his hands and knees in the dirt and dark, Moze quietly weeps, and Will kneels next to his friend to hold and console him in his pain and sorrow. We look on, impotent and mourning, for an eternity of forty seconds of screen time. Evil has again done its pleasure, and its work crushes and breaks the best of what God intended.

By the time Edna comes home from the dance, Moze has already packed his meager belongings, for it's obvious that he can't stay in Waxahachie. He quietly explains that he has to leave, even though he has gotten far more "attached" to this place than he had planned. And though he's in a hurry to leave, he has bothered to assemble parting gifts from his meager belongings: a rag doll he made for Possum, a rabbit's foot Frank admired, and for Edna, a keepsake lace handkerchief that had belonged to his mother. Before he walks off into the night, Edna in return bestows on the bruised and cowed man his dignity, reminding him that, given all they have accomplished, he is surely the best cotton farmer around. A grateful Moze, though now again a vagabond, smiles and disappears into the night as a train whistle sounds in the distance.

A New Creation

And so ends the story of the film. Sadly, as is the way of a broken, sorrowful world, the new family cannot last in the face of the relentless malignancy of evil; Moze, who had perhaps thought his wandering had ceased and he'd found a home, is again wandering into the night. Tragic and mournful, yes, but Benton, for the last time, changes direction yet again. Just as in the sheriff's death at the beginning of the film, he has refused to leave these people in defeat in the end or in glib triumph. He changes course for a last time, providing a stunning epiphanic close to the film.

In this third abrupt turnaround, Benton appends one of the most surprising and peculiar endings in film history. Exactly what to call it is a puzzle because it is largely a thing unto itself. Postscript, epilogue, parable, fable — whatever it is — it both completes the film and works retroactively to give added clarity and poignancy to all that has gone before, especially that central current of the search for trust and solace among the tragedies that romp through human life. Perhaps the best term for what transpires in this final sequence, however discordant or incongruous it may seem in light of the persistent tragedy in the lives of the characters, is benediction. Here Benton dramatizes a markedly Christian view of the culmination of human well-being within the painful mess and riddle of human history.

The last sequence begins by harking back to the Waxahachie of the film's beginning. We again see the settings and sounds that opened the picture, especially the small stucco church and the singing again of "Blessed Assurance," whose title summarizes Benton's understanding of the human story. The singing of that hymn comes from the small pink church, which viewers remember from the film's beginning, and inside parishioners sit in the pews. The minister reads 1 Corinthians 13:1-8, St. Paul's radiant hymn to love. In the third row of the somewhat sparsely attended church sit Edna, her children, and Mr. Will. The camera moves in to focus on Edna's sister, Margaret, who sits stonily in the front row next to her cheating husband, whom she has earlier thrown out of the house for his infidelity. As the minister reads of love's traits and its everlasting nature, the camera comes in close as Margaret lays her hand on her husband's, then and there wordlessly forgiving him; the marriage is repaired, for which he heaves a huge sigh of relief.

Then follows a Holy Communion, whose hallmarks — repeated over and over again — are forgiveness, reconciliation, love, and blessing.

While the choir sings "I Come to the Garden Alone," a hymn that speaks of intimacy with God, and the minister recounts the words of the Last Supper ("This is my blood . . ."), the camera follows the trays carrying the bread cubes and the small goblets of grape juice, the symbolic body and blood of Jesus Christ. Members of the congregation serve one another, some reciting to themselves or saying to others "The peace of God" (a shortened version of the blessing "May the peace of the Lord be with you"). For mainstream Protestant church-goers, the ingredients and progress of the ritual seems ever so normal and regular; but along the way, Benton increasingly deviates from churchly mores and conventional liturgical practice. Slowly he detaches the scene from historical realism to push toward a luminous and transfigurative transcendence, at once surreal and exultant. First of all, in rather a surprise, just about every character in the story seems to be in attendance, and they all partake of the sacrament, row after row, good and bad alike, giving and forgiving: mean bankers, widows, children, mill owners, adulterers, blind men, and, more than likely, even Klan members (except for one, we are never sure who they are among the townspeople). In the communion sequence itself, Benton overlays and conflates elements that would normally be sequential: in the customs of 1935, the minister would not have read the words of instruction while the choir sang, and he certainly would have read them before the distribution of the bread and the wine. Nor would children have been allowed to share in the sacrament. In melding these together, Benton on the one hand concentrates religious intensity and, on the other, begins to loosen the scene from historical realism to prepare us for his extraordinary conclusion.

Benton's intentions for this long church service and the film as a whole become clear as the communion juice passes to the back rows of the sanctuary. The first clue comes when the camera shows an elderly homeless woman whom we have seen three times in the film, but very briefly each time, and for a total of only about fifteen seconds of screen time: once in the opening montage, in the car she lives in; again, when she beckons young Frank to take refuge with her as he tries to make it home ahead of the tornado; and finally, when she lies dead in her overturned car after the storm. If her implausible return to the land of the living in the church slides by the audience, as well it might, there is more inescapable outlandishness to follow. Benton thrusts it smack into his viewers' faces with a directness and force that make the meaning of the film and the church's "story," as the hymn proclaims, utterly unmistakable. On the aisle of one of the last pews, receiving the platter of tiny glasses, is Moze, who was not present when we saw Edna's family and Will in one of the front rows at the beginning of the service. The story proper has him fleeing Waxahachie for his life, the victim of bigotry and hatred; but here he reappears in that same town and, at that, in a segregated church celebrating — of all the preposterous things — communion with white people. Again, as with the violence, the camera handles it matter-of-factly: Benton refuses to remark on Moze's presence in any way. Instead, Moze simply takes a glass, drinks it, and soberly turns to serve Mr. Will, who then serves Possum, who drinks and in turn serves her big brother. Frank drinks the juice and then mutters to himself, "The peace of God," as if thinking that the symbolic wine itself contains and bestows the very peace of God. When the juice — and the camera — move to his mother, she repeats the process, drinking and muttering, eyes straight ahead, as if in private communion with God and her own soul.

At this point, Benton throws over the constraints of realism to urge a wholly different view of the nature and ends of human life, and especially of God's purposes therein, the "blessed assurance" of the hymn. Edna turns to her right to hand the tray to someone not seen since the first scenes, her husband, Royce, who receives the tray, drinks, and passes it to the hands of the person next to him, the boy Wiley, who killed him. In turning, he says directly to Wiley, "The peace of God." Wiley drinks and turns to Royce to wish him, with a faint smile and some lilt in his voice, "The peace of God." At the moment of that exchange, the words of the hymn emphasize the nature and consequence of the event: "The joy we share as we tarry there, none other has ever known." This is, after all, what human life is for, this culmination of fellowship, reconciliation, and delight in the fullness of God's blessing. After this exchange between the murdered and the murderer, they both stare directly and soberly into the camera as it, in its habitual reflex in this movie, simply gazes back for a few seconds until the screen fades to black. In a few seconds more, the final credits roll as the hymn continues to assert the joy of reconciliation and intimacy within the precincts of God's love.

Clearly, this closing sequence completely leaps out of any semblance of realism, and that's the point. Within the all-encompassing love of God, the badly fractured world, a storm fraught with enmity and death, again becomes a garden, as the hymn suggests was God's intention for creation and history in the first place. While humans cannot fathom the mystery of the love that is God, that iconic last image of dead

In the film's last frames, the killed (Ray Baker) and the killer (De'voreaux White) exchange Holy Communion and the peace of God, an apt emblem of the nature of the Kingdom of God.

men in forgiveness and reconciliation wordlessly defines what God is. The two men together in new life, imparting peace to one another, radiantly evoke the character of God's inmost self. The point is not to establish the fact of an afterlife, but rather the repair of the world through love and reconciliation within the spirit of God. Indeed, the entire church sequence is the fruition of the new and unlikely family that was anticipated in the storm shelter: in these last scenes the promise of the shelter blooms full. The extremity of divine love manifest in the particular events of this "love feast," as some traditions label the Eucharist, seeks to mend and heal the weary and broken-hearted in a sorely broken world. This is the destination toward which all the story's outcasts, and all people — even the Klansmen — journey. It is the place beyond words that the heart knows, the place where all are reunited by the love of God, and all is made whole. It is not a rapturous cosmic dance as befits the end of history. But then, God goes everywhere, even in the midst of history, even — perhaps especially — to the bloodied hardscrabble soil of depressed Texas.

Benton Filmography

Films Directed by Robert Benton
The Human Stain (2003)
Twilight (1998)
Nobody's Fool (1994)*
Billy Bathgate (1991)
Nadine (1987)
Places in the Heart (1984)*
Still of the Night (1982)*
Kramer vs. Kramer (1979)*
The Late Show (1977)*
Bad Company (1972)*

*indicates that Benton also wrote these films

CHAPTER 6

THE LAUGHTER BEYOND TEARS

Love's Redemptive Call in *The Mission*

At the top of an enormous waterfall, Captain Rodrigo Mendoza (Robert De Niro) finds a great surprise, what he and no one around him ever guessed was possible — and all the more because of his broken-down condition, which is an apt emblem for his profound inner debilitation. Mendoza, the former conquistador, arrives at the top of that falls mud-soaked and bedraggled, crawling exhaustedly on all fours like a giant bug; tethered to him is a large bag of the armor and weapons by which he has made his living. He has survived days of a penitential climb up this sheer rock face through pouring water and then up rain-slick mountain-sides through mud, all the while dragging that bag of woe. And that's not even the half of it. The more profound burden that he will always carry with him is the ravaging guilt for killing his brother over the woman they both loved.

Mendoza's ascent is his penitential attempt to find a way to forgive himself; at least that's what the priest Father Gabriel hopes it will ac-complish. It is more of a challenge than a promise, for Mendoza does not believe it will work. And then, midway through *The Mission*, comes this daunting surprise, a wild, incandescent moment that stuns everyone — Mendoza, the other characters, and the audience. That is no small feat in what is a glowing film from first frame to last, both in the story it tells and in the manner of its telling. And as is often the case in *The Mission*, this scene is wordless: the camera, acting, and music do the telling, save for a few words in Guarani that go untranslated. Furthermore, there is hardly anything like it in cinema anywhere, this cogent, plausible, and full-blown religious conversion whose wrenching effect shows what it means to run head-on, unexpectedly, into the love of God, a love that for all its compassion and ecstasy is nonetheless relentless and not altogether tame. But getting to the top of the falls, where light engulfs Mendoza in that transfixing moment, has been an intensely difficult journey. And that is but the beginning of a still more arduous one.

Darkness Itself

In the middle of the eighteenth century in central South America, a Spanish mercenary and slave-trader, the volatile, passionate, and brutal Rodrigo Mendoza, has slain the brother he dearly loves after learning that his own mistress has for six months been his brother's lover as well. Like Cain, the original fratricide, in his jealousy and anger, Mendoza is afterward so devoured by guilt that he craves the oblivion of his own death. He resorts to a monastery cell, not in any hope of forgiveness or redemption — for he believes that his crime is unforgivable — but as a quiet place to excoriate and starve himself. The monks are not enthusiastic about their guest, for Mendoza has scorned everything the church and its Jesuit priest-missionaries represent. Nor do they care for his resolution to die there; but their rule of hospitality bids them to welcome and care for this woebegone criminal. The measure of their kindness is made clear by glimpses of the excesses of Mendoza's evil acts.

Viewers first meet Mendoza in his raid into the forests to capture indigenous Guarani, women and children included, to sell into slavery. He traps these largely defenseless people as if they were animals, using airborne snares and plain brute force; those who try to escape he rather matter-of-factly kills, apparently for the mere pleasure of taking life. Then he herds his human booty into town, leading the degraded parade as if he were some conquering hero. Finally, as the film visually emphasizes his similarity to Judas, he takes payment for these slaves in gold coin from one of the wealthy Spanish plantation-owners. The pillage and slaughter mean nothing to Mendoza; he celebrates power and coercion as the sole arbiters of justice in human affairs. Indeed, his raids on the Guarani seem devoted as much to dispensing sheer terror as to making money. And throughout the first part of this movie, in everything from the way he carries his body to his horsemanship, Robert De Niro's superb display of physical acting conveys the character's relish of his own physicality and his capacity for domination. As one character puts it, "Might does make right," and that is the way Mendoza sees the world and comports himself within it, even to the point of killing his own flesh and blood.

The Mission (1986)

Producers:	Fernando Ghia, David Puttnam
Direction:	Roland Joffé
Screenplay:	Robert Bolt
Music:	Ennio Morricone
Cinematography:	Chris Menges
Editing:	Jim Clark
Production Design:	Stuart Craig

Cast

Robert De Niro	Rodrigo Mendoza
Jeremy Irons	Gabriel
Ray McAnally	Cardinal Altamirano
Aidan Quinn	Felipe
Cherie Lunghi	Carlotta
Ronald Pickup	Hontar
Chuck Low	Cabeza
Liam Neeson	Fielding
Bercelio Moya	Indian Boy
Sigifredo Ismare	Witch Doctor
Asuncion Ontiveros	Indian Chief

Academy Award

Cinematography:	Chris Menges

Additional Academy Award Nominations

Art Direction:	Stuart Craig
Costume Design:	Enrio Sabbatini
Director:	Roland Joffé
Editing:	Jim Clark
Original Score:	Ennio Morricone
Picture:	Fernando Ghia, David Puttnam

Though Mendoza thinks otherwise, his murder of his brother is not an exceptional crime but rather a pure, straight-on expression of who he is at his core; it is an unsurprising, even predictable, product of his cruel and predatory nature. What is at the center of Mendoza's life is Mendoza, and throughout he wears the same impassive look on his face, no matter what he's doing — marauding for slaves in the jungles, hearing his mistress tell the hard truth, or killing his brother.

The filmmakers demonstrate Mendoza's predatory core with wonderful cinematic flair: when Mendoza leads the procession of human booty into town for sale, jaunty on his prancing horse, the camera lingers, as it often does in *The Mission* (this time for a full minute), in tight shots on the yoked prisoners as they struggle to keep up with Mendoza's procession of horses. These alternate with low-angled telephoto shots of Mendoza that give his figure both mass and menace. The score turns cacophonous and forbidding, as it often does in the story's dire circumstances, such as the "crucifixion" that begins the film and the massacre that concludes it. Townswomen gather their children, and everyone runs from the dreaded Mendoza. His only gesture of human vulnerability is a nod to his mistress as his parade passes below her balcony. Shortly after this, Mendoza sells his cargo for the handful of gold to the equally brutal Spanish ambassador, Don Cabeza (Chuck Low), a heavy, bald, and thundering figure. The don's sole concern is to spirit away his human purchases, for he and his country deny that they either engage in or condone this slave trade. This transaction in human beings introduces in bold terms the subject that will dominate this story soon after Mendoza's conversion: the imperial inhumanity of Western nation-states in their colonization of any part of the non-Western world that might have any economic value.

The truth of Mendoza's predatory nature culminates shortly after he hears about his lover's preference for his brother Felipe (Aidan Quinn). The mistress, Carlotta (Cherie Lunghi), fears that Rodrigo will hurt his brother, and this proves prophetic when Rodrigo finds Felipe and Carlotta together, and in a subsequent duel stabs his brother with a hidden knife. In a chilling sequence, Carlotta arrives immediately after the slaying; she screams and screams as the camera, for a long thirty seconds, fixes on the impassive face of Mendoza. While this murder is a shock to Carlotta, the deed itself is entirely consistent with everything the audience has seen of Mendoza.

But almost immediately Rodrigo is filled with remorse and retreats to a monk's stall, sleeping on straw and refusing to eat. His initiation

The score turns discordant and percussive as Mendoza (Robert De Niro) parades his new captives into town for sale.

into crushing grief and repentance, a wholly new experience for him, overturns everything he thought he was: all his prior beliefs about the sufficiency of power and his revered notions about the autonomous personal will, specifically that power and revenge will satisfy the heart. Suddenly morality, crime, and death have become real and pressing to him, and the strange sensation of self-condemnation seethes within. For this avalanche of guilt, he believes, there can be no remission; for his crime, he declares to Father Gabriel, "there is no forgiveness." In effect, what strikes Mendoza in the depth of his remorse over killing his brother is the reality of the soul, that psychic region where one calculates the joys and costs of living, though he is loath to so much as suggest the existence of either the soul or any kind of God with whom he might have something to transact.

Indeed, the full measure of Mendoza's dark path is revealed when this everyman of the rod comes to realize the enormity of his crime and turns toward death as the only escape and propitiation for his horrors. That is, after all, the only reality Mendoza has understood and venerated in his long history of pillage and slaughter. Finally, though, the fratricide itself, as well as his persistent depth of guilt and despair, place him in the company of the biblical Cain, who preferred death to life after his crime (Genesis 4:14). Mendoza is not only part of Cain's murderous brotherhood as a typical archvillain whose livelihood is the embodiment of mankind's essentially predatory nature; but he is also Cain's brother in regretting his deed unto death. Indeed, he would probably die in that monk's cell were it not for the spiritual gambit thrust before him by an

166

opponent every bit as fierce and resolute as he, Father Gabriel (Jeremy Irons), one of the Jesuit missionaries who has opposed Mendoza's ravages in the mission villages of the Guarani that so far have been protected by the Vatican. These two previously confronted each other in the forest when Mendoza was ambushing a native hunting party. On a visit to the monastery from his outpost in the jungle, Gabriel learns of Mendoza's crime and his present despair.

Light Comes

Mendoza has already spent six remorseful months in a monk's cell wishing for death when Gabriel shows up to give him a daunting penitential challenge. What follows this is, in simplest terms, Mendoza's long arduous passage to conversion. It must be long and arduous given the hard case he is. Gabriel designs a specific physical journey over terrain that perfectly defines the religious-theological challenge before Mendoza and, for that matter, humanity as a whole. Mendoza must ascend an enormously steep waterfall, a torrential cascade that is both geographically real and — at the thematic center of *The Mission* — also profoundly moral and spiritual. In addition to surmounting the falls, Mendoza must also somehow haul up that symbol of all his predatory nature, the large sack of armor and weaponry. The falls is literal in its immensity and relentless force; but at the same time it suggests the biblical Fall, that predilection toward darkness that humans must overcome and which Mendoza has come to represent in his enmity toward all things divine and human. This falls is an obstacle that Mendoza must pass beyond.

That's hardly the end of the meaningfulness of the falls, which is seen in full shots regularly throughout *The Mission*. In literary-cinematic terms, the waterfall suggests multiple meanings depending on dramatic context. In addition to alluding to the biblical Fall, they are the Mount of Purgatory, which Dante must climb to reach paradise. At other times, depending on whether one ultimately interprets the film as hopeful or despairing, the falls suggests Sisyphus's futile attempts to surge beyond human limits. But most often the falls becomes — religiously and experientially — what Franz Rosenzweig calls an "enigmatic signifier," the presence of an enormous force whose meaning remains uncertain or elusive. At the beginning of the film, when the martyred priest drops over the falls on his cross, the cascade seems to be, in its visual magnificence and its gentle horseshoe curve, the welcoming bosom of an infinite divine; or, more darkly, it suggests at the very least the vexing mystery of history and of life itself.

Like his biblical namesake, the angel Gabriel, announcer of good news, the Jesuit priest Gabriel is in every way a match for Mendoza — and then some. While he is the consummate bearer of peace, Father Gabriel is himself by no means timid or frail, for he lives the radical gospel robustly and fearlessly: he and his Jesuit brothers carry that gospel to both the Guarani and the predatory Europeans who casually enslave and slaughter the indigenous people of South America. As much as Mendoza and Gabriel differ from one another, in some ways they form a perfect symmetry. Both are very intense, tend toward silence, and share equal measures of great resolve and fierceness. The opening sequences make this clear. Gabriel has chosen to be the replacement for the missionary who was martyred by those Guaranis living above the falls. He bids farewell to his brethren and begins his own torturous ascent up the wet rock face of the falls, barefoot and alone, inching himself up by his fingertips over the water-slick walls, his journey every bit as perilous as Mendoza's will prove to be (Gabriel goes by himself; Mendoza carries his bag but is occasionally aided by the priests). For three minutes of screen time Gabriel climbs through the torrent of the falls straight up the rock face, with the camera cutting back at times to show him to be but a speck against a vast expanse of water and vertical rock wall. The travail is long and very scary; Gabriel almost plummets to his death on one occasion. His destination is the heavy mountainous jungle of the Guarani, and once he is there, he walks fearfully — and with good reason — through the alien ground where his confrere was killed. Gabriel's fear seems very sensible, for as much as he embraces the task of bringing the fiery love of God to all people, he relishes his own life and does not wish to become a martyr himself. As he walks cautiously through the heavy mountain jungle, he startles and twitches at the slightest noises from the underbrush.

Gabriel's coming to the jungle contrasts starkly with Mendoza's raids on the Guarani. Gabriel ventures into the forest to give of himself and to bring light, not to pillage and enslave; nor does he bring traps, muskets, or armed compatriots along with him. Instead, he carries only the simple ceramic cross he took from the body of the martyred priest and an oboe, on which he will play a gentle tune to entice the justly wary Guarani toward the sweet love he so passionately feels and brings to them, cannibals though they be. Eventually, Gabriel sits on a rock and plays his lilting air for forty-five seconds until the listeners hidden in the undergrowth slowly emerge. The chief grabs the instrument from Gabriel's hands, breaks it over his knee, and throws it to the ground. But then another picks up the broken pieces and tries to put the oboe back together; failing that, he hands them to Gabriel.

Such is the effect of the gentle lilting music Gabriel plays — which is at the heart of Ennio Morricone's magnificent score — that it, like the man who plays it, seems to reflect the luminous and tranquil grace of God that the Jesuits wish to impart to the violent Guarani. As Gabriel first plays, the camera cuts to an aerial view of the mountainous terrain and the vast jungle, and the music seems to wash over the landscape as if bathing it in an infinite tenderness and quiet elation, suggesting the expansiveness of a divine love that goes everywhere and blesses everything. Then the same delicate music, now orchestrated more fully to suggest its embrace by others, overlays the next sequence, in which the Guarani labor to construct Gabriel's new mission. By such means of attraction, says the narrator, "the Indians of the Guarani were brought finally to the account of the everlasting mercy of God." Indeed, he wryly adds, "with an orchestra the Jesuits could have subdued the whole continent." The pure fire of Gabriel's resolute courage and kindliness "bear[s] the beams of Love," as English poet William Blake put the matter deftly not long after the events of this story took place. (Blake knew nothing of the Guarani and their fate, but he saw similar human predations in the streets of London.) These beams of love profoundly affect the Guarani, and eventually they affect Rodrigo Mendoza, an even tougher case, who against all odds will also come to know the reality of and, more than that, the loving character of God.

When Gabriel first meets Mendoza in his monastery cell, the priest skips pleasantries and gets directly to the point. He quietly recounts Mendoza's violent and predatory history and then taunts him as a coward now that he is running from life because of one monstrous error. Mendoza responds that he has no choice because "there is no forgiveness" for such a wrong as his. In turn, Gabriel challenges Mendoza to a penance so arduous and extreme that it promises to assuage the grief and guilt that fuel Mendoza's death wish: the immense pain in completing it, Gabriel promises, will make Mendoza think he has paid enough for killing his brother and allow him to return to the land of the living. Gabriel implores Mendoza to risk the venture, staking his challenge on the traditional Roman Catholic notion that appropriate penance can effect divine forgiveness and reconciliation of the person with God and the self. Ever defiant, Mendoza taunts back, asking whether Gabriel dares "to have it fail."

Gabriel's idea of penance seems particularly suited to accomplish its goal. If anything can redeem Mendoza, this looks like a good prospect; either that or Mendoza will die trying. This ultimate spiritual wager is the ascent of the same Niagara-sized Iguazu Falls over which the martyred priest catapulted at the very beginning of the film and which Gabriel himself later climbed to take the place of the dead missionary. Like Gabriel's ascent before, Mendoza's will be perilous: a steeply vertical climb up a water-slick rock face, under torrents, and then up mud-sogged mountains. In addition to getting himself up the mountain, the barefoot Mendoza must haul behind him, tethered to his chest by a long rope, that large bag of armor and weaponry, the implements of domination and death by which he made his living and defined his life — and which led to the murder of his brother. Throughout this many-days-long penance, the camera simply watches, alternating between close-ups and distance shots of Mendoza and the bag. On one occasion Mendoza hangs by his fingertips on the cliff face, and on another he slogs and slips through mud and mire, only to be rescued by Gabriel. Director Roland Joffé devotes an enormous amount of screen time (fifteen minutes in all, and all of it virtually wordless) to detailing the terrible risks and excruciating physical rigors of this climb. Nor is there any music to make Mendoza's tortures more melodramatic; the images speak well enough by themselves. Amid the visual chronicle of this long torture, the only words are the petitions of Gabriel's brother monks to ease the penance, one they deem unreasonable and very likely fatal. When Father John Fielding (Liam Neeson) finally intervenes by cutting the rope that attaches the bag to Mendoza's neck, Mendoza himself retreats down the mountainside to retrieve and reattach the bag. Indeed, for Mendoza as for Gabriel, this is combat over his soul, and, by his own free choice, there will be no easy grace.

The lengthy sequence culminates with the arrival of the missionaries at the top of the waterfall, which is the home of the indigenous tribal people that Mendoza has murdered and enslaved and Gabriel has risked his life to convert. The villagers give the monks a warm welcome, and then a few of them recognize the bedraggled, mud-smeared figure bringing up the rear, his desperate condition and huge burden again symbolizing his moral condition. He staggers along on his hands and knees dragging along that large bag of crime, guilt, and woe, much like John Bunyan's famous Pilgrim, an allusion no doubt intended by the screenwriter, Robert Bolt. And in this scene Mendoza also parallels the figure of the biblical prodigal, the runaway son, here mired and lost in the mud of self and violence, alienated and cast out from himself, humankind, and God.

When the Guarani finally recognize the figure for Mendoza, one member of the tribe runs up to him, pulls back his head by his hair, and puts a knife to his throat. The audience has every reason to expect that this native will cut Mendoza's dirty throat for his mountainous crimes. Indeed, by most standards of common sense and justice, Mendoza deserves execution: he has enslaved and killed Guarani people, and he has also murdered his own brother. But then, to the viewers' amazement and relief, after a brief untranslated exchange between Gabriel and the tribal chief, the chief commands the native with the knife to slit the rope around Mendoza's neck rather than his neck itself, thus freeing him from the burden of his bag of weapons. The would-be assailant then promptly drags Mendoza's bag of armor, that apt symbol of his aggression and despair, to the side of the cliff and dumps it into the river below. This is absolution beyond anyone's imagining, and it comes from those most justified in taking revenge by cutting his throat on the spot and dancing in his blood. Instead, they do just the opposite, wordlessly dramatizing how that musical air played by Gabriel has transformed their deepest sense of the world.

At the end of his climb, now among the Guarani, Mendoza himself has clearly expected to die; this is what he has longed for all along, even more so now that he seems to have defeated Gabriel's challenge to embrace suffering as a path to finding forgiveness and ridding himself of his crushing load of guilt. Notably, there is no indication that Mendoza has found that the agony of his penance has eased his anguish or given him a sense of triumph. Now, though, Mendoza is profoundly shaken and astonished by this unforeseeable gesture of gratuitous mercy. He is astonished, not by what his penance has wrought, but by the forgiveness that has been extended to him by those from whom he least expects it, those he has so sorely afflicted in the past. In medium close-up, and with the same deliberate patience with which it has chronicled Mendoza's climb, the camera watches the incredulous Mendoza glance over his shoulder at the fate of his heavy burden of armor and then look at his liberator; then on his knees, appropriately enough, in the mud above the falls (and the Fall), before God and the Guarani, he begins to weep and then sob. And as the tribal members and the monks gather round him, caressing his face and embracing him, Mendoza begins, amid his sobs, to laugh. Or as the film's technical advisor, the Jesuit priest Daniel Berrigan, put it in his book on the making of *The Mission*, Mendoza seems, as the "scene builds,

Amid his tears and laughter after being forgiven by the Guarani for his crimes against them, Mendoza is embraced by Father Gabriel.

layer on layer, take after take, to an almost unbearable pitch," to be torn "between wild laughter and wilder tears."[1] Indeed, the prodigal has found welcome and rest, a home in the most unlikely place imaginable. Novelist and apologist Frederick Buechner's sense of the comedy of grace seems to catch the manner and nature of this peculiar light, particularly as it typically arrives in the world of the Bible, whether with Abraham and Sarah learning of the geriatric Sarah's pregnancy or in Jesus' parable of the Prodigal Son: "With their laughter something new breaks into their darkness, something so unexpected and preposterous and glad that they can only laugh at it in astonishment."[2]

As all this happens, we hear again the lilting, quietly exultant musical coda of the film, one that seems to catch the exquisite texture of the relentless, but ever-delicate love of God, and the camera goes in close on the bearded, long-haired Mendoza, who now looks to be a dead ringer for popular artistic renditions of the suffering Jesus. The suggestion seems not that Mendoza is suddenly transformed into a figure akin to Jesus but perhaps that the love of Christ has gone into him, remaking him into another person; for he has come to know, in the forgiveness and welcome, the heedless, go-for-broke love that in Christian theology Jesus brings into the violent tangled world that Mendoza has so wholeheartedly perpetuated. The radical embrace Mendoza encounters suffices to flip his

1. Berrigan, *The Mission: A Film Journal* (San Francisco: Harper, 1986), pp. 150-51.
2. Buechner, *Telling the Truth: The Gospel as Tragedy, Comedy, and Fairy-Tale* (San Francisco: Harper, 1977), p. 56.

perception of the world and self upside-down and inside-out; never did he dream it possible, nor did anyone else. This turnabout is every bit as radical as St. Paul's on his journey to Damascus. This is — again as Buechner deftly penetrates its paradoxes — the "comedy of grace," where what happens is "what needn't happen and can't possibly happen because it can only impossibly happen and happens in the dark that only just barely fails to swallow it up."[3]

Just how extreme this love is comes clear in the considerable theological irony at the heart of Robert Bolt's screenplay. The setting for the story is thoroughly Roman Catholic: it is full of Jesuit missionaries, a papal emissary's message to the Vatican is its narration, and there is much talk of penance. Yet what Bolt propounds at the center of his tale is a distinctly Protestant view of forgiveness and redemption. There are no signs at all that Gabriel's design for Mendoza's redemption has worked; in fact, the opposite seems to be the case. At the top of the falls, Mendoza is unflagging still in his struggle to defeat Gabriel's penitential scheme. Instead, the love that retrieves Mendoza from despair is unforeseen, unlikely, gratuitous, and entirely beyond human volition or imagination — either Mendoza's or Gabriel's. It courses through people and is in its own nature wild, intractable, and, as Buechner insistently argues, preposterous. It is God's grand loving joke, the thing "too good not to be true."[4] Its effect is to "reverse" Mendoza, to effect in him an about-face that repudiates the past and seeks the way of peace spelled out by Jesus, the monks who follow him, and the aggrieved and once-murderous Guarani — which is the incredible part.

Lest there be any doubt about *what it is* that Mendoza meets atop the Iguazu Falls, the movie goes out of its way both to clarify and underscore the nature and reality of the mystery. This is not spectacle or bluster for its own sake or for big grosses; this is exacting religious precision in exposition. The most immediate indication of this — and simultaneous with the visual story — is Ennio Morricone's jubilant music, which itself becomes an aural display of the sort of transcendent reality that Mendoza encounters. On the one hand, it reflects the criminal's own feelings in the aftermath of forgiveness, the music slowly rising as Mendoza slowly comes to realize the magnitude of the forgiveness from the Guarani people and also, by extension, from a God who has long been offended by Mendoza's trespass on his creatures. There is in this

3. Buechner, p. 58.
4. Buechner, p. 71.

reprise, just as in Gabriel's rich oboe music in his initial approach to the Guarani, a deep yet delicate joy, at once ravishing and winsome. The music plays on and on as Mendoza weeps, and then eventually laughs, as the Guarani and the priests embrace him and even caress his face, just as they might a small child, which is exactly what the formerly fearsome Mendoza has become. The "feeling content" of the music not only mirrors Mendoza's reaction but also implies the essence of the God that instigates it, a God of unreasonable appetite for human well-being, especially for that fathomless part of the human that houses his or her deepest perceptions and attitudes toward life and being — the soul.

There is no candidate, no matter how unlikely, not even the marauding Mendoza, to whom this hungry divine embrace does not extend. It is, in its deepest character, as Buechner suggests, preposterous — going to those most grievous and unlikely, much beyond human reasonableness or expectation. The fact that Mendoza is caught by it and then laughs in response makes the point rapturously clear. Once again, this is the truth too good not to be true, as Buechner put it. The character of this God is further displayed by the sort of open-hearted reception that Mendoza subsequently receives among the Guarani, who have been grasped and shaped by this same Love. Indeed, their now pacific world seems Edenic, full of a gentle relish of life and one another. On one occasion, *The Mission* becomes blatant in its declarations, just in case the viewer has not yet gotten the point. When Mendoza asks Gabriel what he might do to repay the Guarani and the priests for his welcome, Gabriel hands him a New Testament with the instruction: "Read this." And for a full minute thereafter, the voice of Mendoza reads aloud, slowly and meditatively, from St. Paul's great hymn to love, 1 Corinthians 13, as the camera cuts between glimpses of Mendoza reading and scenes of the idyllic life of the Guarani village that has fully welcomed and embraced Mendoza. Immediately after this recitation of 1 Corinthians 13, Mendoza applies to join the Jesuits as a novice and is duly accepted; Father Gabriel fittingly closes the ceremony with the words "Welcome home, brother."

Mendoza's ascent up the falls to the Guarani and God culminates in his full-blown Christian conversion and his request to become a Jesuit. Joining the order and taking the novice's vows of obedience is no small gesture for the formerly willful, self-consumed mercenary and slave-trader. And throughout the rest of the story, submission will prove difficult for the passionate Mendoza, though all that passion is now turned to the defense of the weak, the very people on whom he previously preyed. So it is that the fruition of Mendoza's long movement toward a radically different concept of the world — from macho domination to all-encompassing love — results in a potent counterforce to the powers of darkness of which he was an agent in his former predatory darkness. Those respectable and ostensibly Christian forces are arrayed against the vision of life and God that has been developed by the Jesuits in central South America; and there is holy irony in the fact that the imperial lords seeking to destroy that vision will encounter a formidable foe in the very man who was previously their willing servant.

What proves to be mortal conflict between these two metaphysical agencies constitutes the primary focus of the remainder of the film, for which Mendoza's personal history is but a prelude, albeit one that infuses the second half of the story with enormous thematic and emotional depth. What is at stake is nothing less than the fate of the Jesuits' vast metaphysical claim that the love of God rules the universe. Mendoza remains prominent in the story, his choices — along with others' choices — crucially forging the final outcome. But he becomes, instead of the story's prime focus, one of many in this story whose actions have consequences. The question of exactly how far Mendoza will go to sustain his newfound love suspends throughout the rest of the story to its very end. For now, though, it is clear that Mendoza's hungry soul has at last found rest, welcome, and joy: an idyllic place, an unlikely home, among the obscure and powerless Guarani, and with these, for whatever it might mean, redemption and new life such as he never dreamed.

"Such as We Have Made the World"

The story of Mendoza and Gabriel is only a part of the whole story. Screenwriter Robert Bolt successfully imbeds the story of Mendoza's conversion and questions of transcendent love within a sweeping — and harrowing — examination of eighteenth-century geopolitics on the frontiers of Western imperial expansion. That unremittingly dark history makes up the second half of *The Mission*, and it does not make for a happy tale. It does, in fact, run counter to the gist of the hopeful first half, and it ends as sadly as any major Hollywood release ever has. Indeed, one of the problems with *The Mission* is that it splits into two halves, one hopeful and the other tragic: the halves seem disconnected, and even some otherwise astute critics have lost patience with the film. What does unite the two, though, is the depth of thematic unity: the first half clarifies what is at stake in the second, and the second reiterates the point of the first within a fuller frame of reference — perhaps like two movements of one symphonic suite. After all, for historians, and for the Guarani in particular, it is not just Mendoza's or Gabriel's fate that matters but also the fact that their personal histories pour into histories of larger scale and of far greater import. On one hand, Mendoza is a ruthless mercenary, slave-runner, and brother-killer, and the story makes it clear that his curse was as abominable as anybody could conceive. Yet, at the same time, Mendoza serves and participates in a vast historical juggernaut whose chief aims were power and profit through global pillage, integrally part of a project to dominate the powerless. In short, as evil as he is personally, Mendoza is also a fit emblem institutionally of the larger devouring darkness of colonial exploitation.

For Robert Bolt, there is no essential moral and spiritual difference between Mendoza the person and the international powers that he represents — indeed, those that employ and pay him: that is, the Western imperial enterprise is no less ruthless, devouring, and evil than any "personal" malevolence Mendoza himself musters. Mendoza is simply an individual actor in a limitless series of exploitative calculations. Indict one, indict the other. Evil is evil, whether done by individuals or by kings, popes, or nations. Indeed, one of the remarkable achievements of *The Mission* is to show the inextricable intertwining of the personal and the social, the private and the political, the religious and the cultural. *The Mission* is not a story of private or quietistic conversion that prepares for a tidy afterlife of blessing and individual contentedness. The renewal of the self is a crucial matter, to be sure; but the vision here is far more expansive, suggesting that Christian conversion "saves" the individual self mostly to labor for the renewal in the here-and-now of the whole earth and all that dwells therein. It is delusion to think that personal morality is somehow neatly separated from corporate or national culpability. Bolt's social vision here suggests that all people live communally and complicitly, no matter how "pure" the individual life. Everyone participates with the principalities and powers, as St. Paul names them, that daily despoil the human and natural Eden that God made. Ultimately, the personal spiritual combat between Gabriel and Mendoza simultaneously takes place on a large, supra-personal scale, for it goes hand in hand with the profound cosmic moral-spiritual conflict between the forces of light, represented by the love that envelops Mendoza, and the forces of darkness, the principalities and powers that — respectable and "legal" though they may be — enslave, maim, and devour the powerless for mere money. Thus *The Mission* is as timely as every morning's headlines.

The Mission deftly accomplishes this conflation by placing Mendoza's personal history within a larger narrative and historical frame. The first words of the film are an unspoken text on the screen, a brief historical prologue that locates the story of the film's second half within a larger frame of very real human time: "The historical events represented in this story are true, and occurred around the borderlands of Argentina, Paraguay & Brazil in the year 1750." The film then cuts to a solitary figure looking intently into the camera as he stops to think in the midst of dictating a letter, a missive that is addressed to no less a personage than "Your Holiness," the Pope. The speaker's first statement is too abrupt and acerbic, a terse ironic formulation that bitterly indicts both the Vatican and himself because "the little matter that brought me here . . . is now settled, and the Indians are once more free to be enslaved by the Spanish and Portugese settlers."

This is the larger tragic story that the film will describe. The speaker breaks off, noting that this tack fails to set "the right note," and he begins again, backtracking to the beginning of those events that have culminated with this "freedom" for the indigenous "Indian" people of the region. The new beginning describes the success of Jesuit missions that have not only saved the souls of the Guarani but, ramifying the religious into the political, "provided a refuge for the Indians against the worst depredations of the settlers and have earned much resentment because of it." All of this plays somewhat cryptically, for the viewer has no idea what events the speaker is writing about, and it will take the whole film and even the credit sequence to learn about them. In this instance, the open-endedness of the comments and the speaker's obvious passion on the subject function to hook the viewer, especially as his dictation becomes the voice-over narration for the splendid visual and aural retelling of the story that is *The Mission*. In effect, the whole film is this letter, this epistolary confession that the narrator dictates to the Pope.

The story he tells begins with the Mission of San Miguel, a lovely small city of red adobe buildings from which comes the sound of violins being played by those Indians who have found God and, at the same time, refuge from relentless and remarkably vicious European predators. (The actual historical characters were known as the "Paulistas," a name derived from their home in Sao Paolo, Brazil, which was the South American center for Portuguese, Spanish, and Dutch slave traders.) Complete with lawns, farms, violin-making workshops, music rooms, and children

The Jesuits and the Guarani

The history of the Jesuits depicted in *The Mission* is not romantic prettification. In fact, in the early seventeenth century the Jesuits were beginning to have a major presence in the region, which lasted for approximately 150 years. They evangelized the Guarani, protected them from the constant threat of slave traders, and established model communities. It was not only one of the largest utopian experiments in history but also one of the most successful.

The first Christian missionaries to the region were Franciscans, who soon gave up their labors because of continuous raids by Paulistas, the mercenary slave traders who were centered in São Paulo, Brazil; the latter were a mix of Spanish, Portuguese, and Dutch pirates and businessmen. The protection of the King of Spain made little difference, for the slave traders continued unabated, and this was no small threat. One source estimates that, over the course of 130 years, more than two million natives were slain or carried into captivity. Needless to say, friendly Europeans willing to protect the Guarani and others from the marauding bands of predators proved attractive, and within a few decades over 40,000 Indians lived in twelve different mission communities. Unfortunately, the Paulistas saw this success in evangelization as a great convenience to themselves, because now they no longer had to scrounge through thick forests for slaves. Now potential slaves were all concentrated in several places, and in 1629 the Paulistas devastated mission after mission, in effect wiping out the missions and carrying off tens of thousands of natives into captivity. After some time, the network of missions mustered their own army.

Eventually there were thirty-one missions or "reducciones"; the ruins of many still stand in what is now Argentina, Paraguay, southern Brazil, and Uruguay. The missions proved to be a kind of haven between two worlds:

running about — all bathed in a reddish-gold light — this mission seems almost like Eden and is clearly about more than saving souls. Tough-minded and learned, and very much inspired by Thomas More's *Utopia*, the Jesuits have sought to create a distinctly alternative culture, not only to the one the native people have lived — itself violent and predatory — but, just as importantly, to the European culture from which the missionaries themselves came and against which the native people need to be protected. (The historical record indicates that the Jesuits protected

one world was that of a primitivism that practiced human sacrifice and can-
nibalism, and the other exhibited, as the papal legate puts it in the film, "the
worst depredations of the European settlers." Some of the missions grew
into communities as large as 20,000, and under Jesuit guidance they established an advanced system of law, even doing away with capital punishment;
a public system of birth control, a welfare system for the poor, and hospi-
tals; communal holdings of property and enterprise; workshops in sculpture, wood-carving, and stonework; and mercantile farming and crafts.
Through all of this, the workday averaged about six hours (the workday in
European societies at the time was twelve to fifteen hours). The remainder
of the time was spent in prayer, dance, music, sham battles (football), bow-
shot contests, concerts, fireworks, and worship. In addition to common
farms, every family had its own garden. The assorted tribes were taught and
educated in their native languages, and as a whole this became the first fully
literate society in history. By 1732, as many as 140,000 South American
natives lived within mission communities.

The beginning of the end came in the 1750s, when Spain, which had
protected the settlements, ceded part of the missions to Portugal, which
was simply interested in the economic potential of the region. Portugal
promptly ordered everyone to vacate the missions. Following a seven-year
guerilla war, the Jesuits finally convinced Spain to annul the edict of transfer
to Portugal. A series of wars followed, ending with the defeat of the Guarani
in 1756 and the expulsion of the Jesuits in 1767. Franciscans tried to sal-
vage the missions, but they lacked the support of the government and of the
Guarani. The sorrowful truth is that by 1801 there were only 45,000 natives remaining, roughly the same number as today. The evidence of the Jesuit venture can be seen in the splendid stone remains of the missions and
in the fact that the official language of Paraguay is Guarani.

the Guarani in more than thirty communitarian missions for well over a
hundred years, until imperial greed crashed in on them. See sidebar.)
Nor do the fervent Jesuits rest on their accomplishments; they restlessly
strive to expand the benison of their love. As the papal legate narrates,
"It was from these missions that the Jesuit fathers carried the word of
God to the high and undiscovered plateau to those Indians still existing
in their natural state and received in return martyrdom" — which is
where the story proper of the film begins. At the word "martyrdom," the

camera cuts in close to a swirl of bodies of indigenous people bustling a large object through the jungle to a riverside, where they set it afloat. By the time the group reaches the water, it has become clear that the object they are carrying above their shoulders is a man wearing a crown of thorns and strapped to a cross.

The native people have taken the Jesuit missionary's symbols rather too literally and are giving him the medicine he has recommended to them — sacrificial death on an instrument of torture. For well over a minute, accompanied by discordant, percussive music, the camera watches the priest on the cross, alive and still very conscious, float and then bounce along the river as it turns from a broad gentle current to rapids and, finally, to the crest of a waterfall. The camera leaps back and reveals this to be the top of an immense horseshoe waterfall. For another seven seconds the cross-bound priest plummets, and the camera catches his descent from different distances and angles, even repeating portions of the fall, Eisenstein-style, to deftly expand time and momentousness. Afterward, the camera fixes on the giant waterfall for another fifteen seconds while the opening credits appear on the screen. It is as though the priest falls into eternity itself, or the fallenness of human history itself, or whatever else the falls might represent; for the waterfall comes back over and over in the film and soon assumes assorted kinds of symbolic weight. Here, at the beginning of the story, the falls provides at the very least an apt and fitting stage for the *gravitas* of all the glad and wrenching history that follows. (The notes for the film identify the waterfall as the Iguazu Falls, lying on the border of Brazil and Argentina: 259 feet high and four times the width of Niagara Falls.)

The narrator comments that the death of this priest was to bring to these same murderous people, the Guarani, another "priest whose life would become inextricably intertwined with their own" and in whose sad history "I now find myself a part." Here the story turns to Father Gabriel bidding farewell to fellow priests as he prepares to climb the same giant waterfall over which the martyred priest plummeted to his death. Before he ascends, Gabriel dons — as if assuming another's life and calling — the small and plain pendant cross worn by the dead priest, which now adorns the stones that cover his grave. Later, before the climactic battle in the film, Gabriel gives that same cross to Mendoza, who leads the effort to defend the natives against the invading Portuguese soldiers. Gabriel's ascent leads to his confrontation with Mendoza, and from there to Mendoza's ascent and, eventually, to Mendoza's taking on that cross of loving, sacrificial martyrdom.

The narrator of this tale assumes a pivotal role in the second half of the story: he is Cardinal Altamirano (Ray McAnally), a papal emissary sent to mediate the mounting dispute between the Vatican, under whose protection the Jesuits do their work in the highlands above the falls, and Spain and Portugal, both of whom wish to exploit the lands and "civilize" the "savage" people. Altamirano arrives in Sao Paolo, Brazil, with an entourage and amid much hoopla from his Spanish and Portuguese hosts, who wish the cardinal to do their bidding as swiftly as possible. Indeed, that is exactly what the cardinal expects to do, though not without some twinges of conscience. The matter is very thorny, for the Vatican wishes to keep both Spain and Portugal as allies in the vast complex business of international colonial expansion. Altamirano is above all a realist, one who is adept in the crass and bloody games between geopolitics and the kingdom of God. And he will do the Vatican's bidding at all costs, for on that rests his own continued political viability and his privileged life of luxury. He even goes so far as to threaten the local Jesuits with the claim that the Pope will shut down the whole order if they fail to obey the Pope's command to abandon the territory, the missions, and their protection of the indigenous people.

However, to his great discomfort and consternation, the cardinal runs into a wholly different and unexpected kind of trouble in his encounter with the Guarani and their Jesuit fathers. In this he is much like Mendoza: despite their hugely different callings, they do have basically the same employer and serve the same masters. Still, as expert and comfortable as he is in the sordid ways of the world, the cardinal eventually arrives at the point where he can no longer ignore the reality of the same ravishing love that has become manifest in the lives of the Guarani and of Mendoza, both of whom display a clear measure of the Jesuit accomplishment in the region. Over and over again, as he tours the missions, the cardinal is astonished by the palpable joy that emanates from the Guaranis' apprehension of divine love.

While the cardinal knows about the success of the missions (if they had failed, his presence there would not have been necessary), he is hardly prepared for "the beauty and the power" he finds in the remote regions of South America. To the destruction of the missions and their people — this rare efflorescence of love in actual lived human history — he will but reluctantly assent; for a while he tries, if not to save them all, which he considers impossible, to at least prolong their existence. Thus, to forestall the impending tragedy, and hoping against steep odds to effect some kind of compromise, he agrees to a tour of the missions themselves, an exercise in fact-gathering and decision-making that occupies the third quarter of the film. First he travels to the oldest and largest of the missions, "the great mission of San Miguel," a huge and autonomous mission-city where he witnesses a thriving and congenial community. Upon arriving, he is struck by the physical attractiveness of the mission, a place of red adobe buildings and broad green lawns. Shortly thereafter, when he enters its cathedral-sized church, a very large yet simple building of pure white stone, full of shafts of light from its clerestory (gorgeously lit and shot by cinematographer Chris Menges), he is greeted and astonished by an exquisite native choir of many scores of voices, ethereal and pure, full and exultant, that fill the building with *Ave Maria*. The camera rises to the ceiling to take in the whole magnificent scene as the cardinal walks slowly to the front. When he turns to survey the whole expanse, the camera closes in on the look of stricken alarm on his face at the splendor of what is displayed before him, the radiance of translucent love and adoration that he has been asked to extinguish. Even so jaded a conscience as his is shaken into an awareness of the reality of what the church says it seeks and reveres. Perhaps he had this awareness long ago because, for the cardinal, as for viewers of this film, the glory of the holy, ineffable, and loving One has seemed to come to earth to dwell in and among people. In short, the cardinal has been enveloped in what Jewish theology refers to as the *shekinah* of the Lord, the nimbus of the visible manifestation of divine presence.

The life of the mission is no less amazing than the simple church and its grand choir. Under the direction of native and European Jesuits, the arts flourish there, as do agriculture and worship, and all seem to thrive in zeal and delight. Moreover, the diverse commercial enterprises are for the common good, and the profits, a native priest explains to the cardinal, are distributed equally among all the members of the mission community. When the cardinal says he has heard of this radical practice, a socialist system advocated by a contemporary French political group, the priest informs him, much to his chagrin, that it was also a doctrine of the early church. During the cardinal's tour of the mission's farms, the Spanish ambassador who is accompanying him, the blustery Don Cabeza, declares that there is no difference between these peaceful cooperative plantations and his own. However, the Jesuit novice Rodrigo Mendoza, who is also with the cardinal's tour, counters that there is one huge difference: he quickly unshirts one native, an escaped slave, to expose a back covered with scars from Spanish whips. Cabeza fumes in response and declares, in the film's starkest distillation of the colonial powers' views, that all property should be private and that the church's obstruction of free enterprise is scandalous. He further remarks that the natives who work the farms really need the whip instead of compassion and conversion: "The work of the missions is the work of the devil. They teach contempt for property and lawful profit, and they are disobedient to the king's authority."

The effect of Cabeza's many tirades is to make the cardinal's choice all the more stark and difficult. On the whole, the cardinal's dose of the wonder-filled life at the missions is terribly unsettling, and he proposes to undertake a prayer vigil in the church to help him clear his mind so that he may make the right decision. He sits alone for five hours, solitary in the cavernous dark church while outside, in a prayerful vigil in the large cathedral courtyard, hosts of native people await his decision, lighting the pitch darkness with torches of golden-white light. The scene is beautifully staged and lit, and it seems to foreshadow the postscript from the Gospel of John that comes at the calamitous end of the film: "The Light shines in the darkness, but the darkness has not overcome it" (John 1:5).

After Altamirano's many hours alone, Father Gabriel intrudes on his vigil to plead quietly with him to venture into the jungle interior — and perhaps his own interior — to visit the San Carlos mission, the latest outpost above the falls that is the site of Gabriel's and Mendoza's missionary labor among the Guarani. There perhaps, says Gabriel, away from all distraction, "your prayers will meet with better fortune. I think there God would tell you what it would be good to do. And give you the strength and grace to do it. Whatever it costs you." What follows is a lengthy and exhilarating arrival at the San Carlos mission, and then a tour that repeats but far surpasses the cardinal's earlier survey of the San Miguel mission. The cardinal's entourage and the Jesuits arrive by dugout on the river to whooping and cheers from the banks. Ennio Morricone's score is jubilant and driving, leaping and twirling, as it records a royal welcome by the cheering yet respectful crowds, who then dance and sing, including another rendition of *Ave Maria* as the choir stands, appropriately, before the newly completed thatch-roofed church. The whole sequence is altogether beautiful and ecstatic, suggesting village life that is Edenic in its tranquility and elation, a place where God has come and dwells in rare transparency. If his visit to San Miguel startled the cardinal, he is now utterly stricken, both by the pure spiritual beauty of the mission life and by guilt from the terrible reality that awaits both him and these people — one that he alone is privy to at this point.

The cardinal's tour of the mission proves to be, in fact, a ruse. In truth, the cardinal has made this journey to San Carlos simply to convince the Jesuits to abandon the mission to make way for the coming of the Portuguese armies, who will do the bidding of Cabeza: they will subdue the native people "by the sword" and bring them to "profitable labor by the whip," a fate that the last part of the film depicts with unsettling directness and honesty. Before that apparent inevitability takes place, however, the community of San Carlos — the Guarani and the Jesuits alike — goes through its own wrestling of conscience and soul, because a great deal is at stake. When the cardinal informs the tribal leaders that they must abandon the mission to return to life in the jungle, they protest with a stream of trenchant questions, asking whether God has changed his mind about his will for them and whether the cardinal speaks for God or for the Portuguese. The children tell him that they don't want to go back to the forest because "the devil lives there." And the "king" of the Guarani communicates to the cardinal, as Gabriel translates: "They were wrong ever to have trusted us. They are going to fight." If this does happen, the cardinal warns the Jesuits, "it is absolutely imperative that no one of you should have even seemed to have encouraged them to do so, and therefore all of you will return with me to Ascuncion . . . tomorrow. If anyone should disobey this, he will be excommunicated, cut off, cast out. . . ." In making this fierce and arrogant demand, the cardinal seems less concerned with the personal fate of the Jesuits, either temporal or eternal, than with the future of the Jesuit order. If these particular Jesuits resist, he says, all Jesuits will be expelled from Portugal and then from all of Europe: "If your order is to survive at all, the missions here must be sacrificed. . . ."

And so the contest begins, with its dire terms made clear. There is no hesitation in the choice these Jesuits make: down to every last priest, they refuse to abandon their new friends in this faith community to whatever their fate might be. In the aftermath of this decision, the camera silently watches the boy who has become Mendoza's particular friend retrieve the former mercenary's sword and rusting bag of armor that has remained in the river below the mission ever since it was dumped there. Reluctantly, Mendoza decides to take up his sword again and to train others in defense of the village. The pacifist Father Gabriel will have no part of this, because his experience of God's love forbids doing violence. Then, in an interlude before the invasion, the two talk for the last time. In what proves to be a moving farewell (beautifully lit by Menges), Mendoza quietly asks Gabriel for his blessing and a release from his

vows so that he can become a soldier with the natives. This Gabriel refuses: "If you're right, God will bless, and if wrong, my blessing won't do
any good." He urges Mendoza not to fight but to "help them as a
priest. . . . You promised your life to God, and God is love. . . ." Mendoza
makes clear to Gabriel that his choice is in fact informed by love, because
fighting for these people will reassure them that God has not left them,
which is their view of their current plight. Gabriel confesses that if might
and power do vanquish love in this world, he does not "have the strength
to live in a world like that," and while he cannot bless Rodrigo, he silently transfers to him the martyr's cross that he has carried around his
neck from the beginning of his ascent up the falls at the film's opening.
This is a gesture that, on the one hand, forecasts their soon-to-be-met
mutual fate and, more than that, displays their profound sacrificial love
for the people around them, regardless of what means of expression they
choose. The one fights, and the other prays, but both go bravely to certain death. Whatever God these two have come to know, that God has
utterly transformed them, producing what Yeats called the "terrible
beauty" of self-sacrificial death ("Easter 1916").

Regardless of their personal course, either to fight or to resist passively, it seems clear that none of the Jesuits thinks they will survive the
coming of the Portuguese, an expectation that is fully confirmed as the
camera cuts to shots of the aggressive Portuguese onslaught on the beautiful San Miguel mission: there, amid rain, mud, and blood, babies are
torn from mothers' arms and the native people are herded together to
face life as slaves. The remainder of the story, as the same evil destroys
San Carlos, is even more grim, a graphic portrayal of human predation
indiscriminately devouring the good and the powerless.

While Gabriel broods on the future and how best to help without
taking up the sword, Mendoza and other priests prepare the village and
its people for war: they lay strategy, set defenses and booby-traps, and
train fighters. These activities are interspersed with shots of a splendidly
equipped Portuguese military, along with their own native recruits, haul-
ing men, cannons, and other supplies up the vertical falls. It is now clear
that whatever redemption Gabriel and Mendoza achieved by means of
that arduous ascent is now wholly reversed: the climb now seems to be
the ascent of hell itself, a final evil that will utterly consume innocence
and light. This montage runs, again wordlessly (except for Mendoza's
brief conversation with Gabriel), for twenty-six minutes, allowing the inevitability and dread of the action to soak into even the most jaded
viewer's awareness. Similarly, Morricone's score, heretofore full of lilting

and exuberant tunes of both native and Christian joy, turns piercingly cacophonous. Hardly music at all, it is full of irregular percussion and the grating, screeching bursts from an array of wind instruments. Finally, as villagers die and the village itself burns, music returns to a slow, pained lament.

"And the Darkness Has Not Yet Overcome It"

The last eye contact of Gabriel and Mendoza — two God-taken, fearless, love-bound souls — comes in the last seconds of their lives. From the far side of the river, the Portuguese bombard the village with cannon and musket fire. The village resistance fighters engage the invaders in the forests and on the river; Guarani and priests alike die with devotion and courage. But the Portuguese invaders are too powerful and too many. Dressed in his priestly white gown and carrying before him a large golden cross, Gabriel himself offers his own passive defiance as he leads a host of worshipers away from the thatched church, which has been set afire by the flaming arrows of Portuguese-aligned natives. As Gabriel's large group of unarmed villagers walks toward the river and the soldiers, musket fire hits women and children indiscriminately, the soft thwop of fifty-caliber musket balls striking flesh and flopping victims to the ground. Throughout this scene there is an extraordinary, almost surreal, measure of realism. The fighting villagers' primitive weapons do great damage, largely because of the ingenuity and courage of those using them; but the superior technology and force of the Portuguese succeed in massacring almost everyone, even those they successfully capture.

Filmed with extraordinary realism, this long sequence is difficult to watch: it is both gruesome and mournful, made especially so by the percussion that tolls like a death knell throughout. When a booby trap Mendoza has set fails, in a sequence that plays as dark comedy, he is himself struck by multiple musket balls, and as he lies on the ground dying, he lifts his head to fix his eyes on Gabriel and the procession marching from the church. Resolute in the face of his fear, Gabriel walks forward until a musket ball strikes him in the chest and he falls dead, after which Mendoza concedes his own death, his head sinking to the ground. To the sound of now slow and mournful percussion, the camera slowly withdraws from the village to brood on the mayhem and sweep of the slaughter. Now full of smoke and flame, the decimated village resembles popular images of hell, which it surely has become for those who once lived in its Eden. Indeed, the whole dire sequence looks as if the fires of hell have come to consume the kingdom of God. And all the while the children of the village watch the carnage from their hiding places in the surrounding forest.

This ending is not at all happy. Here, as one viewer once complained in consternation, the Christians lose — horribly. From the massacre, the scene changes to a luncheon where Cardinal Altamirano hosts the ambassadors of Spain and Portugal to discuss their report on the takeover of the missions. When Altamirano complains of the death toll, the worldly-wise Hantor, who feigns a similar disgust, tries to console Altamirano with notions of pragmatic expedience in which the number of dead was unavoidable. He says that "the world is thus," full of grim necessity and injustice. The cardinal demurs from such easy nostrums of absolution, instead insisting on confessing the stark moral truth of his own complicity: "Thus have we made the world; thus have I made it."

In what seems to be the film's last scene, a young girl walks naked from the burned-out church in the abandoned mission village. In the shallow river that runs by the village she picks from the water a broken violin to take into the jungle with the small remnant of surviving children who await her in the background in a dugout canoe. But what she leaves in the water, lying on the river bottom below the floating violin, is also telling: a large golden, cross-shaped candlestick from the church, a piece of ecclesiastical and symbolic iconography that came from outside this community — perhaps from Rome, whose hands are now demonstrably bloody. This image is conjoined with the final words of Cardinal Altamirano's letter to the Pope. The gist of the young native girl's abandoning of the symbol of the church's opulence and worldliness is repeated in Altamirano's words to the Pope, words that excoriate the church and himself, full of irony, animus, and self-loathing: "Now your priests are dead, and I am left alive. But in truth it is I who am dead, and they who live, for as always, your Holiness, the spirit of the dead will survive in the memory of the living."

And thus ends the film, or so it seems. The credits play over a black screen as Morricone's choral music returns; and then, three minutes into the credits, the face of the cardinal reappears. Hunched over his writing desk, he simply looks directly at the audience and stares, a stern searching expression on his face, implying that the audience should do better than he did or meet the fate of his own tortured soul. The inclusion of that look suggests both the vision and the power of *The Mission*.

The Mission on DVD

In 2003, Warner Home Video finally released *The Mission* on DVD, featuring a new digital transfer of the video and audio; together they set the film forth in all of its spectacle and majesty. Again there is hardly a comparison between this DVD version and VHS versions. The new release shows off why Chris Menges won the Academy Award for cinematography and Ennio Morricone a Golden Globe for the soundtrack.

The DVD edition also features an audio commentary by director Roland Joffé that leaves much to be desired, even by the gushy standards of moviemaking egotism sometimes on display on audio commentaries. Little of what he says has anything to do with the actual film, and very often his comments seem just a bit loopy, as the one that suggests that *The Mission* has nothing to do with religious questions.

A second disk contains an intriguing hour-long documentary entitled *Ominibus,* which deals with the making of the film, although once again Joffé takes center stage. The most interesting portion focuses on how they located actors to play the Guarani. For this, the producers imported the remote and largely un-Westernized Waunana Indians hundreds of miles to the location. Tensions between the production crew and the Waunana over the length of the shoot and money are treated in the documentary.

Accomplishment

All told, *The Mission* is a remarkable achievement in constructing a lyrically brilliant film that manages to evoke both the ferocity and delicacy of God's love for humanity. At the same time, it renders in searing detail, in Oscar Wilde's memorable words from *De Profundis,* "the tears of which the world is made, and of the sadness of all human things."[5] Rampant evil ravages the world, particularly by means of the church's abdication of the call to be the living bride and body of the loving Christ that the film exalts. Throughout, *The Mission* ingeniously uses the unique resources of cinema to portray the character of this love that besets Mendoza. Indeed, the sweep and the depth of the story seem to demand the expansive "spectacle" treatment the filmmakers lavish on it. This is

5. Wilde, *De Profundis* (New York: Modern Library, 2000), p. 24.

grand cinematic spectacle for a reason: it is nothing less than trying to evoke through story, setting, photography, and music, all gorgeously rendered, the experience of the shape and texture of God's immense care for the universe. The extraordinary talents of Puttnam, Bolt, Joffé, Menges, and Morricone have converged to achieve a stunning rendition of a historical moment that pretty well defines the spiritual and moral plight of the Christians who seek to haul divine love, what John Updike refers to as a "cavernous capacity for caring," into the tangled conflicts of self, family, church, state, and God. The consequence is that audiences glimpse — amid music, setting, light, and event — this limitless metaphysical passion blazing clear and bright against that devouring darkness. That light is what the prey and predator alike, the Guarani and Mendoza, come across in the "beams of Love" borne by the fiercely resolute Jesuit missionaries who venture barefoot through the world with no more than simple crosses and oboes, the latter a fitting instrument for catching the exquisite wild reality of a Love that lies beyond words themselves. To their mutual everlasting surprise, after that Love embraces them, the Guarani and Mendoza embrace both that Love and one another. And then, against even greater odds, the same is reiterated in the amazement of Cardinal Altamirano as he tours the Jesuit missions and, after their destruction, as he sits in sorrow, self-recrimination, and warning. It is no small thing to refuse that ravishment by a Love so radical and consuming that only the divine could dream it. Ultimately, the grail of power is supplanted by the unforeseeable gift of Love and redemption.

The Mission Filmography

Films Directed by Roland Joffé
Vatel (2000)
Goodbye Lover (1999)
The Scarlet Letter (1995)
City of Joy (1992)
Fat Man and Little Boy (1989)
The Mission (1986)
The Killing Fields (1984)

Films Written by Robert Bolt
The Mission (1986)
The Bounty (1984)
Lady Caroline Lamb (1972)
Ryan's Daughter (1970)
A Man for All Seasons (1966)
Doctor Zhivago (1965)
Lawrence of Arabia (1962)

Notable Films Produced by David Puttnam
Memphis Belle (1990)
The Mission (1986)
The Killing Fields (1984)
Local Hero (1983)
Chariots of Fire (1981)
Midnight Express (1978)

CHAPTER 7

"IN THE REGIONS OF THE HEART"

The Meeting of Art and Belief in *Babette's Feast*

Babette's Feast is delicate, lyrical, haunting, and complex — a seemingly simple fable about the ancient conflict between flesh and spirit. This round in that old contest takes place over several decades in the late nineteenth century amongst a pious and ascetic Lutheran sect in a tiny Danish fishing village on the barren coast of Jutland. In the last third of the film, an aged and fractious remnant of the founding generation enjoys a long sumptuous feast, provided and executed by an exiled Parisian chef, Babette Hersant (Stéphane Audran), which magically and gracefully restores their lost amity, as well as their well-worn religious faith.

Predictably, with an ending such as this, aesthetes argue for the power of art, and religionists for the power of communion. And both are right — mostly. But each of these exclusive responses fails to take into account the whole story, either the visual one or the narrative one; there's more going on in this film than the dogma of either camp will allow. With an enchanting use of cinema's resources — direction, palette, lighting, and music — screenwriter-director Gabriel Axel transforms Isak Dinesen's fetching short story into a luminous plea for the inescapable interdependence of these supposed "antagonists" of body and soul, art and religion.

The gist of the story argues that neither of these achieves its full capacity, the grace it is intended to give, without considerable help from the other; in short, they need each other — body and soul, art and belief — to make real their own deepest purposes, which accord with God's intentions for creation and human history and from which neither art nor Christianity could be excised without a profound loss. Ultimately, *Babette's Feast* not only resolves these apparent contrarieties but sets forth, in delicate splendor, its own unique vision of materiality, art, and the art-

191

ist's work within both the world at large and Christian communities. Axel's telling of Dinesen's story suggests that, because of its notions of divine love, the Christian community is the group most capable of imbibing and grasping the artist's adoration of a world steeped in sensuous beauty, a beauty that is graceful in its own right and betokens the love of the God who put it there in the first place. It is this notion of a world framed by divine love and for love that lies at the center of *Babette's Feast*.

This vision of *Babette's Feast* contends that God made the world in love for the delight of all creation, including God's own self, angelic hosts, and humankind — the whole grand show. God infused inexhaustible splendor into the deepest fabric of the world, doing so at God's own good pleasure and, more than that, for the delight of humankind and all creatures. The whole world, including and especially the entire carnal world, from food to music and other people, all feasts in their own right, was made in love and merits endless relish and praise, a foundational notion that is often overlooked by both otherworldly — that is, highly "spiritual" — renditions of Christianity and by "aesthetized" formalist notions of art. To live with this exultant apprehension of the world and life is to know love and find humankind's purpose and "home," an image that pervades the story and music of *Babette's Feast*.

Of course, the stark contrast to this is the enormous problem of the way the world is, the reality of crushing evil, as Babette has suffered, which is not the way life is supposed to be. These onslaughts of evil pose terrible impediments to arriving at the heart's home, the belief that love finally rules the world, as one sophisticated and cynical character comes to realize in the course of Babette's banquet. Human life does not, by any stretch of the imagination, happen in Eden, "home," or any place like them. There is instead the pervasive dark mess of history, full of malice, tragedy, blindness, confusion, and pain — of lostness in general. In the vision of *Babette's Feast*, people live their lives as exiles, inexorably far from Eden, longing and looking for "home." Always, as life informs everyone soon enough, the destination called "home," that elusive realm of delight and relational wholeness, is a hard place to get to; but against considerable odds, the welcome feast does happen, and a wondrous one it is, as Axel's film luminously displays.

In *Babette's Feast*, artists help in this journey "home" because they joyously serve and celebrate the extravagance God has lavished on creation. The artist's work, according to the film, is to lay bare the created world's original bedrock beauty, the beauty marred and covered over by evil and darkness of different kinds. Art allows its creators and partakers

Babette's Feast (1987)

Director:	Gabriel Axel
Screenwriters:	Gabriel Axel, Isak Dinesen
Original Music:	Per Nørgaard
Cinematography:	Henning Kristiansen
Editing:	Finn Henriksen
Production Design:	Jan Petersen, Sven Wichmann

Cast

Stéphane Audran	Babette
Birgitte Federspiel	Old Martina
Bodil Kjer	Old Philippa
Jarl Kulle	Old Lorenz Lowenhielm
Jean-Philippe Lafont	Achille Papin
Vibeke Hastrup	Young Martina
Hanne Stensgaard	Young Philippa
Pouel Kern	The Minister

Academy Awards
Best Foreign Language Film

to glimpse the original beauty and rapture of the created world: in this defined role, the artist becomes a hierophant — a priest of sorts — of that original beauty, recalling it and restoring it. But *Babette's Feast* also makes it clear that artists can accomplish only so much. While beauty in its own right can bring bystanders to "attention," delight, and gratitude, it proves insufficient to transform the moral or spiritual character of those who imbibe it, no matter how devoted to beauty they may be. That is, unless they embrace its power within a specifically Christian vision of the world that views divine love as the source, purpose, and command of human life. Then beauty attests, as it does for the aged parishioners and the worldly-wise General Lowenhielm, to the possibility of a radiant lovingkindness at the heart of reality. For those disposed to see it, the reality of beauty and the delight it affords assume a redemptive, sacramental function that culminates in reconciliation and an affirmation of the goodness of the flesh and the world. In *Babette's Feast,* all of this brings about soul-shaking surprise, overturns reigning conceptions of the self and the world, and ends in thanksgiving, specifically in the quiet glad dance that provides one of the closing images in the film.

At Babette's banquet, and at God's, no one has the least idea of what he or she is getting into, and the outcome is profound surprise. After all, despite a darkly tragic world, divine love still makes itself known by any means possible so that all may know that the world was made in and for love. Only those whose hearts are tuned to notions of reconciliation, ancient and ascetic Christians though they be, are likely to apprehend the full meaning of the adoration of sensuous beauty that art pursues. As *Babette's Feast* makes eminently clear, the fancy denizens of Paris's faddish art world had not a glimmer of the Light that art celebrates.

Prelude

The film's journey is long, covering decades and a diverse array of characters; yet the telling of the story is engagingly simple and seamless. From the beginning and regularly thereafter, the soft but resolute voice of a female narrator provides context and summary, always attending to those junctures that affect what she calls, early in the narration, the "hidden regions of the heart," the vital places in the soul where, as Emily Dickinson put it, "the meanings are." Always there is the reassuring note of a fairy tale, where all things end happily: "There once lived two sisters . . ." goes the first sentence, and somehow the viewer knows that, come the end of the story, as with fairy tales, all will be well. The film's first shot surveys the tiny slate-gray fishing village on the harsh shores of Jutland, a "remote, desolate place." We then see the village's minister, "a priest and a prophet, and the founder of a religious sect," along with his radiant daughters, Martina (Vibeke Hastrup) and Philippa (Hanne Stensgaard), making their way to church. Once there, the sisters sing their souls out gladly and jubilantly, setting forth the notion that divine love cares deeply for simple but central human needs, whether physical, emotional, or spiritual:

> Jerusalem, my heart's true home
> Your name is forever dear to me
> Your kindness is second to none
> You keep us clothed and fed;
> Never would you give a stone
> To the child who begs for bread.

Only four minutes into the film, and repeated often thereafter, the words of the hymn initiate the film's predominant thematic chords, defining the inescapable foundational terms of the human condition: the soul's homelessness and deep craving for a place of welcome, shelter, and concord: God's holy city of "Jerusalem," the heart's true home, which the central characters, all exiles of one sort or another, yearn to locate. By the end, in a very real sense, Jerusalem does arrive, for at least a time, and almost everyone comes to know its profound sweetness. This is particularly true in the satisfying of their longing to recognize a divine love that itself thirsts after humankind and prompts reconciliation — between humans and God and between people themselves. Everything that follows this opening hymn of *Babette's Feast* moves steadily toward Babette's loving gift, the sumptuous feast, magnanimous and surprising as it is, that satisfies the depths of the "child who begs for bread." As the story makes clear, all are children, especially the elderly of the tiny remnant, lost now in acrimony and hunger.

That note of deprivation and longing is seen in the starkness of the initial setting, which is no less severe than the plight of the young sisters. Both possessed of beauty "extraordinary, akin to the flowering of fruit trees," yet devoted to their elderly father, the sisters turn away suitor after suitor. For one thing, their widowed and aging father (Pouel Kern) now needs them to carry on his work; furthermore, his particular strain of pietism denigrates earthly ties in general, love and marriage in particular, which are, says the narrator, "considered to be of scant worth and merely empty illusion." So Martina (named after Martin Luther) and Philippa (named after another great reformer, Philipp Melanchthon) seem destined to be spinsters. That is, until two strangers appear, each a Prince Charming in his own way, and both seeming to promise hope and fulfillment. The first, Lorenz Lowenhielm (Gudmar Wivesson), is a young officer, handsome, rich, and very profligate; his father has sent him away to stay with a wealthy aunt in this desolate countryside so that he may reflect on his debts and the general runaway dissolution of his "merry life." Out riding one day, he chances on the lovely Martina while she is fetching milk for the household. Instantly enamored, and simultaneously suddenly fascinated for the first time by religion and piety, Lorenz begins to envision "a higher and purer life without debt or parental lectures and with a gentle angel at his side," as the narration wryly puts it.

The young soldier even goes so far as to join the small community of believers; but it is to no avail in winning the affection of Martina. After one devout meeting, in which the pastor/father speaks of how one day "mercy and truth" will meet and "righteousness and peace shall kiss one another," Lorenz concludes, nevertheless, that he and Martina will never kiss, at least not on this earth — and he takes what he assumes is his final leave of her. As she bids him silent farewell in the dark entryway of the pastor's home, a single candle between them lighting their faces, he declares that he is going away forever and will "never, never see you again. For I have learned that life is hard and cruel. And that in this world there are things that are impossible." In the aftermath, feeling rejected and angry, Lowenhielm turns cynical: returning to the Danish court, he vows to reject his hunger for love in order to someday "cut a brilliant figure in the world of prestige." He does so by marrying a lady-in-waiting to the queen and by brokering the piety he learned in the village to ingratiate himself at the royal court, which is now undergoing a "piety craze."

This farewell sequence will reprise near the very end of *Babette's Feast*, when Lowenhielm, now a well-mannered and sophisticated general, coincidentally visits his aunt in Jutland during the centenary of the sect's founder, which is the immediate occasion for Babette's feast. The aunt, now very elderly, has been invited to the small celebration planned by the sisters, and Lowenhielm accompanies her, largely to determine whether his life course has been prudent or in vain. The answer he receives at the feast surprises him more than anyone. His sophistication and achievement, though it has now become somewhat world-weary, has not prepared him for the holy astonishment that awaits him. After all, he — as much as anyone there — is also a child begging for bread.

The second visitor to the village is the French opera singer Achille Papin (Jean-Philippe Lafont). He has been thirsting for solitude and silence, and he has traveled to remote Jutland on the recommendation of an admirer. But while he is there, he is seized by a bout of severe melancholy brought on by a vision of himself as a forlorn "old man at the end of his career," a foreboding that will be more than realized. In his despair he hears, as though in a dream or fairy tale, a powerful angelic voice coming from the nearby church, a voice that soars above the rest of the congregational singing:

> Lord, our God, Thy name and glory
> Should be sung throughout the world
> And every soul Thy humble subject
> And every wayfarer shall sing aloud Thy praises.

What a singer is this! This particular wayfarer, Achille, though by no means humble, hastens to enter the church just as the last line sounds and identifies the beautiful female voice as that of Philippa. Papin falls into a virtual swoon, immediately savoring the fact that he has found a diva to awe Paris. The camera surveys the church's singers and its interior, regularly alternating between Philippa's singing and Papin's admiration. But her father stands at the front of his congregation, with light from the high windows pouring in on him, as befits a master of praise; and as the singing continues, the hymn emphasizes God's ultimacy in history and in beauty. Something does transcend the desperate temporal busyness of fame and mating, and Papin would do well to heed it; but he is fixed on Philippa's vocal success in Paris and — as soon becomes clear — on the person of Philippa herself, as the hymn continues:

> God is God even if all lands be deserts.
> God is God even if all life were ended,
> If the people should vanish, and you, divine heavens,
> Will reign over the countless and play the harp so beautifully.
>
> Highest mountain and deepest vale shall vanish.
> Heaven and earth as well will perish.
> Each height and peak shall be no longer,
> But the Lord's glory shall rise again in a thousand hearts.

During the last two lines of the hymn, the camera lingers on the large and unusual crucifix that hangs in the front of the church: roughly carved in wood and painted, the softly lit face of Jesus is turned to the side, serene and gently smiling, almost bemused. Coinciding with those last two lines of the hymn, the shot suggests that in this look of love and delight somehow lies the lasting transcendent glory that "shall rise . . . in a thousand hearts" and "play the harp so beautifully." This is a smiling and tender Christ, and it is exactly this note that sets the tone for the amour between Philippa and Papin and, for that matter, for the film as a whole.

Immediately after the worship service, Papin is at the minister's door asking to give singing lessons to Philippa; she will, with some training, he assures the father, "sing like an angel." To appeal to the pastor's sensibility, he adds that "that is important when one sings God's praises." The singing lessons soon commence, but Papin does not tutor Philippa in a Bach cantata toward the splendor and praise of God but with a titillating love duet from *Don Giovanni*. (In the film's funniest sequence, the old pastor and his other daughter, Martina, listen anxiously to the "lesson" in an adjoining room, as well they should.) Though middle-aged and slightly plump, the baritone Papin is nothing if not the exuberant duetist, telling Philippa that she "will be a star in the heavens" and that no one has sung as well as she sings. But he clearly comes to be as interested in her person and beauty as he is in her talent, and it is also clear that Philippa herself feels considerable emotional agitation. Sensing the cascade of her own affections for both the music and for Papin, she soberly informs her father that she wishes to end her singing lessons. The gleeful old man, having triumphed over yet another suitor, delivers a note to Papin that sends him away utterly disappointed — about both the prospects for art and his own prospects. We later see the measure of Philippa's loss in the silent look of remorse on her face as a single violin plays. Papin disappears from the story, except for a brief cutaway, decades later, as the writer of a letter introducing the third visitor to this obscure village.

The Stranger-Guest-Servant-Cook

After Philippa's brief and thoroughly chaste dalliance with Papin, the story abruptly leaps forward thirty-five years to September of 1871. A rainstorm pelts the village as a solitary cloaked figure goes from door to door looking for the now elderly spinster sisters. Hearing the knock on the door, they take in an exhausted and half-numb middle-aged woman and warm her with tea and concern. The stranger, Babette Hersant, bears a letter of introduction from none other than Achille Papin. As the storm rages outside, an apt metaphor for the world from which Babette has come, the elderly ladies read aloud Papin's letter explaining that its bearer has lost her husband and son — "killed like rats" — to one General Galliffet during an abortive revolution in Paris. Babette has fled the wrath of Galliffet, and now she seeks refuge in this obscure place, sent there by their old friend Achille Papin. The circumstance is made all the more poignant by Papin's long and mournful addendum to Philippa, his "beautiful soprano of the snows." He regrets that her voice has not filled the concert halls of Paris, but he assures her, imagining her surrounded by adoring grandchildren, that she has chosen the better path in life, for his own fate amongst the fickle aesthetes of Paris has not been happy. He is now "a lonely, graying old man forgotten by those who once applauded

198

and adored me. . . . What is fame? The grave awaits us all." Papin's rueful reflection echoes the gist of the hymn sung in the church when he first heard her angelic voice there. He closes the letter in something between a lament and an epitaph, signing himself "a friend who was once Achille Papin." Before closing, he tersely adds that "Babette knows how to cook." And so, though the sisters insist they have no money to pay her, they agree to take Babette in, for she pleads, "I will simply die if you will not let me serve you."

Babette occupies a small attic room in the sisters' small house, and they set about teaching her how to cook the drab fare they prepare daily for the poor and infirm of the village: fish like shoe leather and soup like gruel, grim victuals that the camera goes out of its way to emphasize. Slowly Babette, though she is foreign and above all French, fits in with the provincial life of the very small village: she bargains gamely with local shopkeepers and fishmongers and seeks to improve the taste and variety of the food the sisters dispense to the needy. A polite distance remains between the sisters and their servant, who receives only room and board for her labors. Still, this world is comfortable for everyone, and they all appear to take pleasure and comfort in the satisfactions of their daily work and the routines of a secure life. While their remote location, far from the "excitements" of big cities such as Paris, provides no more than bland routine, it also ensures their safety from the perils that inhabit the big and exciting places. And this life goes on, quiet and spare, as is usual in the course of small towns, for more than fourteen years, the narrator informs us.

This is not to say that nothing changes in this tiny outpost on the sea. For one thing, the amity and general spiritual confidence of the small remnant of the religious sect founded by "the minister" has slowly diminished. As is often the case, insurgent religious groups have difficulty sustaining their initial clarity and urgency of vision, especially after the passing of a charismatic founding figure, and this inevitability has beset this community. Some worry about past sins or the coming of death; others turn "testy and querulous," revisiting old jealousies, swindles, and infidelities, whole lifetimes of wrongs both trivial and large. The sisters observe this fraying in the community and feel powerless to do much about it. At the close of one meeting of the gathered remnant, all of whom now fit comfortably around a single dining table, the sisters suggest singing "Thy Kingdom come, O Lord," because they know very well that it may take that "coming" to restore harmony to the now fractious group. In any case, the sisters hope that a celebration on the hundredth anniversary of their long-dead father's birth will restore some of the concord of the original community, and for this they plan a small gathering over cakes and coffee. That is about as exciting as things get in Jutland.

But there is an event of greater moment. Each year a friend has renewed Babette's subscription in the French lottery, and now a letter from France — itself a major event in this little village — arrives to indicate that Babette has won the sizable sum of 10,000 francs in the lottery. Everyone in the town, including Babette, is astounded by this good fortune, and they all expect that the penniless Babette will use this largesse to return to France to take up the remains of her former life. The sisters consider her departure a sure thing, and the poor in the village dread the prospect because it will mean a return to the barely edible sustenance of the pre-Babette era. Indeed, leaving is an option that Babette apparently considers very seriously: the camera shows her in solitary deliberation, sitting alone or standing pensively on the shore. Thus it comes as something of a surprise when she suddenly makes up her mind. She turns from the shore and strides with resolve to the sisters to tell them, with evident delight, that she wishes to prepare a "real French dinner" for the centenary celebration.

The sisters had intended no more than a "modest supper followed by a cup of coffee," since it is a matter of principle and taste that they never provide more than that for guests. From the outset, though, Babette is insistent. When she first asks, her right hand rises to clutch the cross she wears around her neck; this gesture identifies the context in which she situates her request, if not her art as well, and is one of the critical gestures in the film. When the sisters reluctantly agree, Babette then asks that she be allowed to pay for the meal with her own money. The sisters protest this as well, until Babette reminds them, in terms consistent with her grasping the cross pendant, "Have I ever asked you for anything? Hear my prayer today. It comes from my heart." The sisters concede her point, and Babette responds with quiet delight as she asks for time off to travel to Frederickshavn to order ingredients.

Making Ready

The climactic portion of *Babette's Feast* begins, appropriately, with a lightly comic tone as the ingredients for the meal begin to arrive: cages full of chirping quails, a live tortoise of eighty pounds or so, crates of forty-year-old wine, and so on — all sufficient to incite nightmares in

Babette (Stéphane Audran) sits before the sisters as she prepares to ask them if she may prepare a feast to honor their father. In the next instant, as if to clarify the nature and purpose of her request, she grabs the pendant cross that hangs from her neck.

Martina and Philippa of satanic sensuality in which Babette is the temptress. The sisters, already frightened by the mere mention of the word "French," accepting all its associations with atheism and decadence, watch the procession of goods marching into their humble kitchen, and it stokes their fear of perdition. So they forewarn their pious parishioners of the decadence to come, and all the churchly diners agree neither to taste, enjoy, nor praise the food or drink in the least. The sisters warn of "dangerous, maybe even evil powers" in what promises to be a "witches' Sabbath." At the end of this little meeting, and with more than a little irony, the community again sings "Jerusalem, the Heart's True Home," completely failing to connect their coming celebratory meal, or physical pleasure in general, as celebrated in the hymn, with the goodness of God or God's promises of care for humans. Throughout this sequence, filmgoers on the one hand share the sisters' incredulity at the parade of ingredients; but unlike them, viewers anticipate the splendor of what likely awaits, of which no one in the film, except Babette, has any idea at all. Even so, though more movie-wise and sophisticated than these old characters, viewers may have less of an idea than anyone of the full measure of surprise that is afoot, both temporal and religious. After all, what transpires approaches a revelation in its unexpectedness as much as it does in the strangeness of its content; and no one sees the full import of what approaches, not even Babette.

So as not to stretch credulity for the surprise to come, and to whet viewers' culinary and dramatic appetites, the camera dotes on the many elaborate preparations for the feast, beginning with the setting of the elegant long table, enough to seat twelve, an appropriate number for those who relish biblical allusions. Table settings, candlesticks, and wine goblets abound, all spread on a fine linen cloth. In the kitchen, in quiet but obvious joy, Babette goes about preparing the different courses of food on the wood-burning stove. Meanwhile, in humorous counterpoint, fearing that their father's eyes might witness some desecration or infamy, one of the sisters quietly relocates his large portrait from the dining to the small living room, where the guests will gather after the meal for a chaste cup of coffee.

In a moment of pre-banquet conflict — one that focuses on the religious meaning of the feast — the audience's attention is drawn to Lorenz Lowenhielm, who had left Jutland and Martina decades earlier to achieve power and fame in the military and politics. Now a general and successful in all the ways he had hoped to be, and once again visiting his aunt, he will also attend the feast. Alone in his room, the old man (now played by Jarl Kulle) converses with his younger self, who sits impatiently in a chair while the old man questions the correctness of his life's central choice. The older, wiser man suspects that, in the language of Ecclesiastes, "all is vanity" (also the complaint of the aging Achille Papin). He sees tonight as an occasion — observing again his lost love and the virtue she represented — for resolving the soul's conflict over that central choice: "I have found everything you have dreamed of and satisfied your ambition," he says to the young man he was. "But to what purpose? Tonight we two shall settle our score. You must prove to me that the choice I made was the right one." Or, as he asks his aunt as they ride to the dinner, "Could many years of victories result in defeat?" The feast will prove him wrong on both counts.

While a storm blusters outside, again the apt metaphor for the human circumstance, guests gather in the snug living room, the camera playing lovingly on their aged faces as they again sing "Jerusalem" while awaiting the summons to dinner. The camera cuts repeatedly to the final food preparation and presentation, especially to Babette's delicate construction of the roast quail (Cailles en Sarcophage). Finally the guests enter the dining room to encounter the first surprise in a litany of ever-mounting astonishment: the glowing table, replete with three ornate silver candelabra and each place with three crystal wineglasses, silver tableware, delicate plates stacked five high, and all adorned with large fan-shaped napkins. The camera adoringly tracks the full length of the brilliant light-filled table. The general is quietly taken aback by how his senses are being overwhelmed, having had no expectation of such elegance in this rough back country. When he takes his first sip of wine, he is startled, then astounded, and then he savors each subsequent sip, rolling it over his tongue. "Amazing!" he proclaims, "An amontillado! And the finest amontillado I've ever tasted." Next comes the turtle soup, "quite definitely real turtle soup, and what a turtle soup," pronounces the pleased general. And so it goes, on and on, course after course, wine after wine, and all the while the parishioners respond — by previous agreement — as if they eat this fare every day and that none of it merits the least comment. One diner even reminds them, in egregious theological error, that the food is of no importance whatever, just as at the wedding at Cana, the occasion of Jesus' first miracle, when he turned water into the best wine of the party.

For a long while their studied indifference, though they eagerly down every last morsel, plays humorously off Lowenhielm's increasingly perplexed amazement. The only other character to express pleasure, spontaneous and unfettered, is Mrs. Lowenhielm's carriage driver, who sits in the kitchen while Babette scurries about; he, too, drinks and eats, despite his humble status, like the invited guests, and he is also utterly incredulous and overwhelmed at what comes his way. Magnanimous Babette lavishes on the delighted humble servant all the same exquisite fare that those in the dining room receive. Here the story echoes Jesus' parable of the king who invites anyone and everyone to dinner when his invited guests do not show up. Just in case the audience does not grasp the outlandish notion that this exquisite cuisine is for everybody, even those who refuse its "taste," director Gabriel Axel pushes hard the notion that this is the universal meal, the feast intended for everyone and from which no one is excluded. Meanwhile, taken aback by Blinis Demidoff, the pastry appetizer, the general is then once again startled by the wine, a twenty-year-old champagne: "This most certainly is Veuve Clicquot 1860!" To another member of the religious sect, it is but some wonderful kind of "lemonade."

Fruition

From this initial chain of astonishments, the feast moves to a different, more reflective, phase that supplies the context for understanding its

A look of astonished incredulity comes over General Lowenhielm's (Jarl Kulle) face as he reacts to the "finest amontillado I have ever tasted."

meaning. In other words, the story returns to the "regions of the heart" and, in the most pointed terms, of miracle. As Lowenhielm relishes the blinis and the champagne, the delicate, reflective sound of a single violin rises, and the minister's followers, now clearly warmed by the food and wine in spite of themselves, begin to reminisce about "the minister" and his teachings. The dominant note of those teachings has thus far in the film been asceticism, the denial of the pleasures of this world for a vision of the new Jerusalem that is to come. But contrary to expectations, all these current recollections make clear that the core of his message, one that melds with the mood and meaning of this feast, has been not so much worldly denial as quite another intense spiritual demand: "Little children, love one another," as one ancient follower recalls. The profound human yearning of a small child begging for bread, as an early hymn paraphrases the Bible, is here satisfied in the common meal. This is the note above all others that the daughters have tried to sustain in both practice and spirit, and it is evident as well in the lyrics of the hymns. To followers' recollections, Lowenhielm adds that the minister's collected sermons were a favorite of the queen. A tiny lady in the crowd tells of an apparent miracle that accommodated the minister's pledge to preach across the fjord one Christmas morning.

Concluding this sequence, the appearance on the table of the main course, Cailles en Sarcophage, is the occasion for General Lowenhielm's anecdote about the Café Anglais, a tale whose improbability and eventual serendipity suggests the workings of a strange and remarkable providence. During his youth in Paris, he was feted by his French hosts, for winning a riding competition, with a dinner at the celebrated Café Anglais. The head chef there, he recalls, was a woman, and the group ate the café's specialty, Cailles en Sarcophage, a dish of her own creation. General Galliffet, the host for this celebratory dinner, explained that this woman, this head chef, had the ability to transform a dinner into a kind of love affair, a love affair that made no distinction between bodily appetite and spiritual appetite. General Galliffet said that in the past he had fought a duel for the love of a beautiful woman. But now, he said, there was no woman in Paris for whom he would shed his blood — except this chef. She was considered the greatest of culinary geniuses. (This General Galliffet was the same one who would later kill Babette's husband and child.)

That Lowenhielm should eat this same exquisite Parisian dish here in the rural outback of Denmark, decades later, is beyond explanation; but for him it fits perfectly with the other guests' stories of unexpected evidence of divine action in obscure lives and obscure places. Indeed, this culinary "love affair" brings to mind a love affair from earlier in his life, when he courted Martina and encountered the strange world of piety that she inhabited and in which she chose to remain. In the backdrop to this feast, then, lies a history of the mutual exchange between spirit and flesh, and between art and belief. Each can help the other prosper.

The context suggests that superb food speaks of love in a variety of ways: the love for the sensual pleasure derived — substantial, valid, and full of marvel; the love of the artist's craft in transforming the raw ingredients into something glorious; the love of the giver of the feast for its splendor; and finally, the love and gratitude returned by the recipients. Most of all, though, thanks to the artist's craft, the feast's exquisite perfection and delight suggest the possibility of a world made perfect and whole in every way, the "Jerusalem" of their song. Of course, the prototype for this "love feast" between body and soul is the Last Supper of the Lord and the ritual practice of the Holy Eucharist, which has run through the liturgical worship of the church from its beginning. In the ever-mysterious but inexorable economy of the soul, the supposed boundaries between body and spirit quickly blur, and a dinner transfigures itself "into a kind of love affair" that at once transcends and absorbs all other loves.

Of the two responses to Lowenhielm's tale of the Café Anglais meal, the first — and more telling — comes from Christopher, now old and deaf, who appropriately pronounces his "hallelujah," his habitual, all-purpose rejoinder to anything he doesn't quite hear. Like so many of the comments during the dinner-table conversation, this remark plays humorously, but at the same time it is an incisive assessment of the theological gist of Lowenhielm's story. Another old gent agrees nonchalantly that, yes, it certainly is Cailles en Sarcophage, as if there were nothing extraordinary about the dish for these folks and, really, could there be any doubt about it? The humor has a point but also dilutes the high seriousness of the drama that might otherwise spill over into portentousness.

The final phase of the banquet displays another variety of miracle, the toughest one and one that is crucially important to almost everyone attending. Here the mood turns openly festive, a difficult feat for these aging ascetics. The gladness created by the exquisite meal spills into the texture of the relationships between almost everyone in attendance: lost trust is restored, new understandings and bonds form, and the world is again made new and whole, at least for a time. The most obvious recipients are the surviving members of the minister's dissenting sect. Now, savoring the ripe blessings of the flesh and the delight of being alive, they individually move to overcome the pettiness and acrimony that has slowly eroded their historic mutuality and concord. The message that they should "love one another" was, after all, their minister's central message and no doubt his greatest accomplishment. One businessman quietly confesses to a rival that years earlier he cheated him on a lumber deal; the other admits that he knew about it, and that he cheated in return. The first man responds by saying that, if that was the case, well, then he deserved to get bilked.

Over coffee and champagne in the living room, the folks exchange individual blessings with one another. Solveig and Anna bless each other and then rest their foreheads together, just as small children would. From across the room, John blesses Christopher, and the latter responds with the greeting "my brother." After Lowenhielm and his aunt depart, the whole group gathers quietly in the dark under the bright stars; they encircle another apt symbol, the town well, and sing hand in hand. The two sisters stand apart, watching the "little children" as they exult in gratitude for their recovered harmony, the fullness of their lives, and — at their age — the approach of their hearts' "true home":

The clock strikes and time goes by;
Eternity is nigh.
Let us use this time to try

To serve the Lord with heart and mind,
So that our true home we shall find,
So that our true home we shall find.

And they have indeed found that "true home," a glad domain of love and reconciliation, even as they contemplate death. Throughout the long scene in the living room, the camera has doted lovingly on each of the aged faces, relishing their lives and their magnanimity, as Philippa sings her song of recollection and mortality, a benediction and petition:

Oh, watch the day once again hurry off,
And the sun bathe itself in water.
The time for us to rest approaches,
O God, Who dwelleth in heavenly light,
Who reigns above in heaven's hall.
Be for us our infinite Light in the valley of night;
The sand in our hourglass will soon run out.
The day is conquered by the night;
The glories of the world are ending,
So brief their day,
So swift their flight.
God, let Thy brightness ever shine,
Admit us Thy mercy divine.

As they approach "the valley of the night," the present "glories" of the feast merge with the "brightness" of "mercy divine." In this present brief moment of glory and reconciliation, they imbibe a foretaste of the divine feast that is the Christian afterlife, where all is made whole and well. Indeed, they have found the shelter of love in their communion on this stormy winter evening, and in this haven "righteousness and bliss" have indeed kissed.

The second locus for fruition is the relationship of Lorenz Lowen-hielm and Martina, the woman he left behind more than forty years earlier. Over the meal they exchange kindly glances at one another, even wordlessly toasting each other, and near its end Lowenhielm rises to offer a formal tribute. It is somewhat cryptic, but it parallels and anticipates the reconciliation that will come about between the members of the flock. He clinks his glass and rises to address the guests. He begins and ends with the same words — "mercy and truth have met together" — and in between confesses the limits of his own life choices as he hopes to explain to the other guests what he now understands to be the purpose of human life, which parallels the central promises of the long-departed minister:

> Mercy and truth have met together. Righteousness and bliss shall kiss one another. Man, in his weakness and shortsightedness, believes he must make choices in this life. He trembles at the risks he takes. We do know fear. But no.
>
> Our choice is of no importance. There comes a time when our eyes are opened. And we come to realize that mercy is infinite. We need only await it with confidence and receive it with gratitude. Mercy imposes no conditions. And, lo! Everything we have chosen has been granted to us. And everything we rejected has also been granted. Yes, we even get back what we rejected. Mercy and truth have met together. Righteousness and bliss shall kiss one another.

With his eyes now opened by the surprise and magnificence of Babette's feast in this unlikeliest of places, Lowenhielm does come at last to "realize that mercy is infinite," that there is no foreclosing or binding of divine love for the world. Love, that "brightness" of which the flock sings, overcomes everything. Here spirit triumphs over the "flesh" and all earthly pursuits, a realization Lowenhielm has had, oddly and ironically enough, by the extraordinarily material and "fleshly" meal he has just relished. That this should have happened is not surprising, however, given his early assertion that meals at the Café Anglais blurred the lines between flesh and spirit. The beauty and splendor of those meals was to move otherwise jaded, power-hungry diners, such as Galliffet and even Lowenhielm, into wonder and gratitude before the loving mysteries of the world, including the transforming alchemy that art attains. Here the actual beauty of the meal transforms the occasion into a love affair that culminates in spiritual community. And in this regard, the meal echoes the surprise and munificence of the Incarnation.

Lowenhielm's response is particularly important, for he may be the only character who has sufficient thoughtfulness and sophistication to articulate, as he indeed does, the nature and meaning of the "miracle" of Babette's feast. He has come to the feast with that weighty question about his own life: whether it was better lived in the courts of Europe or, as it might have been, in the small village by the sea in humble piety at the side of the lovely Martina. What he encounters in the feast answers his question, and then some, and in ways he never dreamed. Each course of the meal takes Lowenhielm as if by storm; his mildly cynical understanding of the world and how it works, an understanding bordering on despair, turns upside-down and inside-out. But the great surprise and sumptuousness of the feast brings him to recognize that a loving metaphysical reality does embrace the entirety of this world, himself included. If this delicate majesty, itself a gesture of love, might occur here, of all places, then matter does not limit "reality," for the world is suffused with constant remarkable displays of divine love. Lowenhielm goes to the feast wondering about the questions of human love and runs smack into the reality of a pervasive cosmic love that subsumes and resolves all of the questions of the heart. His mind and soul are overturned, and he leaves knowing that "all things are possible in this beautiful world of ours." The parishioners overcome their skepticism of the body, and Lowenhielm overcomes his skepticism of "spirit" and goodness.

This assertion of the ultimacy of love replays in Lowenhielm's farewell speech to Martina. In a moment alone in the entry hall of her tiny home, a single candle again burns between them, in the very spot where they had said good-bye decades before, when he declared that he would never see her again and that some things in this world were "impossible." He now gladly renounces his youthful assertion, admitting instead the supremacy of a kind of love that affords lasting spiritual intimacy and indicts the tawdry baubles of passion and romance that usually pass for love. He tells her, against all sense, "I have been with you every day of my life," and asks her if she knows that, to which she assents. Lowenhielm then vows, or prays, "You must also know that I shall be with you every day that is granted to me from now on. Every evening I shall sit down to dine with you. Not with my body, which is of no importance, but with my soul. Because this evening I have learned, my dear, that in this beautiful world of ours, all things are possible." It is, paradoxically, the palpable, material splendor of "this beautiful world of ours" that often bespeaks the ultimacy of the spirit. He has found that "all things are possible" rather than "impossible," as his youthful self had believed. For Lowenhielm, apparently, the feast confirms what his misgivings have tried to tell him through all the intervening years.

This admission by the general constitutes for him, as for the viewers, a wild metaphysical leap. The cultural sophisticate and political realist had apparently never wholly discarded his intimations of religious reality; if he had, his private internal debate would not have taken place. At this dinner he receives an answer to his lifelong query — even more than he had contemplated. The impossible can burst forth, whether it be the Café Anglais appearing on the shores of a harsh northern sea, the persistence of old affection, or, even more, the possibility of trust and intimacy of spirit, that "mercy and truth" and "righteousness and bliss" all conflate within a single glowing recognition of the centrality of the divine love that infuses "this beautiful world of ours."

That assertion prepares the way for the last segment in the film's three-part conclusion. Attention shifts from the flock, Lowenhielm, and Martina to Babette and Philippa, the two remaining principals whose fates have yet to be decided and who, up to this point, have remained relatively disconnected from the reconciliations achieved by others. After all the guests depart, the sisters, all aglow, enter the kitchen to thank Babette for the wonderful meal ("a very good dinner indeed"); all their apprehensions have not only been dispelled but transformed into delight and enormous gratitude. Sitting alone and quiet, but very satisfied, in the kitchen after her labors, Babette calmly makes an amazing announcement: "At one time I was the head chef at the Café Anglais." The wonder of this fact eludes the inexperienced sisters, even after Lowenhielm's dinner tribute to Babette; they only remark that they will remember this evening long after Babette has returned to Paris. But Babette's response to that does genuinely amaze them: having no money and no one waiting for her there, she says, she will not return to Paris. The news of her pennilessness startles the sisters, but Babette calmly explains that "dinner for twelve at the Café Anglais costs 10,000 francs."

Like the woman who lavishes precious oil on the feet of Jesus to express her gratitude and love, Babette has made a similarly extravagant gesture, one that begins with her grasping the cross and ends with her bestowing her windfall on the poor and, in terms of her art, the unknowing. Countering their protest ("you shouldn't have given all you owned for us") she admits, "It was not just for you." While she gave freely and sincerely in gratitude for the sisters' years of hospitality, she undertook the feast so that she could once more practice the art she had put aside when she fled for her life from Paris. And though she will now be poor for the rest of her life, she also knows that "an artist is never poor," a nugget of truth she learned from Papin. No matter what ill fortune befalls the artist, there remains the relish of the exercise of God's gift to make the world more "happy" by creating beauty. And this she will continue to do for the sisters and for the poor of the village, whose pleasure in her cooking is no less than Lowenhielm's. As Papin, Babette, and Lowenhielm understand art, it is a gesture of love, adoration, and gratitude for the goodness of the world that the artist both returns to God and bestows on those for whom she has undertaken it. At the Café

210

Anglais, Babette "was able to make them happy" when she gave her "very best." Exactly how happy is seen in the devotion, though short-lived, of those such as Galliffet and Lowenhielm. And that is the delight of the artist, simultaneously self-giving and self-fulfilling, to do that for which she has been called. In Papin's words (quoted by Babette), "Throughout the world sounds one long cry from the heart of the artist: Give me the chance to do my very best."

Babette recites all of this with supreme confidence and calm, as if the work she had done that evening confirmed all her recollections of the pleasures and purposes of her long-neglected craft. Sensing that that evening's feast was the end of Babette's artistic career, and recalling Papin's words to her, Philippa assures her, slowly and tenderly, that there is more: "But this is not the end, Babette. I'm certain it is not. In Paradise you will be the great artist that God meant you to be. Ah, how you will delight the angels!" These two great but obscure artists, the singer and the chef, then tenderly, even achingly, embrace one another in their mutual understanding and sympathy. As they hold each other, each smiling, the camera cuts to a solitary candle on the sill that flames out as snow begins to fall outside the window, and so ends the film.

Dessert: Art and Love

More than she herself realizes, Babette's work has fallen on thirsty but fertile soil, unlike the reception of her art in Paris — or that of Papin. To be sure, both Babette and Papin achieved fame, but there is no indication that their art was much understood or appreciated beyond the momentary pleasures it brought. It made their patrons happy for a little while, as Babette herself explains; but beyond that, it apparently had no lasting or deep consequence whatever. In fact, it is notable for being inconsequential, which the screenplay takes pains to point out. By the time Papin writes his letter of introduction for Babette, he is old, forsaken, and bitter; his letter is mostly a lamentation about the fickle nature of fame and the abandonment by those who had seemingly cared about him and his work. Worse still is the instance of General Galliffet, who broadly announced his devotion to Paris's greatest chef, swearing he would fight duels only for her: tragically, this same culinary devotee killed Babette's husband and son and was in hot pursuit of Babette herself when she fled to the shores of Jutland. So much for the redemptive potential of art, even among its most ardent admirers. It does not suffice to ennoble or transfigure the soul of those who consume it, even with relish.

Something quite the opposite from this fickleness transpires in that small cottage in the Danish outback. All the diners, save for Lowenhielm, are utterly unsophisticated, completely untutored in the culinary art of anything. It is likely that this very naiveté and innocence opens them to some extent to the pleasures of the food; but that inexperience hardly accounts for the measures of delight and meaning that overflow, culminating in reconciliation, profound gratitude for their lives and for one another, and even calm acceptance of the sure approach of death. That is a long way from Galliffet's blood-drenched treachery. An enormous difference lies, as it does for Lowenhielm, in the lenses of perception and interpretation brought to the feast: that is, the disposition to see the world, history, and human life as formed by divine love and summoned to communal love. It is this frame of understanding that allows art to bloom fully.

The sect members bring to the feast a slightly skewed view of this, notably in their somber view of the flesh as somehow evil, a path to sin and perdition, a distraction from the soul's pure "spiritual" contemplation of love. It is a notion more Platonic than Christian, but it still has sway over them. Nonetheless, these aging ascetics are fertile ground for the art of the meal. When they finally sing and dance around the well under the bright stars of God's sky, there is hardly a lovelier vision of a holy felicity anywhere in film. For the sisters the feast makes real what they had always hoped, believed, and hung onto with tenacity — from feeding the poor to urging the flock.

The greater astonishment comes for Babette in this place that has become "home," her own Jerusalem. Surely she could start again in Paris with a new restaurant with her lottery money, but she concludes that the real "prize" of existence lies in this remote tiny place of humble people. Here she has found safety, welcome, and love — in other words, "home" — a reality very unlike the fickle and sometimes deadly fashions of Paris. So she donates her new fortune and lavishes the best of her long-dormant artistry on the unsuspecting, knowing that she is unlikely to receive much in either comprehension or appreciation from them, but also learning that they are sufficiently "holy" to welcome her. It is worth repeating that in this she resembles the woman who lavished the costly perfume on Jesus' dirty feet and dried them with her hair. Babette's gratitude extends to the two sisters, who took her in with magnanimity, an exile from Paris and a Roman Catholic in this conservative Lutheran place; but it is also gratitude to God for the wonder of taste and for the skill she has to create culinary marvels that she bestows on others.

All of this follows on her fingering of the crucifix she wears as she makes her initial request to prepare the meal for the commemoration of the minister's centenary. That wordless gesture clarifies context and intention, and then it ramifies through everything that follows, giving those events a meaning that resolves the false conflict between art, the domain of the senses, and Christianity, the supposed conduit to a fleshless spiritual world beyond. Babette's best suffices for the courts of God, where the angels will sing in praise, the only place, Philippa sadly reminds her, that any artist will ever be fully understood and revered. The earth is, after all, an imperfect place, especially among the cognoscenti who think they know better.

Babette's Feast is a quiet, lyrical drama, slow and painterly in style, packed with delicate but potent images that go to where words cannot stretch, even though virtually the whole story is set in the unpromising setting of a remote and unexciting place among mostly obscure, unexciting people. But it covers a great deal of territory — cinematically, intellectually, and religiously — as only a few rare films have. In giving visual life to Isak Dinesen's fetching story, screenwriter-director Axel makes plausible the toughest of all propositions, whether in cinema, literature, church, or anywhere: that God shows up in human affairs, that divine light does indeed shine, even in the most unexpected places and amid the manifold disappointments of human life. That comes as great surprise to the characters, including the religious ones, and even more to viewers, especially the jaded among them. The three elements that bind the whole of *Babette's Feast* together are surprise, splendor, and love. The divine light becomes in this film a palpable manifestation of divine love.

As in Jesus' miracle at Cana, love changes ordinary water into exquisite wine for the relish of all. Moreover, that such carnal delight is a gift displays the love of the miracle-maker for the people to whom he gives it. Similarly, in this "love affair" that Babette prepares, grace inheres in the ordinary matter, the food itself, just as love inheres in the loveliness of the created world. Mary Elizabeth Podles suggests that this alone suffices to work the change in the parishioners, but more is afoot than just "the supreme goodness of the created order," no matter how resplendent that might be.[1] It is by virtue of Babette's artistry that that

---

1. Mary Elizabeth Podles, "*Babette's Feast*: Feasting with Lutherans," *Antioch Review* 50 (1992): 564.

supreme goodness of the ordinary is enhanced, "blessed," and imbued with a second grace, namely, an artist's love for the food itself and her skill in realizing its glorious potential. In the sort of art Babette practices, sensuous relish of the material world becomes a redemptive agent, for it brings to light the splendor of the world as it was first intended and displays the love that was first imbued in the creation, the world as it was before darkness obscured its original luster.

The guests at Babette's feast in Jutland will, unlike those she served in Paris, actually "get it" by virtue of their lifelong religious habit of seeing love as the central point of human existence. The thirsting for Jerusalem that echoes throughout the story, especially in the music, disposes these diners to profit from this culinary gift, even in spite of themselves. It is this prior disposition toward love that inclines these aging ascetics to turn the good cheer they find in the food toward others, and the lost accord of the small community is wondrously restored, culminating in the delicate image of their "love dance" around the town well, itself an appropriate emblem of human nourishment. In this regard, Babette's feast is genuinely eucharistic, a love feast that transfigures ordinary elements, bread and wine, into agents and portents of divine love for the world.

The full wonder of all this is grasped only by General Lowenhielm, who had eaten this meal before but now again relishes its elegance in this most unlikely of places. This time the feast assumes a different character, and the light it casts, miracle that it is, brings him a radically different understanding of his own life and human life in general. The sophisticated general has encountered an outlandish and improbable love, and he glimpses the lineaments of the mystery that has graciously come his way. If this feast can happen in this near-wilderness, then anything can happen — even transcendent Love. The delight and love the meal occasions shows the insubstantiality of the material and the supremacy of the spiritual, the physical mediating the religious. And it is here, in this exultant kingdom of love, that the cryptic lynchpin of the story, namely, the conflict between the material and the religious, between art and belief, is resolved. For in the end, "righteousness and bliss shall kiss."

PART THREE

FABLES OF LIGHT

A farther stage of the comedy of Christian grace is the radical surprise of the fairy tale, what is here called "fables of Light." To the ordinary human world of distress and woe come miraculous beings and forces that proceed in fantastic ways to transfigure the reality of the mostly human characters. As narrative, these stories inhabit a territory somewhere between parable and fable, and far from being mere "kid-stuff," these tales reside on a short list of enduringly popular films in recent American cultural history. The reasons for this are arguable, but one of the more conspicuous possibilities is the persistent emphasis in these films on human longing for the coming of divine help for the human circumstance. For example, Steven Spielberg repeatedly returns to what I call the "lost boy" story wherein a distraught young (or child-like) man yearns for home or some special something that will repair his bland or fractured world. That same appetite for a realm of heroic meaning drives young Luke Skywalker in George Lucas's *Star Wars* saga. It is perhaps not coincidence that these fables have soared to popularity in a time when institutional religion tends to tame or channel the splendor and exuberance of the divine; in these films, human longing and the divine are let loose, so to speak, and then anything can, and usually does, happen. The fantastic and implausible become real, and throughout there is help from beyond for all kinds of human misfortune. Worlds float, the dead rise, evil is vanquished, the lost are found, and small green creatures bear the wisdom of the ages. The perennial struggle between good and evil goes both magical and metaphysical. This is not a world without serious peril, even though it is clearly pitched toward children. Rather, as Buechner points out with regard to fairy tales in general, the fantastic is a realm "full of

215

Film and "Reality"

In fiction film, what appears before the camera is a wholly contrived world, spun in the imagination and staged before the lens; in documentary film, it is a world that, though very much "real," is nonetheless selected, filtered, and arranged. Regardless of genre, most moviemakers set out to convince viewers that the stories they etch with light in some way "show" the world as it is — or could or should be. The camera catches light to "picture" a story about the fascinating, perplexing venture called human life.

We watch because we still have, running full-force through us, the human appetite for story. On the most fundamental level, there is the pure pleasure of being told a story and of "entertaining" its possibilities, mystery, and power. For some reason we relish the sensation of "losing ourselves" in a tale of some kind, of being seduced away into another sort of reality, at least for a time. People like to travel, to see the world and to get away from life's ordinary woes and aggravations, and stories offer a means for getting away. Movies in particular, with their enormous big-screen and big-sound immediacy and realism, envelop viewers in their imagined kingdoms that seem so real. Most filmgoers are more than a little susceptible to this, easy marks, ready for that quick trip away; if a motion picture is even half good, it offers an excursion of sorts, at least for a while, from the usually untidy world of daily life. To be sure, diversion, or what is sometimes nastily called "escapism," is necessary and not all bad, at least once in a while.

darkness and danger and ambiguity."[1] Into a world fraught with evil breaks Light, and rescue happens, and with it comes unimaginable joy, as if from Heaven itself. In books it is Oz, Narnia, Middle Earth, or Hogwarts. And in the movies it is Tatooine *(Star Wars)*, cookie-cutter suburban California *(ET)*, and Metropolis *(Superman)*.

In their high regard for the fantastic, these fables of Light partake of the same penchant for the fabulistic that shapes much contemporary avant-garde literary fiction, as argued by Robert Scholes in his well known 1967 book, *The Fabulators*. Scholes's specifications for fable sound like a blueprint for the popular fables of Light. There is, first off, extraor-

---

1. Buechner, *Telling the Truth: The Gospel as Tragedy, Comedy, and Fairy-Tale* (San Francisco: Harper, 1977), p. 78.

But most movies have a lot more going on than mere diversion or distraction. Like all the arts, traditional and avant-garde, elite and popular, hip and kitsch, movies sometimes offer a way of exploring life's larger riddles and testing out possible solutions to them. On the one hand, the light the movies throw up on the screen can clarify or illumine the conditions of living, can tell what human life was like, or is like, or will be like — hard or easy, happy or sad, exultant or tragic, light or dark, ad infinitum. And stories do not stop at description alone; the objective or neutral narrator, whether camera or author, simply does not exist. Given that, filmmakers also provide their hungry audiences with some "take" on what the task of survival requires, "showing" on the big screen or in the flickering home video box some emotion or truth that might help people better understand and survive their real world. That, to be sure, has always been one of the chief attractions — and promises — of any kind of art. Whether art does this in fact is the central question in a long-running debate that shows no indication of fading away or being resolved. In a way the question is moot, and we are simply stuck with what we've got — images, melodies, and tales. Love them or leave them, the arts, including movies, offer as good a navigational instrument as we have, and people steer by them more than they are likely to admit. That they do shed some measure of light on murky or bothersome reality is clearly true; how much they illumine a path through the wilderness or darkness is another question.

dinary delight in the simple plot design that pits the hero against towering odds. The tales are also heavily didactic, but they nonetheless delight and refresh. Most of all, though, there is a calculated loss of realism in order to fashion a world of fantasy where the primary concerns are ideas and ideals. In short, while these tales may begin in a constrictive empirical world with its surfeit of tragic reality, they quickly move toward an unimaginable realm of supernatural power that operates to repair the woebegone world in which the central characters travail. In this regard, they mimic the "once upon a time" wild hopes of some fairy tales, save here the fairy tale becomes "Long ago in a galaxy far away" of *Star Wars* (1977). From this genre come not only the most popular stories of our time, but also some of the most potent religious stories of modern culture.

There is, of course, *Star Wars*, the film that begins the story of young

Luke Skywalker, restive teenage boy, who finds himself on an unimaginable journey that culminates, incredibly, in his embrace of Jedi servanthood and, simultaneously, the rescue of "peace and justice" from the devouring evil Empire (Episodes IV-VI). Central to Skywalker's progress is his developing capacity for faith, patience, and, for lack of a better term, love. *The Return of the Jedi* (1983) concludes with a moving portrait of redemption as a son's love saves a fallen father and a new world erupts in celebration and hope. Lucas's current project, the completion of the first three episodes of the saga (I-III; 1999-2005), examines the means by which cosmic evil, the dark side of the Force, seduces the innocence of young Anakin Skywalker, the future father of Luke Skywalker. At its core is Lucas's long meditation on the nature of evil and good. What he has to say is not new. Evil thrives on anger and hatred; love sacrifices and exults.

The serio-comic *Superman* (1978) "fabulates" the Christian story of Incarnation, the coming of a mysterious savior "friend" who rescues humankind from perils both earthly and otherworldly. The film remains the best of all adaptations from a comic book and stands as one of the best Hollywood films of the 1970s. The film story alters the comic book tale to conform with the gist of the New Testament, mines its many plot details from the story of Jesus, and thieves crucial portions of the script from the New Testament Gospels. Best of all, though, it catches the wild, even preposterous comic spirit of the cosmic surprise at the heart of the New Testament. The wit, music, and splendid physical acting of Christopher Reeve collaborate to give the whole alternately sad and jubilant tale a fetching sort of realism.

The most persistent theme in the work of Steven Spielberg dramatizes the plight of the lost "every-boy" who must find his way to a new home. That begins with restive middle-aged boy Roy Neary (Richard Dreyfuss) in *Close Encounters of the Third Kind* (1977) and continues on with the woe of young Elliott (1982) in *E.T.* after his father has run off with his secretary. In both cases alien creatures arrive, resplendent in light, who first beguile and in the process provide hope for a new home of sorts, one that satisfies the deepest human longings for reconciliation and intimacy. Spielberg's preoccupation with the theme recurs so late as 1999 with *A.I.*, in which the "lost boy" is a sentient and feeling robot "child substitute" that is too easily discarded by a fickle humanity. All these films emphasize the relentless human search for connectedness, an appetite that seems to find surcease only by help from transcendent otherworldly powers from beyond the human circumstance. As such, the stories of these "lost boys" become affecting metaphors for the human predicament in general, one that will take Light from beyond to cure. Spielberg relentlessly pushes the question of what it will take to satisfy the human heart. His "lost boy" films provide apt, searching parables for humankind's search and, in his portraiture of super-natural aliens, compelling facsimiles of what divine help might look and feel like.

CHAPTER 8

TRACKING THE FORCE

Meaning and Morality in the *Star Wars* Saga

Thus far the still-unfolding *Star Wars* saga, now amounting to about ten hours of film story, features three big surprises, one in each of the three original pictures, *Star Wars* (1977), *The Empire Strikes Back* (1980), and *The Return of the Jedi* (1983). All three of these bright and revealing moments prove to be turning points, amazing ones, on which the progress of George Lucas's whole remarkable saga depends. The first takes place amid quiet conversation and, because the context is so unremarkable, it is easy to overlook; after all, the scene is mostly talk and, furthermore, talk of abstract forces about which the audience has no idea. Soon after the talk, though, comes the surprise that the hidden realities of which old Obi-Wan Kenobi has spoken actually shape the cosmic conflict at the center of the *Star Wars* chronicle. The second surprise, coming early in *The Empire Strikes Back,* offers even greater revelation, but this time it takes a notably comic turn, namely, the incredulity of the young hero in response to the farfetched notion that a puny, pesky, and funny-looking creature, the now legendary Yoda, trains warriors and, more than that, carries in his mind and soul the extraordinary powers of the universe.

The last glowing instant comes in the spectacular, unforeseeable, and wildly revealing climax of *The Return of the Jedi.* This is the conclusion nobody guessed, the full blossoming — or, more aptly, eruption — of the Force about which Obi-Wan quietly spoke to naive young Luke Skywalker long before. Two completely unexpected and stunning acts of selfless bravery, one fast upon the other, defeat the vast metaphysical evil that is a hair's breadth from completely extinguishing the slowly dimming light of human kindness.

Against all odds, then, wrapped in the pop space western that is

Star Wars, lies a fetching, luminous, and finally exultant fable of holy trust, apprenticeship, and pilgrimage that culminates in a resplendent vision of servanthood, reconciliation, and a winsome portrait of the new creation that awaits the cosmos. At its core, the very heartbeat of the *Star Wars* saga offers a riveting melodrama of redemption by love, the unforeseen wild Force that runs all galaxies both near and "far away." To be sure, much in this saga is digressive and self-indulgent, especially chase sequences and the special effects ad infinitum; but throughout the saga Lucas deftly displays in fresh, crisp images the hidden forces whose conflict drive the story. From beginning to end, Lucas's wild and fetching claims about the supernatural spangle forth, going where few films even dream of venturing, turning the whole of his story on the lathe of intergalactic metaphysical mystery.

The Sacred Journey

That first surprise comes twenty minutes into *Star Wars*, after an opening sequence that pumps its importance. It is clear from the story's prologue that the stakes are very high — in fact, the world depends on it — for the evil depicted is neither tepid nor readily contained. That is immediately obvious even without the graphic violence of the kind that so many films now use to get an audience. The ship of young Princess Leia (Carrie Fisher), an emissary for the besieged Republic, is taken over by the forces of the Empire's ominous Darth Vader (the acting of David Prowse and the voice of James Earl Jones), whose character, appearance, and sound comprise one of Lucas's many strokes of imaginative genius. This first glimpse of the towering Vader as he strides down the ship's corridor — large sculpted black helmet over his entire head, long black cape flowing behind, and a resonant, diction-perfect, razor-sharp voice — tells audiences all they need to know about the great measure of evil now afoot in the universe. Hardly ever has there been a classier, more striking, or more fearsome villain conjured on film. Though young Princess Leia Organa is feisty enough, she is hardly a match for the ruthless might of Vader. For one thing, the conspicuous difference in size between the tiny princess and the gigantic dark "Lord," as his minions call him, is striking. Furthermore, the utter darkness of Vader comes across in his clothing, and even more in the remarkable tone of his voice, full of anger and venom. And his actions speak even louder than his words when he lifts a Republic soldier off the ground by his neck with one hand (we see his feet dangling) and then crushes his throat (we hear the crunching) and throws him aside. Princess Leia, while by no means a traditional damsel in distress, given her moxie, is nonetheless in a terrible fix. The only hope for Leia's rescue and, it seems, the survival of the old Republic now rests on the shoulders of a most unlikely person, a kind of last resort, who dwells in a remote corner of the galaxy. Before her capture, the princess has managed to launch an escape pod that carries a faithful droid who bears a plea for rescue to an elderly friend on the distant desert planet of Tatooine. The droid turns out to be the stalwart R2-D2, and the old friend is Obi-Wan Kenobi (Alec Guinness), a once famous Jedi knight who now lives, in a barren wilderness, the purposefully obscure life of a hermit and, as his attire and words suggest, a monk. Most of his few neighbors refer to him simply as "old Ben Kenobi" and think of him as a half-mad eccentric. The unexpected begins to happen when the droid, safely landed on Tatooine, comes into the hands of young Luke Skywalker (Mark Hamill), who works on his uncle's hardscrabble moisture farm. When the droid escapes to look for Obi-Wan Kenobi, to whom he is to deliver the princess's message, Luke goes in search of the droid, only to be ambushed by nomadic bandits known as Sand People. Wounded and unconscious, he is rescued and magically restored, in Good Samaritan style, by old Obi-Wan. The pair take refuge in Obi-Wan's simple desert dwelling, where the old monk explains to young Luke the princess's message and the destiny that beckons Luke to join him, Obi-Wan, on what he acknowledges to be a "damn fool idealistic crusade."

And here, in this quiet moment of refuge and talk, comes the first huge — and lasting — surprise in *Star Wars,* the central element that transforms the epic from a dreary space-western into a tale of transcendent wonder and delight. As Obi-Wan talks to Luke Skywalker, it slowly becomes clear that there is more at stake than simply rescuing a princess or defeating the bad guys, though those are certainly conventional and worthy plots. Obi-Wan is after nothing less than the defeat of Darkness itself, the metaphysical power that seeks to destroy all that is good in the world. For this to happen, young Luke must join up with the old man, who now seems well past his prime physically and certainly no match for the fearsome Darth Vader. But joining up — and here's the rub, as Obi-Wan tells Luke — involves far more than learning to shoot a blaster or wield a light saber. To succeed in the task set forth by Obi-Wan, Luke must reckon with many difficult truths, which are at the same time, paradoxically, wonderful truths.

The first and greatest of these is Obi-Wan Kenobi's challenge to

Star Wars (1977)

Director:	George Lucas
Screenplay:	George Lucas
Music:	John Williams
Cinematography:	Gilbert Taylor
Editing:	Richard Chew, T. M. Christopher (special edition), Paul Hirsch, Marcia Lucas, George Lucas (uncredited)

Cast

Mark Hamill	Luke Skywalker
Harrison Ford	Han Solo
Carrie Fisher	Princess Leia Organa
Alec Guinness	Ben Obi-Wan Kenobi
Anthony Daniels	C-3PO
Kenny Baker	R2-D2
Peter Mayhew	Chewbacca
David Prowse	Darth Vader
James Earl Jones	Darth Vader (voice)

Academy Awards

Art Direction:	John Barry
Costume Design:	John Mollo
Visual Effects:	John Stears, John Dykstra, Richard Edlund, Grant McCune, Robert Blalack
Editing:	Paul Hirsch, Marcia Lucas, Richard Chew
Original Score:	John Williams
Sound:	Don MacDougall, Ray West, Bob Minkler, Derek Ball

Additional Academy Award Nominations

Picture	
Supporting Actor:	Alec Guinness
Director:	George Lucas
Original Screenplay:	George Lucas

Luke's picture of himself and his world; for if Luke is to succeed in his combat with the Empire, his superficial notions of what the world is like must radically change. Luke's first substantial shock is learning the truth that he is born of a distinguished spiritual parentage. His long-dead father was not, as Luke's uncle has told him, an insignificant navigator on a spice freighter, but was, like Kenobi himself, a Jedi knight, a member of a famed brotherhood like King Arthur's Round Table or Robin Hood's Merry Men. "For a thousand generations" this brotherhood protected peace and justice in the old Republic before the tyrannical reign of the dark Empire, which "hunted down and destroyed the Jedi knights." Luke's father, Anakin Skywalker, was "the best star pilot in the galaxy" and a "cunning warrior" until he was murdered by the Emperor's agent named Darth Vader, the same man who now threatens Princess Leia. For Luke, this is jolting news: he had always seen himself as unexceptional, just an ordinary kid. Now he has more heritage and promise than he ever dreamed.

Then, in news bigger and stranger still, Obi-Wan tells Luke that, in order to free the captive princess and do battle with the evil Empire, he must go with Obi-Wan to learn about something Luke has never heard of, "the ways of the Force," a mysterious and invisible energy that bonds and animates all matter and spirit: "It surrounds us, it penetrates us, it binds the galaxy together" (a quote that sounds strikingly similar to St. Paul's language in Ephesians 4:6, which invokes "one God and Father of all, who is over all and through all and in all"). The notion of anything spiritual at all surprises Luke, for he lives in a thoroughly secular age and has never had the least notion about the possibility of anything metaphysical — anything beyond the tangible world.

Nor is Luke's common-sense empiricism at all uncommon. The same skepticism is later prominently displayed by Han Solo (Harrison Ford), the vagabond adventurer who Luke and Obi-Wan hire to transport them to the hidden rebel base. While Obi-Wan is instructing Luke in his first lessons about the Force, Solo volunteers that in all his roaming of the galaxy he has never seen anything that has prompted him to believe in the existence of a "mystical energy field" or "one all-powerful force controlling everything," including one's personal destiny. Obi-Wan's bemused response to Solo's claim that everything is chance and luck is that "there's no such thing as luck." Clearly, Lucas intends to pose hard questions about the foundation of knowledge, metaphysical reality, and personal human destiny — questions of fate or providence. These questions and other important ones become more insistent as the series progresses; indeed, they become the matters on which the outcome of the whole story hinges. Viewers of the trilogy know that it will take virtually the entire saga for Luke Skywalker to fully trust the reality of the Force, in other words, to arrive at faith in something he cannot detect with his senses. Indeed, argues Lucas, there is more to the world than what meets the eye, and that makes all the difference, despite the persuasiveness of common sense and reductionist science. For the time being, though, sitting there in Obi-Wan's desert hermitage and for the first time hearing of such strange notions, all Luke can think about is that he's late for dinner and "can't get involved" in an old man's "damn fool idealistic crusade."

Luke's reasons for not following Obi-Wan reveal much about him and forecast major obstacles to a quick and happy outcome. The biggest of these is that Luke has a lot of growing up to do — emotionally, intellectually, and spiritually. This is no small task because of who Luke is at this early stage, and Lucas works from the film's beginning to show how unlikely a candidate for any kind of heroism Luke is. His origins and experience do not promise much: an orphan farmboy on an obscure desert planet on the fringes of the known world (for those inclined to read *Star Wars* as Christian allegory, Tatooine is the equivalent of the biblical Galilee, Jesus' own obscure home territory, and by the end of the film Luke Skywalker will emerge, given the sacrifice he offers, as something of a Christ figure). Furthermore, his character and temperament seem ill-suited for valor or selflessness: he's impatient, brash, short-tempered, dreamy, and full of wanderlust. Unfortunately, his dreams stretch no further than the macho ideals that his culture glorifies, and here the filmmaker undertakes a quiet but persistent strain of social criticism. Luke's great ambition in life is to attend fighter-pilot school to become a "top gun" and then go off to war. But he doesn't even have much hope for that because his uncle wants to keep him, quite literally, "down on the farm" for at least another year. Lucas deftly dramatizes Luke's unrest in a couple of brief scenes; most effective, though, is the wordless shot of Luke simply gazing at the horizon, yearning for who knows what as John Williams's music of plaintive longing adds texture and depth to the boy's frustrated desires.

Then comes this chance, out of nowhere, for more adventure and life than Luke ever imagined. There is the strange droid his uncle buys; the meeting with Obi-Wan and the secret message from a captive princess; Obi-Wan's history and his own father's history; the strange potent something called the Force (the audience has already seen it operate in

The Appeal and Popularity of *Star Wars*

Episode I — The Phantom Menace, the prequel to the *Star Wars* saga (the story that preceded the first filmed episode, entitled *Star Wars*), finally made it to the screen in 2000, and this super-hyped mega-event has prompted much rumination by movie critics and the standard oracles of culture. Two questions seem to have interested everybody: 1) Does George Lucas, after a seventeen-year hiatus, still have his magic movie wand? 2) What explains the lasting popular captivation with what skeptics deem just a tech-fancy space western? The answer to the first question is easy, and it is a fudging "well, maybe," because *The Phantom Menace* is in many ways very uneven, full of seriousness of purpose but lacking in the exuberance and warmth of earlier episodes. It is nonetheless impressive, especially as it somewhat ploddingly lays out the scenario that prepares for vital conflicts in the story to follow, which presumably is the story of how good turns bad, the perennial mystery of iniquity, of how evil happens in the first place.

The second question is more interesting and complex: it asks what Lucas supplies in this film and this whole saga that so many, young and old alike, seem to want so desperately. There are many small answers, and one big one. The many small ones have to do with the freshness and pizzazz of the film-making itself. Back in 1977, no one had ever seen anything close to the kind of intergalactic adventure that the original *Star Wars* offered. There had been Stanley Kubrick's *2001: A Space Odyssey* (1968); but as gorgeous as that looked and as magnificent as it sounded with all that Strauss, it was a pretty serious, even somber undertaking. With his own strokes of genius,

Obi-Wan's healing of Luke and Darth Vader's vengeance on a skeptic of its powers); and the possibility of leaving home to become, of all things, a "knight." That's a lot of news for a young fellow on an ordinary morning on Tatooine to absorb, and Luke is understandably wary. But, whatever reasons he has for his reluctance to follow Obi-Wan, they disappear when he returns home to find his aunt and uncle slain by the storm troopers of the Empire, who have tracked the escaped droid R2-D2 to this planet. Now nothing remains for Luke where he has grown up. Perhaps seeking revenge for the destruction of his home, Luke decides to ally himself with crazy Obi-Wan Kenobi.

226

Lucas meshed those cinematic splendors with an array of stock movie-genre conventions, added a host of story twists, and made them all come alive in John Williams's triumphal score. In crowded, airless theaters everywhere during that summer of 1977, hordes took in *Star Wars* and left with wonder and a good feeling, having been given a happy ending to make kids glad. Nothing profound, to be sure, but a sense of "whoa and wow — where'd that come from?"

Who had seen a plausible ray gun or blaster anywhere up until then, not to mention Lucas's full catalog of wild invention: light sabers, talking monster menageries, Mutt-and-Jeff droids, clunky hotrod space ships, feisty fighting princesses, tractor beams, giant worm gullets, storm troopers, furry eight-foot puppy-dog sidekicks, and, yes, black-caped, oxygenated bad guys with masks by Max Factor? Just the strange argot of names and terms in the film was fascinating enough: Wookiee, Millennium Falcon, Leia, Skywalker, Darth Vader, Obi-Wan Kenobi, Death Star, protocol droid, evil Empire — language that somehow got down to the feel of the worlds that *Star Wars* imagined. This was really cool new stuff and a very long way from how space tales had looked and felt in the past, even for Trekkies, with their odd thing for pudgy Captain Kirk and funny-eared, soulless geniuses. No one had seen anything like it before, not Buck Rogers or Arthur C. Clarke. The only fiction maker to come up with anything at once so original and so authentic, so fully made and fresh, was J. R. R. Tolkien in his medieval-like saga of hobbits, orcs, and wizards. Ultimately a parable of hope and renewal, *Star Wars* was more incantation than movie — a wondrously funny, fresh, and exultant tonic for an America wounded and weary in soul from assassinations, civil strife, war, and high crimes.

So begins Luke Skywalker's long struggle: it is on one level a splendid martial contest, with light sabers and star fighters and plain old guts, but that is not nearly the half of it, as the audience soon discovers. For the rest of the film Luke will roam the cosmos, suffer many close calls, and meet a host of new friends; but no part of his experience proves more crucial than his decision, in the midst of the star fighter attack on the Empire's Death Star, to turn off his targeting computer and trust the Force to guide his natural instincts. The result is triumph, and a grand victory celebration follows, one that will be reprised in even grander fashion at the end of *The Return of the Jedi* and also at the end of *Episode I — The Phantom*

Menace (1999), which is where the whole grand story starts (the Jedi knighthood's discovery of a young Anakin Skywalker, Luke's father).

The truth is, as *The Empire Strikes Back* (1980) makes clear, what tentative trust in the Force's reality Luke has found at the end of *Star Wars* is insufficient to defeat the dark might of the Empire. It sufficed to destroy the Death Star and foil the Empire in this one encounter, but that victory, both spiritual and military, amounts to little when measured by the scope of the military and spiritual struggle that lies ahead. This is especially true of Luke's understanding of the religious reality that infuses his world: he has much to learn about the Force, especially its very nature, to which the first installment in the trilogy offers but the barest introduction. In that film Lucas was concerned primarily with the necessity of belief in the numinous reality of the Force; that vital leap of faith allows Luke to destroy the Empire's Death Star. In *The Empire Strikes Back,* Lucas continues to push the necessity of that belief but expands his treatment of the Force to dramatize its essential character, elements only hinted at in the first film. This shows the Force as something other and more than mere force or supernatural power. Through the teachings of Yoda, the Jedi master who has trained Jedi novices for centuries, Lucas imbues the Force with a notably deeper and richer personality. It soon becomes clear — again to Luke's astonishment — that there is unfathomably more to the Force than mere power for human exploitation. The Force does not simply flow into people for them to use for whatever purposes, much like positive thinking's assertions about reservoirs of divine power that aid people if they simply believe in them.

The Force is far more than another weapon for the macho superhero to add to his blaster-belt; rather, it has a very demanding spiritual and moral content. Believing in the Force is easy enough, especially after witnessing its power, as Luke already has; it is quite another matter to understand and embrace — in short, to live — its deepest intentions. These purposes boil down to two inextricable components, though Lucas never uses these specific terms, no doubt for fear of making his script hackneyed, sentimental, or overtly moralistic. While the Force first counsels "faith" in the reality of its abiding presence and power, its inmost character is far more than power for human disposal. What it is really about is radical love for all things, a posture its devotees must take deeply into themselves if they wish to become full-fledged Jedis. Beyond all the blasters and monsters and space heroes, the genius and ultimately the lasting appeal of the *Star Wars* saga lies in Lucas's ability to dramatize the necessity, cogency, and poignance of this sacred existential posture in

228

both the lives of his characters and the history of their fictional galaxy. Ultimately, the history of the universe depends not on Luke Skywalker's physical brawn, combat prowess, or strategic wiliness but on the extent to which he has imbibed the lessons of love.

This emphasis gathers steam and clarity in the story of Luke's formal training for Jedi knighthood in *The Empire Strikes Back,* which is the most imaginative and visually stunning of the five *Star Wars* films so far. From an eerie ice planet invaded by giant attack walkers, the story leaps to its opposite, the steamy bog of Dagobah, the home of the solitary Yoda, the unlikeliest warrior-mentor-master ever concocted. Once again, these never-dreamt-of worlds took viewers by utter surprise and gave enormous delight when that movie came out. And here on Dagobah, Lucas shows for the first time just how weighty his intentions about myth, plot, and the significance of religious belief are, specifically as they play out in Luke's struggle. Far from being a superior Jedi hero, the impression given at the end of *Star Wars,* Luke is shown in *The Empire Strikes Back* as still very much the same callow youth he was at the beginning of his story back on Tatooine. And he is, to be sure, still very much a novice in opposing evil — and not a promising one at that. He has a great deal to learn, all of it spiritual, and his growth depends wholly on his comprehension and acceptance of the nature of the Force. The Force has moved from a largely magical plot gimmick, a *deus ex machina* contrivance, to a complex conception that within its posture of love demands an attitude of nonaggression — an odd, even paradoxical, stance for would-be warriors. It is emphatically clear that the only hope for combating the evil Emperor and his dastardly henchman, Darth Vader, lies in this posture of nonaggression.

The primary focus, then, of *The Empire Strikes Back* is the education of Luke Skywalker in the nature and ways of the Force, which in Lucas's vision are one and the same. Along the way, audiences not only learn more about the character of the Force, needless to say, but also see at length the character of Luke, the impatient angry one. The spirit of the dead Obi-Wan Kenobi (who sacrificed himself in *Star Wars* to help Luke) has told Luke to journey to a mysterious planet to seek a Jedi master named Yoda, teacher of candidates for the Jedi knighthood. Once there, Luke finds the second great surprise on his path to Jedihood, and it is one shared by viewers, since we have been influenced by many of the same glib attitudes about power and majesty that Luke has imbibed. If Luke is surprised by the *reality* of the Force in *Star Wars,* here he is surprised by its *character.* His typical childish notions of the Force as simple power and domination lead

229

him to expect a resplendent mighty warrior, a shining John Wayne figure. Instead, in his first lesson about the nature of the Force, he finds the unlikeliest of figures, the last sort of creature one would envision as a teacher of warrior knights, one who seems to be the very antithesis of power. This Jedi master stands two feet tall, is green, reptilian, has big pointed ears, frog-like eyes, and a raspy voice, and, as he limps along with a staff, is clearly aged. Living where and how he does, Yoda is notably humble and "unworldly," so much so that in his homely, comical looks and voice, his lack of physical might, and the obscure remoteness of his home he echoes the prophecies of Isaiah about the coming Messiah. If Yoda is indeed who he seems to be, then the last are indeed first, the humble are exalted, and the obscure are the luminaries.

This all becomes clear when, in that second great surprise in the saga, Yoda suddenly reveals himself as the Jedi master he is. Luke has allowed himself to be sheltered and fed by the impish creature because this troublesome little being, looking for all the world like an overgrown frog, has promised to take him to Yoda, the Jedi master. Luke has taken so little note of him that so far he hasn't even bothered to ask his name, even after Yoda has ministered to him, just as Obi-Wan did at the beginning of *Star Wars*. Luke is a slow learner, but the painful joke and lesson is on him when Yoda finally reveals himself, complaining aloud to Obi-Wan, whose spirit in turn answers. Upon hearing Obi-Wan's voice, Luke is for once dumbstruck as the camera cuts to Yoda: the small creature straightens up from his habitual stoop, and the camera takes in his resolute look of quiet, profound dignity. During this brief episode, Yoda's demeanor plays directly off Luke's — and the viewers' — glib presumptions about the nature of power. (The centrality of these character roles to the thematic core of the films justifies Lucas's extraordinary pains in keeping plot details absolutely secret until the film's release; much of his point would have been lost if audiences had known beforehand that the Jedi master was a frog.) The humble obscurity of Yoda speaks volumes about the nature of the Force that Luke must come to understand.

Luke's chagrin is just a foretaste of what is to follow. Yoda's lessons for knighthood consist, not of better sword play or karate, but of humility, patience, tolerance, calm, and trust, a group of traits starkly opposed to those Luke manifests and, to some extent, venerates. In effect, Luke must put on a new mind and see himself and the world as never before, or go further into a "larger world," as Obi-Wan Kenobi bade him in *Star Wars*. To succeed, Luke must put aside fear, anger, and aggression, which constitute, Yoda emphasizes, the sure path to the dark side and all the usual meanness of the world. Always, Yoda tells him — and Lucas repeats insistently in the subsequent films — these sensations and attitudes precede the act, the actual doing of evil. To feel these, then, is already to have started down the path that leads to evil, darkness, and damnation. This ethical-spiritual matrix Yoda puts most succinctly in *The Phantom Menace*, where he tells ten-year-old Anakin Skywalker, Luke's father, that "fear is the path to the dark side. Fear leads to hate, and hate leads to suffering." Here Lucas simply echoes Jesus' repeated counsel for spiritual purity in all aspects of life, from sexuality to hostility.

Along with this counsel of love for all things, Yoda advises Luke to revere the spiritual and intrinsic goodness of all life, which is an extension of recognizing the reality of spirit and the Force as continuous interdependent realities. In his most eloquent speech in *The Empire Strikes Back* — and perhaps in the whole saga — Yoda insists that we are not "crude matter" but "luminous beings," and Luke must arrive at the place where he embraces this truth. In Lucas's fictional universe, spirit controls the very limits of physical reality, and those trusting the Force, either its dark or light side, control and direct matter as they wish. Spirit runs the world, not physical size and might, as the tiny Yoda shows when he, by the power of his soul, raises Luke's submerged star fighter from its mucky home in a bog. During his long and difficult training with Yoda, Luke begins to absorb these truths, though he still has a long way to go before he can overcome the concentrated evil of the Emperor and Darth Vader. Lucas emphasizes Luke's great susceptibility to evil in numerous instances where Luke's impatience and anger defy the wisdom of Yoda. As Yoda initially points out, Luke is impatient like his own father was, the Jedi knight Anakin Skywalker, who was seduced by the dark side and became Darth Vader (as we come to learn in *The Empire Strikes Back*). The most striking example of Luke's vulnerability comes in his imagined confrontation with Darth Vader, in which Luke lops off Vader's head but sees behind Vader's mask his own face. It is a potent reminder — and an uncharacteristic departure from the surface simplicities of melodrama — that the enemy lies as much within us as without, and that poses a daunting moral and spiritual challenge.

Luke's apprenticeship ends when he chooses to interrupt his training with Yoda to rescue his friends Leia, Chewbacca, and Han, who have fallen into Vader's clutches. The difficulty with this decision, which is opposed by both Yoda and Obi-Wan, is that, with his training only partially completed, Luke must confront Vader without being fully prepared. In fact, Darth Vader has captured Luke's friends for the very purpose of using them as bait to lure this young apprentice into an encounter; he knows that Luke is his son and is "strong with the Force," and he wants to interrupt Luke's apprenticeship before his power and skills increase. When their meeting finally takes place, the match between them is close, for Luke has become a skilled and wily opponent. Vader succeeds only when he literally disarms young Luke and then, as the two stand on a windblown parapet, tries to lure him to the dark side by revealing that he is in fact Luke's father. Horrified at the revelation that this monster of evil is his father, Luke chooses death rather than to embrace evil, a potential for selflessness that forecasts the climax of *The Return of the Jedi*. That choice is a tribute to Luke's fast-growing maturity, especially when contrasted with the petulance of the young man who is initially worried about being late for dinner. Luke's self-sacrificial end is averted, however, when he is miraculously rescued — again, thanks to the power of the Force — by another one who, unbeknownst even to herself, shares in the lineage of the Force.

Finding Home

Nor did Lucas disappoint in the third episode of the initial trilogy. In *The Return of the Jedi* (1983), Lucas pulls off stunning surprises that retroactively illuminate and enrich the whole of the trilogy. Not only does that primary issue of Luke's maturation and fate, and of the Rebellion, arrive at a crisp resolution, but many related uncertainties are resolved and themes come to happy fruition. Lucas does this all in very plausible ways that no one anticipated. Indeed, only at the very end — that is, in the last ten minutes of six hours of film — does the ultimate focus of the saga become entirely clear. There has been enough, to be sure, to whet audience curiosity about what will happen next; but in *The Return of the Jedi*, Lucas's intergalactic leap in plotting gives his story a depth that moves it from amusing and affecting kid stuff to a mythic religious tale of lasting appeal. Finally, at the end of a long pilgrimage, Luke Skywalker gets it right, and that makes all the difference. Indeed, the conclusion of *The Return of the Jedi* explodes with a depth of meaning that no one thought possible. One way of getting at that is to examine the history and implications of Lucas's selection of a title for the last installment of the trilogy.

For a long time during production and pre-release hype, the movie was entitled *The Revenge of the Jedi;* indeed, posters with that title adorned the walls of many movie theaters. That seemed to be an unexceptional choice: the usual Hollywood formulaic happy climax, a standard "kill 'em all," justice-is-done conclusion. It fit well enough with what most viewers wanted and expected from the story Lucas had told up to that point: the good guys vanquish all the bad guys, sending Darth Vader and the Emperor to painful death and perdition. Still, to those who had been paying much attention to the struggles of Luke Skywalker and to the theology and code of the Jedi as laid out in *The Empire Strikes Back,* that "get even" recourse just did not make sense. After all, at the heart of the Jedi code lay a kind of quasi-pacifism: the Jedi never sought vindication, aggression, or revenge but used the Force only for defense. The Jedi used the Force to wish the world well and to protect its inherent goodness from destruction by evil. The apprehensions of devotees about the seeming departure from the theme of the saga that was implied by the title of the third episode were partly dispelled when, not long before its release, Lucas changed the title to the one we now have, and what a difference that makes.

Still, if the earlier title sounded frustratingly predictable and thematically contradictory, the new one seemed cryptic. The return of what Jedi? The story had none about to return: Obi-Wan Kenobi was dead, Jedi master Yoda was decrepit and never the physical match for Darth Vader, and brash Luke Skywalker was not yet a Jedi. So where was there a Jedi to return? One possibility was that a new Jedi knight would show up to supplant the aspiring Luke, who seemed so uncertain and rash in *The Empire Strikes Back.* There was the ancient Yoda's prophecy in *Empire* about yet another Jedi, another Skywalker, unknown to all, who possessed the potential to enter the Jedi knighthood and save the day if the immature, ill-prepared Luke should go the way of his traitorous father. The title meant, surely, that some new, old, or lost warrior, heretofore completely unknown, would emerge to take up the Jedi mantle and finally vanquish the dark Lord Vader and the vile Emperor. But others in the first two parts of the story seemed highly improbable, even preposterous for this challenge. Han Solo was still very much, as his name suggests, the posturing macho vagabond, and Lando Calrissian (Billy Dee Williams), another handsome scoundrel, just did not seem up to it. The Wookiee Chewbacca and the droids were never serious candidates (Jedi presumably need to be human, although rather special humans, as *Episode I — The Phantom Menace* later made clear). In hindsight, indeed, the matter of the title suggests that Lucas went far out of his way to encourage mistaken expectations, if only to teach viewers a lesson about hope and redemption. The truth is that nobody really got it, certainly no elite critics or reviewers, even though the revelation and the full power of surprise lay out in plain view right in the title itself, *The Return of the Jedi*, where Lucas told audiences all they needed to know about the likelihood of the marvelously improbable.

The most obvious candidate for a returning Jedi is the apprentice Jedi Luke Skywalker, who at the start of *Return* is looking and acting very much like a full-fledged Jedi, venturing into the habitat of Jabba the Hutt, the sadist monster grub and captor of Luke's sidekick, Han Solo. Luke performs impressively in this scrape, and audiences hope that he might have the right stuff after all. But then the dying Yoda tells him he has yet to pass one final test: he must face Darth Vader again before achieving full Jedi knighthood. With no one else seeming very suitable, the audience is stuck with Luke, even though he perhaps doesn't have the mettle. About halfway through *The Return of the Jedi*, Lucas complicates the story once again by making known the identity of the other potential Jedi foretold by Yoda: Princess Leia, the mysterious one whose identity comes as much as a surprise to her as to anyone. She is the "other Skywalker" and stands ready but unschooled in the Jedi knightcraft and wisdom necessary to joust with Vader. It says something unfavorable about audience attitudes concerning women that no one imagined that Leia would be a candidate for Jedi-hood or that a woman would be a galaxy savior, despite many early hints, especially at the end of *The Empire Strikes Back*, when she senses Luke's distress and initiates his rescue. Indeed, Leia has from the beginning seemed a far more suitable candidate than her impetuous brother.

With the revelation of Leia's identity, Lucas scored major points for surprise and for feminism, but the momentous surprise of the title comes in the very last scenes. It turns out that Lucas's allusion is not at all to the emergence of a new, uninitiated candidate for the holy Jedi brotherhood that ceased with the deaths of Obi-Wan Kenobi and Yoda. Another Jedi, now fallen and traitorous, still lives: the shrouded Darth Vader, servant of the evil Emperor and the father of the two potential Jedis (Luke and Leia are brother and sister, separated in childhood to protect them from their fallen father). The momentous surprise is that the fearsomely evil lord, Darth Vader himself, returns as a true Jedi. This radical reversal in devotion comes when Vader witnesses Luke's utter submission to the spiritual-moral heart of the Force, which is a mirror image of his own servile submission to the Emperor. It happens this way: midway through *Return*, Luke surrenders to Darth Vader, convinced that he will have to meet him again, as foretold by Yoda, but convinced also that there is still goodness lingering in his father and that he can be persuaded to forsake the malevolent Emperor before whom he abases himself. Vader himself rejects Luke's pleas, explaining in a voice touched with sorrow and remorse that Luke has no idea of the power of the dark side and that it is "too late" for him to turn back.

Darth Vader then brings his son to the Emperor, and in the final mortal conflict, the loathsome Emperor — his vile look and manner matching his moral stature — repeatedly tries to goad Luke into anger, hatred, and revenge, knowing full well that, if Luke so much as flirts with those attitudes, he has already gone far down the path to the dark side, as Yoda had warned. In the psycho-moral realm of the Force in *Star Wars*, and the New Testament, the deed inexorably follows the thought; morality is measured by spirit as much as by deed. Luke disciplines himself well, even though the Emperor has told him that the rebel forces led by Luke's friends are falling into a fatal trap that will kill them all (the partially completed Death Star is operational). Luke only caves in to his anger when Vader intuits that Leia is his missing daughter and says that he will seek her out and lure her to the dark side. Only then does Luke strike out in full fury, which is apparently permissible since he wishes to defend and protect, which Jedis are allowed to do.

In a lengthy combat with his father, he finally manages to disarm Vader, literally, just as Vader had earlier disarmed him. To his great credit, however, he then refuses the Emperor's offer to make his "hatred complete" by killing Vader and taking Vader's place at the Emperor's side. The Emperor even invites Luke to kill him, the Emperor, for that self-gratifying act would cost Luke — insofar as it is an act of aggression — his own soul. It is in this moment, finally, that Luke becomes a full-fledged Jedi, and he seems to know it. In a choice of solitary kenotic self-denial, and in full fidelity to the Force, Luke throws down his light saber and announces that he is "a Jedi, like my father before me." It is a gesture of faith, love, and sacrifice. Knowing that he has lost his chance to win Skywalker's soul, the Emperor executes Luke by sending wave after wave of lethal electrical current through him. The camera cuts regularly to bystander Vader as he watches both the agony of his son's loving self-sacrifice — a crucifixion really, and the trilogy's only graphic violence — and, in contrast, the Emperor's odious delight in torture and murder. In short, Luke chooses to die because he has at last comprehended and embraced the heart of Yoda's teachings: that the universe runs by love and that love should pervade all thought and action (for the theologically minded, it is a perfect rendition of the notion of substitutionary atonement).

235

His witnessing of Luke's strength, faithfulness, and care recalls Vader to the good person he once was as Anakin Skywalker, before his still-mysterious seduction to the dark side (Lucas depicts the beginning of this very process in *Episode I — The Phantom Menace* and *Episode II — The Attack of the Clones* [2002]). Seeing his son's willingness to die rather than use the power of the Force for aggression and murder, Vader musters the faint remnants of love and goodness of his days as a father and as a Jedi. On the verge of death himself, Darth Vader rises to destroy the Emperor in order to save his own son. In perfect symbolic appropriateness, the waves of electricity that fell on Luke now devour Vader and mortally wound the already weakened man. At the cost of his own life, Vader acts to save his son, and in doing so — as the last scene of *Return* makes clear — he is restored to full spiritual brotherhood with Obi-Wan and Yoda. In destroying the evil that first seduced him, Vader once again becomes a Jedi. Thus the title *The Return of the Jedi:* it points in a straightforward way to the transformation that no one guessed was likely or possible. Through the son's witness of love, the father is redeemed, and the father and son meet in reconciliation and true communion.

This is aptly symbolized by Vader's dying request that his son remove that stark black mask, itself a potent visual symbol, so he might at last see his son with "my own eyes" or, as 1 Corinthians 13 puts it in the rapturous image of reconciliation and intimacy, "face to face." As the son was willing to die for his father, the father in his last gesture willingly dies for his son. When Luke tells his mortally wounded father that he will die if he removes the mask and that he must get Darth Vader from the Death Star in order to save him, the hideously maimed old man, whose appearance is an apt visual reflection of his inner distortion, replies simply to his son, "You already have." Luke has given his father salvation and, as we soon see, redemption. In this expression of love, both father and son realize the good and holy identity for which they were made. Evil as manifested in the Empire and in Darth Vader has been defeated; goodness reigns.

Partly because the *Star Wars* saga is melodrama, and partly because human instinct tends to prematurely separate the sheep from the goats, the potential for the redemption of Darth Vader never crossed the well-set minds of most viewers. For some, the redemptive ending was not entirely plausible. The *Time* magazine reviewer, for example, thought it corny. But the very surprise it occasions effectively uncovers the bad manners of contemporary cynicism and hopelessness. That is admittedly a preachy point to make, but the effect of the ending of *The Return of the Jedi*, the unlikely return itself, pivots on the audience's usual gullibility about the way the world usually works, which is badly. Sinners, whores, and late grape-pickers all the same, contemporary imaginative habits are constrained to see judgment and doom, to turn away from the possibility of renewal.

The fullness of the redemption of Darth Vader, which is the final fruition of the motives and actions of the Force, is best seen in what happens in the last scenes of *The Return of the Jedi*. From the exploding Death Star and the Endor moon, where Leia and Han Solo await the return of Luke, the camera cuts abruptly to a gorgeous shot of the head of a burning torch against a black background. The camera moves with the torch as it ignites a funeral pyre where the body of Darth Vader lies, still attired in black helmet-mask and black cape. The camera cuts to Luke Skywalker, who holds the torch and watches the flames engulf the pyre and the body. Here light and fire burn in the darkness to consume darkness, an apt visual evocation of the first chapter of the Gospel of John, with its rhapsodic fugue on light and darkness. The camera stares for a long time at the fire consuming the darkness of evil, this ancient Christian symbol for purification (and in the work of modern poet T. S. Eliot). The camera tilts upward to the darkening Endor sky where, with still more imagery of light in the darkness, fireworks explode in celebration of the victory over the Empire. For the film's last scene the camera tilts down to take in the twilight Valley of the Ewoks, where small fires light many parties of celebration. At one of these we find the familiar crew of characters dancing and backslapping in celebration. Luke Skywalker arrives to hugs and congratulations from his sister and compatriots, including his old rival Han, who has finally come to understand that it is he, and not Luke, whom Leia wishes to marry.

Still mourning his dead father, Luke wanders off to view a consoling vision of two nearby shimmering figures, a ghostly Obi-Wan and Yoda, gentle and smiling; they are then joined by a third Jedi, someone not seen before in the film but also dressed in the monk's robes of the Jedi. Slowly it dawns on viewers that this unfamiliar face resembles the maimed suffering face of Darth Vader; indeed, it is he, but he now appears healed and renewed in the person of the redeemed Jedi Anakin Skywalker. The malevolent Lord Darth Vader is dead. Evil and death have not conquered; the good man who Vader once was lives again — forever. He joins the others to smile on Luke, who will hereafter always have with him these guiding presences, emblems and agents of the abiding care of the Force, which is love itself. A spiritual brotherhood reigns over all, giving solace and hope, pointing the way for the future.

Star Wars on DVD

Fox and Lucasfilm finally released the original *Star Wars* trilogy (1977-1983) on DVD in September 2004. Before that, the best source for those films was the out-of-print laser nine-disk boxed set called the "Widescreen Collectors Edition" (of the "Definitive Collection"). While this edition is now hard to obtain, it remains a model for the use of supplementary materials. Fortunately, the set includes a detailed printed guide to the audio commentary by various members of the production team, mainly by Ken Ralston and Dennis Murren, and to the supplementary materials that accompany each film. These range from interviews with Lucas and actors to award ceremonies, and these supplementary materials sometimes even have audio commentary on their significance. A large coffee-table book by Charles Champlin, *George Lucas: The Creative Impulse, Lucasfilm's First Twenty Years* (1992), is included in the set.

Typically, the laser disks, a now extinct forerunner of DVD, display the films with an immediacy and freshness not available on VHS versions. The first two installments in the second trilogy, *The Phantom Menace* and *The Attack of the Clones,* are available on DVD with audio commentary by Lucas and special effects directors. Supplementary materials include a rich array of featurettes on different aspects of the productions, deleted scenes, theatrical trailers, and production stills.

The New Creation

The central story in the *Star Wars* epic culminates in these sequences of redemption and reconciliation, completing and clarifying the thematic heart of Lucas's trilogy. As Luke finds reconciliation and intimacy with his godforsaken father, the ragtag assembly of characters ends up forming a new family of mutuality that looks a lot like what the New Testament envisions as the constituency of the family of God. From the very start, the high purpose of the Republic draws together a host of strange and unlikely prospects into one huge cooperative crew that moves increasingly toward interdependence and caring. In the first episode, for example, Obi-Wan is a mentor and father to Luke Skywalker, the orphan from podunk, as they go off together to rescue the endangered Princess Leia and — beknownst to and undreamt by childish Luke — to rescue

238

the Republic and, with that, the very fate of the galaxy. For transport, Obi-Wan and Luke hire Han Solo, a smuggler with a price on his head in the underworld. A prototypical prodigal scalawag, a hard-bitten and self-interested loner, as his name reflects, Solo reluctantly comes to a new vision of life beyond self-interest. His tough-guy prowess demands that he rescue Luke and others from tight scrapes; yet he is overwhelmed when the same is done for him, when, in *The Return of the Jedi*, Luke and his compatriots risk life and limb to retrieve him from Jabba the Hutt's pit of torture. The gang had earlier picked up a man of dubious morals, Lando Calrissian, buccaneer and black-marketer. So it goes, time after time.

Perhaps there is no greater surprise than the abundant help the group receives from the unlikeliest of all allies, the diminutive Ewoks, the ingenious teddy-bear race whose backwoods booby traps reduce the high-tech Empire troops to helplessness. The cute and furry little beasts, an unlikely source of any help, prove as game and vital in defeating the Empire as Han Solo and his machismo. Wookiees, droids, Ewoks, crooks, princesses, con men, orphans, and priests — all join up to smite the foul and unholy Empire. All this wild unexpected collaboration by natural antagonists is beautifully portrayed in the closing celebrations on Endor, where Ewoks and droids dance with humans and Wookiees. They have come to know one another as the compatriots they were made to be. More than that, brother now knows sister, and son now knows father. The sky explodes in gladness, as trust and harmony again pervade the world, making it a home for all.

Past and Future

The future of the *Star Wars* saga lies in its past. The original *Star Wars*, now officially entitled *Episode IV — A New Hope*, the first of the original trilogy to be filmed, showed how light comes out of darkness. The trilogy now underway shows how darkness emerges from light, how people and societies come to lose harmony and hope; it is George Lucas's attempt to explain how the knighthood of Jedis was dislodged and the old Republic fell into the "dark times" under the tyranny of the Empire. But he does not in the least diminish those religious elements so prominent in the first trilogy. In *Episode I — The Phantom Menace*, Lucas makes more obvious and heavier still the mythic freight at the heart of his adventure. We begin at the apprenticeship of a younger Ben Obi-Wan Kenobi (Ian McGregor), the old man who dies in the first *Star Wars* film. He becomes the mentor of the boy Anakin Skywalker, another obscure kid on the desert planet of Tatooine who is strong with spiritual potential, just as his son after him will be. More portentous still is the possibility that the boy Anakin is of mysterious virgin birth and might be one to fulfill ancient prophecies about the coming of a potent savior figure. Indeed, the ten-year-old shows remarkable intelligence and physical prowess. Still, the Jedi Council, headed by a relatively youthful Yoda, is uncertain of the wisdom of accepting the boy as a Jedi novice-apprentice, given his age (he's too old even at age ten), the murkiness of his background, and his personal volatility. That is where *Episode I* ends, a clear set-up piece for the conflict that follows in *Episode II — The Attack of the Clones* (2002). In that prequel Lucas further explores the personal sources that make Anakin Skywalker, now a young man rashly in love with the Princess, susceptible to the vile Emperor and the dark side of the Force. Presumable the still untitled *Episode III*, slated for release in 2005, will dramatize how Anakin finally succumbs to the blandishments of hate that comprise the dark side.

In attempting to create an enticing prequel for a movie myth that just about everybody knows and very many downright love, Lucas set for himself a great challenge. Those first films were so good — and now are so legendary — that Lucas has had a difficult time measuring up, especially to the expectations of *Star Wars* junkies waiting with bated breath to dissect every bit of the endless pre-release gossip and hype. To its credit, *The Phantom Menace* tells its story pretty efficiently, dispensing with the frequent lengthy diversions that diluted the dramatic impact of the central conflict in *The Return of the Jedi*. Yet, while there is much to appreciate in this first of a new trilogy for the twenty-first century, especially its visual splendor, it has by and large fallen rather flat because it lacks the steady humor and visual wit of the earlier films. The primary figure for comedy, a new creature named Jar Jar Binks, is difficult to understand and, compared to the Wookiees and droids, painfully unfunny. Nor is the film as effective in establishing another ragtag "family" of interdependent relationships, which provided much of the warmth and emotional magnetism of the first trilogy; we end up caring less about these creatures and their collective fate than we did about those in the first *Star Wars* films. Some of that lack no doubt comes from Lucas's strenuous effort to explain the origins of later characters, and so far neither they nor the crises that will bring them together have reached full bloom. The first *Star Wars* film started *in medias res,* the middle of a pivotal crisis, while the *Phantom* prequel is busy constructing the pieces that will

George Lucas and Religion

For George Lucas, as becomes clear in the *Star Wars* story, imagery, and verbal text, the Force is an ever-present supernatural reality whose inmost character is a love that bids all to heed and embrace its redemptive call. Its sacred purpose is to bring everything — the whole of creation, in fact — to reconciliation, and thus to harmony and felicity, as the last wondrous scenes of *The Return of the Jedi* so emphatically demonstrate. Renewal and restoration make a difficult destination, and people struggle mightily, as the history of Luke Skywalker illustrates, to arrive at that triumphant end. Fear, anger, and hatred — the very essence of darkness itself — must be excised from the self, and love must take its place.

In this strange and demanding pilgrimage, the Force mysteriously cooperates, pushing and shoving the unlikeliest of people in the most unexpected ways toward remarkable ends. For Lucas, as for Christian apologist Frederick Buechner, in his remarkable little book *Telling the Truth: The Gospel as Tragedy, Comedy, and Fairy-Tale* (1977), the tragic world is full of surprise, especially of a heart-splitting joy that argues that everything is infinitely more mysterious than the skeptical empiricism of modernism allows. As Yoda declares midway through the first trilogy, and then promptly demonstrates by lifting Luke's ship out of the swamp, we are creatures of spirit, "luminous beings, not this crude matter," and we live in a world bound and pervaded by spirit. Lucas cloaks all of this in the trappings of science fiction/fantasy lingo about energy and the like. But the gist of it is Yoda's declaration, and everything depends on one's recognition of the reality of the Force. Only by that means does the soul complete the arduous journey home. To be sure, Lucas takes elements from other world religions; but the central terms and structure of his story, as well as his verbal and visual language — all dramatizing the reality of redemption — suggest that Lucas's God in large part resembles the one depicted in Judaism and Christianity.

lead to that decisive moment. The crisis it constructs — again, the peril of another young female royal — is rather tame, visually static, and narratively arcane. In a way, having experienced the pleasures of the original three films, we know too much for Lucas's own good. Overall, though, *The Phantom Menace* is a pretty good adventure, a real genuine kid movie for all ages, full of visual magic, moral contest, and anticipation — for

241

the next *Star Wars* movie. That next one, *The Attack of the Clones,* just about killed interest in the series, due to poor casting, even poorer direction, and pedestrian camera work. It is clear that, while Lucas is a great myth-maker and story-shaper, he sadly lacks facility as a director (Irwin Kershner directed *Empire,* and Richard Marquand directed *Jedi*).

Mostly, though, we already know what we need to about the central mystery of the *Star Wars* saga, both present and past. At its core is a complex and fetching portrait of what Lucas in his fantasy world labels the Force, by which he means, as he has said directly in interviews, God. With studied restraint, he does not go so far as to specify which God he is depicting; but his prime purpose, he says, is to show his audiences what it is like to believe in God.[1] More than ever, as *The Phantom Menace* makes clear, Lucas seems intent on making that goal overt so that audiences cannot mistake his point. Indeed, it is easy to see Lucas trying to construct his own sci-fi versions of J. R. R. Tolkien's *The Lord of the Rings* or C. S. Lewis's protracted fantasy in *The Chronicles of Narnia.* Some conservative religious people have fretted extensively about supposed "New Age" influences. But it is best to take the series as Lucas intends it: an exploration of what it is like to live amid invisible realities that shape individual lives and that care, radically, for the fate of this whole world.

1. *Time* (April 26, 1999).

Films Written and Directed by George Lucas

Star Wars: Episode III (2005)
Star Wars: Episode II — Attack of the Clones (2002)
Star Wars: Episode I — The Phantom Menace (1999)
Star Wars (1977)
American Graffiti (1973)
THX 1138 (1971)

Additional Films Written by Lucas
Radioland Murders (1994) (story)
Indiana Jones and the Last Crusade (1989) (story)
Willow (1988) (story)
Captain Eo (1986) (story)
The Empire Strikes Back (1985) (story)
Indiana Jones and the Temple of Doom (1984) (story)
Star Wars: Episode VI — Return of the Jedi (1983) (story)
Raiders of the Lost Ark (1981) (story)
Star Wars: Episode V — The Empire Strikes Back (1980) (story)
More American Graffiti (1979)

CHAPTER 9

THE SUPER-MAN

Displaying the Incarnation in *Superman*

It finally happens, almost exactly halfway through, a whole hour and a quarter in. Viewers know it's going to happen sometime, sooner or later. After all, the movie is *Superman* (1978), and there really can't be a flick about him without him showing up eventually. It's a long wait: the film-makers do a lot to stoke expectation even while clearly eager to bring the hero out of the boy and the cape out of the suit. Despite this hyped antic-ipation, and though audiences had a brief glimpse of Superman leaving his "fortress of solitude," the sudden appearance of Supe to do his air-borne hero rescue of Lois Lane erupts in heart-stopping surprise. Part of that jubilation (or is it relief?) comes from the long and very necessary preparatory story of the life of young Kal-El, the sole survivor of the late planet Krypton and the adopted son of the childless Kents of rural wher-ever. Viewers wait, in a way, for their own good, getting to know the im-patience of unrealized promise.

Still another reason for that measure of "joy" — that "catch of the breath" or "beat and lifting of the heart," as J. R. R. Tolkien put it — is that by the time Superman shows up, viewers have learned about the kind of world where he makes his appearance.[1] At its heart, or lack of it, is a weary and befuddled "collective humanity," a species that lives a be-wildering mixture of comedy and sadness, passion and cruelty, dreams of bliss and harrowing tragedy. In this world, kids are mean, and fathers and planets die young; and in Metropolis, that very frazzled human city, the best are either naive or confront their lives with measured cynicism,

---

1. *The Monsters and the Critics and Other Essays*, ed. Christopher Tolkien (Boston: Houghton, 1984), p. 154.

as does blustery Perry White, editor of the *Daily Planet*. The viewer gets the sense throughout that just about all people in this world are but a half-breath away from drowning in a soup of deep woe, either through their own doing or through the way life treats them. Indeed, this is a vale of quiet desperation always on the verge of tears. Surprisingly, in this comic-book superhero fantasy, there's a good deal of tough realism about the plight of humanity and its darkness; that "verisimilitude" was, apparently, part of director Richard Donner's vision for the film from the very start (see discussion of audio commentary on DVD in sidebar).

A good deal of the success of *Superman* lies in its affecting portrait of various kinds of woe, but then also in its wonderfully agile and witty movement from that painful real world of fear and sorrow to a happy comic-book realm where hope abides and everything might just turn out okay in the end. To a large extent, the latter works because of the former. As Frederick Buechner suggests in *Telling the Truth*, the sweetness of the good news when it finally comes depends to a large extent on one's intimate experience of the sorrowfulness of the bad news. To this end, the filmmakers take great care to show enough real human tragedy and grief so that when the palpable superhero does finally show up with hope, viewers feel that shimmering deep-down thrill, that profound heart-quake, of what it is like to realize instantly the improbable dream of in-the-flesh supernatural deliverance from humankind's tear-sodden befuddlement. And so dire and constant is the latter, though displayed with both poignance and comedy, that it will indeed take some sort of miraculous intervention to rescue humanity from its sad fix. So when the superhero does finally show up, we not only expect it but welcome it with open arms.

Superman is, to be sure, thorough-going fantasy; but the fantasy, as with *Star Wars*, is neither escapist nor Pollyannaish. Again, as Tolkien explained, good fantasy literature does not by any means "deny the existence of . . . sorrow and failure." Rather, contends Tolkien, "the possibility of these is necessary to the joy of the deliverance; it denies (in the face of much evidence, if you will) universal final defeat." Only in knowing the harrowing pains of tragedy can anyone apprehend the "fleeting glimpse of Joy" that lies "beyond the walls of the world, poignant as grief."[2] And then there is the disclosure itself, that grand high comedy of transfiguration that is at once hilarious, preposterous, and exhilarating.

From start to finish, both *Superman: The Movie* and its sequel, *Super-*

2. Tolkien, p. 153.

Superman (1978)

Studio:	Warner Bros.
Producers:	Pierre Spengler, Ilya Salkind,
	Charles F. Greenlaw
Screenwriters:	Mario Puzo, David Newman,
	Leslie Newman, Robert Benton
Director:	Richard Donner
Cinematographer:	Geoffrey Unsworth
Production Designer:	John Barry
Editor:	Stuart Baird

Cast

Marlon Brando	Jor-El
Christopher Reeve	Superman/Clark Kent/Kal-El
Margot Kidder	Lois Lane
Gene Hackman	Lex Luthor
Ned Beatty	Otis
Jackie Cooper	Perry White
Glenn Ford	Jonathan Kent

man II, shot mostly simultaneously, are campy but serious fun. In the first, there are broad hints all around to prepare the way and whet the appetite. And it's worth the wait. Few sequences in movie history rival the wild magic of the moment when the bumbling *Daily Planet* reporter, the "mild-mannered" Clark Kent (Christopher Reeve), metamorphoses into a palpable rescuer of humans in their peril and distress: Lois hanging from a helicopter that is dangling from a skyscraper; those threatened by a madman who wants to sink most of California; a whole planet taken over by invaders exiled from Krypton *(Superman II)*; and even someone as humble and insignificant as a small girl whose cat is stuck up in a tree. There's hope and help, a new "friend" to humankind, as Supe himself puts it to Lois Lane (Margot Kidder). And he saves them from more than physical peril, as the slow redemption of Lois demonstrates.

The grand surprise, when it bursts forth — a lesson to all not to underestimate anybody — is made the more emphatic and heart-rending by what we've seen heretofore of Clark Kent, the doofus clown from whom

Valerie Perrine	Eve Teschmacher
Phyllis Thaxter	Martha Clark-Kent
Susannah York	Lara
Jeff East	Young Clark Kent
Marc McClure	Jimmy Olsen

Academy Awards

Special Achievement	Les Bowie, Colin Chilvers, Denys Coop,
in Visual Effects:	Roy Field, Derek Meddings, Zoran Perisic

Additional Academy Award Nominations

Sound:	Gordon K. McCallum, Graham Hartstone,
	Nicolas LeMessurier, Roy Charman
Editing:	Stuart Baird
Original Score:	John Williams

Although very successful at the box office, *Superman* did not do well on the awards circuit, mainly because it was seen as a comic-book/television rip-off pitched toward kids. And in 1978 it was up against a great number of very good, certifiably serious films, including *The Deer Hunter, Coming Home,* and *Heaven Can Wait.*

the caped wonder will emerge. Indeed, the delight of finally seeing Superman's superheroism is made all the greater by the comedy of Clark Kent's ineptitude. Up to the moment of Superman's appearance in Metropolis, the Clark Kent we've seen is not so much an ordinary fellow as he is ever so much less than ordinary; it is difficult to imagine how this fumbling and inept person could possibly be Superman. What we've seen of his whimpish youth is not much cause for hope; and uncertainty only heightens once Clark Kent appears in Metropolis at the *Daily Planet.* Even though editor Perry White (Jackie Cooper) thinks Kent possesses a "snappy prose style" and is the "fastest typist" he's ever seen, young Clark is personally just plain clownish, a bumbling chaos of ineptitude, both physical and social, one who seems flummoxed by the simplest obstacles, such as negotiating any kind of door.

The façade is a brilliant "cover," and this movie version of Clark Kent, markedly less competent than the ordinary and pleasant fellow of the 1950s television serial, is a brilliant creation by the screenwriters,

247

Superman on DVD

The Warner Video 2001 DVD edition of *Superman: The Movie* is a model for DVD production. The video and audio qualities are exceptional, especially with its digital transfer and remixed digital audio. In addition, there is an entertaining and informative audio commentary by director Richard Donner and "creative consultant" Tom Mankiewicz, who apparently gave the multi-versioned script a final rewrite. The disk also includes twelve scenes deleted from the original, ranging from the very brief and incidental to a further development of Lex Luthor to a long conversation between Superman and his father following his first appearance in Metropolis. Of special interest (and fun) are numerous screen tests. An early test has an entirely unmuscled Christopher Reeve, showing the clear difference between the pre-Supe Reeve and the actual Supe. (Reeve spent many months lifting weights before and during the shooting of *Superman* and *Superman II;* the two films were shot simultaneously, and some early takes had to be re-shot in order not to disrupt visual continuity in the film). Also included are some recently discovered screen tests of actresses for the role of Lois, including one by Stockard Channing and another by Margot Kidder. The impact an actor can have on a role becomes quite clear. And last, there are three documentaries on the making of *Superman,* giving particular attention to the special effects that won an Academy Award. Of course, there's the movie itself, 154 minutes of abundant humor, deft acting, and metaphysical hijinks.

costumers, and, most of all, by Christopher Reeve himself, whose splendid physical acting and nuanced manipulation of voice and face make the Chaplinesque Kent plausible. This persona as clown is a far cry from what anyone might expect of a would-be superhero. Contrast the various brooding Bruce Waynes of the *Batman* series (1989, 1992, 1995) or the sweet Peter Parker of *Spiderman* (2002). Concealing the identity and putting on a charade, yes, but this? Then again, less of this masquerade would no doubt have revealed Kent's identity to the canny intuitions of Lois Lane (in *Superman II* she catches on). Furthermore, that very gaping disjunction between the shambling Kent and his super alter ego imparts, when the disclosure at last comes, the great heart-springing delight. It is ultimately a song of hope: if this can happen to him, the befuddled klutz, then there's hope for anyone, and anything can happen.

There's no understating the measure of drama and exhilaration within what is perhaps the finest comic moment in a golden age of American film, 1970s American cinema. For a full two minutes the audience has watched the realistic and scary events culminating in Lois Lane's hanging by a phone cord from a helicopter dangling from the top of the *Daily Planet* building. This is an apt metaphor for the fragility inherent in the human predicament: people hanging onto safety and sanity by a mere string. The stumblebum reporter Clark Kent emerges from the *Daily Planet* tower to find Lois's purse on the sidewalk, fallen from the helicopter dangling above. He instantly recognizes it as hers because he has earlier, with his x-ray vision, observed its contents: "Ten dollars, two credit cards, a hairbrush, and a lipstick." He looks up, concludes that it is Lois dangling from the helicopter, and immediately starts to run toward the camera, the first beats of John Williams's magnificent score beginning to come through the noise of the excited crowd of onlookers. Kent stops in front of a boothless public telephone, looks the device up and down, does a double-take, and dismisses it as an unsuitable place to shed his suit for the cape (in the 1950s TV serial, Kent relied on the nearest enclosed phone booth, the only kind of phone booth at that time, for a quick changeover). From across the street, the camera watches Kent begin to sprint for the cover of a building, and in the next moment the full majesty of what Clark Kent has been hiding for exactly half the story suddenly emerges. Transformation happens. Instead of being hunched and maladroit, Kent now runs with shoulders and head thrown back, chest and neck bursting with resolve and power, and as he crosses the street to run straight toward the camera, he tears open his dress shirt to expose the "S" on his now expansive chest. For the first time since the credits, Williams's majestic score reaches orchestral fullness to celebrate the transfiguration.

And it is all done in high comedy. Finally, Kent spins a revolving door and emerges in his cape, chats politely with an incredulous observer, and rockets upward to grab the falling Lois and then to grasp the plummeting helicopter — one-handed. "Don't worry, miss, I've got you," says Superman to the astonished Lois, and her astonished perplexity echoes the viewers' own: "Who's got *you?*" There is the smack of pure kid-happy elation that this frog is a prince after all. No matter the joke, or the fantasy, the message is clear: in the midst of the peril and despair that hounds people everywhere, there is at long last cause for hope; more than that, there is this appearance here and now of tangible help for the human mess, as utterly improbable as that may seem. There can be no better news than that; nor can there be greater deep-down satisfaction for the world-weary, whether child or adult, for this is what humans at their core wish the world to be.

"Who are you?" The Riddle of the Divine

Exactly what sort of hope this is — and it is here that the success of the first two *Superman* films lies — comes clear in the narrative design of the original. Like the other enormously popular fantasy/science-fiction tales of our time, such as *E.T.* and the ever-unfolding *Star Wars*, *Superman: The Movie* and *Superman II* are imbued with all sorts of religious freight, though it is ingeniously and wittily disguised. The appeal of the first Supe film rests in large part on its deftly "cloaked" retelling of the Christ story, Western culture's central narrative of fall, sacrifice, transformation, triumph, and return to Edenic harmony. As usual, the filmmakers do it through fable, as the introduction to this section spells out. The fact that the substance of the Jesus story can still elicit such waves of delight and heartfelt elation says two things about efforts to communicate the well-worn and by now hackneyed story of the New Testament Gospels: first, the tremendous need for narrative freshness, and second, that this much-abused old story still retains an enormous amount of lasting fire, if only told with that freshness.

How innocuous the story has become is apparent in the fact that all kinds of people, many of them lifelong Christians, took great pleasure in the tale without recognizing it for what it was, even though the filmmakers fell all over themselves laying out hints concerning the source of this very modern superhero's life. And these viewers left the theaters more buoyant than they were after any church service. It is no less amazing that if many viewers, religious and secular alike, had been told beforehand that *Superman* was a Jesus story — significantly, not *the* Jesus story — most would not have bothered to go see it.

The best brief designation for the shape and substance of these contemporary religious fables, one that applies equally well to Spielberg and Lucas, is "christomorphic," a term devised by Roman Catholic film scholar Neil Hurley in an essay on "cinematic transfigurations of Jesus."[3] Hurley observes that in a number of enormously popular films, the central dramatic progression depicts the protagonist moving from

---

3. Hurley, "Cinematic Transfigurations of Jesus," in *Religion in Film*, ed. John R. May and Michael Bird (Knoxville: University of Tennessee Press, 1982), pp. 61-78.

an initial position of obscurity and lowliness to ascend through a tribulation-filled narrative to some sort of savior status, whether as actual rescuer of the distressed and imperiled or as an inspiration to a band of followers after a sacrificial death. Hurley's paradigm emphasizes the improbability or unlikelihood of such humble figures assuming any kind of salvific role; consequently, their ascent, typically against imposing odds, elicits surprise and elation at their triumph, followed by gratitude and hope, for if the likes of these can succeed, then no one is lost or foreclosed from the goodness of life. Indeed, these fables usually become parables of hope. Hardly any single film, unless it is *E.T.*, fits this mold better than *Superman*.

The filmmakers take enormous care to sustain and embellish a specifically Christian theme straight through to the very end; and this same care, along with wit and ingenuity, accounts for much of the film's enormous success. In this regard, *Superman* is far more than a pastiche of portentous allusions, pious claptrap, and melodrama, which are usually the results of Christians' trying to make popular films or of pop-culture, myth-making movies such as *The Matrix*. In the case of the first two *Superman* films, which were shot simultaneously, Superman as a Christ figure is not a random allusion or image simply pasted over the top of displays of special effects or old-style heroism. Rather, in what is a rare accomplishment in Hollywood, the whole of the film serves to elucidate and impart the surprise, wonder, and delight of the fantastic possibility of an incarnation of divine love itself. And that characterization is no simple miracle-working trickster in a cape or spider webs but a notion of God that features an extravagantly loving servant who comes out of nowhere, whether it be Krypton or Kansas, to suffer and triumph for bedraggled human creatures. To the filmmakers' credit, they do indeed, in Frederick Buechner's words, "get the joke," the high humor of the Incarnation, "the hilarious unexpectedness" of the impossible actually happening.[4] Most of this gleeful christomorphic "work" in *Superman* comes at pivotal moments in which the filmmakers borrow freely, and usually with great wit, from biblical language and events to shape and deepen the history of Kal-El/Clark Kent/Superman.

Five sequences from the beginning to the end merit attention, and several of those at some length: (1) the departure farewell from Krypton; (2) the arrival and discovery on earth; (3) the brief interlude in the arctic

---

4. *Telling the Truth: The Gospel as Tragedy, Comedy, and Fairy-Tale* (San Francisco: Harper, 1977), p. 61.

desert; (4) the emergence in Metropolis; and finally, (5) the triumph in reversing history itself.

Leaving Home

It all starts, as any full-blown Christ-story does, with the mysterious circumstances surrounding the hero's origin, circumstances that are usually both royal and tragic. In the Bible, Jesus is divine, about as royal as one can be, but his difficult task on earth is to rescue a benighted humanity from itself, and that will cost him mightily, "not less than everything," as T. S. Eliot calls the sacrifice in *The Four Quartets*. That sort of trouble seems to play double for Kal-El in *Superman*. Not only will his servanthood on earth cost him plenty, as *Superman II* dramatizes (though not quite the full death and descent Jesus endures); but the circumstances of Kal-El's birth and infancy on Krypton are as sad as they could be, loudly echoing those surrounding Jesus' birth: stable, exile, and particularly Herod's Slaughter of the Innocents. The screenwriters seem to conflate the biblical Fall and the advent of messiahship. For one thing, Kal-El himself seems born to a manifold fall: evil has come to the previously idyllic Krypton. *Superman* begins, somewhat oddly, with the trial on Krypton of three aristocratic villains who, in marked parallel to the biblical Fall in Eden, sought to grab full control of the democratic planet. This utopian planet has been disturbed, and necessity demands the exile of the unholy trinity. However majestic technologically, morally, and religiously, the world into which Kal-El is born is flawed, though still vastly superior to earth, and in *Superman II*, Superman will contend directly with these exiled villains (in fact, the good he does at the end of the first film inadvertently frees the three from their captivity).

Worse still for Kal-El personally is the imminent demise of his home, specifically the physical destruction of the planet Krypton that will kill all those who remain, including his parents. To avert the same fate for their son, Jor-El (Marlon Brando) and Lara (Susannah York) choose to send him on a three-year voyage through space to the planet earth, whose environment will allow not only survival but mastery. Clearly, then, Kal-El himself will begin life as an exile and, worse still, an orphan whose parentage is entirely unknown to either his adoptive parents or himself (Mary and Joseph at least had explanatory visits from angels). When he does finally land on earth after his three-year voyage, it is in a remote and obscure place that — with a nod to Frank L. Baum —

looks a lot like Kansas: empty, flat, and remote, more or less the equivalent of the biblical Galilee, a place for which Jesus' Jewish contemporar-
ies had nothing but contempt. (The location of these scenes of Clark
Kent's youth is actually Calgary, Alberta, Canada). Fittingly, he is
adopted by humble parents, themselves childless, and his own adolescence is fraught with confusion about his origins, his remarkable abilities, and his purpose.

Needless to say, all this time the audience knows more about young
Kal-El, alias Clark Kent, than he does. Thanks to the title, everyone
knows that this uncertain young fellow will become the fabled superhero,
the man of steel, faster than a speeding bullet, able to leap tall buildings
in a single bound, and also, probably, the world's "fastest typist." Still, if
the audience is paying attention and is attuned to biblical language and
concepts, they cannot but suspect he is intended to be much more than
simply the next virtuous super-fellow, a la Batman and Spiderman.

From the start, the filmmakers broadcast their christomorphic intent. His youth is far more than a very powerful human being who will
do good deeds, and his origins show it: the first shots of Krypton show a
place that has but the faintest resemblance to anything earthly. The
whole thing, from costumes to interiors, is splendid production design,
and while it may not be heaven itself, it surely suggests what a mildly futuristic one might look like. All is science fiction: surreal, pure angular
form, pure white, and amid the pervasive eerie whiteness of the set, the
attire of the "good" characters does in fact actually glow, dressed as they
are in iridescent white (their costumes were made of the same highly reflective fabric that movie screens are made of). And none more so than
Jor-El, the white-haired and white-suited father of Superman, who belongs to the leadership council of the planet. Brando gives his speeches
dignity and emotion, pausing often and savoring his words, and throughout he pitches his voice to its lower, more resonant registers to add
gravitas and rhetorical force. And when he arrives at his benedictory farewell to the infant son who rests, appropriately, in a star-shaped capsule
bound for another world, his language turns to that of the King James Bible, which was screenwriter Tom Mankiewicz's intent (see sidebar for
commentary on Superman DVD). Indeed, saying the words he does,
Brando ends up sounding and looking an awful lot like God envisioned
by the Jewish-Christian tradition, albeit a bit British. Added to Brando's
imposing physicality, the voice seems to emphasize the paradoxical center of the Christian God, a transcendent being whose attributes are simultaneously majesty and tender lovingkindness.

What the look and voice does not make clear, the words unequivocally do, exploring in sophisticated terms the mysterious notion at the heart of the Christian conception of God: the Holy Trinity, the idea that the godhead, while one and unitary, is also in fact a co-indwelling of three distinct persons or personalities — God the Father, Jesus Christ the Son, and the Holy Spirit (who later in *Superman* gets into the act as the abiding green crystal that accompanies Kal-El to earth). Achingly delivered by Brando, Jor-El's last living words to his earth-bound son (he will reappear later by means of memory in the crystal) lay this all out, and they resonate throughout the rest of the story:

> You will travel far, my little Kal-El. We will never leave you, even in the face of our deaths. The richness of our lives shall be yours. All that I have, all that I have learned, everything that I feel, all this and more, I bequeath you, my son. You'll carry me inside you all the days of your life. You will make my strength your own, see my life through your eyes, as your life will be seen through mine. From the son comes the father, and the father the son. This is all I . . . all I can send you, Kal-El.

The effect is to imbue the child Kal-El and the whole ensuing drama with an additional frame of meaning, one that is more specific and precise than are other popular film fantasies that have some christomorphic suggestions, such as *Terminator II* and *The Matrix*. And if there is any doubt about who this Kal-El/Superman really is, Jor-El's crystal-bound words to his son shortly before the thirty-year-old rejoins his earthly world tell the whole of the tale, so to speak: "They can be a great people, Kal-El; they wish to be. They only lack the light to show the way. For this reason, above all, their capacity for growth, I have sent them you, my only son."

The language of light, redemption, spiritual aspiration, and, most of all, of biblical messiahship — "my only son" clearly being cribbed from the famous John 3:16 passage ("For God so loved the world that he sent his only begotten son . . .") — fastens clearly and tightly to the Christ story. The sequence not only supplies parents and son with enormous affective depth, namely, heartfelt love, but ascribes the same to whatever divinity they manifest. And that is only a small part of what distinguishes *Superman*.

Jor-El's grief-laden exposition of the Christian mystery of the Trinity makes an appealing initiation into both the narrative and emotional

Played by Marlon Brando, Superman's father, Jor-El, not only looks and intones like God but speaks King James' English.

depths of the film's incarnational theme. From the beginning that theme emphasizes the centrality of relational bonds and the pain they frequently inflict on people. The parents clearly feel the loss of their son far more than their own impending death; their only concern seems to be for him. Until the very last moment they debate what may offer the best destination for him, Lara protesting that earth is a planet of "primitives . . . thousands of years behind." The father responds that Kal-El will be stronger and wiser than earthlings, but his mother foresees that he will also always be "alone," cut off by his superior wisdom and intelligence from real intimacy with any human being. That Kryptonians, and Kal-El in particular, do yearn for emotional and spiritual intimacy is evident in that they do marry, breed, and rear; when Clark Kent arrives in Metropolis, for example, he immediately and lastingly flips for Lois Lane, eventually going as far in *Superman II* as to sacrifice his superhuman status in order to marry Lois.

In any case, despite the prospect of the enormous cost of perpetual solitude for his "only son," Jor-El sends him off to earth to "serve its collective humanity." It is no surprise that Clark Kent grows into a doting son. Of course, his call and his capacity to care inform Kal-El's earthly mission of protecting the weak and innocent and restoring justice and peace to the whole creation, restoring the norm of the original Edenic (and Kryptonic?) harmony and beauty. Indeed, Kal-El will be, as his father forecasts, the "light" to show the beings of the earth how to care. How intentionally the filmmakers constructed the theme of the Incarnation appears in one drastic departure from the story told in the original

255

Marvel comic-book *Superman* series (which originated in 1938). In that account of Superman, Kal-El is simply sent randomly into space away from Krypton just so he can survive; he lands on earth entirely by happenstance. In this film version, Jor-El's steadfast resolve is to send Kal-El to a place where he might do much good with his extraordinary powers.

The New Home

Through the three-year-long ride in the star-shaped capsule to that blue sphere called Earth, Kal-El matures physically and learns much, by means of the crystal, of Krypton's vast store of knowledge about the physical universe and also, near the end, the "matters of the heart." The story per se, Kal-El's life on earth, begins with the crash landing of his star capsule in a wheat field. The roar of the capsule and crash so startle a middle-aged couple in a truck that they almost lose control and in the process blow a tire. Jonathan Kent (Glenn Ford) is kicking the flat tire in exasperation when Martha Clark Kent (Phyllis Thaxter) sees the long scorched channel in an adjoining field. Then, as the film's winsome musical leitmotif quietly sounds, just below the rim of the crater appears — stark naked, smiling, and arms outstretched — the small boy. While Jonathan changes the tire and Martha holds the child next to her, the couple debates what to do with their find. They have no children themselves, and Martha suggests they keep him as their own because he clearly has no parents, "at least from around here." They can tell others, she says, that he's been orphaned by the death of Martha's cousin in North Dakota, which is closer to the truth than she realizes. The sequence is played with warmth and affectionate humor as the two go back and forth on the subject: at one point Martha reminds Jonathan of his weak heart, and he asks her, as she moves the conversation to the possibility of keeping the boy, "Martha Clark-Kent, are you thinking what I think you're thinking?"

The answer to this question emerges when the farm couple's rickety truck slides off its jack, and then, to their utter astonishment, the rear end of the truck rises into the air, as the small child, smiling broadly, holds it high above his head. Looking back at the scorched crater behind them, Mr. and Mrs. Kent slowly comprehend the wonder of what they have witnessed. In this first demonstration of the boy's powers, audiences chuckle with relief and awe at the comedy of it; no guffaws or cheers, no buildings leapt in a single bound (not yet, anyway) — only the

Jonathan (Glenn Ford) and Martha Kent (Phyllis Thaxter), aka Joseph and Mary, have their first encounter with the miraculous powers of the intergalactic orphan they've come across.

picture of the small boy holding a truck high over his head. Quiet, affecting, and profound, it is a foretaste of what mere humans are in for.

It is just this kind of sequence that contains the enormous "fun" and appeal of *Superman*. It is a rare cinematic feat insofar as it induces audiences to marvel and applaud the possibility of a divine intervention of care and love, and in that sort of accomplishment, repeated many times in *Superman*, lies the great achievement of this movie. Far more than its number of allusions to the Jesus story — and they abound — or its graceful flight sequences, the film's great religious feat comes in delivering audiences to that unique "zone" of awe-filled experience occasioned by even so little as the prospect of an incarnation of a specifically Christian kind. Insofar as this telling of the Superman story elicits this wonder and elation, similar to what was occasioned by the original promise and appearance of Jesus, it gets to the very mystery and heart of the matter, an experiential wellspring that brings forth amazement, contemplation, and, for some, devotion. This is a benign smiling face of the Holy, indeed, and it's a long way from the fearsome incursions of Spielberg's aliens in *Close Encounters*. It succeeds because, on the one hand, though it is a comedy, it takes into full account the depth of woe that besets humanity and, on the other, it expresses the soul-shaking exhilaration that follows on the coming of "a friend" to a weary humanity.

That Kal-El is more than just any super-kid was apparent in Jor-El's trinitarian closing speech. That same pattern of biblical allusion follows the toddler to earth. First off, there's the place he lands: Kansas, or maybe North Dakota, a vast empty middle-of-nowhere place, the demeaned boondocks from which no good thing ever came, as the Pharisees and other arbiters of taste in Jesus' time complained. And then there are the parents: not only are they vital names from the Bible — Martha and Jonathan — but they are about as close to Mary and Joseph as the filmmakers could get without giving away the whole joke. While this mother is not virginal, she is childless; and the strange coming of Kal-El, if not exactly miraculous, is still supernatural, at least as earthlings might understand it. And there could be no kindlier parents than this pair, who suggest the attributes of the Christian God: Jonathan communicates endless compassion and understanding, and Martha shows quiet but passionate love for her otherworldly son. They remain humbly and gratefully perplexed by the phenomenon of their adopted son, fearing others will discover his extraordinary powers and take him away; yet at the same time they sense, though dimly perhaps, that he has a purpose to fulfill on earth. When the adolescent Kal-El, now named Clark after Martha's family, complains of having to restrain and conceal his superhuman powers, Jonathan insists that, while he does not know why Clark was sent to earth, he does know that it was to do something "more than score touchdowns."

Clark (played as a teenager by Jeff East) is next seen as a tall, rather awkward, and even sissified teenager: at school he wears a solid bright red shirt, khakis up high and too short, and high-top basketball shoes. There's even a slight pout to his walk and a tinny whine in his voice. Instead of playing football, he's the lowly team manager and reluctantly submits to the hazing of the local heroes. Though he can kick a football into orbit and could score constant touchdowns, young Kent withholds himself in order to conceal his identity until his purpose in this world becomes clear. That stance does not mean he is not frustrated by the restraint, for he takes pleasure in his special abilities, such as outracing trains and cars, always pushing the envelope when nobody is looking, testing out what he seems made to do. That same conspicuous pleasure in his wondrous powers will abound when he eventually takes to the air. Now, though, scenes of Clark spreading his wings, so to speak, provide occasion for some wry homage. The parents riding on the passenger train that Clark outruns are played by Noel Neill, who played Lois Lane in the 1950s television series, and Kirk Alyn, who played the man of steel in 1940s Hollywood movies (the 2001 expanded DVD release of *Superman* identifies the little girl who sees Clark outrunning the train as Lois Lane, the very girl who will grow up to be the woman Clark will fall in love with). And when Clark runs off down a country road, the dust cloud he leaves behind recalls the signature trail of the animated Road Runner of cartoon fame.

This is great fun: the picture does not take itself too seriously, yet it simultaneously treats its concept with utmost respect. Then, as if to acknowledge that this is serious business after all, the hijinks abruptly stop dead with father Jonathan's actual death of a sudden heart attack just as he starts to run with his only son. At the hilltop cemetery, Clark fervently laments to his mother that, despite all his special powers, he was unable to save his father, a recollection that will motivate his actions near the end of this film and then again at the conclusion of *Superman II*. Early one morning, not long after the death of his father, Clark awakens and goes to the barn, as if mysteriously drawn to a pit beneath the floor, where lies the glowing green crystal sent with him to earth by Jor-El, his father on Krypton.

On another early morning, Clark bids a sob-choked farewell to his mother as they stand together atop a lovely wheat-covered hill, the camera wheeling and closing around them. He has arranged for a neighbor to help on the farm, and all he can tell her, all he knows, is that he's headed "north," as the crystal has presumably bid him to do. He sobs the word "mother" from deep within himself, and the two embrace and watch the sunrise as the camera circles around in the midst of the vast wheat field. The substance of the scene is highly reminiscent of the peculiar relationship Jesus had with Mary, and his necessary parting from that remarkable woman. Nor is Clark's reaching his destination any lighter in mood or substance. Way up in the ice-bound north, he throws the magical crystal far into the distance, and from its landing springs a huge white modernesque structure that resembles the architecture of Krypton. The crystal then generates the talking, glowing visage of the long-dead Jor-El, who identifies himself as Clark's father and has much to say about his long history, humankind, and Clark's "special heritage."

What follows is a novitiate of sorts in saviorhood. Kal-El/Clark will spend a full twelve years in what his father calls a "fortress of solitude," during which his father will tutor him in the great mysteries of existence, earthly and otherwise. On the relatively insignificant issues of history and science, "matters of mere fact," his son has already been instructed during his three-year voyage to earth. These twelve years will delve into the thornier riddles of the human heart ("more fragile than your own") and the "various concepts of immortality and their basis in actual fact." Each of these will receive a full year of study. Most of all, though, Jor-El clarifies the reasons he sent his son to earth "to serve their collective humanity." He bids Kal-El to "live as one of them . . . to discover where your power and strength are needed." While his powers are enormous when compared to human capacities, Kal-El is forbidden, as he was already told on his voyage to earth, "to interfere with human history" but is rather to "let your leadership stir" human potential for change: "They can be a great people, Kal-El, they wish to be, they only lack the light to show them the way." It is "for this reason, above all, their capacity for growth, I have sent them you, my only son." It is all very stirring, and it is dramatized by mesmerizing special effects that are all the more remarkable considering that they were devised before the age of digitalization.

Everything in the life of Kal-El/Clark Kent/Superman so far has played as advent. At the very end of his twelve years in his educational "fortress of solitude," viewers have gotten but a glimpse of what is to be. In the distant open-air ice fortress stands a tiny figure that suddenly becomes airborne and then for ten seconds flies straight toward the camera. John Williams's score goes into a full-throated trumpet fanfare, and a resplendent and powerful Superman, his out-stretched cape fluttering in the wind and a look of pleasure and resolve on his face, flies toward the camera and then banks off to the right. It is a breath-taking scene that makes audiences gasp, as they realize that, yes, a man can fly.

And so ends this intergalactic orphan's novitiate, the exile that prepares him for his life and calling as Superman. It has lasted twelve years, as the script repeatedly — and somewhat clumsily — emphasizes, making Clark Kent exactly thirty years old when he shows up as a mild-mannered reporter in the busy urban heart of humanity. It was at precisely that age that Jesus began his ministry of healing and rescue in the busy first-century crossroads that was Palestine. As editor Perry White exhorts his reporters after Superman has completed his first miraculous night of work in Metropolis, "I tell ya, boys and girls, whichever one of you gets it out of him is gonna wind up with the single most important interview since God talked to Moses."

Emergence

Once he arrives in Metropolis, the Clark we get is certainly not the one we expect, for he seems not quite up to the task, to put it mildly; in fact, he's rather a decline in basic competence from the very mild-mannered reporter of the 1950s television series (George Reeves) or the boyish young Clark (Dean Cain) of the *Lois and Clark* television series of the 1990s. Despite their calculated blandness, both of these "other Clarks" proved appealing, each exuding a personal solidity and even forcefulness. They seemed like they could get along perfectly well in an ordinary world, and viewers trusted them to know when Superman's help might be needed. In *Superman: The Movie*, Christopher Reeve's Clark is not nearly as competent as an ordinary functional human being; but he is also a lot more fun, once one gets the joke of his clown-like persona. This Clark is in fact a bumbling, inept naif who is hardly equipped with any of the finesse or savvy necessary for success — or even basic survival — in the hard-bitten world that is Metropolis. The first time we see Kent, on his first day at the *Daily Planet,* gives us about as much as we need to know. While he is properly dressed in a three-piece business suit (this is the era of polyester leisure suits), the thing could hardly be more ill-fitting: his shirt collar is both too large and worn too high; his suit coat seems to pull his shoulders forward and, while not too small, could use more material and a different cut. And when we finally see him full from a distance, his trousers fall at least two inches too short. Add to that the heavy black-rimmed eyeglasses that continually slide down his nose and his well-oiled hair, and even Christopher Reeve's striking good looks and "presence" are mildly clouded. All of this simply seems to be a continuation of the image of the adolescent Clark in the boondocks.

Clark's lack of poise, presence of mind, and coordination is most obvious in his desperate attempt to manage everything he carries around with him. There is his hat, slightly too large (and a somewhat odd item for the 1970s), his briefcase, his raincoat, and those continuously slipping eyeglasses, all of which he tries to shuffle every time he tries to shake hands or hold the door for someone. Moreover, he has great trouble with entrances, ranging from elevators (whether they're going up or down), revolving doors (getting his hand stuck in one), and restrooms (is it the men's or women's?). His slumped, hemmed-in shoulders and short trousers only accentuate his stiff, choppy walk. In personality, Clark is socially "out of it," using locutions such as "Gee, Miss Lane . . ." and "swell," and always acting the role of the good boy scout who lacks any trace of sarcasm or of the rogue that would make him appealing to Lois, to whom he takes an instant liking. All these bumbling shortfalls are aggravated by his high-pitched, nasal voice that soon starts to grate on even those viewers inclined to like him. The overall impression is that, regardless of his typing skills, he should probably not be let out by himself in a big scary place like Metropolis.

261

Though he knows it is an impediment to romance with Lois Lane, Superman cloaks himself in the clownish garb and ineptitude of mild-mannered reporter Clark Kent.

And this is Superman? Even given the demands of disguise, the filmmakers seem to have gone a bit toward the ludicrous — unless one gets the joke, or several of them. One obvious cause for this extreme of physical disguise is that this version of *Superman* has a very well-muscled Christopher Reeve in the lead. When cast for the role, Reeve had the looks, voice, and height (6′4″) to do Superman, but he was very lean, as is clear in some of the newly released screen tests in which Reeve suits up as Superman. Lack of muscle was not a problem in the 1950s TV series, in which George Reeves's Superman possessed a normally muscled male physique even when he wore the tights and cape. For this version, though, the filmmakers wanted a statuesque Clark Kent, and they sent Reeve off to the weight room; the actor put on more than twenty pounds of muscle through the long course of shooting *Superman* and *Superman II*. (In fact, due to the length of the shoot, some of the first scenes had to be reshot to cover the discrepancy between the earlier and later Reeve.) One way to conceal all of Reeve/Clark's conspicuous strength was to shroud it in suits, posture, and ineptitude.

Three other reasons are more dramatically sensible and compelling than cosmetic foolery, and these go to the heart of much of what the film manages to pull off in achieving the look and "feel" of an incarnation. On the one hand, the stark contrast between the Clark persona and Superman covers his true identity; but also long familiarity with the clownish Clark stokes up expectation, as viewers steadily become more and more eager to see the "super" side they know is coming. That mix of waiting and expectation is the meaning of advent. And then comes amazement when Superman finally does show up, soaring skyward to save Lois, full of regal charm and mastery. The delight and elation of that moment of help for humans in distress pretty well approximates the psycho-spiritual clout that the Incarnation of Jesus should have for those who actually believe in its truth. In this regard, the film has much to tell the church about the gladness and exultant unexpectedness of What and Whom it celebrates.

The audience's first sense of the coming "revelation" occurs when Clark and Lois are mugged as they walk not far from the *Daily Planet*. Kent is at his nasal, silly worst when an armed gunman motions them into an alley; and yet, though he seems terrified, he shields Lois and pleads that violence solves nothing and that the miscreant should turn over a new leaf. The thief snidely agrees to do so — right after he "rips off this lady's purse." In contrast to Kent's jittery grovel, Lois proves far more feisty, dropping her purse to make the mugger reach down so she can kick away his weapon. Startled by her attempt, the fellow fires the gun and then runs away.

The outcome for Lois would not have been happy if the seemingly dimwitted Kent had not reached out to catch the bullet barehanded. Then to conceal his protection of her, he fakes a faint, falling into a di-sheveled heap against the wall. Lois thinks he's been shot until he begins to stir, soon confessing that he must have fainted. Lois is incredulous and humiliated: some chivalrous knight in a three-piece suit he's turned out to be! When Lois walks disgustedly away, the camera remains on Kent for a few seconds as the musical leitmotif quietly reprises; he opens his hand to look at the bullet, toss it aside, and smile at the loving joke he has played on Lois. Walking out of the alley and again talking nasally, he chastises her for her recklessness in risking her life, and all for "ten dollars, two credit cards, a hair brush, and a lipstick," the exact contents of her purse, as Lois incredulously informs him. "Lucky guess," he tells her as he walks away smiling.

This is all great fun and whets the appetite for more; indeed, view-ers don't have long to wait for the full "glory," when Lois reacts to her first encounter with the actual Superman. She falls from the helicopter dangling from the *Daily Planet* building but is caught midway down by Superman. His comment is nonchalant, to say the least: "Don't worry, Miss, I've got you." Lois's incredulity, and her girl-reporter instincts, ask the pertinent question, one as metaphysical as it is practical: "Who's got *you?*" This query repeats and expands when Superman deposits her, along with the helicopter and its injured pilot, appropriately enough, on the top of the *Daily Planet* — because he has now assumed ascendancy over the planet as a whole. Again, the contrast between Clark and this "superman," as Lois will eventually dub him, could not be more stark. His physical power now clearly displayed in his massive chest and neck, his ever-sliding spectacles now gone, his voice now deep and resonant (indeed, an Americanized version of Jor-El/Brando), decked out in super suit and cape, a jaunty curl now covering his high forehead, his manner now relaxed and confident — Superman calmly, and with teasing humor, reminds Lois that flying is still the safest way to travel.

For once in her life, "something" has rendered the jaded, talky, know-it-all Lois speechless and full of awe; the best she can muster is a nod of fervent assent to Superman's innocuous comments. As he begins to walk off, she poses the cosmic question, eking out the words one by one: "Who . . . are . . . you?" Superman's answer is direct and simple, "a friend," which he delivers with a warm smile, and then he slowly ascends, waving as he says a playful "bye" on his way up. The camera cuts to Lois, who watches the ascent and then promptly crumples into a dead faint. At last, and to her immense good fortune, the rescue, the answer, and the grand aplomb of Superman himself bring her to a dead faint, this hard-bitten girl reporter who is uncowed by anything in heaven or on earth, at least until now. Fearless in the face of the mugger, she is in this scene fully done in, reduced to a faint by real goodness, the one thing Lois in her cynicism and irreverence (and likely despair) had never dreamed possible. She is dumbfounded by some mysterious "something" that lies very far beyond the ken of her considerable street savvy. To that question from time immemorial, "who are you?" comes the answer: "Too good not to be true."[5]

The last rather surprising thing about the two sides of this incarnation is that there is no great difference in the intentions and effect of the two personalities of Kal-El as clown and savior-hero. There is, to be sure, the "super-friend" who will use his super powers to defend and help humanity, whether it be in stopping street thugs, the grandiose evil machinations of Lex Luthor, or the ravages of the natural disasters, such as broken dams or the earthquake that will bury and kill Lois Lane. Superman rescues and affirms humanity, and he fends off evil with humor and utmost gentleness. But the fact is that this Superman is virtually a pacifist, defeating enemies and bad guys with a minimum of force. What

5. Buechner, p. 71.

there is of force, is comic. In the first two *Superman* films, the only real visceral violence done by Superman comes when Clark settles the score with the bully truck driver; even then he handles the matter with appropriateness and wit. The violence in his combat with the evil exiles from Krypton is always stylized and outsized, as if from a comic book. In truth, both these figures, Clark and his super self, are surpassingly kind. Superman is always gentle and, at worst, only mildly indignant with his foes, and Clark Kent is nothing but "nice," even though he takes much abuse for the clumsiness of his personality.

Last, the purpose of Kal-El's careful construction of Clark's personality seems to have one other benign function. Clark is a wonderful cover for Superman, but the disguise also seems intended simply to make others feel better about themselves. Clark comports himself in a manner so clownish that those around him seem relieved that, whatever their own deficiencies, they are at least not so discombobulated and inept as he is. Once in that "role," Kal-El stays fixed within it, though he repeatedly is tempted to reveal himself, at least to Lois, who clearly adores Superman but is completely indifferent to Clark. The cost is high since it consigns Kal-El/Clark to perpetual isolation without prospect of intimacy, at least in his life as Clark Kent — or even as Superman (which *Superman II* details). Apparently, as decreed by father Jor-El, Kal-El's extraordinary powers depend on his living in the world but not as an ordinary human being, which in this case entails celibacy. And in this chosen path, the filmmakers stipulate still another striking parallel to the life of Jesus.

Fighting the Evil One . . . and Triumphing

The primary conflict in *Superman* comes in the contest between Superman and the evil genius Lex Luthor, who wishes to use nuclear weapons to sink the California coast in order to turn his own worthless inland desert property into valuable beachfront real estate. The scenario is preposterous and comic in the extreme, as is the characterization of Luthor, played with pompous, ham-fisted relish by Gene Hackman. Indeed, Luthor's nature seems to come from hell itself, albeit a comic one, and one from which he is likely to be kicked out for being so insufferable. He currently lives in garish opulence many stories below Metropolis's Grand Central Station. The "greatest criminal genius" of his time, as Luthor fancies himself, he recognizes Superman as a formidable foe and tries to neutralize his superpowers by exposing him to kryptonite, which in earth's atmosphere will kill anyone from Krypton. Superman is freed (resurrected?) from slow death in a watery grave by the intervention of the vampish Miss Teschmacher (Valerie Perrine), Luthor's buxom live-in girlfriend, who removes the fatal kryptonite from around his neck.

This incident echoes the kind of magnet the virtuous Jesus was for women of dubious repute, whether Mary Magdalene, the woman at the well, or the adulterous woman he saved from stoning. It is also a replay of the standard "whore-with-a-heart-of-gold" motif in Hollywood film. The characterization of Luthor and his buffoonish entourage, particularly Ned Beatty as his assistant, Otis, defuses whatever real-world peril Luthor poses. Altogether, the evil in *Superman,* cast in the mode of comic-book ludicrous, adds considerably to the pure fun of the film. And *Superman* is rather unusual in this approach, especially when compared to other ostensibly viewer-friendly comic-book villains, such as those in the Batman series, particularly Jack Nicholson's Joker and Jim Carey's Riddler or Willem Dafoe's Green Goblin in *Spider Man* (2002).

At the center of *Superman's* second half is the dramatization of Kal-El's temptation to use his superpowers for the wrong ends. The first of these is Luthor's rather crass suggestion that they join forces to rule the world. Only a fool would join up with Luthor, if only because of the villain's dreadful taste. The faint echo here is of Jesus' temptation in the desert, in which the Power of Darkness offers him control over all the kingdoms of the earth. The more serious threat, again echoing the desert temptations, is the opportunity to contravene his father's instruction not to use his powers to "intervene in human history," though exactly what constitutes an intervention is somewhat uncertain. (As the recent DVD audio commentary by Tom Mankiewicz and director Richard Donner suggests, it does not seem that the filmmakers themselves were all that clear on what they intended by the term "intervene" [48:20].) And there is the deleted scene between Jor-El and son Superman after he has saved Lois: the father chastises the son for intervening as much as he has. Exactly what he is allowed to do, in contrast to what he does in that first night of his emergence, is a bit mystifying; it is thus no surprise that the scene was removed from the final cut. In the released version, in any event, Superman is apparently allowed to do whatever he can to protect people, such as Lois, or to stymie bad guys such as Lex Luthor; but he may do so only within the metaphysical boundaries of humanity's earthly existence. Jor-El has forbidden him to break through realms of time and space in order to reverse or disrupt the boundaries that limit humans. Apparently, Superman can do what he will within this frame, but he cannot reverse the laws of physics.

That limit becomes agonizingly burdensome when Superman confronts Lois Lane's death near the end of the first film. Lois's car, with her in it, has been swallowed up into a crevasse opened by the earthquake set off by the explosion of one of Luthor's stolen nuclear bombs. Superman pulls Lois's car from the earth, but Lois has already died. His agony is acute, and he bellows an earth-shaking scream of anguish and anger. There also seems in this excruciating *de profundis* a good deal of anger toward his own real father, Jor-El, for consigning him to grief and renewed isolation, and this scene seems to hark back to Jesus' protestations about being "forgotten" while he was suffering on the cross. Lois's dismal fate, despite his love and superpower, clearly reminds him of the impotence he felt at the death of his adopted father. And as if to expiate for that death and vent his own rage, he sets out to return Lois to life. The only way to do that is to reverse time itself, to turn back the clock by reversing with his immense speed and power the rotation of the earth; and this is what Superman does, thereby resurrecting Lois — in the manner of Lazarus. And there seem to be no negative consequences of this radical act, even though he has defied his father's injunction not to mess with human time or history. The filmmakers might have intended this to be a major theme, as the materials on the new expanded DVD edition suggest; but either because it made the plot overcomplicated or the screenwriters wrote themselves into a dramatic dead end, the final release of the film for theaters pretty much dropped the topic as a thematic issue.

Superman II follows similar christomorphic territory, although the sequel, shot simultaneously with the first film, inverts the thematic thrust of the first one. Where Kal-El overreaches the limits set by his father in the first film, in *Superman II* he relinquishes all claims to being "super." Consigned to solitude and celibacy by the terms of the servanthood specified by his father, Kal-El chooses to sacrifice his superhuman powers in order to live with Lois, with whom he has fallen irretrievably in love. Since he is utterly unable to interest her in his Clark Kent persona, he decides early in the film to reveal himself to her in order to attract her to him. He then petitions his father for permission and the means to enter into full humanity, a metamorphosis he accomplishes via some kind of techno-booth apparatus. Married to Lois in his fortress of solitude, he finds happiness with her in a place that is no longer solitary. Meanwhile, as they honeymoon in the arctic, the "real world" pays a high price in horrendous events as a result of Superman's retreat into self-pursuit, though those events remain unbeknownst to him. But soon enough he discovers that the three villains from Krypton have themselves arrived on earth and have no desire but to dominate the planet. Also, once they know that the son of Jor-El also lives there, they will now seek revenge on the father by humiliating and killing his son. Now completely human, and much like the biblical Samson, Superman suffers the agony of human pain and defeat for the first time, first at the hands of the bully truck driver and then from the three exiled villains from Krypton, who delight in the humiliation and suffering of the son of their old nemesis. At the very end of the film, having retrieved his superpowers to vanquish the three Kryptonian villains, as well as his old foe Lex Luthor, Superman faces the necessity of living out his days in anguished separation from Lois, because with Clark's re-embrace of his superpowers comes the obligation of celibacy. In a concluding gesture of sacrificial love, Clark kisses Lois one last time in order to erase from her memory all knowledge of their past together and of his Superman alter ego. Clark will feel as he does about Lois forever, but she at least will not carry the burden of unfulfilled longing.

Conclusion

Superman is perhaps not so much "holy fable" as parable, a plain tale that makes palpable and memorable a stunning and mystifying reality. The motivation for using parable is to find the terms that make a concept understandable both intellectually and experientially. In the New Testament, Jesus' stories convey unreasonable, even preposterous truths about the nature of God by talking about servants who hoard money and masters who invite street people to the feast when invited guests do not show up. The genius of *Superman* is that it begins as fable and becomes parable, smartly melding the fantasies of the fable with the realism of the parable. The filmmakers haul the fantastic through heart-sore everyday life in such places as Metropolis, and by means of parable, paying close heed to the depletions of contemporary urban life, test the cogency of its wild appeals to humanity's deepest longings.

The great achievement of *Superman* is that its comic/christomorphic fantasy makes wonderfully clear and palpable what it is like, against all of earth's tragic odds, to find a measure of divine help for the human mess. In Superman the inmost character of the divine appears as a "friend" who offers rescue and succor. Insofar as this help comes by surprise and

Richard Donner Filmography

Lethal Weapon 4 (1998)
Conspiracy Theory (1997)
Assassins (1995)
Maverick (1994)
Lethal Weapon 3 (1992)
Radio Flyer (1992)
Lethal Weapon 2 (1989)
Scrooged (1988)
Lethal Weapon (1987)
The Goonies (1985)
Ladyhawke (1985)
The Toy (1982)
Inside Moves (1980)
Superman (1978)
A Very Special Place (1977) (TV)
The Omen (1976)

displays lovingkindness, it bespeaks the loving intentions of God that occasion deep gladness, the kind of "joy" that Tolkien saw at the core of, not only fantasy, but of the Christian story itself.

Superman pronounces these intentions in the antic comedy of buffoon-cum-Christ, the reality that is "too good not to be true," the utter preposterousness of an incarnation of love itself. In just about every aspect, then, from its witty use of Jesus allusions to its music, alternately delicate and sublime, *Superman* conjures up festive, campy "showings" of the Holy One that do address the strangest wild hopes of bedraggled humanity and, when fulfilled, gladden the heart and soul. In this story, and in their way of telling it, the filmmakers not only dramatize the lineaments of the Incarnation but also convey the very exultant texture of the encounter with the inmost spirit of God — surprise, amazement, relief, laughter, love, and hope.

CHAPTER 10

"EARTH'S THE PLACE FOR LOVE"

The Lost Boy's Search for Home
in Three Steven Spielberg Movies

In Steven Spielberg's most memorable films, the ones that made his
fame and fortune, the same thing keeps happening over and over. These
are all "lost boy stories," tales in which boys, young and old, search desperately for a home, for what Robert Frost in his poem "Birches" called a
"place for love." For Spielberg, the nature of the self and the nature of
the world in which people find themselves make this the central human
quest. But this is not an easy place to find. Ultimately, that elusive domain of home is the place that promises both to satisfy the self's deepest
thirsts in one fell swoop and to counter the harshness, sorrow, and tedium of ordinary human life. This home has little to do with traditional
associations of the term, for home is not primarily based on blood relationships, such as family or clan; and it has even less to do with the geog-
raphy of a particular place, such as a town or a house.

Instead, for all of Spielberg's boy heroes, this hard-to-find destination is always, first and last, profoundly relational: it is a place of intimacy,
harmony, and trust — and a joy in these qualities that is made all the
more precious by the prevailing harshness of the world in which the lost
boys find themselves. Compared to this "place for love," simple physical
safety in the hostile world hardly seems to matter, though matter it surely
does. After all, as a chronicler of the horrors of Normandy Beach and the
Holocaust, Spielberg clearly knows that evil is terrifyingly real and incal-
culably monstrous, that it destroys not only those vital "places of the
heart" but life itself. Global calamities are real, but they are no less harrowing, Spielberg's many movies contend, than the innumerable withering fears of childhood, of lostness and abandonment. From these, as
much as from wars and dreams of scary villains, children need shelter.

270

Typically, Spielberg's boy heroes are at first simply lost, looking hard for something, though they usually fail to realize either the reality or depth of their hunger for a haven of some sort. Difficult circumstances of various kinds beset them, inside and out, and range from diffuse restlessness amid materialistic monotony to the deep sadness caused by the desertion of a parent. At least some of the drama in each of Spielberg's lost boy films derives from the central character's struggle to figure out what ails him. That is no small task, for these boys, still being boys, still coming to self-awareness, scarcely have a clue — initially at least — about their malady and even less of an insight about what it might take to repair it. Usually, though, all of it comes clear in a flash, sometimes quite literally, as Roy Neary discovers when he is lost on the road to Cornbread in *Close Encounters of the Third Kind* (1977). The epiphany for these lost boys comes unexpectedly, suddenly, and sheathed in light. Mired deep in loss, alienation, and aloneness — in short, exiled and homeless — they are suddenly hit with a mysterious, unexpected flash of some sort that clears the dark muddle and sets the boys off in hot pursuit of more of the same. Something in the moment strangely and mysteriously connects, promising somehow to restore heart and soul. This is heavy terrain, and emotional; but it is also — when tangled with questions of human meaning and purpose — spiritual, though that is an imprecise term for the deepest parts of the self.

Usually, in Hollywood movies, this sort of profound restoration happens within romance; but all of Spielberg's boy stories take a different turn, of necessity, for these young males have a ways to go before romance and eros come upon them. Instead — and in stark contrast — what helps these boys find their hearts' content comes, very literally, from out of this world; and what these boys ultimately come to know over the course of the story (and it does take them a while) greatly surpasses anything human experience itself contains. It is unambiguously otherworldly, and while it is fully beautiful and not carnal, the connection that transpires in this flash is immediate and compelling, as is the certainty that somehow "this is it," that is, this is what the deepest self most wants in a darkly forbidding world. The downside of this is that Spielberg's stories repeatedly suggest, somewhat grimly, that the best human life offers cannot completely satisfy the self's deepest longings or repair the wounds suffered during its earthly travail.

The gist of the matter is that human life requires something from beyond life itself, some force from a half-magical, out-of-this world realm to save the woebegone individual self. The distinctive note in

Close Encounters of the Third Kind (1977)

Studio:	Columbia
Screenwriter:	Steven Spielberg
Director:	Steven Spielberg
Cinematographers:	William A. Fraker (American Scenes), Douglas Slocombe (India Sequence), Vilmos Zsigmond (Director of Photography)
Production Designer:	Joe Alves
Editor:	Michael Kahn

Cast

Richard Dreyfuss	Roy Neary
François Truffaut	Claude Lacombe
Teri Garr	Ronnie Neary
Melinda Dillon	Jillian Guiler
Bob Balaban	David Laughlin

Academy Awards

Cinematography:	Vilmos Zsigmond

Additional Academy Award Nominations

Supporting Actress:	Melinda Dillon
Director:	Steven Spielberg
Sound:	Robert Knudson, Robert J. Glass, Don MacDougall, Gene S. Cantamessa
Art Direction:	Joe Alves
Editing:	Michael Kahn
Original Score:	John Williams
Visual Effects:	Roy Arbogast, Douglas Trumbull, Matthew Yuricich, Gregory Jein, Richard Yuricich

Spielberg is the extent to which he persistently locates the home for which his heroes search in a relationship with a transcendent Other, a supernatural or, as Martin Amis puts it, a "superevolved" Other.[1] Only in such a relationship do these boys seem to find the measure of trust and communion, the "at-homeness" that will renew their hopefulness about life, heal the heart's wounds, and restore their weary souls. In these science-fiction tales, alien forces show up to introduce a supernatural power, as in *Close Encounters,* or a variety of gentle and transcendent love, as in *E.T.: The Extra-Terrestrial.* Only by such transcendent supra-human means may people achieve the mythic home Spielberg so persistently celebrates.

Because these tales are redemptive for their boy protagonists, moving them from despair into a new fullness of life, and because the source for this redemption comes from beyond the earth, the stories immediately become quasi-religious, at least as parables of the contours of religious experience: their religious nature becomes full-blown in the overtly religious trappings with which Spielberg dresses his stories. For one, he steeps his tales in traditional Jewish-Christian story and imagery, freighting his tales with religious heft even when audiences do not recognize the nature of the cinematic substance that moves them. Moreover, as I will argue in this chapter, Spielberg continually uses his considerable cinematic brilliance to show the depth of human tragedy and longing, but also amid these deficits, the numinous character of the divine in both majesty and gentleness. In his chronicles of the experiences of his protagonists, Spielberg dramatizes what it is like to encounter the divine up close and personal. Indeed, he manages to suggest the "look" and "feel" of the divine, and from those we get what students of religion call the "feeling content" of the characters' experience of the holy. This is no small accomplishment, and this kind of cinematic effectiveness is Spielberg's particular gift, one that is acknowledged even by those who disapprove of his work, such as scholar Robert Kolker: "He is so proficient — so efficient — at structuring his narratives, controlling his mise-en-scene, and positioning the spectator within these structures, that all his films all but guarantee the viewer will surrender herself to them at some point during the narrative."[2]

The full import of Spielberg's religious sense is fully and clearly dis-

1. Amis, *The Moronic Inferno and Other Visits to America* (New York: Viking, 1987), p. 3.

2. Kolker, *The Cinema of Loneliness: Penn, Stone, Kubrick, Scorsese, Spielberg, Altman,* 3rd ed. (New York: Oxford, 2000), p. 256.

Children and Violence in Spielberg's Films

One critical ingredient has always informed Spielberg's best work. That is his own deep sense of the tragic, that life is full of perils and that not everything turns out well, no matter how good people are or how hard they try. That is an uncomfortable vision of the nature of human life and the world. Admittedly, this claim runs counter to the prevailing notion that Spielberg is a rank sentimentalist who is unable to stare straight into the teeth of the inescapable ugliness of this world's constant diet of suffering and death. In fact, Spielberg has proved markedly inconsistent in how he uses violence in his films. On the one hand, his Indiana Jones series (1981-1989), particularly *The Temple of Doom* (1994), has drawn justifiable fire for pitching toward children large quantities of remarkably graphic, even titillating violence. On the other hand, in films for adults he has often been plainly uncomfortable with the harrowing realities of evil, regularly choosing to dilute or mince the full impact of the evils his films depict. That was certainly the case in *The Color Purple* (1985), *Amistad* (1997), and even *Saving Private Ryan*. In those films Spielberg seemed skittish concerning the hard realities of emotional anguish, regularly choosing to dilute its impact with sentiment, beatific lighting, or too-quick comic relief.

That said, it is also true that Spielberg has at times mustered the courage and ingenuity to make pain and the fear of it both palpable and moving. That is nowhere more true than in Spielberg's films about children, in what I

played near the end of *E.T.: The Extra-Terrestrial* (1982), when Elliott and his friends escape in the panel truck with E.T. inside, and they stop at the park from which they will take their bicycles into the mountains for E.T.'s rendezvous with the spacecraft that will return him to his home. The rear doors of the truck swing open, and clouds of white vapor from the dry ice in which E.T.'s body was packed billow out. Then, emerging from the cloud is E.T. himself, red heart again glowing brightly, white sheet draped over him and along the sides of his head, looking calm and resolute, as well he should, since he has just defeated death itself. The image of the resurrected E.T. recapitulates a long tradition of popular Christian art that has meditated on the miracle and mystery of a resurrected Jesus, particularly on that moment of his emergence from the tomb. The image of E.T. emerging from his mobile tomb summons a call "lost-boy stories." The theme has from the start exerted an enormous attraction, and when treating it he has done his best work. So powerful has it been that Spielberg has filmed the fairy tale of the pre-eminent lost boy, Peter Pan himself, the perpetual ambivalent boy who never wants to grow up but himself yearns for a home of his own as he makes a home for other boys, his gang of "Lost Boys," all of whom are disconnected and yearn for a real home. The outlandish *Hook* (1991) gives the theme a grotesquely comic turn — actually a mix of the mawkish and ludicrous, making it one of Spielberg's worst ventures. But in numerous other films that treat seriously the emotional plight of children buffeted about by the harsh "adult" realities of an unfriendly world, Spielberg captures the deep emotional-spiritual longings that profoundly affect children and persist into adulthood, by and large defining the human predicament.

For reasons that are not entirely clear, Spielberg seems at his best cinematically and philosophically when he's treating the plight of vulnerable innocents rudely thrust into recognitions of tragedy and evil. Thrown into a new hard world, typically alone and disconnected, these subjects have not only lost a safe, warm world but are ill-equipped, in their experiential and moral innocence, to find their way back to a serene world of emotional security. In this regard, the lostness of these boys is far more emotional and relational than physical or geographic, though those kinds of lostness factor in as well. The task in the tale is to restore these displaced young souls to a realm of emotional trust and care, to bring them back to the tenderness of home.

storehouse of symbols that mark the presence of God and divine miracle: tomb, cloud, grave-cloth, beatific calm, regal music, and, above all, surprise at the improbable working of transcendent divine love, which is just what it takes to bring the dead to life.

This scene is a culmination of what precedes it in the film, a long sequence showing that Spielberg was well aware of E.T.'s religious freight. The resurrection comes immediately after two events: first, E.T.'s choice of sacrificial death so that Elliott may live and, second, the news delivered to him by some means that his desperate call for rescue from earth has been answered, meaning that he has not been abandoned and will soon be going, in E.T.'s signature word, "home." Both of these events track down the thematic and narrative center of Jesus' death and resurrection: in short, in the giving of love is the coming of love. The emergence from the truck tomb emphatically reiterates the story's thematic and emotional core: love resurrecting one whose sacrificial love gave life to another, both emotionally and physically. It is a stunning turn of events and a stunning image, and nothing in the film quite prepares us for it. While constituting the dramatic climax of the film, it also largely defines the trajectory of Spielberg's career as a filmmaker in search of a defining vision of life. Admittedly, *E.T.* is an odd story for the Jewish Spielberg to tell (the script was co-written by Melissa Matthison, a product of Catholic schools); but such stories of love as the route to new birth and life have remarkable power and attractiveness quite apart from the particular creedal formulations they generate.

It is clear that, outside of specific theological claims, Spielberg feels, deep in his imagination and soul, the cogency of the metaphysical and the psycho-spiritual promise of the existential formula of love, redemption, and new birth that is displayed most clearly in *E.T.* But there's much that he must first work through in order to arrive at the rich fullness of that vision. From the beginning of his career he has labored to clarify his sense of the nature of the transcendent power in the universe, specifically the nature of God. Simply put, it takes a while for Spielberg to conclude that the superhuman power that clearly displays itself in this very dark world intends first and last to transform all with love, thereby making of life's brambles the home for which his lost boys search. While each of Spielberg's sci-fi lost-boy stories differs substantively from the others, there is always the emphatic refrain that insists that some transcendent Other is necessary to sate the thirstiness that comes from the woe endemic to the human circumstance. This thematic motif continues straight through to the recent Spielberg film *A.I.: Artificial Intelligence* (2001), where once again the human condition requires aid from beyond human power in order to dispel the lostness that is the human condition. It is an invigorating and fascinating journey.

Close Encounters of the Third Kind

Spielberg's first film to focus entirely on this condition of lostness was *Close Encounters of the Third Kind* (1977), an extraordinary tale of, in Spielberg's words, "common everyday people" who find themselves sensationally visited by space aliens who leave the earthlings with a ravenous, half-conscious compulsion to track them down for another meeting. Though now a quarter century old, *Close Encounters* is still a remarkable film for its story and for the striking means Spielberg uses to make palpable the "felt reality" of that story: what it is like to run smack into an enormous and magnificent supernatural power that displays many of the attributes of traditional popular concepts of God — indeed, of holiness itself. For the kind of display Spielberg manages to depict on the screen, words are hardly adequate; but that's the point, because he tries to evoke the *mysterium tremendum* in wide-screen effects and images that words cannot really capture. *Close Encounters* goes a long way toward making the ineffable visible. Just as *E.T.* is a textbook dramatization of the Christ story, Spielberg borrows large chunks of imagery from Jewish and Christian lore to make *Close Encounters* a particularly elegant riff on the Moses story: from the burning bush, to plagues and journeys through the wilderness, to the heights of the mountain, where the protagonist meets up with the immense and very insistent supernatural power that takes him up into itself — just as Moses seems enveloped by God on Mt. Sinai. In depicting all this through his science-fiction lens, particularly the awe and fascination that the encounter with numinous reality occasions, Spielberg makes plausible not only the central physical images of the Old and New Testaments but also the experiential wellspring that gave rise to the core of Western cultural values and dreams in the first place. Using his own verdant imagination, Spielberg, along with his remarkable production crew, devised special effects that are not only genuinely "special" but also serve the story exceptionally well, for the most part eschewing the allure of high-tech gadgetry either for its own sake or for box-office hype. In *Close Encounters*, the bold cinematic conjuring of multiple heavenly effects does prove absolutely necessary to tell the story he wants to tell.

The story itself is simple. The main character, the film's "lost boy," is Roy Neary (Richard Dreyfuss), "the man with the heart of the child," as Robert Kolker has incisively dubbed him.[3] A power lineman in central Indiana, Neary is summoned from home and family one evening to work on a massive electrical power outage that has darkened much of the state. Thanks to an elegant three-part prologue that details previous mysterious visitations by aliens, the audience fully anticipates what will soon happen to Neary: this unsuspecting young father of three is about to suffer — or is it, enjoy? — an encounter of the third kind, meaning a direct encounter with "alien" extraterrestrial visitors. This is an experience that fills Neary not only with awe but also with fear, and this ambivalence will continue through the length of the three-hour film. On the

3. Kolker, p. 300.

one hand, he is utterly fascinated by the sound-and-light spectacle the aliens unfurl like a bright cosmic banner; and he would be entranced by this phenomenon simply by virtue of his own childlike capacity for wonder. The alien-generated techno display Neary encounters ranks as the most marvelous toy ever, and he is as pleased and fascinated by it as little Barry Guiler is later delighted by his own alien-powered toys.

That's the good part. Neary's experience is vastly complicated, however, by the fact that these aliens implant in his brain, as they do in many others, an irresistible compulsion to discover a particular shape, which, unbeknownst to these diverse people, marks the spot where these visitors from space wish to meet humankind. That compulsion soon becomes an obsession that turns Neary's life up-side-down and exacts an enormous toll on his family. And in all of this he has no choice. The story ends triumphantly but sadly, as Spielberg, the family man, now freely admits (DVD commentary). That dark undercurrent aside, Speilberg provides riveting doses of surprise, amazement, and even devotion, all culminating in Neary's "deliverance," like Moses himself, into the heavens, leaving behind a host of other pilgrims who forever search for a promised land. Of all contemporary filmmakers, from De Mille to Zemeckis (*Contact*, 1997), none has come close to Spielberg's conjuring on the screen what it is like to run smack into transcendent power as pure majestic force.

Neary's first encounter happens on a dark and misty Indiana country road in what seems the middle of nowhere. (For some reason or another, most encounters with the divine take place in a deserted wilderness or on lonely mountaintops.) Lost and confused on that dark road as in his life as a whole — though he hardly is aware of the latter — Neary is stopped in his repair truck in the middle of the road, rooftop flashers whirling, trying to shine a flashlight on a large and unwieldy map. A set of headlights approaches from behind, and as they pass, the driver shouts angrily at Neary for blocking the roadway. Neary then drives on in search of some familiar landmark, eventually stopping at a railroad crossing to again consult his maps. Another set of lights approaches, and this time Neary absently motions for them to pass. This time, though, instead of moving to screen right, they move vertically, straight up — to the viewer's surprise and delight. But Neary does not recognize this because the lights are behind him and he is busy studying his map. Abruptly, amid the quiet chirping of the crickets, a long rack of metal roadside mailboxes begins to gyrate and clank loudly for no apparent reason. But that's only the beginning. Just as the mailboxes begin to quiet, and as the camera pulls back to a low-medium distance shot of

Neary's truck, a loud deep roar begins to gather as a bright cascade of intense pure white light flashes downward to engulf the truck in a sort of triangular halo. Inside Neary recoils, as if hit by a blow that has knocked the wind out of him. As he sticks his head out to look upward, squinting and covering his eyes, the camera cuts briefly to the multicolored lights of an aircraft slowly passing over the truck. Several bursts of light coming from within the big light, crackling like lightning electricity, seem to "zap" Neary, forcing him to wince and cower. When these relent, the crossing signal begins to clang and rock violently. Then all hell breaks loose in Neary's truck: the engine spontaneously starts; the assorted stuff on the dashboard and in the glove compartment leaps out at Neary, as if blown by the light; the radio suddenly blasts; the heat gauge soars and smokes; and on it goes, material mayhem blustering forth. Finally, as mysteriously and dramatically as it came, all of this dampens down, and the light suddenly turns off, returning the now terrified, trembling Neary to what hereafter will always be an unquiet darkness. The sound of distant thunder, or what sounds like thunder, prompts Neary to peek skyward from his windshield to see a huge silent airship pass slowly above. Finally, a hundred yards ahead, a light shaft again flashes, more or less beckoning Neary to follow, which he does while his two-way radio chatters of other sightings of something in the sky "as big as a barn."

This is a stunning sequence in ingenuity and dramatic effect, and its impact on everything that follows is decisive. Just this single "meeting" suffices to set Neary on a journey that will eventually bring him to a distant mountaintop to meet this alien power face to face and then finally to leave with these new "friends" to venture into worlds unknown. This light-soaked, supernatural encounter on the road parallels, in kind and in totality, other famous roadside visitations, particularly Moses' encounter with the burning bush in the wilderness and St. Paul's mysterious encounter with the light that blinds him on the Damascus road. Like them, Neary seems to have run smack into transcendent light; in some ways his experience seems even more extreme, engulfed as he has been by pure flame (one glimpse has left half of his face badly sunburned). Still, regardless of intensity and circumstance, these encounters are starkly similar in their impact on the recipients.

More radical turnabouts can hardly be imagined: Moses sets off on a decades-long trek to free the Israelites from Egypt (and themselves); Paul's view of the world and Jesus flips over entirely; and Neary finds himself hauled, unwillingly, to adventures and places he never dreamed of. And his journey is similar to Moses' (whose experience with the fiery bush tore him from a shepherd's life to Sinai to meet with God himself); and, like Moses, Neary suffers a multitude of doubts and problems before he reaches that mountaintop. At first, though, the impact on Neary does not seem nearly as dramatic, and it all comes to pass in a more mysterious, gradual, and ultimately injurious manner, so much so that Spielberg has recently admitted that he does not think he could make the same movie today.

What befalls Neary on that rural route in Indiana is at the very least supernatural — in starkly human and earthly terms — if not flat-out divine revelation. Providing some theological wiggle room for himself, Spielberg doesn't quite deify the aliens; but he does carefully use major images and trappings of the Jewish-Christian tradition that validate occasions of divine revelation, all those palpable displays that traditionally accompany revelations of the divine: light, thunder, fire and flame, searing light within light, wind, earth-shakings, iridescence to the nth power — "Light of Light," as the Nicene Creed puts it. Indeed, in Spielberg's masterful rendering of the eruption of the holy, the display of the *mysterium* itself speaks, revealing through conspicuous splendor the authority of the force that stages these celestial fireworks.

The nature of that force soon assumes greater nuance and clarity as Spielberg adds articulate, affecting music to the mightiness of the light he has constructed. Far beyond mere display, or just "showing off," this mysterious fearsome light from beyond has a voice and wishes to speak; soon after that first "meeting," that lilting five-note coda shows up, and is repeated again and again through the length of the story. It is integral to the "light" that shows up, at once enticing and exuberant, and also carrying within it a code that will tell space researchers where to meet these aliens. It is an inviting, playful set of notes, a combination that goes a long way to obviate the terror that usually comes with encounters with these aliens. The character of this refrain, the "other side" to its personality, is suggested in the film's potent opening sequence in the Sonoran desert, where researchers come across an old man, his face half light-burned as Neary's will be; he claims that "the sun came out last night" and "sang" to him. One critic has gone so far as to suggest that, with this five-tone theme that repeatedly bursts forth, Spielberg is attempting to conjure a mix of notes that is "akin to the music of the spheres."[4] Or perhaps the music, and its eventual overpowering display

---

4. Charlene Engel, "Language and the Music of the Spheres: Spielberg's *Close Encounters of the Third Kind*," *Literature/Film Quarterly* 24 (1996): 376-82.

on Devil's Tower, most resembles the kind of tune that, as the Old Testament Book of Job has it, "the morning stars sang in chorus" when God founded the world (38:7). It is benign, even loving perhaps.

The story takes its time in revealing exactly what has happened to Neary during his long encounter in the Indiana countryside. There is the light that visited him on the roadway, the sunburn, and what his eyes have seen in the subsequent chase of different magical lightships. After the encounter, at four in the morning, he rouses his wife and family and takes them to the hilltop where he and others saw gorgeous lights silently swoop by; but nothing appears. Apparently, the aliens have ended the night's display. The next day, his skeptical wife, Ronnie (Teri Garr), thinks that this is another one of her husband's hare-brained ideas, especially after his employer calls to fire him for not doing his job the previous night. Neary is naturally curious about what's going on, so the next night he goes out to the same hillside to await the reappearance of the lightships, along with a motley assortment of others who have seen the same thing he saw. Instead, to the disgust of this crew of alien seekers, the military stages a flyover of well-lit military helicopters in order to discredit the plausibility of UFOs.

Though Neary does not have another encounter with the ships, there remains the strange and demanding residue of his single meeting, a malign aftereffect that will not leave him alone. To everyone's detriment, his own included, Neary suffers mounting fascination with a particular shape, the same shape that captivates others he's met on the hillside. All these random people find themselves drawn to the image of a cylinder that gradually tapers toward its top. Neary's curiosity about that shape moves from fixation to obsession, culminating in his mad effort to sculpt it in his living room with dirt and shrubbery that he has removed from the foundation of his tract house and thrown in through a window. That deranged gesture — and deranged is what Neary now appears to be — suffices to drive away his wife; she grabs the kids to protect them from her dangerously nutty husband. Alone, recognizing his folly, and now in despair over losing his family, Neary is removing press clippings about UFOs from the family room walls when he sees a TV news report about a chemical accident near Devil's Tower in rural Wyoming.

While Devil's Tower is real enough — and appears to be the very shape that has haunted Neary and countless others — the accident is a ploy the federal government has concocted to scare ordinary people away from the region while its agents meet the emissaries from space in a top-secret environment. The event and image have a certain momentousness for Neary, though he has no clue as to their meaning. This discrepancy between experiential heft and comprehensibility places Neary in the decidedly odd company of Kafkaesque literary heroes, bewildered seekers who have suffered "enigmatic signifiers" that carry with them a "surplus of validity over meaning."[5] These spiritual nomads know that they have come upon a revelatory moment but cannot decipher its import; it is, in short, revelation without content.

From the beginning, Neary has been far from alone in being "haunted" and in his subsequent quest to find the "shape" embossed on his mind. The aliens have imparted this knowledge to countless others, most notably the single mother Jillian Guiler, whose angelic three-year-old son, Barry (Cary Guffey), is eventually abducted by the aliens in what is the film's most terrifying sequence. Neary and Jillian link up for the drive to Wyoming, Neary to satisfy his thirst to "know" what has called him, and Jillian, simply and desperately, to find her lost Barry, one of three lost boys in this movie. He is the one, given his age, who is most beguiled by and trusting of the aliens. The most significant of Neary's fellow questers — and the third lost boy — is Lacombe (played winsomely by the renowned French director François Truffaut), one of Spielberg's against-type scientists who see their work as an extension of childhood wonder and playfulness (another, Keys [Peter Coyote], will appear in *E.T.*). From the start, Lacombe and his large scientific team of like-souled seekers have occupied the fringes of the primary story, Neary's tale; but Lacombe becomes increasingly prominent as the moment of encounter with the aliens approaches. Spielberg goes out of his way to present Lacombe as pure-hearted and spiritual, awestruck and eager to learn, and always in wide-eyed wonder at what he finds. His faith in, and downright reverence for, the reality of the aliens and their benign character, despite significant evidence to the contrary, is unflinching. He seeks knowledge with his heart as much as with his mind, for insofar as he thirsts for intimacy with super-nature, he is profoundly religious, eager to know and venerate a benign power beyond himself and humankind. With only his face and gestures — since he has only a few words in English in the entire film — Truffault creates an enticing Peter Pan–like figure whose deepest appetites do not correspond to popular stereotypes of the modern scientist, who is typically at best reductionist and utilitar-

5. Eric L. Santner, *On the Psychotheology of Everyday Life: Reflections on Freud and Rosenzweig* (Chicago: University of Chicago Press, 2001), pp. 44, 39.

ian, and at worst, a mad Promethean Dr. Frankenstein with no interest in the well-being of humanity.

That negative role Spielberg reserves for the military, both here and in *E.T.* Lacombe seems to be simply an odd duck among his kind, spiritually displaced and very thirsty; and so enticing is his demeanor and deep gentle faith that the audience immediately leaps to embrace his expectations with enormous confidence. The fact that he trusts the aliens ingratiates them to the viewer. In this regard, and in keeping with a religious reading of *Close Encounters,* Lacombe plays the role of John the Baptist, or perhaps Virgil, for Neary and for the audience. But at the very least he is little more than a grown-up version of Barry, trusting fully in the goodness of these mysterious celestial toys that blink, toot, and whirl in joyous playful display.

Though greatly different in background, education, and demeanor, Lacombe and Neary are two of a kind: both are lost boys, still looking for that elusive place that will content their souls. And no matter how grown up they seem, the two share a childlike capacity for wonder and beguilement. The portrait of Neary emphasizes his still pristine boyishness, something that all the work and cares of being a husband and father have not quite wrested from him. The very first shot of Neary sees him in solitary play with the electric train in the family room while the background music is "When You Wish Upon a Star," a sure sign that this is one dreamy grown-up (he'd rather go see *Pinocchio* than play Goofy golf with his kids). The abrupt collision of trains, closely observed by Spielberg's camera, seems to foreshadow the fate of the Neary marriage and family; they will crash in equally dramatic fashion. In contrast to the playful father, the other family members seem distant and unappreciative of his spontaneity and appetite for "fun." Indeed, the other family members, including the children, find Dad rather childish, immature, and in need of considerable patience. It is Neary who is always clowning with his kids, and thus wife Ronnie always has to play the bad cop, making sure Roy behaves as a husband and father should, not as the bumptious boy he is at heart. On the other hand, it is this very relish of fun and exploits, informed by his capacity for innocent curiosity, that makes him the "chosen one" of the aliens.

Nor is there any guile in Neary: what we see is what we get, though that ill equips him for practical life in the real world, where he should be worrying more about work than chasing aliens. He is so utterly fascinated by what has happened to him at the railroad crossing that it never occurs to him that neglecting his job that night in the middle of a major power failure to dash off in mad pursuit of UFOs might cost him his job. And afterwards, with equal obliviousness, Neary musters his family to stand vigil on the hillside, promising the sleepy kids that it will be "better than Goofy golf." And only a person with Roy Neary's predisposition would so quickly turn his living room into a gigantic sandbox for the purpose of creating an enormous mud sculpture of God-knows-what. Both Neary and Lacombe unquestioningly believe in the likelihood of what most would call the magical and divine. They place their hopes — in large part voluntarily — in the techno-glitter of spacecraft and the allure of intergalactic adventure. Indeed, they have faith like that of little children, an ideal that is Christian in origin and romantic in appeal. In this case, given what they both have seen, vesting their hopes in what lies beyond might not be a bad bet.

In this wager, Neary has little choice — at least initially. Lacombe pursues contact with the fearsome aliens for his own intellectual and spiritual reasons. He wants to know more, and he wants to meet this unknown somebody that he, at least, is convinced is benign. He does not express any skepticism about the intentions or character of this cosmic force that is piecemeal making itself known to humankind. On the other hand, Neary — though not actually physically abducted, as is the case with young Barry — has been "taken over" psychologically. After that first nighttime encounter, his obsession with the mysterious shape rises continuously, and, resist it though he does, there is little he can do to fend off the power of the "call" planted deep in his soul by those intense flashes of light-from-within-the-light on that country road. Unable to help himself, he must find the meaning of the shape, the mountain that will prove holy because it will be the place of firsthand revelation with superhuman power. Though knowing full well what is happening to him and that it is costing him his family, he can still do no other, and off he goes on some "damn fool idealistic crusade," as Obi-Wan Kenobi labels the "call" he extends to Luke Skywalker. Some of the more excruciating scenes of psychological delirium and anguish in contemporary cinema come in *Close Encounters,* as when Neary tears up shrubbery to throw in the living-room window, or when he sits fully clothed and crying in the bathtub while water from the shower pours down on him (Spielberg has used either one or the other of those scenes in different versions of the film). The call from beyond splits him and his family wide apart. Ultimately, the call will take him away from earth and earthly ties completely; but at least that decision appears to be a matter of Neary's own choice as opposed to a compulsion.

284

Having just built an enormous mud sculpture in his living room, Roy Neary (Richard Dreyfuss) fears he is losing his mind until he sees the image of Devil's Tower in the bogus disaster report on television.

It is the "call of the shape" that brings him to Devil's Tower to meet the caller; what he does thereafter emerges from Neary's own boyishness, and not altogether a good side of it, though Spielberg does not seem to indicate that Neary's choice to forsake family to soar into space with the aliens is wrong. Once he sees the dazzling armada of spaceships, he's a goner, so to speak; indeed, it is only a short time before he leaves everything behind and goes off with the aliens, so great is the enticement of this ultimate toy. Spielberg, himself a father of many now, can no longer approve of that choice, suggesting that Neary falls victim to an improper and costly enticement. It is rather too easy, and perhaps rather cold, to be Peter Pan, to have all the fun with none of the obligation.

The whole long story culminates in the intergalactic meeting on Devil's Tower, a striking claw-scored, cone-shaped outcropping that rises starkly from the Wyoming flatlands. It is the place that those "called" have seen or heard in their heads, and it is the location communicated in the numbers (geographic coordinates) sent to Lacombe. It is a place of such stark grandeur, it would seem, as Mount Sinai in the Old Testament, designed for meeting gods, as some native American religions have long regarded Devil's Tower. After a long and perilous trek, filled with many obstacles, only Neary and Jillian make it to the top (the Army hunts down all the other civilian interlopers); and then only Neary ventures from the rim into the crater below the summit, where Lacombe's large team awaits the "coming" of the aliens.

285

The whole long sequence, roughly the last quarter of the film, is from beginning to end finely crafted dramatically, visually, and aurally, as befits the coming of the supernatural. Spielberg, his remarkable special-effects team, and cinematographer Vilmos Zsigmond push the boundaries of cinematic possibility. First, there's the warm-up, so to speak: the tower top is visited by playful fly-bys of luminous small blue and red craft that look more like Tinkerbell than the fighter planes one might expect. Then three of them (a sacred number) stop to hover above, eventually responding in color modulation and sound to the musical chimes the Lacombe group beams to them. They then zoom off with their characteristic hum (they are decidedly not big and booming). Thinking these small craft have finished their night's work and accomplished their goal, Lacombe's people applaud their successful, though limited communication. But then, surprisingly, a much bigger show appears: the very sky seems to roil up in cloud and silent lightning, red and gold and white, and then comes an array of ships, all brightly glowing in blue, white, and red, hovering just overhead and then soaring off. It is a profuse and exuberant dance-like display of celestial fireworks. The observers stand agape, as well they should at the might and grace so playfully exhibited. Neary, in particular, who is still hiding behind rocks on the crater rim, can't restrain himself: though he risks capture, he ventures down into the infield to get closer. It doesn't matter because everyone there is too mesmerized to care. Finally, a vast, simply gigantic mother ship, itself towering rings of multicolored light that dwarf the mountain, approaches with a low rumble and does a graceful somersault, as John Williams's delicately jubilant score underscores its breath-taking marvel. Spielberg has slowly ratcheted up the "wonder stakes" to the point of stupefaction at the sheer gloriousness of the spectacle that far outstrips any other screen evocation of the coming of the holy. It is the quintessential Spielberg stylistic signature in a film career that is filled with light.

Slowly the ship descends to rest just above the surface, and the many bystanders don sunglasses and gather around. So benign is the ship's descent that even Jillian ventures down to join the awestruck acolytes. Then comes the remarkable musical conversation: it is initiated by the earthlings, but the mother ship soon turns it into a long progressive jazz riff, a "basic tonal vocabulary," says one of the scientists. It might just as well be a schema for the pure joy of self-expression and creation, as its roaring fantasia even blows a window in the control booth. Religion scholar Jeffrey Goldstein details the way in which Spielberg's aliens "spiritualize" technology by their "play" with its various capacities:

They create music, beautiful light shows, they play with color and sounds like a prankster with the humans. We are terrified and humbled by the mysterium tremendum . . . but . . . fascinated and enraptured by their technology's beauty, artfulness, grace, friendliness, and playfulness. Their mother ship . . . reduces man to puniness. . . . But the center of the ship is aglow with translucent crystalline, citadel shapes drawing us invitingly, like some celestial City of God. . . . This decidedly . . . beautiful and transcendental ship is much like Ezekiel's vision of the menacing four-faced creatures, topped by chariots of wheels within wheels, leading up to the Throne of God's glory at the very peak.[6]

The splendor of the technology is so extreme and compelling that it assumes traits of the divine.

Following the sound-and-light show, after everything has calmed down, the bottom lip of the ship drops down, and shafts of intense bluish-white light pour forth. Robert Kolker catches its characteristically Spielbergian effect: "Blinding light shone directly into the camera lens."[7] The first to emerge from the mother ship are seven figures, all pilots from the planes found in the Sonoran desert at the beginning of the film. While dazed and bewildered, they are unharmed, and they look the same age as they were when they were abducted decades before. (For some critics, the return of the abducted proves the benign character of the aliens; however, that conclusion overlooks the suffering of everyone, especially those left behind, now forty years older than their newly returned loved ones.) Then, before the ramp closes, come many others, civilians among them, including little girls, businessmen, 1950s housewives, at least one dog, and, bringing up the rear, little Barry, who is happily reunited with his mother. Of those watching this procession, only Neary goes toward and into the light, a measure of his unique spiritual thirst and readiness. Standing in front of the ship, Lacombe asks him what he wants, and Neary replies that he only wishes to know that these ships and creatures are "real." Lacombe then hatches the idea of sending Neary, with a cadre of military types who are specially trained for the "mission," off into space with these extraterrestrials. What is needed here is not the technologically smart but the pure-souled, those sufficiently spiritual to understand the character of these visitors. Lacombe has only envy for Neary;

6. Goldstein, "The Spiritualization of Technology: A New Vision for the 1970s," *Drew Gateway* 48 (1977): 30.

7. Kolker, p. 288.

but, selfless man and lover of knowledge and innocence that he is, he intervenes to win government approval for Neary's candidacy, a judgment that is only confirmed by what follows.

For an encore, the ramp descends again, and this time a tall stick-like figure comes out of the ship, a figure whose body seems transparent, no doubt to suggest his ethereal nature. The figure raises his arms in a gesture of welcome, embrace, and benediction, backlit the whole while in prismatic blue-red penumbras with a large red halo looming over his head. This is a prelude to the disembarking from the vehicle of a mob of much smaller, bustling figures, probably children, roughly twenty in number: they have large bald heads and big eyes and appear to be extraterrestrial counterparts to the cherubic Barry (actually they are small girls dressed in tights, ballet slippers, and head masks). Neary is taken off for a quick briefing, is suited up, and prayed over: "God has given his angels charge over you. Grant these pilgrims . . . a happy journey." Of the ten or so astronauts lined up outside the ship, two of these small figures choose Neary and lead him into the ship; the other small ones gather around him as if he were Jesus suffering the little children to come unto him (Matthew 19:14; Mark 10:14; Luke 18:16). They all cling to him as he raises his arms outward, just as the stick figure had, so they can touch him. As he walks into the intense light of the ship, Neary pauses to look back at the world he is leaving, apparently with no regret, and then walks up the ramp, contented and whole, a lost boy having found a home at last. The last alien left, looking far more palpable now, is that stick figure, angular body and long thin neck topped with a large trapezoidal, hairless head, with large eyes dominating his face. (The size of the extraterrestrials' eyes, in contrast to their small mouths, noses, and ears, suggests that these creatures see far more than humans do.) The creature exchanges the now-familiar hand gestures with Lacombe and smiles faintly before retreating into the ship. The ramp closes, and the giant ship ascends upward, looking very much like a star, or the oil refinery that was the inspiration for Spielberg's visual design of the ship.

Spielberg's thematic turn here is clear enough. On the one hand, he honestly depicts the ambiguous condition of the drab sort of contemporary domesticity Roy Neary experiences; yet he endows Neary with more than a mild dose of puerile restlessness. Rather, what troubles Neary is something in his soul, a thirst that he himself has been scarcely aware of. The dreary mores of middle-class life not only constrain his natural childlikeness but diminish his considerable capacity for wonder, play, and delight. Even with his extraordinary appetite for the miraculous, Roy is lost from the start in a routinized and desacralized society. The path to a heart-resting home depends on supernatural intervention, and that encounter succeeds only because it displays a splendor that is "commensurate" with Neary's — and humanity's — "capacity for wonder," as F. Scott Fitzgerald writes in *The Great Gatsby* of the Dutch explorers' response when stumbling across "the fresh green breast of the new world" that was the North American continent.[8]

In *Close Encounters of the Third Kind,* the only way to this resolution, or salvation, is literally out of this world: by being transported into a vastly more intelligent and beautiful force than anything earth affords. While Spielberg does a good job in *Close Encounters* in catching the way religious hope incorporates the psychological, the essentially otherworldly coldness of his vision is in the end profoundly unsettling. The sort of anti-human sterility that is at its core becomes still more pronounced when we compare it to the Moses story, which comprises the story's primary narrative and visual source. Impressed as he is by the burning bush, Moses leaves his quiet, obscure life, not to seek his own satisfaction, but to liberate a whole people.

In other words, Spielberg's chief error lies in his portrait of the divine, and that in two specific but interrelated ways. To be sure, Spielberg grasps the splendor and power of the supernatural: it is majestic and compelling, especially in the music and light it bestows on humankind. What he misses is what in the Moses account is the inmost character of the divine: majesty and might are but two secondary manifestations, more or less conveyances of the divine's own most profound nature; put in simplest terms, that nature is love. In *Close Encounters,* these aliens spend most of their energy and time scaring the daylights out of people, abducting small children and the unsuspecting, sometimes for decades, and terrorizing and devastating those left behind. No matter how shiny and mighty, this is techno-power without morality, and it is a far cry from Moses' account of the divine, in which power acts in history for people, consoling and liberating them from captivity. To be sure, there are divine fireworks aplenty in the Moses account — burning bushes, plagues, miracles, and law-giving thunderstorms — but those always appear in behalf of the liberation and well-being of the Israelites. In *Close Encounters,* the only route to this dearer life is, quite literally, "out of this world," away from the earth and its bothersome people, its confining bourgeois culture that denies and stymies Neary's quite healthy natural

---

8. *The Great Gatsby* (New York: Scribner, 1995; 1st ed. 1925), p. 189.

appetites for wonder and delight. In short, the light and splendor of *Close Encounters* is detached from any significant moral-spiritual content. The redemptive *caritas* at the heart of the Jewish-Christian tradition is here reduced to glitter and tinsel, to what Jeffrey Goldstein has called a "spiritualization of technology."[9]

Spielberg tries to temper the moral gist of his film by giving the aliens, once we meet them up close, a winsome nature, largely by using playfully enticing music and visual imagery that gives them some warmth and gentleness. Unfortunately, this strategy does not go far enough to obviate their ominous and hostile mien throughout the full length of the film. At best, Spielberg is inconsistent, even contradictory, in his portrait: on the one hand, these creatures seem to "sing" in light and sound in a way that suggests ecstasy; on the other hand, they mortify and kidnap. Worse still, as Steven Spielberg has recently admitted himself, there is something deeply troubling in Neary's ready decision to leave this world behind, especially his wife, his needy children, and even his soul-mate Jillian, in order to fulfill a boyish fascination with things that sparkle and go bump in the night. There's more at stake here than the enjoyment of a fancy electric train — albeit intergalactic — such as Neary plays with in the film's first views of him. (Recall that he plays with the train by himself, with "When You Wish upon a Star" playing in the background; his children already seem to have outgrown him.) He is indeed a "lost" boy, but not quite in the romantically sympathetic sense Spielberg intended. What Spielberg intends to be a spiritual search and a benign supernatural visitation ends up being narcissistic, demeaning humanity's deepest thirsts and bonds. That runs directly counter to the Moses account, where the supernatural comes in lovingkindness to free, enrich, and guide human experience into the depths of this-worldly love.

E.T.: The Extraterrestrial

In many ways *E.T.* (1982), released only five years after *Close Encounters,* is Steven Spielberg's best film, largely because the story repairs the glaring thematic inconsistencies in *Close Encounters.* Plot circumstances, themes, and many of the characters echo those in *Close Encounters,* but this time Spielberg places at the story's heart the centrality and necessity of love as the wellspring of cosmic meaning. In *E.T.,* there are two

9. Goldstein, p. 27.

lost boys: one human child, Elliott (Henry Thomas), and the other an extraterrestrial "adult," even though he is roughly the same size as the boy. Each is in his own kind of exile, and both need each other desperately; and they bond completely, giving a whole new spin to the word "interpersonal."

Ultimately, however, despite the depth of their mutuality and love, sacrificial unto death, they conclude that, given who they are, the place for love is certainly in their own respective worlds, not away in a glittery sanctum of intergalactic escape, such as Roy Neary embraced. So, at the end of the movie, each chooses to remain within his own world. Moreover, at the core of the story — the story within the story that gives *E.T.* its depth and resonance — is the Christ story, particularly in E.T.'s redemptive sacrifice for the lost and lonely Elliott. The extent to which E.T. becomes, despite his painful lostness at the story's beginning, a fullblown Christian savior figure, even including a glad and glorious ascension, is more than a little eerie. In this regard, *E.T.* partakes fully in the christomorphic pattern spelled out by Neil Hurley.[10]

The first lost boy in *E.T.* is clearly E.T. himself, abandoned by his extraterrestrial compatriots in their hurry to escape from a research team of scientists scrambling up the mountainside to the aliens' forest landing site. From these first moments, Spielberg thrusts his woebegone alien directly into the viewers' attention, and certainly by the end they cannot avoid reckoning with what kind of creature this is. This clarity and persistence of focus stands in stark contrast to the murky gradualism of *Close Encounters*. Appropriately, then, *E.T.* picks up where *Close Encounters* left off: the very first scene is an encounter of the third kind, at least for viewers, and it, too, takes place on a mountaintop, the usual place for appearances of the divine. The landing place is also something of a wilderness, though it is close to mile upon mile of the cookie-cutter "little boxes" of the suburban sprawl that so hemmed in Roy Neary. The approach of the posse of scientists is very scary to E.T., and to the audience, since it is shot from E.T.'s perspective — about the same as the perspective of the ferns on the forest floor. Before the intrusion, all is very quiet and dark; the only light comes from the warm golden glow of the landing craft and, of course, from the glowing red heart of E.T.

The sequence emphasizes that, whoever these strange visitors are, they are not predatory but are in harmony with the world around them.

10. Hurley, "Cinematic Transfigurations of Jesus," in *Religion in Film*, ed. John R. May and Michael Bird (Knoxville: University of Tennessee Press, 1982), pp. 61-78.

E. T. the Extra-Terrestrial (1982)

Studio:	Universal
Screenwriter:	Melissa Mathison
Director:	Steven Spielberg
Cinematographer:	Allen Daviau
Production Designer:	James D. Bissell
Editor:	Carol Littleton
Music:	John Williams

Cast:

Henry Thomas	Elliott
Dee Wallace-Stone	Mary
Robert MacNaughton	Michael
Drew Barrymore	Gertie
Peter Coyote	Keys

Academy Awards:

Sound Effects Editing	Charles L. Campbell, Ben Burtt
Visual Effects	Carlo Rambaldi, Dennis Muren, Kenneth Smith
Original Score	John Williams
Sound	Robert Knudson, Robert J. Glass, Don Digirolamo, Gene S. Cantamessa

Nominations:

Best Cinematography	Allen Daviau
Best Director	Steven Spielberg
Editing	Carol Littleton
Best Picture	Steven Spielberg, Kathleen Kennedy
Original Screenplay	Melissa Mathison

Their presence does not spook forest animals as they quietly go about their task of collecting botanical samples (their gentle nature is far more benign than all the gratuitous abductions and terrors in *Close Encounters*). Indeed, they seem a whole lot less intrusive, even though they are aliens, than the noisy and clumsy humans who soon arrive in hot pursuit of these invaders. Into this idyllic tranquility charges an ominous black-garbed posse, the NASA guys — or whoever they are — first in their roaring SUVs and then on foot charging through the quiet forest glen. In this, Spielberg's second take on human-extraterrestrial relations, it is the humans who pose a threat, setting out to abduct whatever or whoever they can get their greedy scientific hands on. These government "scientists" bear an uncomfortable similarity to the crass bureaucrats in *Close Encounters*. In contrast to the warmth and light that radiate from the extraterrestrials, the humans simply don't look that good; and they scare off these visitors, who in their rush to escape must leave behind one of their mates, the one who becomes known as E.T., who now is alone, lost, and terrified. There is some merit in one critic's suggestion that, if *E.T.* is a Christ story, then these "scientists" become, thematically and dramatically, the soldiers of Herod who scour the countryside to murder the new-born Jesus so he cannot grow up to rival Herod's authority.[11] Whatever the case, the scene is remarkably effective in eliciting sympathy for the endangered E.T. and in constructing one kind of ominous peril that the newly abandoned creature will face in his sojourn on earth.

The other lost boy in the story, Elliott, is an actual human boy, at least in age: a seventh-grader, Elliott still has the vulnerability of a child; but throughout the film, this emotionally stricken child shows the sense and maturity that adults are supposed to achieve. If Roy Neary is a grown man but childish, Elliott is a child who is "grown" beyond his years in sensitivity and thoughtfulness. His particular lostness lies in the fact that he has been abandoned by his father, who has just run off to Mexico with his secretary, leaving Elliott, his mother, Mary (Dee Wallace-Stone), younger sister Gertie (Drew Barrymore), and older brother Michael (Robert NacNaughton) to fend for themselves in a sprawling California suburb. While Elliott is still very much at home, he nonetheless feels his loss acutely, apparently far more than do his siblings. Henry Thomas portrays him with a sort of wondering tenderness, full of longing for what is now gone (the physical presence of his father) but also for lost

11. David Bruce, "Hollywood Jesus," 3 September 2003. http://www.hollywoodjesus .com/et.htm.

innocence and faith in the goodness of this world. Indeed, in the early scenes Elliott, unlike his siblings, goes around in what seems like a sustained state of quiet mourning. This is somewhat more difficult for Elliott because, from the start, he seems to be a loner, rather distant from his teasing peers and his older brother, who takes refuge from his feelings in a pose of adolescent sarcasm and machismo.

It is Elliott's natural curiosity, amplified now by a great yearning in the aftermath of his father's departure, that brings him to pursue the mysterious creature he detects in his backyard toolshed one night. He leaves gifts to lure E.T. into his trust (David Bruce sees the shed as an evocation of the stable and Elliott's gift-giving a mimicking of the magi). Spielberg gives the slow process of their coming to trust each other a particularly good pace. A loner and now very sorrowful, Elliott needs a friend badly, and he has empathy for those who share his lostness; no wonder he shelters and "adopts" the lost creature whose plight is like his own, but much more extreme. And E.T. seems to be a mirror image of Elliott, showing as much compassion and care for Elliott as the latter lavishes on him. A chief difference, of course, is that while both love those around them, E.T.'s power allows him to heal parts of the broken world. The measure of their kinship shows up most clearly in Spielberg's play with names and initials. It is no accident that the letters "E.T.," the name Elliott gives his new friend, are the letters that enclose Elliott's own name. Spielberg later underscores this deep connection in a poignant sequence where the two very sick creatures muster their failing strength to call to each other with affecting tenderness from their separate hospital gurneys.

The big surprise comes in just how close these two do get, how much of a home they make for one another, and this is largely due to E.T.'s remarkable empathic powers, which extend all the way to the telepathic. What is unique about E.T.'s extraordinary mental capacities, even in the world of science fiction, is that these powers only come into play as a by-product of E.T.'s compassion and love. E.T. does not display these powers to flaunt his might or splendor; their uses are entirely functional, and he brings them out only to accomplish particular ends, such as showing the children where he is from or healing stricken plants or bleeding fingers. Moreover, there is E.T.'s remarkable spiritual capacity — that is, his capacity for empathy and tenderness. The more these two care for one another, the more intellectually and emotionally symbiotic they become — especially emotionally. More than simply knowing or thinking what the other thinks, each feels what the other feels. When

E.T. inadvertently becomes drunk on beer when he raids the refrigerator, Elliott does the same sitting in his science classroom. And that inebriation emboldens Elliott, who has also seemingly assimilated E.T.'s enormous charity and generosity, to free the frogs that the class is about to dissect, no doubt partly because of their striking physical resemblance to his new friend from outer space. The sequence is richly comic, full of surprise and warmth; but it also thematically reveals the mutuality and profound emotional empathy between these two, an intimacy so great that it ends up in a kind of co-indwelling between the two. Indeed, as Michael explains at one point, "Elliott feels his feelings."

The strongest indication of this mutuality is Elliott's increasing use of "we" when he refers to E.T. His brother questions him about this early on, but the practice increases and intensifies to the point where Elliott explains E.T.'s declining health in collective terms: "We're sick; we think we're dying." By the end, the two are so psychically symbiotic that E.T.'s physical condition elicits similar symptoms in Elliott — that is, until E.T. relinquishes their intimacy, choosing to disconnect from Elliott. As for Elliott himself, he realizes that E.T. has finally died "because . . . I don't know how to feel." To be sure, Elliott and E.T. remain distinct individual beings and personalities, but they are also very much one, which has overtones of the mutuality and co-indwelling that characterizes Christian notions of a three-part godhead, a Holy Trinity of three distinct "persons" who are nonetheless of the same substance and "one." This notion of a tripartite godhead has always been one of the stranger doctrinal mysteries in Christianity; but *E.T.* goes a long way toward demystifying it by dramatizing how the co-indwelling might function psychologically.

E.T.'s empathy and power extend not only to his intimacy with Elliott but to actual control of the rest of the physical world, especially in healing its flaws and effecting rescues of endangered creatures, including himself. We first see this when E.T. telepathically lifts into thin air and spins an array of balls to show the three siblings where in the galaxy he has come from. So extraordinary is E.T. that he makes whole worlds, at least small ones, float by the agency of his power. What follows only sustains that initial impression. Soon E.T. will propel the cycling Elliott and Michael high in the air to speed their way to the rendezvous site on the mountain, and will replay the same trick to spectacular effect when he and the other boys escape a horde of police cars that are in hot pursuit of the kidnapped "corpse" of E.T. Further, a mere casual glance from E.T. heals a wilting flower, and later he heals Elliott's bleeding finger with the touch of his own glowing finger, a source of radiant light humming with power that heals instead of terrifies, as it did in *Close Encounters*. And oddly, when E.T. dies, the flower he restored wilts, at least until he is resurrected. E.T. seems to be a life force, pervading everything around him, just as the Force in *Star Wars* flows through and binds all matter and in so doing sustains the world in love.

Spielberg adds countless small story details and visual details that exalt E.T., in good christomorphic fashion, from ignoble and abandoned frog figure to a figure of Christ-like majesty and grace. Humor is a part of this, certainly, but even that is revealing of E.T.'s remarkable character. One of the wittiest moments in the film takes place when Elliott's mother, Mary — who is now in effect, like her biblical namesake, a surrogate single parent to an alien fugitive — ventures upstairs to check on strange noises. She looks in the large walk-through closet that connects two rooms. Along the wall is a neat pile of stuffed animals, at which she glances. But she fails to see E.T., who has concealed himself right in the middle of the pile, looking cute and perfectly appropriate among these funny stuffed creatures. The point is that this outer-space fellow is as benign in nature as any stuffed animal, a toy whose primary purpose is to bring comfort, joy, and friendship to small children. But the film shows well enough that this is exactly what adult humanity also needs much of the time: in this specific instance, the needy adult is the single mom Mary, whose plight demonstrates that calamity can also befall adults. The christomorphic distance E.T. travels is shown at the end of the film, where Mary falls to her knees, weeping at the feet of the resurrected E.T. while he is bidding farewell to her children just before he ascends to the stars in a glowing light ship that trails a rainbow, a traditional Western cultural symbol of hope since Noah. Earlier in the movie, the three children, like the three magi, together lean in wonder and love over their new guest, who will, though they don't know it yet, bring them together as never before. Above their heads, in another instance of fine visual wit, hangs a glowing star-shaped, red-and-blue stained-glass window.

The strongest chord of association comes in Spielberg's very direct specification of E.T. as divine, particularly identifying him with a redemptive Christ, beginning with the advertising for the film: posters adapted a portion of Michelangelo's Sistine Chapel ceiling showing the finger of God reaching across space to touch the finger of Adam and infuse him with life. In the poster, E.T.'s magical finger replaces Adam's, suggesting a direct link between Jehovah, the Creator-Father, and whoever E.T. is supposed to be. Such religious imagery pervades the story. On numerous occasions E.T. wears a hooded cloak: first, when he huddles in the blankets that Elliott wraps him in, and then later when he dons the dress-up clothes Gertie puts on him for Halloween. He looks like a monk in that garb — in fact, somewhat like the Jedi knight Obi-Wan Kenobi. That strain of imagery comes to a resounding conclusion in the film's climactic moment, E.T.'s emergence from the tomb. He has come back to life either because Elliott has pronounced his love over his body or because he has somehow received word that he has not been abandoned, for his compatriots are coming to rescue him. E.T.'s lasting fear throughout, like Jesus' fear at his crucifixion, is that he has indeed been abandoned. In either case — whether from Elliott or from "home" — the power of love and hope has returned E.T. to life. The risen E.T. is ecstatic at the prospect of going home, as he yelps over and over; but Elliott and Michael must first get him to the landing site, no small task given the hordes of government techno-goons hovering around. The two human boys steal the panel truck carrying E.T.'s casket and rendezvous with their dirt-bike comrades at a nearby park before undertaking the trip up the mountain. The comrades wait as the truck approaches and comes to a stop. The back doors fling open, and emerging from the clouds of vapor produced by the dry ice in which his "dead" body was packed is E.T., the white grave-cloth draped over his head, standing in sober dignity in the door of his mobile "tomb," luminously transfigured in the midst of a billowing white cloud. And to cue the proper response, the mildly nasty young boys on the bikes stand in wide-eyed wonder. As for the resurrected E.T. in the door of the van, there could hardly be a more direct summation of the complete arc of the Jesus story.

Spielberg fittingly concludes this messiah story with a mountain-top ascension. Just as E.T. and the boys arrive in the forest after their successful E.T.-sponsored getaway flight, his rescue ship gently descends to the forest floor. This arrival obviously contrasts sharply with the fireworks and power displayed by the mother ship in *Close Encounters* and, for that matter, with the recklessness and violence of the police pursuit of the boys. Soon Mary and Gertie arrive, along with "Keys" (Peter Coyote), the one space researcher who seems to care about E.T. as a being other than a specimen for dissection. Fully healed now, either by love or hope, and his return home assured, E.T. assumes a new measure of dignity and authority, a kind of regal gentleness. His farewells to the three siblings are touching and poignant. To the mischievous Gertie he says, "Be good," repeating the line she has often addressed to him. To Michael, who now dares to caress E.T.'s head, he simply says, "Thank you."

His farewell to Elliott is far more complicated, as befits their history together. E.T. petitions Elliott to come with him, something Elliott says he cannot do, a marked departure from Roy Neary's eagerness to take off with the aliens. Elliott's response to E.T.'s invitation is a simple declaration of "stay" (during this exchange Mary has fallen to her knees). It is E.T. who first confesses his sadness at their parting, holding up his finger and pronouncing "ouch," elongating the word into many syllables. On the verge of tears, Elliott responds in kind, confessing his own "ouch." The two then embrace for a long time, and E.T. tries to comfort Elliot by rubbing his back during the long hug. As the camera looks over Elliott's shoulder at E.T., one of the ship's landing lights casts a bright white halo directly over E.T.'s head, and John Williams's mushy score mounts and swoons.

E.T.'s last gesture is to raise his hand to Elliott's face, and his potent healing finger virtually ignites, casting its bright white light into Elliott's face, apparently anointing and blessing Elliott with light itself. His words are both haunting and explosive: touching Elliott's forehead, E.T. says, "I'll be right here," an echo of Elliott's pronouncement at E.T.'s casket: "I will remember you all my life, every day." That recollection will now be made immediate and constant because some portion of E.T. will dwell in Elliott, apparently much in the way E.T. "dwelt" in Elliott during the days of his sojourn on earth (the words are a close gloss on Jesus' last words on earth, "I will be with you always" [Matthew 28:20]). This is a clear reference to the orthodox Christian notion of a Holy Spirit, a divine comforter and guide who abides with believers after the ascension of Jesus, who is, after all, God come to earth.

But despite this promise of future close communion, E.T.'s departure for his home is sad indeed. His "disciples" watch him climb the gangway, and the family dog even follows him up. The door closes, and the ship silently rises from the earth and then, like Jesus ascending in clouds, streaks like light through the sky, a meteor in reverse, trailing another rainbow.

Even though in the end young Elliott is again abandoned, it is not the kind of destitution that seems to afflict Roy Neary or cast-out David in *A.I.: Artificial Intelligence,* Spielberg's 2001 reprise of the theme. The love realized between the helpless Elliott and the hapless E.T. will persist, especially with the endowment of spiritual kinship that E.T. has promised ("I'll be right here"). Even before E.T. has promised his abiding spiritual presence, Elliott has concluded that his proper place is on earth, tragic and pain-ridden though it is. Thanks to his relationship with E.T., he has discovered that he has his own capacity for love and that he, too,

His magical finger aglow, E.T. tells Elliott (Henry Thomas) that he will always "be right here," thus asserting a continuing in-dwelling presence in Elliott's mind and soul.

is worthy of care and love. Whatever it was that transpired between Elliott and E.T. — and love realized and expressed is always something of a mystery — it has proved restorative, if not fully redemptive, imparting spiritual renewal and hope for the goodness of life and love. In the film's reenactment of the Christ story (divine visitor, love, communion, sacrificial death, and resurrection — all clearly emphasized), Spielberg endorses the indispensable centrality of love for life here and now, the one ingredient that might possibly satisfy the restless human self and make for a genuine "homecoming." At the very least, it's clear that, in making *E.T.*, Spielberg turned away from the promise of escape into otherworldly adventure as an antidote for the tragic human condition.

The element absent from Roy Neary's consideration, and maybe his experience, lies at the heart of *E.T.*: Spielberg here seems to meditate on Robert Frost's claim in one of his most famous poems, "Birches."[12] Amid a torrent of mid-life travails, "weary of considerations" and when "life is too much like a pathless wood," the narrator recalls his childhood delight in swinging to the ground on limber branches from the upper reaches of birch trees. But even while savoring his nostalgic reverie of

12. *The Poetry of Robert Frost*, ed. Edward Connery Lathem (New York: Holt, 1969), p. 122.

swinging birches, he is mindful that he does not want permanent escape from the present, and he admonishes fate to leave him where he is: "Earth's the right place for love: I don't know where it's likely to go better." There is in Frost, and in Spielberg, a kind of resigned hopefulness, one fully cognizant of how cruel life can be but also acutely aware of the fact that, given humanity's deep hungers, there is no other place that might yield personal wholeness and completion. Instead of Neary's escape into transfixing displays of supernatural power and splendor, *E.T.* places its hope in the coming to earth of another sort of splendor, one that casts the light of love into the darkness of human alienation and despair.

A.I.: Artificial Intelligence

In 2001, after a three-year filmmaking hiatus following his blockbuster *Saving Private Ryan*, Steven Spielberg returned to making movies and, after a very long hiatus indeed, almost twenty years, to the "lost boy" theme. Since *E.T.* in 1982, Spielberg had increasingly turned to heavy-duty, fully adult subject matter, notably the Holocaust (*Schindler's List*, 1993), slave ships (*Amistad*, 1997), and Normandy Beach (*Saving Private Ryan*, 1998), all seeming to prove that he had actually grown up. Having established this "grown-up" ability to treat difficult adult subject matter, a maturity that Hollywood had been reluctant to recognize, Spielberg returned to the familiar territory that had made much of his reputation. *A.I.* shows a Spielberg, now in his mid-fifties, who has in the intervening years matured into a writer-director who is a good deal wiser, braver, and perhaps darker about the prospects of human life.

Judging from the account in *A.I.*, the human predicament is neither happy nor hopeful, largely because of people themselves; and there is neither timely nor ready divine rescue for the deeply agonizing psycho-spiritual fix in which sentient creatures, whether human or android, find themselves. This darkening of his vision Spielberg freely admits, acknowledging that he would not have made *A.I.* twenty years before. In fact, the film is so somber in its conclusions that it hardly seems to belong to Spielberg at all. No doubt his own increasing sense of the fragility of human life and affection has played a role. While hard to measure, there is certainly a far greater awareness of the profound tragedy of human life and death, which may well have resulted, at least in part, from his long friendship and collaboration with the late filmmaker Stanley

A. I.: Artificial Intelligence (2001)

Studio:	Warner Bros.
Screenwriters:	Steven Spielberg, Ian Watson, Brian Aldiss
Director:	Steven Spielberg
Cinematographer:	Janusz Kaminski
Production Designer:	Rick Carter
Editor:	Michael Kahn

Cast:

Haley Joel Osment	David Swinton
Jude Law	Gigolo Joe
Frances O'Connor	Monica Swinton
Sam Robards	Henry Swinton
William Hurt	Allen Hobby
Jake Thomas	Martin Swinton

Nominations and Awards:

Academy Award Nominations:

Visual Effects	Dennis Muren, Scott Farrar, Stan Winston, Michael Lantieri
Original Score	John Williams

Kubrick. Kubrick originated the first treatment of *A.I.* from a story by Brian Aldiss, "Super-toys Last All Summer Long" (1969), and thereafter collaborated with Spielberg on it. Kubrick's sudden death in 1999 put the project squarely in Spielberg's hands; whether he chose to make the film out of regard for Kubrick or from his own deepening awareness of life's perilousness, it is impossible to say. Spielberg himself has not indicated his motives for going ahead with the project, nor has he suggested how much of the final product is Kubrick's and how much his own.

In any case, under Kubrick's tutelage — and in comparison to those adult works in which Spielberg set out to grapple directly with the darkness of the Holocaust, slavery, and the world at war — *A.I.* is indeed sober, perhaps even dire, in its conclusions. Gone, or at least greatly modulated, is Spielberg's bent for what one prominent critic bluntly called "ruthless sentimentality," including his taste for deus ex machina endings, an inclination that reappears shamelessly in the otherwise harrowing *Minority Report* (2002).

Nor do special effects overwhelm the story in *A.I.*; more importantly, the cinematography is muted, as Spielberg contains his penchant for visual pyrotechnics, especially lighting, that invariably make climactic scenes look like the transfiguration of Jesus. Also diminished is his haste to deflect uncomfortable emotion with a joke, a habit he has long had. As effective as *E.T.* is, Spielberg shied away from complex or harrowing emotion in it; in *A.I.* he seems far more willing to let characters' fear or sorrow have their way with viewers. There is, in fact, remarkably little humor of any kind, and what there is of it is mostly darkly satiric. Spielberg seems more interested in simply telling the story instead of humoring or sweetening audiences through the hard stuff — of which his films have always had plenty. Most notably, though, *A.I.* simply lacks either a hero or a clearly happy ending. Perhaps due to the influence of Kubrick, *A.I.* has as mournful an ending as Spielberg has managed, verging on stark pessimism about the human capacity for fidelity or the sensibleness of humans' inextinguishable longing for relational intimacy. Though it is too early to judge with certainty, this may signal a distinct movement in Spielberg's mood toward tragic realism, if not outright pessimism. His next film, *Minority Report* (2002), a futuristic horror story about government surveillance, is also very dark and is "saved" only by a tacked-on blissful ending that rings as hollow as anything Spielberg has ever done.

Right from the beginning, *A.I.*'s emotional tonality moves between indignation at human cupidity and wistful melancholy about the impossibility of achieving a modicum of relational trust, not to mention unconditional love. Throughout his long career, Spielberg's negative characters have always seemed more troubled or deluded than plainly evil, more oblivious than selfish in their wrongdoing. From the very start of the narrator's prologue in *A.I.*, it is clear that the human historical prospect has turned very bleak: global warming has melted the ice caps, submerged coastal cities, and caused catastrophic climate change worldwide. What remains of America now prospers because of strict population control and the use of very smart robots. In most ways, these robots, or "mechas" (from "mechanicals"), are completely indistinguishable from people in either their look or behavior, and they go about their narrowly designated tasks — whether as nurses, nannies, or gigolos — with pleasantness and efficiency. These humanoid creatures care about neither their own fate, whether they continue to function or expire, nor that of those around them. In short, what they lack is "feelings," meaning the capacities for empathy and affection, that mysterious inner stuff that makes people people. The rub comes when the leader of Cybertronics, Inc., Dr. Hobby (William Hurt), wishes to create a mecha who can feel and love, specifically a child-bot, for which there is a large market among childless couples. Twenty months later, bingo, the first prototype is ready for testing. His name is David (Haley Joel Osment), and he goes to the upscale home of the Swintons, whose own ten-year-old son, Martin (Jake Thomas), has died — sort of. For five years he has lain cryogenically frozen, awaiting a cure for the disease that killed him. Martin's mother, Monica (Frances O'Connor), still hopes for his revival and steadfastly goes and reads to him every day, even though he is frozen. One day her husband, Henry (Sam Robards), an employee of Cybertronics, surprises Monica when he comes home with young David, the child-bot.

Monica's initial aversion to the creepily serious "child" slowly erodes, and eventually she decides, as the instructions have it, to imprint the child's circuitry; after that she becomes his "mommy," and he will devotedly live and breathe for her forever — irretrievably. The only way to erase this imprinting is to kill the bot-boy. At first quirky, David soon adapts to the modes and mores of people, and all goes well until doctors find a cure for the frozen Martin, who proves both jealous and nasty. Misadventures prompt the fickle parents to "return" David, even though they know Cybertronics will destroy him; this is because, once his circuitry has been imprinted, he will not be able to change his affections. The tearful Monica chickens out, however, and instead abandons David in the woods, Hansel-and-Gretel-style, and tells him to run away. Distraught, confused, and forlorn, the newly orphaned boy soon encounters a host of badly disfigured mecha fugitives who congregate in the woods at a "mecha dump," where they scrounge around for spare body parts that might restore greater function to their diminished selves. These mechas have apparently broken the mold, so to speak, because they do care — at least minimally — about preserving their own lives. The scene is both comical and grotesque as the different bots go about searching for an eye or a better hand.

The only thing that concerns David, however, is finding his mother again; he is technologically bound to her, but he also feels an enormous affection and need that is very human. And so begins his long quest to find Monica once again, the one who is supposed to care for him as much as he cares for her. The "child" can't help caring, wired as he is for this bond, even though Monica, given her fickleness and rejection of him, does not seem to be the mommy to die for. Here the question of who's more human, the robot or the human mother, gets dicey and stays that way throughout the picture. The predicament and stakes are vintage Spielberg; the dark conclusions come from Nathaniel Hawthorne or, in movie terms, Kubrick, the director who made *2001: A Space Odyssey* (1968), *A Clockwork Orange* (1971), *Barry Lyndon* (1975), and other notably dark masterpieces (in theme and mood, *A.I.* feels most like *Barry Lyndon*). At their best, Spielberg's dramas display the deepest human longings for love — trust, care, affection, and delight with others and God — all that we pour into the notion of home, both personal and cosmic.

This is the same turf that Spielberg covered in *Close Encounters of the Third Kind, E.T.,* and fairy tales in general — everyone's initiation into the terrors and dreams of humanity — at least until Disney began to tame the genre. In *A.I.,* the fairy tales evoked are Hansel and Gretel, The Wizard of Oz, and, at its very core, Pinocchio, the tale of the manmade puppet who wants to be a real boy so everyone will love him. Like it or not — and sophisticates of various stripes usually don't — this is the simple inexhaustible stuff of which humans are made, and it is this very craving for relational mutuality and "at-homeness" that is a large part of the image of God forged onto the human psyche. When done well, as Spielberg has often done it, this drama of psyche and soul recalls everyone's deep longing to find the haven (and heaven) of home, the ever-elusive realm of complete and unconditional love that completes the hungry human soul.

David's hope of becoming a "real boy" is the Blue Fairy's promise to transform Pinocchio, a fragment of the Pinocchio story David remembers from bedtime reading. He takes this fairy-tale dream literally, just as people take promises of divine care and personal redemption literally; and he sets out to find this magical being who will make him a real boy so that he can then win back his mother. Here Spielberg stumbles badly, complicating David's quest with digressions that ploddingly reiterate the film's central thesis — just in case the primary story line is not entirely clear. There is, for example, the case of the mecha Gigolo Joe (Jude Law), whose designated task is to sexually satisfy the lonely women who've been neglected or unloved. Joe's very purpose in life acknowledges the limits and distortions of human propensities of various kinds. Despite this programming, Gigolo Joe chooses to care for the lost and searching David, even to his own death. Joe's faithfulness exceeds that of every human in the film, including Monica's, David's erstwhile mother, and Dr.

Hobby, the brilliant narcissist who created David to assuage his personal grief over the death of his own son. And these refined folks fare no better morally than the "bot-hunters," whose fun and profit lies in destroying the race of mechas for the entertainment of those hordes of dispossessed people who've lost their livelihoods to the robots. Apprehended by these bot-hunters, David is to be tortured to death before a large crowd of cheering spectators. In Joe and the human desire for the destruction of the mechas, Spielberg makes his case for intrinsic human meanness.

Eventually, though, David does end up at Hobby's headquarters on the top of a skyscraper that eerily rises out of the deep waters that cover New York City. There David finds countless other Davids just like himself: many, many child-bots in various stages of construction, some already packaged in snazzy boxes for store shelves, the advertising pitch splayed in big letters across the child-size box: "DAVID — AT LAST A LOVE OF YOUR OWN." This discovery of his ordinariness only exacerbates David's sense of insignificance and meaninglessness. There follows an unsettling conversation with the self-congratulating Dr. Hobby, who has lured David to his headquarters by cruelly manipulating David's dream of transformation by the Blue Fairy. Mainly, Hobby triumphs in his own accomplishment in creating David, assuring David that he is different from all other mechas, for he has "the ability to chase down . . . dreams, and that is something that no machine has ever done till you." Technophile that he is, Hobby is oblivious to the toll those dreams have taken on the humanness he has programmed into David's "psyche"; for with the capacity to feel and love comes the capacity to suffer, which Hobby himself has clearly done after the death of his own human son, David, after whom he has named and closely modeled the mecha David. In fact, Hobby shows himself to be crassly utilitarian in fostering technological advance: he is the unfeeling creator who doesn't care in the least how that creature feels; but he creates longings aplenty, particularly the hunger for intimacy, not bothering about whether those longings are ever satisfied. This does not disturb Hobby, though he himself has long supped on grief.

When David complains about Hobby's use of the Blue Fairy to lure him to his headquarters, Hobby rationalizes his ploy with the observation that "the Blue Fairy is part of the great human flaw to wish for things that don't exist." The idea that this deception on a matter so crushingly important to David violated the human heart, as Nathaniel Hawthorne put it, never occurs to Hobby (for whom the business of creating "humanness" seems to be no more than an elaborate hobby). As the god figure, Hobby is downright terrifying in his indifference to human emotion, despite his own very real mourning. Hobby and his world depress David so much that he seeks to kill himself, or at least escape from creatures such as Hobby, and he casts himself into the waters that cover New York. Given what he has learned of humans, his choice seems justified, and his self-destruction would seem to make an appropriate end to the film.

At that moment, though, Spielberg's story takes yet another surprising turn. Instead of drowning, David is carried along by currents amid schools of fish. All the while a bright light shines behind him as if he is pursued, or protected, by some sort of a benign presence. Eventually he arrives, now in a submersible craft, at the long-submerged Coney Island amusement park. Inside it he finds Pinocchio-land and comes to stand before a statue of an angel-like Blue Fairy, wings and all, who in appearance seems to be a cross between a starlet and the Virgin Mary. Still urgent in his quest, and with his voice and face full of eager expectation, David repeatedly beseeches the plaster statue, "Please, please, please, make me into a real live boy." And he continues this "prayer," as the voice-over narrator names it, even after his "amphibi-copter" is trapped inextricably under a collapsing Ferris wheel.

There David remains, in endless futile petition, beseeching an impotent figment of humanity's imaginative thirst for intimacy and permanence. This continues, as the narrator tells us, for two thousand years and into a new ice age, which has caused the complete disappearance of humankind. Through all of this, David keeps his gaze — in a haunting phrase — on the "blue ghost in ice." Until, that is, a new elegant species of creature, descendants of David's own kind of artificial intelligence, and now possessed of extraordinary genius and technological power, arrives to awaken him from his slumber. When he does awaken, he walks straight to the Blue Fairy, who, now brittle from the long deep freeze, crumbles into a heap at David's touch. So much for the human dream of superhuman help, as Dr. Hobby earlier warned. How much Kubrick-Spielberg intend this consequence to reflect the true nature of humanity's quest for God is not altogether clear; the scene could certainly be read that way, especially in light of what follows.

These rescuers of David from his entombment in ice, an apt symbol of the coldness of the human enterprise, quickly access the memory of his entire long sad history of disappointment and frustration, and they promptly set out to repair his sorrow. Tall, thin, shapely, and shining, these comely creatures, each gently touching another, surround David in a circle that magically transports him to his home of long ago. What stands out is how much more concerned these nonhumans, strangers all, are about David's inner self than Hobby ever was in his reckless tinkering with emotion and love. Hobby endowed his mechas with the capacity to love but not the freedom to escape fruitless or cruel attachments; for those first "feeling mechas," enslaved as they were, the only way out of the bondage of longing was the oblivion of death. Indeed, this new species of mecha — a new species of "life" itself — seems more humane than humans ever were, whether as scientist or parent. These new mechas value David for himself and for the fact that he was alive when people were. Strangely, they view humans in their wild longings and visions as a vital piece in deciphering the puzzle of existence. These advanced techno-creatures of spirit revere humans for their "heart sense" in valuing love, even if the latter failed miserably in their efforts to satisfy their thirstings. Through the Blue Fairy they tell David, "You are so important to us. . . ." For now, though, they simply say, "So we want you to be happy."

They manage to give David the comfort of his long-lost home and, in their immense compassion, they give him the comfort of a living, talking Blue Fairy, who seems to exude all the compassion and understanding David has so long sought. In short, they give him a single day of his heart's deepest desire, which is to be reunited with his "mommy," though she's been dead for two millennia. They would make this blissful interlude permanent, but that exceeds even their technological capacities. With but a shred of Monica's DNA, they can re-create Monica for a day but no longer.

So David has his day with his mother, "the everlasting moment he had been waiting for," as the narrator puts it. And a perfect day it is, one without the distractions of her husband, without other children, and, the narrator adds, "without grief." David dotes on Monica, and she on him, a perfect day of hide-and-seek and birthday parties, ending with David tucking Monica in at night as she drifts into the sleep of death. In a last gesture, mother and "son" confess their endless love for one another. David curls up beside her, and for the first time ever, mecha David sleeps, his hungry heart now sated and glad. It seems that at last — mysteriously and perhaps miraculously — David has become the real boy he has yearned to be ever since his human brother, Martin, showed up. At last, after millennia of longing, he has known unconditional love, if only for a day, and this fullness of love has imbued him with full humanity. The notion is that only in the full exchange of love do creatures, humans

The spectral figures from the distant future, having a remarkable physical and spiritual similarity to those in *Close Encounters,* watch the revivified David beseech the Blue Fairy.

and mechas alike, find completion, meaning that the restless heart at last knows the calm and fulfillment that derive from mutual trust and delight in the other. In the first flush of this new deep reciprocity of love, peace descends on David, for that moment and forever; and the same is true for the fretful, conflicted Monica, who, having given fully of herself to David alone, is newly whole, calm, and content. And as David falls asleep, something his machine-based being has never allowed, the narrator concludes the film noting that David "for the first time in his life . . . went to that place where dreams are born."

While we cannot be sure of the exact meaning of that evocative phrase, it suggests some sort of supernal afterlife of bliss that joins one to the wellspring of what we nebulously call the "spirit," whether resident in humans or mechas. As for how this fulfillment comes about, apparently it takes the new god-like species of "mecha" to provide what no humans, or their assorted cultural gods, ever managed to pull off. Here *A.I.* seems to offer the completion, both narratively and visually, of Spielberg's thematic preoccupation from his first days as a filmmaker. The superior new beings who manage to sate David's thirsty heart emphatically resemble the delicate ethereal aliens in *Close Encounters,* and Spielberg borrows imagery from the advertising for *E.T.,* such as the finger extending out to bring life. But in *A.I.,* Spielberg has traveled a long way from those noisy bullying creatures in *Close Encounters*. This evolved techno-species knows better than humans themselves what it will take to satisfy the human heart's deep cravings for intimacy, those cravings instilled in David.

With *A.I.*, Spielberg arrives at full clarity on a theme that resonates through all his films but is especially prominent in the science-fiction tales of lost boys treated in this chapter. These tales offer Spielberg's simplest and clearest expressions of his understanding of the human creature; and for reasons that are not altogether clear, this kind of story also seems to bring out his best filmmaking. The plight of boys either abandoned (Elliott and David) or dislocated (Roy Neary) offers a telling, and wrenching, dramatic prism for displaying what the human creature, young or old, most wants from life. For Spielberg, there is in each person a great and profound thirst for intimacy with others. He envisions this intimacy as encompassing not only a mutuality of affection but a relationship of unconditional sympathy, acceptance, affirmation, and trust. In achieving this full measure of love — for that is what it's most often called — the restless heart satisfies its longings and finds as much a bulwark or "home" as this life provides from the ominous dark forces that invariably threaten to devour safety and innocence. Despite this deepest of human appetites, it is tragically true that people are not very good at constructing or sustaining intimacy, finding and preserving a condition of "at-home-ness." In fact, people most often prove mean, demanding, or just plain fickle, as did Elliott's father and David's mother.

Nor does Spielberg place much hope in the liberal dream of a vast caretaker government that will satisfy all human thirsts, for the selfishness that prevails in individual people is writ large in the impersonality and self-interest of government. This theme begins in *Close Encounters'* treatment of military deception, continues in *E.T.'s* portrait of scientific ruthlessness, shifts slightly to mega-corporate exploitation in *A.I.*, and reiterates all of these in *Minority Report*. Despite Spielberg's reputation for sentimental optimism, it is not really true of his best work, though it does certainly impair films such as *The Color Purple* (1985), *Amistad* (1997), and even *Saving Private Ryan* (1998). For reasons that are not clear, the science-fiction lost-boy tales bring out in Spielberg an affecting balance of realism and emotion that resonates with children and adults alike.

What makes these tales religious is that, in all of them, Spielberg entertains the notion that, given general human flakiness, especially among adults, only the supernatural — specifically some transcendent compassionate Other — seems capable of finally satisfying that unfathomable human longing for intimacy. In *Close Encounters of the Third Kind,* Roy Neary finds his domestic and work worlds prosaic, devoid of anyone — even his own children — who relishes the fun and wonder of life quite as much as he does. The only things that finally capture Neary's whole heart are the bells and whistles, so to speak, of the vast techno-power of the alien spaceship that comes to rest on Devil's Tower. For no good reason at all, other than his capacity for childlike wonder, the aliens choose Neary to ride off with them in their gigantic light ship for who knows how long. And for no good reason, other than his fascination with things that "go bump in the night," Neary blissfully chooses to go off with them, leaving fatherless his very needy family. It is a gesture of supreme narcissism for Neary to leave and for the director to romanticize this desertion by the first intergalactic deadbeat dad. The situation is worsened by the fact that, up until their landing, these aliens seem decidedly lacking in any enviable qualities whatsoever.

Why so many smart people, such as Lacombe, are so eager to meet these scary aliens constitutes the great logical flaw in the story's motivational structure. After all, when these aliens do show themselves, it is mostly to terrify, kidnap, and obsess hordes of innocent bystanders. If they had displayed themselves in the gentle manner of E.T. and his cohorts, audiences could perhaps understand Neary's readiness to elope; but without that attractiveness, the film remains deeply perplexing, though it is riveting filmmaking from beginning to end. The aliens come with godlike power; bathed as they are in light and music, they seem to manifest quantities of divine majesty, save for that bothersome moral posture. Bringing nothing but their techno-blitz and doing nothing to help out this earthly sphere in any way whatsoever, they simply grab their new specimen and make their getaway after the scantest of hellos.

E.T.: The Extraterrestrial seems to set out to redress the manifest shortcomings of *Close Encounters.* This time Spielberg presents a far more satisfying, and affecting, portrait of the human circumstance and a plausible antidote for its ills. Overall, *E.T.* offers a trenchant metaphor for specifically Christian notions of the Incarnation. Elliott's father running off with his secretary sounds like Neary in *Close Encounters,* and *E.T.* is best seen as a sequel that tracks the lives of those left behind. Bereft and alone, Elliott comes upon another abandoned soul, the marvelous alien he dubs E.T., who has been left behind by compatriots in their hurry to escape a marauding search party of human astro-scientists. And E.T. is about as benign an alien as Hollywood has ever come up with. He clowns, gets drunk (inadvertently), heals, and, most of all, cares deeply about the young boy who has sheltered and befriended him. Their bond of mutual sympathy is so profound that E.T. effects telepathic communication between the two. Intimacy and trust can hardly go deeper than that. Along the way he performs various small miracles, from floating a small world to healing dying flowers and cut fingers. Nothing is too small or insignificant for his attention. Slowly this lost alien, unlikely redeemer though he is, transforms the world around him, teaching everyone a new measure of gentleness and love that culminates in his self-sacrificial death so that Elliott may live. And so great is his care for the earth and its people that it seems he would do the same for the whole of humanity.

And then comes the resurrection and ascension, leaving little doubt about what sort of supernatural being this alien creature is supposed to suggest. The now transfigured and very "Christ-like" E.T. invites Elliott to go with him, but Elliott, unlike the crazed Roy Neary, chooses to stay; both members of this symbiotic pair know that the demanding ties of kinship and obligation surpass whatever pleasant prospects escape might hold. Spielberg seems to argue that it will take the supernatural intervention of Love itself for people to know love, and that the human task is to stay on this earth to try to realize that love in the here and now. This recognition of the depth of the human yearning for love and the necessity of a transcendent agape to display its lineaments place *E.T.* a good galactic distance from *Close Encounters*. Indeed, in *E.T.* Spielberg seems to have come upon the recognition that the perceptual and moral limitations of the human creature are so profound that any measure of redemption or healing of human wrongness and sorrow depends on the approach of some transcendent Other. And in many ways a large part of *E.T.*'s success derives from Spielberg's masterly narrative and visual distillation of central elements of the Christian story. He at once mines the potent enticements of the story itself, supplies a storehouse of that story's most beguiling images, and then deftly pitches the whole brew at humanity's personal thirsts for reconciliation and intimacy.

In *A.I.*, Spielberg becomes blatantly insistent on the prominence of the human thirst for intimacy and again suggests that the only way that might be satisfied is with the intervention of a grandly benign supraphysical compassion. The exact metaphysical status of the strange new "mechas" that come at the end of the film is never made even proximately clear, though they seem to comprise a sort of self-creating techno-spirit, a new kind of divinity that differs markedly from tradi-

Spielberg DVDs

The filmmaker in Hollywood who has always taken the greatest care in the video release of his films is Steven Spielberg, and that is especially true of the three films treated in this chapter, even before the coming of DVD. One of the early benchmarks for extensive supplemental material was the early laser disk edition of *Close Encounters of the Third Kind* (1977). The disk contained extensive commentary by Spielberg and his expert crew of special effects people. The new two-disk DVD "Collector's Edition" is nicely supplemented, but it fails to rival the laser disk. One disk contains the film, and the other a recent documentary on the making of the film, a 1977 featurette on the same, and a collection of deleted scenes.

The digitally enhanced 20th Anniversary DVD "Limited Collector's Edition of *E.T.: The Extra-Terrestrial* (1982)" is similarly equipped with a twenty-five-minute "making of" documentary. Of equal interest are a strong collection of production drawings and photos, a documentary of a twenty-year reunion of cast and crew reminiscing about their experience on the film.

The two-disk "Special Edition" of *A.I.: Artificial Intelligence* is a film buff's dream, carrying more supplemental material than the earlier films, including interviews with Spielberg, Haley Joel Osment, and Jude Law. There are useful featurettes on acting, lighting, design, special effects, visual effects, robots, and music.

As always with Spielberg, the visual and sound qualities of the disks are superb.

tional human conceptions of transcendent divine love. Humans play mecha child David (and others like him) grievously false, either abandoning or destroying these creatures whom humans themselves have contrived for their own convenience. The mecha destruction fair, where violence is done for entertainment, differs little in impulse from the purposes of creating mechas in the first place — that is, human pleasure. And once again, human lostness can only be repaired through intimacy availed by some sort of transhuman intervention. There is the great human dream of care that is only fully satisfied by intimacy with some sort of transcendent Other.

A.I. is enchanting, haunting, challenging, and vexing, a rueful meditation on what's best and worst about being human and the huge bother

312

of expecting very much out of life. That's a grim homily, however lovingly dreamed and etched it is in *A.I.* Nonetheless, in an era of mounting triviality in the cinema, Spielberg's accomplishment recalls what movies can do, and what Hollywood never even so much as thinks about attempting anymore, enamored as it is of gimmicks and rank profit.

Each of the three movies discussed in this chapter concludes with moments of fulfillment of the deep thirst for intimacy, although each is bittersweet in its own way, either for its moral implications, the brevity of its intimacy, or its bleak irony. Still, together they form a penetrating diagnosis of the intricate hungers and contradictions of the human creature; and together they provide a fetching portrait of what it will take to resolve the cravings of the restless human heart. In this regard, Spielberg posits the necessity of some sort of transcendent love, for that is what it will take to address and heal the pernicious self-absorption of humans and the limits of human longing. Most of all, though, in these sci-fi films, drawing heavily on the central narrative and intellectual currents of the Jewish and Christian traditions, Spielberg makes credible the "encounter" with divine love, its shapes and consequences, though it does take him a while to come clear about the nature of the transcendent presence that he dramatizes. Since the mid-1980s and the appearance of *E.T.*, Spielberg has been consistent in his claim that some sort of transcendent love is necessary in order to show human creatures the path to love and to the recognition that, when all of earth's tragic darkness is reckoned, earth is still "the place for love."

Spielberg Filmography

Catch Me If You Can (2002)
Minority Report (2002)
A.I.: Artificial Intelligence (2001)
Saving Private Ryan (1998)
Amistad (1997)
The Lost World: Jurassic Park (1997)
Schindler's List (1993)
Jurassic Park (1993)
Hook (1991)
Always (1989)
Indiana Jones and the Last Crusade (1989)
Empire of the Sun (1987)
The Color Purple (1985)
Indiana Jones and the Temple of Doom (1984)
Twilight Zone: The Movie (1983) (segment 2)
E.T.: The Extra-Terrestrial (1982)
Raiders of the Lost Ark (1981)
1941 (1979)
Close Encounters of the Third Kind (1977)
Jaws (1975)
The Sugarland Express (1974)

PART FOUR

FOUND

This last section includes films that seem not to fit tidily into Buechner's categories. All the films here tell stories of full-grown, more or less "normal" people who are at some point abruptly struck by some sort of Light that they do not expect, look for, or comprehend. The tales culminate with clarity and profound gratitude for the measure of Light that has come their way. The films end with manifold praise, though it comes in one instance in the form of tears. This category differs significantly from those films treated in the second section on Christian grace. The critical difference comes in cultural setting, for all these people live in a world that is markedly secular. Consequently, when Light smacks them in the face, so to speak, they don't know what to make of it because the culture no longer provides either a fetching or cogent religious prism for viewing their experience. For the characters in *Tender Mercies, The Mission,* and so on, that is not the case. When good or bad comes along, it usually transpires in a specifically Christian culture, one that is informed by the theologically interpretive riches of the Judeo-Christian tradition, and as a result, characters readily understand their experience in those terms — if only broadly so. And further, the bright gift they receive often comes from the church itself or from loving Christian people. These provide the winsome prism through which characters understand their personal experience.

In the three films in this last section, that is decidedly not the case. When light of some kind does strike them, they lack a ready frame of reference or perspective that will help make sense of it all. As a result, they misread, protest, or simply puzzle over it. In *Grand Canyon* and *Blue,* the meaning of the benign riddle in which the central characters find them-

315

selves enmeshed at first baffles them; it only becomes entirely clear in the last frames of the film. In *American Beauty,* the dismally besotted main character so woefully mistakes the exit from his life of tedium and quiet despair that his wrong-headedness in effect kills him, although not before a string of last-minute epiphanies dispels his delusions of meaning. Only his regular voice-over commentary and an alternative vision of life by a shadowy minor character intimate that in the end all will be well. For all of these folks, the last sort of thing they expect to have happen does, and it takes a long time for their cognitive capabilities to catch up to their experience and the sixth sense of the soul. The full meaning of the Light takes a long time to dawn, and all three films, as different from each other as they are, end in quiet exultation. I entitle this last section "Found" because, in the end, all these folks come to realize what in their lostness has found them.

How much these stories differ from each other is immediately clear. Lawrence Kasdan's *Grand Canyon* (1991), co-written with his wife, Meg, features an ensemble of diverse characters caught in the urban cauldron of contemporary Los Angeles: film producers, lawyers, secretaries, tow-truck drivers, white and black, male and female, rich and poor, young and old, and so on. Regardless of their work, race, or home location, they are all beset by the woes of modern urban life: traffic, crime, loneliness, poverty, competition, gangs, and meaninglessness, to cite only a few. They are even vulnerable to a few of the perennial disasters, such as earthquakes (this is Los Angeles, after all). Despite these perils, or maybe because of them, most come by assorted routes to conclude that a largely unseen Providence labors to help individual people and then brings the whole diverse lot of them together in a new sort of trust and harmony. As a result of this divine action, most end up affirming that, as the last words of the film put it, life is "not all bad." This is a judgment that takes them a good long while to arrive at, for all these characters start in hostility toward any such conclusion, grudgingly move toward bafflement, and then, finally — in a subdued but sincere "Gloria" — embrace what they can no longer deny. A few, given how smart they are, should have caught on much earlier than they do, but their sense of privileged sophistication keeps the blinders on.

American Beauty (1999), directed by British stage director Sam Mendes and written by Alan Ball, tracks the sad but very funny history of a middle-aged public relations man, Lester Burnham (Kevin Spacey), who mistakes the sexual fantasies of American male adolescence for the holy grail, only to discover otherwise in the very last minutes of his life.

316

The satire is biting and relentless: on Lester, his wife, Carolyn (Annette Bening), the real-estate entrepreneur, America's hyper-sexualized youth culture, and a catalogue of lesser targets as well. For some viewers, Lester's awakening from somnolence to randy self-awareness seems, for a long while, to be a good thing: at least Lester is no longer asleep, and male viewers in particular cheer him along in his dogged pursuit of his teenage daughter's best friend. How wrong he is in his exaltation of this sort of American beauty finally bursts on him in the last moments of his life, when he arrives at a radically different apprehension of beauty. That is, beauty as a luminous splendor that pervades all of life, transfiguring the commonplace into pronouncements of divine love in and for the created world. When Lester abruptly dies, his face wears a smile that he carries into death. The film won Academy Awards for Best Picture, Best Director (Mendes), Best Actor (Kevin Spacey), Original Screenplay (Ball), and Cinematography (the late Conrad L. Hall).

Though very similar thematically to *Grand Canyon*, the late Polish filmmaker Krzysztof Kieslowski's *Three Colors: Blue* (1993) could hardly be more different in story and style. The first film in a trilogy derived from the colors of the French flag, *Blue* inspects the "afterlife" of a French woman (Juliette Binoche) whose young daughter and famous composer husband have died in a traffic accident that she has survived. Though she struggles to eradicate all feeling and attachments within a self-fashioned half-life, her escape from life is repeatedly disturbed by austere but resplendent bursts of music, heard only by Julie herself and the audience, which beckon her to foreswear her numbness and to embrace life again, along with the risks of loving a gorgeous world. Even as she seeks anonymity and non-life in Paris, the music, people, and events will not leave her alone; eventually she grasps the importance of the music that periodically disrupts her self-induced anomie. Almost a silent film, *Blue* makes extraordinarily complex use of cinema's resources, particularly palette and soundtrack, to show how the divine pushes Julie toward resurrection and a re-embrace of the goodness of life. Indeed, for Julie, blue is the color of love, and the music that intrudes on her inner life is the sound of the color of love.

All the characters in these films end up, albeit by different means, at a place where they never expected to be, one full of gratitude and love for this world and the people around them. And as all the films in the end acknowledge, this is the unforeseeable gift of recognition of the unimaginable beauty of a world cast into being by the exultant love of God. By one means or another, Light has found them.

CHAPTER 11

OF ANGELS AND HEADACHES

The Unexpected God of *Grand Canyon*

In a brief scene midway through *Grand Canyon,* a well-to-do middle-aged housewife sits by her backyard swimming pool. She gazes fondly at the baby she holds in her arms, a child abandoned under a bush whom she found that morning while on her morning jog through her posh neighborhood. As the scene closes, she says to herself, quietly and contentedly, relishing both her find and this moment, "Surprise, surprise." Bound together as they are, the scene and the phrase go to the heart of *Grand Canyon,* and they are about as close as writer-director Lawrence Kasdan and wife Meg, who cowrote the screenplay, come to an outright declaration of the substance of their sprawling chronicle of the perils of survival in contemporary Los Angeles, a city that looks and feels like it has been spewed up from hell itself. As good filmmakers do, Kasdan trusts the power of the story — itself full of many surprises — and his own cinematic ingenuity to convey his suspicion that prospects for life in Los Angeles, and for life in general, may not be nearly so grim as a lot of evidence suggests, a good deal of which Kasdan graphically details in the fear and turmoil that dominate the first part of his story.

By the end, though, it is clear that the Kasdans believe that amid the dark tangles and pitfalls of living in this world come shining surprises, unexpected but out of somewhere, suggesting that people, even though they little sense it, are not alone in the consuming darkness of their sometimes dire circumstances. As bleak as human life can be, amid that very darkness there courses a relentless lovingkindness that attends to human well-being and, to that end, continually intrudes in unforeseeable ways to save people from physical peril, isolation, confusion, and meaninglessness. Near the end of the film, the mother who has found

318

the abandoned baby declares that miracles — signs of divine involvement and care — abound but go unobserved because no one expects or looks for them anymore, to borrow from T. S. Eliot's *The Four Quartets*. Horror and glory mix together, and even though much of the time evil and destruction prevail, divine care moves above and through the despair and mess of life. It is a high and holy kind of love, albeit ever mysterious, that repairs the wreckage between people, even the most unlikely people, to bring about reconciliation, mutuality, and wholeness. And it is a grand vision of what life should be like, one that culminates in the rousing last scene of this movie, where brokenness is wondrously healed and made whole — at least for a little while.

That is a lot for any film to tackle, and *Grand Canyon* is far from perfect, having its own share of miscues and digressions. Nonetheless, it is remarkable in constructing a plausible, cogent cinematic portrait of how and why the divine, in both small and spectacular ways, shows up in human affairs. The story is such that both the characters and audience come to ponder the possible meaning of those events usually called coincidence, good fortune, or lucky stars. *Grand Canyon* wonders aloud in its script, through events, and especially in its visual style whether these surprising rescues, recognitions, and connections are not in fact the hand of a supernatural guiding love that moves and cares unceasingly. To that end, the film depicts numinous moments of outright revelation, the kinds of insights we usually dub "epiphanies," when the fog that typically engulfs human experience briefly clears and the stubbornly opaque world turns translucent and glowing, infused with divine care and purpose.

Both the characters' histories and those revelatory moments clarify the Kasdans' supposition about the possible reality and purposes of God, the how and why of God's activity. For them, what makes the holy holy — the very purpose of these displays of supernatural power and fireworks — is not that these moments show the existence of some divine power but that they display its inmost nature, an incessant care for the well-being of people, particularly for bringing disparate people into deep bonds of trust and care. It is this holy action that turns alien and threatening parts of the world into domains of welcome and joy, turns destruction into healing, and turns lost places of fear and discord into something akin to home. This vision shows reconciliation as a chief feature of the otherwise somewhat amorphous notion of redemption. In the Kasdans' vision, human life was made for intimacy and delight, and it is to these ends that God acts.

319

"Not the Way It's Supposed to Be"

A great part of the emotional power of *Grand Canyon* comes from the Kasdans' utter — and graphic — honesty about how bad human life can get, which is the story's beginning and a reality it never forgets even as it turns to happier possibilities. Indeed, the Kasdans seem to go out of their way to emphasize innumerable threats to life and the pursuit of happiness, if only to avoid making whatever hopefulness they do come to offer feel like pablum or mawkish optimism. Their honesty about the way the world is, to wit, a dire worst-case scenario, sets the bar high for whatever counter-evidence they offer, specifically for the hard task of depicting experience that might allay our worst fear about the intrinsic meanness and meaninglessness of life. They people their story of life in the hard times of Los Angeles with a diverse group of lost souls. Just about every kind of character and type is there, about a dozen in all, covering the social spectrum from glitzy movie producers to gang members and the homeless. And in their own ways they are all sorely confused, aimless, scared, and solitary — usually for good reason, given when and where they live. This is urban malaise writ large. By the story's end, though, almost all have arrived at better places, though their routes there have not been easy or direct.

At first, though, they start from where they are, and that is Los Angeles, a place that bears little resemblance to a city of angels. Despite its Hollywood-soaked mythic status as a golden land, the last frontier of the good life, America's paradise of sun and celebrity, it is, in fact, quite the opposite. As *Grand Canyon* sets out to make perfectly clear, all the Hollywood happy endings cannot paper over its harsh contemporary reality, one just about everybody in the city knows too well. The harsh truth is that, despite the glamor and glitter, Los Angeles seems worse off than other American cities. Instead of a fabled Eden, it has become a killing zone, physically and psychically, a place consigned to death — muggings, drive-by shootings, child abandonment, eternal traffic, terror, and gory flicks that celebrate it all. And what people don't do to each other, nature takes care of in earthquakes, brushfires, heart attacks, and any number of other natural disasters. The predominant emotion in Los Angeles is fear, as Davis (Steve Martin), the B-movie producer, points out; and he should know because, as a film producer, he has made a killing exploiting the mayhem with guns-and-gore movies. When a helicopter traffic reporter looks down on its hydra-headed freeway system and comments, "It's hell down there," he is talking about far more than the traffic.

To make sure everyone gets his point about the frightening disarray of modern urban life, Los Angeles-style, director Kasdan bothers to articulate it in the good crisp language of the dialogue, making his point unavoidable even for theater-goers numbed to film chaos. In an early scene, after narrowly escaping an urban gang, the well-heeled white immigration lawyer Mack (Kevin Kline) talks with his rescuer, tow-truck driver Simon (Danny Glover), about life in the city. He concludes that Los Angeles and the world in general have gone to "shit," and he marvels that, given the innumerable ways in that city to "buy it," anyone is left alive at the end of the day. Indeed, this world is "not the way it's supposed to be," as Simon tells the spokesman for the small gang of thugs. It is Simon, a lay philosopher of sorts, who has thought long and deeply about life and survival, and he is quietly eloquent about the insignificance of humanity in an indifferent universe, which for him is symbolized by the muteness and ageless perdurance of the rocks of the Grand Canyon, rocks that "laugh at me and my troubles." Humanity, he thinks, is akin to the fly on the rear end of a cow by the side of the road as whatever intelligence there is in the universe speeds by at seventy miles an hour. Apparently, Darwin is alive and well and living in L.A.!

Los Angeles is a grim place where fear is warranted, even necessary, and the filmmakers never let viewers forget that this is a world of caprice and predation. Indeed, it is a major, and memorable, point of the film: evil abounds, erupts, and surrounds. This sense of "uncontrolled evil," as Kasdan has put it, has always been a strong current in his movies, from *Body Heat* (1981) to *The Accidental Tourist* (1988), and it seems to shape much of the narrative structure through the first portion of this film. The story constantly juxtaposes the safety of normality with abrupt graphic eruptions of devouring evil from which no one, no matter how "normal" or rich, is immune. This looming evil goes everywhere, resolutely ignoring neighborhood or social status. Evil erupts in a drive-by shooting in a poor neighborhood, but the rich also get mugged and shot while shopping on Rodeo Drive. And earthquakes and heart attacks strike everywhere, indiscriminately and pervasively.

The opening sequence signals the pressure of this inescapable and enveloping reality, starting in gray (or rather black-and-white, in which gray predominates), and very soon thereafter the story enters the full darkness of night itself. The opening credits play over a gray-sepia slow-motion basketball game on a playground in the inner city. While black men play pick-up ball, a teenager buys drugs from a passing car across the street and then walks toward the camera, which then cuts to a heli-

---

Grand Canyon (1991)

Studio:	Fox
Producers:	Michael Grillo, Lawrence Kasdan, Charles Okun
Screenwriter(s):	Lawrence Kasdan, Meg Kasdan
Director:	Lawrence Kasdan
Cinematographer:	Owen Roizman
Production Designer:	Bo Welch
Editor:	Carol Littleton

Cast

Danny Glover	Simon
Kevin Kline	Mack
Steve Martin	Davis
Mary McDonnell	Claire
Mary-Louise Parker	Dee
Alfre Woodard	Jane
Jeremy Sisto	Roberto
Patrick Malone	Otis
Randle Mell	The Alley Baron
Sarah Trigger	Vanessa

Academy Award Nomination

Original Screenplay:	Lawrence Kasdan, Meg Kasdan

---

copter slowly traversing the sky high above. (This is the first of many shots of helicopters hovering throughout this movie.) As the ball bounces lazily on the rim, the camera cuts to a very different kind of ball game and to a very different world: from the gray sepia of the sandlot game, the ball now bounces into the garish full color of a Lakers game in the Los Angeles Forum. "Magic" Johnson leads a fast break, deftly passing the ball off to a teammate for an easy basket. Sitting in the high-priced courtside seats are three figures: a flashily dressed, silver-haired man of middle age (whom audiences recognize as Steve Martin), an attractive female, and a distracted man dressed like a businessman (Kevin Kline). Despite his proximity to the basketball action, this last fellow seems to be spending most of his time eyeing the assorted groupies who parade through the stands. After the game, outside the fancy Forum Club, the silver-haired Davis harangues his friend, the distracted Mack, about life in Los Angeles, particularly about the extent to which fear hounds everyone. Davis himself seems untroubled by such fears, flamboyantly dressed as he is in an orange duster coat, with a comely blonde on his arm, and his red Ferrari Testarossa in the parking lot. He tells Mack, his "best friend," that they have to talk more about fear, even as he revs up his sports car and the camera cuts to his California license plate, which spells out GRSS PTS, a double-entendre reference to how profit shares are computed in Hollywood and, aptly enough, to the kind of films from which Davis makes his enormous income.

Mack himself is not so lucky, at least on this night: he will soon come to know fear firsthand and full-blown. To avoid the traffic exiting the Forum, he tries a shortcut through the ghettoes surrounding the arena. Realizing that he's lost, with his level of fear rising, he jauntily, yet ominously, sings along with Warren Zevon's "Lawyers, Guns, and Money" on his car radio: "Send lawyers, guns, and money, get me out of here." And then, while he's still lost, his snazzy Lexus sedan breaks down on a dark, empty street. His car phone is also dead, so he has to call for help from a gas station. While Mack waits for the tow-truck back at his car, a gang of five black youths accosts him; the leader even threatens him with a gun to force him out of his car.

Just at the point when some kind of violence seems imminent, up comes the tow-truck, yellow lights awhirl and roaring noisily, and out steps driver Simon (Danny Glover), himself dressed in a yellow tee-shirt (yellow is the color of hope and love in *Grand Canyon*), baseball cap, and, in the style of the hero in western movies, cowboy boots. Instead of a six-gun, he carries a crowbar, and after some tense moments he convinces the edgy young gang leader to let him and his new customer go their way. Soon afterwards, at the service station where Simon has hauled Mack's car, the two chat while Mack waits for a cab. As they sit beneath a streetlight outside the station late at night, a scene that is reprised near the end of the film, Simon quietly lays out the sober Darwinian view of life he has adopted as a black man who has grown up in Los Angeles and now rides its mean streets through countless long nights. Throughout Simon's long confession of despair, Mack hardly dissents, though his life circumstances contrast starkly with Simon's, as viewers have already seen in the brief cuts back to Mack's home (where he has phoned to let his family know about his whereabouts).

There is much more in the movie — indeed, in a vivid chain of horrors — that confirms and even darkens Simon's estimate of the dire prospects for human happiness. From the gas station where they wait, the camera becomes a helicopter searchlight monitoring the ghettoes nearby. It arrives at the home of Simon's sister, who, we've learned, lives nearby. She is waiting up for her teenage son, who is a member of a local gang. Later in the film, her home is the target of a hail of bullets in a drive-by shooting. She and her ten-year-old daughter barely escape with their lives, and when quiet finally comes, the camera watches the terror-stricken mother in close-up as she screams and screams — for a full fifteen seconds of screen time. Still later in the film she curses a door-to-door salesman who is trying to sell life insurance policies to parents for their children.

Nor is the violence confined to high-crime areas. On a sunny afternoon in Beverly Hills, Davis parks his Ferrari on Rodeo Drive. Again dressed to kill, so to speak, in a purple suede coat and white trousers, he is approached by a gun-wielding mugger, who demands his Rolex watch. When Davis misunderstands the mugger's thick accent and instead offers the keys to his car, the mugger shoots him in the leg. Davis falls on the ground next to his fancy car, the camera angle straight down as blood (the same bright red as his car) stains his pant leg, urine stains his crotch, and he vomits. He, too, will survive, but just barely and with a badly shattered leg that will leave him hobbling for the rest of his life. This and the drive-by shooting offer some of the most realistic violence ever put on film, especially as the camera dwells on the toll of the violence in psychic terror and in body function. But these displays are far from gratuitous and customary, as is usually the case in the violent exhibitions that Hollywood so often exploits and enjoys. Instead, Kasdan focuses on the relentlessly sad aftermath of violence, the consequences that movies rarely depict. In place of the usual cartoon violence, the story focuses on the actual grievous conditions of life in contemporary Los Angeles, the city that is perhaps most emblematic of American cultural and social disarray. The film's focus on the benefits but also the toll of life on the living, the sorrows and joys and hopes of mostly ordinary people, gives it a heady dose of realism and takes it a dramatic leap away from adult fairy tales of life in "La-la land," such as *Pretty Woman*.

And there are other kinds of violence, less sensational but no less horrible. Claire (Mary McDonnell), Mack's wife, finds the baby abandoned in the bushes as she jogs through her upper-middle-class neighborhood. And needless to say, no one escapes earthquakes. After one

With stark realism, Davis (Steve Martin), an unapologetic promulgator of film violence, lies gravely wounded beside his red Ferrari Testarossa.

small tremor, Mack and Claire stand laughing in their backyard, relieved that this one is not "the big one." But their relief is shattered when an elderly neighbor runs outside screaming that her husband has suffered a heart attack.

One of the more admirable aspects of *Grand Canyon* is Kasdan's resolve to treat violence with as much honesty as he can muster. After all, he seems to say, in real life in the real world, especially in places like Los Angeles, violence is very real and always looms on the periphery of ordinary life, waiting to erupt and consume, and there is no protection from its pressure. These instances are particularly overt, aggressive expressions of a larger pervasive evil that afflicts human life. Kasdan bothers to film these violent episodes from the outside in, going up close and inside the experience of the victim of the violence. Instead of bringing us close in on the "high," the power rush of the shooters (the usual practice of Hollywood films such as the Dirty Harry pictures, *Lethal Weapon,* and *The Matrix,* and the B-movies Mack's friend Davis makes), Kasdan focuses entirely on the experience of the victims. This tactic ups the stakes for the audience even more by presenting violence just as it usually comes in real life, unexpectedly and randomly.

This pattern, repeated over and over again, underscores the character of an evil that does everything it can to blight and destroy specific human beings and the people who love them. In one notable yet typical instance midway through the movie, the camera watches Claire's sweet recollection of long-ago days with her small son, who has since grown into a teenager now gone for the summer. Even though the sequence has

325

its note of melancholy, its gist is that life is good, despite its inevitable separations and losses. From this lengthy wordless scene, the camera shifts to Rodeo Drive, where the flamboyant Davis, producer of the rankest violence-exploitation flicks, is himself mugged and shot. The mood of sweet nostalgia about how good life can be is abruptly shattered by the reality of arbitrary violence. That is true as well of the drive-by shooting, whose only forewarning, as also with Claire's discovery of the baby, is an insistent percussive prelude in the musical score. And so it goes throughout *Grand Canyon*, over and over again. The routine and apparent safety of ordinary life really cannot be trusted, for evil invades everywhere, even the most benign places.

Less stark but no less troubling in Kasdan's survey of Los Angeles is its toll on the inner life of the whole range of characters. None has an easy time of it, regardless of his or her station in life. All seem in important ways dispirited or confused, disoriented by the flatness or emptiness of their lives. Even so thoroughly amiable a fellow as Mack, the film's central character, seems aimless and bored, coasting along for no reason in particular — which he is just faintly aware of. While he is prosperous, his work seems to annoy him, especially his irritating partner. And perhaps simply because he's male or because his marriage is tired, he has a roaming eye, as the scene at the Lakers game points out. So he flirts with his worshipful, moon-eyed secretary Dee (Mary-Louise Parker), even to the point of indulging in a one-night tryst that we hear about late in the film. To this Mack's wife, Claire, is oblivious, preoccupied as she is with her own busy world, thinking that what keeps Mack at the office late is his work.

Mack seems to suffer the same disconnect in his friendship with Davis. While they do pal around together, the relationship seems to be dominated by the ranting Davis, who mostly fulminates while Mack sits patiently waiting to get a word in edgewise. Indeed, the wonder is that the two are friends at all, given the imbalance in their exchanges and the differences in temperament and values. While Claire is less fully drawn than Mack is, it is clear that she wrestles with her own brand of emptiness, struggling to fill her days with purpose, especially now as she confronts the independence of their only child, Roberto, who has gone off to camp for the summer to work as a counselor. Hyper-organized and something of a control freak, she volunteers to do charitable work, takes meticulous care of their lovely manse, and frets about the mounting indifference of contemporary culture to poverty and street violence.

The film's only other adult of comparable social standing is Davis, the shock-schlock movie producer. He is pompous, rude, and ruthless, especially in his dealings with attractive young women. That his brain and soul have gone awry seems evident in the fact that he actually seems to believe the ideological blather he spouts, the usual Hollywood Joe Valenti line, to defend his rancid films of celebratory graphic violence. So narcissistic is he that when he finally does encounter some transcendent Other — it takes the shooting to dispose him to it — he forthwith turns it to the service of his own ego-drama, and then when change and sacrifice seem mandated by whatever power has laid him low, he discards it altogether, deeming his initial "vision" an illusion or insanity.

On the other end of the economic scale, and in many other ways the complete reverse of Davis, is Mack's new friend, Simon, the black tow-truck driver, who despite his somber pessimism is eminently kind, even heroic, in his humane stoicism. He is as quiet and unassuming as Davis is gaudy and self-promoting. For reasons not explained, Simon's wife left him years before, and while he's lonely, he takes delight in his deaf daughter, who attends Gallaudet University in Washington, D.C. He also tries hard to help his single-parent sister (Tina Lifford) and especially her son, his wayward nephew Otis (Patrick Malone), who runs around with a local gang and does not expect to survive into his twenties. And Simon thinks nothing of his rescue of Mack, even though he could have just as easily, and with considerable justification, driven on by — like a normal Samaritan rather than a good Samaritan — and left Mack's trouble and its aftermath to the police. If Simon has a flaw, it is perhaps an ardent self-sufficiency that borders on arrogance insofar as he is reluctant to concede that he, too, has needs. This stalwart autonomy (or is it self-protectiveness?) keeps him from complaining or demanding more than life is inclined to give. The indifference of the universe and the caution it mandates does not, however, keep him from that unceasing kindness to everyone, whether they be stranded motorists, waitresses, or lost nephews.

Nor is the world more cheerful for the other principal characters in *Grand Canyon*, all of whom are single women. Mack's mid-twenties legal secretary, Dee, is superbly proficient, but with her own life's meaning she is more than slightly muddled, largely because she is so lonely. She has wrongly bought whole the dream of romance as a panacea for all of life's ills. She is told how wrong she is in this assumption repeatedly and emphatically by her good friend and sister secretary Jane (Alfre Woodard) during coffee breaks. Jane herself is single, thirty-five, and with no prospects. Older and wiser than Dee, she is very clear about what is reasonable to expect from a grudging world, and she marvels at Dee's self-deluding dreams of life with Mack "in the big house," as she puts it. While Dee is a comic character for the audience to savor — and far more than she herself realizes — Kasdan suggests at the same time the poignant depths of her isolation. Both Dee and Jane, however, are better off than Davis's girlfriend, the beautiful Vanessa (Sarah Trigger). While glamorous and well cared for, she is no more connected or less isolated than they are, in part because of her own self-destructive past and in part because of Davis's self-absorption. Finally, the most affecting circumstance in the story lies in the plight of Simon's sister, a single mother who works hard as a grocery cashier to put food on her table and keep her two children whole and cared for, responsibilities she obviously takes with utmost seriousness.

Showings

But this grim portrait is not by any means the final word in *Grand Canyon*. The remarkable turn at the heart of the film is that, by the end, this whole diverse lot of lost souls has, like that housewife by the pool, come upon many surprises suggesting that the bleak world they inhabit is not as dark, empty, or withering as they had imagined; indeed, it proves stranger than they think and yet fraught with holy surprise. Many come to sense, and a few directly encounter, the embrace of a kindly protecting Presence that moves in differing wondrous ways to protect, restore, entwine, and enrich their lives. This suspicion proceeds from the experience of fortuitous events whose only likely explanation lies in the activity of a caring, superintending Providence. Much to their credit, the Kasdans are very straightforward in specifying the ways and purposes of this transcendent care, this Presence that constantly intrudes in human affairs to rescue the imperiled and distraught, removing them from harm, and to bring people in general to relish each other and life's goodness. The upshot is that this Providence always wishes to bring the fearful and desolately lonely into the kind of deep intimacy that comprises one of the richest and deepest domains of human experience.

The individual characters in *Grand Canyon* are slow to recognize either the significance or purpose of this reality because from their own "small corner of cognition," as novelist William Dean Howells put it, they have neither the depth nor breadth of sight or experience that would permit them to grasp the portentous nature of what transpires all around them. Compared to the characters, the viewers are relatively knowledgeable: they see the many telling events and note how they affect the lives of the characters, how characters change and come to know one another, and thus the emergence of larger patterns to which no single character is privy, no matter how perceptive. Much of the time the "showings" of this Providence are inconspicuous, though no less real for their subtlety and quietness; at other times, though, this abiding care shows itself in ways that are spectacular and unmistakable, even warranting the term "miracle," as one character argues late in the story.

Talk of this kind of possibility in the Los Angeles setting seems on its face a little ludicrous, given the prevailing mindset of despair and materialistic cynicism. The most conspicuous of these "breakings in" of the transcendent Presence into human affairs are its rescues of the endangered, distraught, or forsaken. Others receive different kinds of visitations, either as epiphanies or revelations, which clarify the nature of human life and set them on different life courses. Both these sorts of divine intrusion have the same purpose: to rescue people from evil and desolation so they may come to relish one another and life's goodness. *Grand Canyon* contends that reality is wilder than any character has imagined, and by the end everyone's sense — on the screen and in the audience — of how the world operates has changed fundamentally and lastingly, though the film does not suggest that its characters will in the future be immune from the usual course of disaster and evil that sooner or later befalls just about everyone.

The first hint that the world may not be as grim and closed as it seems comes early, shortly after Simon rescues Mack from the gang members. The rescue itself is notable, but it also reminds Mack of another rescue years before, one the audience doesn't learn about until further into the film. But Kasdan does give a brief hint of it in a second or two of film as Mack rides in Simon's tow-truck to the service station. As Mack looks into the camera (and at Simon), a quizzical expression comes across his face and then, suddenly and briefly, the sepia-toned image and the noise of a speeding bus flashes before him. There is no explanation for it; it appears and is gone, and only much later, very likely after the audience has long forgotten about it, does Mack explain its origin and meaning. That explanation follows a bizarre dream in which Mack flies, Superman-style, through different aspects of his life, including a visit to the apartment of his receptive secretary, Dee. The nocturnal "fly-through" ends with an airborne Mack exchanging "high-fives" with a beatific, even angelic-looking Simon, who appears dressed entirely in white atop a huge "Holly-mack" sign on the hillside.

But for the dream, Mack would perhaps not have thought about Simon again; but the odd details of the dream suggest that Simon is perhaps something other than what the "conscious" Mack suspects. Then the dream puts him in mind of that first unusual rescue again. The peculiar, even mysterious, circumstances of a prior close brush with death prod him to make sure that this time he expresses the proper gratitude, which was not possible after his first rescue. By the time Mack and Simon have finished the breakfast Mack has insisted on buying Simon in gratitude, it is clear that Mack has looked up Simon partly to figure out the nature of the mysterious good fortune evident in the uncanny rescues that have twice saved his skin.

Over breakfast they discover that, despite their racial and financial differences, they have much in common, notably a love of sports, particularly basketball, and a deep admiration for the late Roberto Clemente (after whom Mack named his son), the great outfielder of the Pittsburgh Pirates who died in a plane crash while doing humanitarian rescue work in Central America. When Simon asks why Mack is bothering to buy him breakfast, protesting that they were in little danger and that Mack owes him nothing, Mack recounts to Simon that other rescue three years before, which has made him wonder about the beguiling strangeness of some events in life. As Mack tells his story to Simon, a reduced-speed sepia flashback recounts it visually (this time in brown and not the gray that opens the film). Thus the experience is refracted through a different perceptual lens and clock, as religious experience often is, and the whole sequence, especially with Mack's apt and haunting voice-over, assumes a certain numinous quality.

At nine in the morning, walking to a downtown meeting and lost in thought, Mack is about to step in front of a speeding bus when a hand grabs his collar to pull him back from certain death (Kasdan himself experienced the same sort of rescue in that very place, a strip of Los Angeles called the Miracle Mile, next to the Mutual Benefit building; therein, he has suggested, lies the genesis of the film). The woman rescuer wears a Pittsburgh Pirates cap (Mack's favorite baseball team), and immediately afterward, smiling broadly, she flits off, saying only "my pleasure" when Mack tries to thank her. Mack wonders aloud to Simon about the origins of this person who has so profoundly and propitiously affected his life: Who was she, and from what realm did she come? And should he have done something more to meet her and thank her? And what about those haunting names, Mutual Benefit and Miracle Mile? He wonders now who Simon is and whether there might be something more he should do for and with Simon. The strangeness of the event is clear enough, and where it will lead — perhaps a new friendship — is foreshadowed in Mack's dream, in their mutual interests, and in the surprise and wonder of the story Mack tells.

Simon is an angel who has come unawares and in disguise, all the more an angel because he would be the last one to think of himself in those terms, because of both his humility and his pessimism. The audience has already heard his sober Darwinian appraisal of the grimness of life, and the story he tells in response to Mack's tale is not at all cheery or hopeful but a kind of counterbalance to what he must see as Mack's blithe optimism about what runs the world. Instead of angels' wings, Simon quietly recounts the hard turns in his father's long life as a black man living all his days amid the silent but hardcore racism of Los Angeles. That personal history affords little occasion for talk about miracles and angels; the implication is that, if they do exist, they more than likely come only to well-heeled white people. Despite that, Simon's character is clear to the audience: at the very least — and this is no small feat — he has a striking kindness to just about everyone. It is a sweetness that radiates, not surprisingly, toward his deaf daughter, and later becomes manifest in his romance with Jane, following the blind date that Mack has arranged.

Still, it is the initial rescue of Mack that most signifies Simon's status. Kasdan's fine visual and musical wit make his point about the unexpected mystery of divine intrusion in human affairs. In his noisy, unglamorous wrecker, with its flashing yellow lights, the tow-trucker Simon, accompanied by an ethereal background score and bedecked in cowboy boots and a golden T-shirt (angel that he is), manages to pacify the gang members and rescue the fancy lawyer in a Lexus from his fix. Indeed, Kasdan supplies all the necessary clues, everything but angels' wings and neon lights, to prod the audience into getting the thinly disguised point that this is not business as usual in a mundane world. (Within the construct of the film, for example, gold is always the signal color of rescue and holy love, and silence or an ethereal, airy music signals some sort of divine presence.) With all this insistently at work, even fatalistic Simon arrives at a measure of hopefulness when at the film's end he proposes the trip to the Grand Canyon that allows for the final rapturous sequence in the film. There he is viewing the canyon, with Jane in his arms, not with fear or despair but with a radiant smile on his face.

331

Mack's two unlikely rescues signal a potent current that runs through the rest of *Grand Canyon*. A host of other conspicuous instances of divine intrusion show the variety of means by which God cares for people and makes himself known. Only slightly less spectacular than Simon's rescue of Mack is Claire's rescue of the baby, though she does not prove nearly as resistant as Simon is to the notion that what transpires somehow derives from the divine. On a bright sunny morning, as Claire jogs along, the soundtrack turns to loud, insistent, and ominous percussion, and given what viewers have just seen, the drive-by shooting of Simon's sister's home, they fear that some similar horror will befall Claire. Instead, an infant's cry comes from a thicket, and Claire responds immediately; deep within the tangle of branches she discovers an abandoned baby girl (much like the pharaoh's daughter's discovery of Moses in the bulrushes). Claire takes the little girl home to feed, bathe, and dress, self-indulgently postponing informing the police of her find. Later that same afternoon she sits by the pool, relishing the sleeping infant in her arms and chanting "surprise, surprise," as if through this child has come revelation, meaning, or purpose — or all three simultaneously.

Nor does it stop there. Claire wants to adopt the child, which Mack finds rather crazy. The script refers regularly to a long-running debate between the two of them about whether or not to adopt (a glimpse of the actual debate comes only once, near the end of the movie). What seals the matter for Claire takes place on another run through her neighborhood, when the divine again shows itself. With that ominous music again playing, Claire stops in mid-stride, for no apparent reason, as she jogs through the business district. She runs in place for a moment and then backtracks so she can run down an alley where in the past she has seen homeless people living in cardboard boxes. A tall, bearded, and scary-looking homeless man, one she has seen before on her jogs, walks toward her; as they pass, a message from the depths of his delirious ravings comes out, clear and resonant, an improbable confirmation of her desire to adopt the baby: "Keep the baby! You need her as much as she needs you." Claire stops dead in her tracks, turns, and stares transfixed in wonder at the man's back as he walks away. The camera takes in her wordless, utterly rapt astonishment, fixing on her face in close-up, and then slowly fades — not to black but, appropriately, to solid white. No wonder Claire is the one who, near the end, tells her thick-skulled husband that all these rescues, connections, and confirmations might in fact be "miracles," events that abound but whose reality we moderns are ill-equipped to discern.

Claire (Mary McDonnell) turns in rapt astonishment after she hears the homeless man tell her to "Keep the baby; you need her as much as she needs you."

The very kind of revelation that comes to Claire also comes to the character who seems least likely to merit it, Mack's friend Davis, the most annoying and problematic character in the story, lost as he is in his tawdry egotism. This intrusion is more traditionally religious than Claire's, but not any less striking for that. In fact, Kasdan manages to pull off Davis's life-changing hospital-room epiphany with flair, beauty, and cogency, making it clear why Davis the egoist is as affected as he is. Glad to be alive after his close call with death, Davis has stayed awake to watch the sunrise over Los Angeles. In masterful editing, the sequence begins with the slow close of the previous scene. The camera pans the walls of Dee's darkened apartment, slowly becoming completely dark, an emblem of Dee's forlorn life, and then as the camera continues to pan right, the frame slowly fills with golden light that then becomes a time-lapse display of a radiant dawn aflame over Los Angeles. The audience witnesses the dawn but does not know who in the story is observing it until the camera, still panning right, catches the light reflecting off the traction apparatus from which Davis's leg hangs. Finally, at the end of this thirty-second sequence, the camera comes to rest on an exultant Davis as he raptly gazes at the light, himself bathed in the intense red-gold glow. When the nurse comes in, he mutters, "I have seen the light." It is, after all, as his nurse sarcastically reminds him, the city of angels, and in farewell she wishes him, with biting sarcasm, "Mazel tov." The profusion of golden light, the script, and the acting speak well enough. Something has happened — even to Davis. For a while at least, the "light" for Davis signals a new direction for his movies; the pompous and rude narcissism of his personality also diminishes, to be replaced, amazingly, by generosity and empathy, self-deprecation and idealism.

There are other unforeseeable and unusual rescues as well. Near the end of the movie, the lovelorn Dee, who is sinking ever deeper into despair over Mack, meets a young policeman who comes to her aid in a road hazing incident. Soon afterward she finds enough common sense and courage to quit the self-flagellation of working with Mack for a far more attractive job. In her case, accident has proved to be the occasion for good fortune. And then there is the case of Simon's nephew Otis, who after a gang fight, scared and hiding, seeks shelter with his uncle, knowing that Simon will give him haven and help him out of the gang life. In Otis's case the rescue is slow in coming, but it does come.

Connections

The purpose of these assorted kinds of rescue is relational, and the second half of the story clearly moves toward an explanation of the nature and significance of these new connections; for from these connections emerge radical claims about the presence that haunts this film from beginning to end. Only slowly, and at first cryptically, do these connections take shape as a pattern by which the divine expresses its care for the world. The most prominent strain of this lies in the emerging relationship between Mack and Simon. Early in the film Mack tries to befriend Simon partly in gratitude and partly in curiosity, though Simon is understandably standoffish because he does not much like or trust wealthy white do-gooders who deign to mess with the lives of the poor. To prove his good intentions, Mack goes out of his way to use his contacts around the city to find a new apartment in a safer neighborhood for Simon's hard-pressed sister, whose home and life has been ravaged by the drive-by shooting. More curious still, following his breakfast meeting with Simon, on a mysterious and zany impulse, Mack arranges for a blind date between Simon and Dee's friend Jane, a woman Mack himself hardly knows. The relationship, wonderfully scripted and played superbly by Woodard and Glover, blooms and so dramatically changes Simon's life that it tempers his ruling pessimism about the nature of human life. We know that this date will turn into something lasting when a downward-looking camera watches Simon pull up to Jane's apartment building in his yellow-gold Camaro, announcing again, with that color of love and hope, that sometimes good things do happen, as Simon tells Mack near the end. For the pessimistic Simon, this is very clearly a sea change in his perspective on life.

An overt response to the question of what to make of this encompassing mystery that brings good into people's lives comes late in the film, and Kasdan clearly chooses to let the viewers wrestle with it on their own to see what sense they make of it. When an answer of sorts does emerge — perhaps more suggestion than answer — it is offered by the story's most admirable character, the clear-eyed Claire. In an evening conversation in their bedroom, Mack wonders aloud about the recent strange events and his own uncharacteristic behavior, such as bothering to find an apartment for Simon's sister and arranging a blind date between Jane and Simon, an event whose beginning and end aptly frames this conversation. Claire argues that the many surprising rescues and new connections between people, including herself and the baby she found, happen for "reasons," reasons that go beyond rational explanation and have their own internal logic or demands: "Maybe I saved her life, just the way Simon saved yours. . . . Some kind of connection has been made; it has to be played out." She wonders if these rescues and connections are plain-as-day "miracles." We don't see them as such because "we don't have any experience with miracles, so we're slow to recognize them." Mack falls backward on the bed, announcing that this miracle talk has given him a terrific headache, to which Claire dissents, denying his right to a headache: "I'll tell you why I reject your headache: because it is inappropriate. If I am right, and these events are truly miracles, then it is an inappropriate response to get a headache in the presence of a miracle." And so ends the scene.

The point is made clearer by what follows: at the end of the scene, the camera cuts abruptly to an aerial shot of Simon's Camaro as he and Jane return from their blind date, an outing that has gone extraordinarily well and marks the beginning of a whole new realm of trust, affirmation, and love for the two of them. When Simon asks if he may call her at work, she responds: "This is a feeling I'd like to have at work." And when she includes his name in her good-night, he asks her to repeat it, which she does with tenderness and relish; and he hears it with relish and relief, as if he has found a new and wondrous resting place. Connection has been made, and it can't be ignored, as Claire has just told Mack. And if that were not enough, the scene that immediately follows this farewell shows Dee, in the aftermath of a road-rage incident, meeting the young police officer who will rescue her from her isolation. Against all odds, then, surprise and miracle — in the form of rescues and connections — take place all the time, and, as Claire informs Mack, we ignore them at our peril.

Kasdan's own image for the action of *Grand Canyon* serves well enough to summarize the gist of the film: "The tiniest little moments" work together to form "a big tapestry," a tapestry of connection that gives warmth and meaning to everyone's path through what is an inescapably dark world. Indeed, the question that Simon's daughter directs to her father and his new girlfriend extends to the film as a whole: "Is there love going on over there?" Against all odds, even in Los Angeles, in quiet sure ways, love constantly breaks in to redeem sundry people from distress and isolation. Sometimes this love even shows off its presence in spectacular ways.

Not all is peachy forever for everyone, however, and Kasdan takes pains to keep his film from becoming a Pollyanna mush of happy-ending sentiment. The glaring exception among the characters is the benighted and narcissistic Davis, whose epiphany has bidden him to relish life and to preserve it. When he at last leaves the hospital, he is humbly taken with the import of his illumination, conducting himself in a kindly and self-deprecating manner and, significantly, refusing to talk about either the illumination itself or its meaning. To explain his deference, he says that he should act and not merely talk about the gist of his new vision of reality. But just a few weeks later, when Claire visits him at his home in the hills above Hollywood, the still convalescing Davis does nothing but talk about what has happened to him, melodramatizing his conversations with grandiose "thees" and "thous." Even though he proclaims his intention to now make only life-affirming films, Claire clearly sees the old pompous Davis reasserting its dominance. The camera even confirms this: at one point we see the skyline of downtown Los Angeles, and it is now, unlike in that golden dawn that has occasioned Davis's epiphany, obscured by a thick blanket of smog.

By the end of the film, after this post-surgery interlude of generosity and gratitude, Davis has utterly turned his back on whatever he encountered in the hospital room with the pronouncement that he must have been "delirious" ever to imagine such possibilities as divine revelation. Months later, in his last appearance in the movie, he has returned to work, and Mack meets him on the studio lot for lunch. Their conversation takes place in a golf cart as Mack drives the permanently lame Davis to a sound stage. As is immediately evident, Davis has returned to his old domineering ways and, more significantly, has plunged into a rank stream of self-pitying fury against the world at large. His lifelong egotism and self-indulgence have again swallowed him; and these are now greatly exacerbated by his venomous complaints about his injury — "his f-----g limp" — an attitude that contrasts with his earlier gratitude at still being alive. Moreover, Davis again mouths Hollywood's standard exculpatory blather about movie violence, even exalting his status as a third-rate producer of movie junk and the possibility of finding life's meaning in the movies. Obviously, Davis now denies the cogency and claim of whatever insight and joy came upon him in his hospital bed, and he is again consumed by egotism and moves in darkness, as the film's imagery blatantly declares throughout his long last encounter with Mack. As the two of them drive to Davis's sound stage, they travel by long black canyons of mounds of studio storage covered in black plastic sheeting. As they pass one such dark alley, Davis instructs Mack to drive the cart down that blackness toward an attractive woman, whom Davis, the soon-to-be husband of Vanessa, proceeds to proposition. For the remainder of the ride, Davis assails the world that has lamed him, ranting about the rage that spews forth from a chasm in American life as big as the "f-----g Grand Canyon." Here Kasdan seems to emphasize Davis's conscious choice to return to his old narcissism, to embrace a darkness that contrasts starkly with the radiant images of the Grand Canyon that most of the other characters will find in the film's closing scene.

Kasdan reiterates this in the film's farewell to Davis, which is laid over by the soft swell of melancholy music. Mack stops the golf cart a hundred feet or so from the huge sliding door of a cavernous sound stage, and the camera follows Davis's slow and painful progress to the door, his extreme limp and his cane symbolizing his deep inner flaw. As he moves toward the door and the camera slowly pulls back, Davis shrinks in size, which is emphasized when he is seen against the enormous door. Like the mouth of hell cranking open to admit the latest miscreant, the enormous door slides open only slightly, and Davis enters its towering darkness, after which the camera lingers and the door slams shut with an enormous echoing boom. Literally and spiritually, Davis has disappeared into darkness.

Transcendental Style: Seeing the All

Kasdan helps his story enormously with his fresh manner of cinematic story-telling, innovating a different and compelling approach to what

Paul Schrader has called "transcendental style," the effort to convey in cinema a sense of divine reality. Kasdan's efforts address two stages of religious experience. The first depicts the experience itself, much of which we have already discussed: the rescue of Mack from the bus, Davis's epiphany, and Claire's alley encounter with the woolly homeless man. With an artful deployment of a variety of cinematic resources — lighting, film speed, palette, editing, and music, to name only the most obvious — Kasdan manages to draw viewers into the astonishment and elation that the characters sooner or later experience. Nothing in the normal course of their world, and especially in the character of Los Angeles, has heretofore prepared them for this elation. Thanks to Kasdan's ingenuity, the audience can glimpse what the characters glimpse. Of still greater importance, and much more difficult to pull off, is Kasdan's accomplishment in bringing the film's viewers to a persistent sense of the mysterious transcendent Presence that observes human affairs and intrudes to rescue, restore, and link people in their individual kinds of lostness.

The primary means to this second kind of religious awareness comes in the sort of knowledge that Kasdan wants to give to viewers, knowledge about what is afoot in the world he constructs, which the characters themselves are aware of only partially at best — except, perhaps, for the clear-eyed Claire. By the end, *Grand Canyon*'s various characters have indeed come, in differing degrees, to understand their world differently and more optimistically. None, though, has the expansive, encompassing perspective that has been provided to the audience. Here Kasdan's style has worked, as good film style does, to clarify and emphasize the thematic gist of this story, just as his plot and script have also worked. In *Grand Canyon,* primarily through imagery, camera movement, and editing, Kasdan does more than simply assert or pronounce the reality of a transcendent Presence. Instead, the director goes so far as to actually create a specific, separate, and numinous "character," nothing less than a divine Presence itself, a Presence that watches, protects, and guides. While the many characters in the film are affected by this Presence, and some, especially Claire, sense its role more than do others, viewers derive some sense of it by observing the characters' experience and reaction. Viewers "get it" more fully than do any of the individual characters, because they are, first of all, privy to the totality of its action in the film and, second, they observe and "travel" with the Presence that Kasdan uses as the film's organizing and interpretive consciousness. This participation is central to enjoying the film, and what has been inconclusive or shadowy in the story comes to full clarity, making the very specific religious implications of *Grand Canyon* clear and unambiguous. At his most inventive in the film, Kasdan manages to evoke the presence of a mysterious, numinous reality of providential care and encompassing Love that goes everywhere in behalf of everybody.

The most prominent visual element in the creation of this Presence is the almost constant evocation of some kind of aerial perspective: this occurs regularly from the very opening shots at the sandlot basketball game to the swooping camera of the credit sequence. We first notice the constant looming presence of helicopters: in the course of this two-hour movie, helicopters appear twelve different times, and there are twenty-two distinct aerial or down-looking shots. Throughout the movie, the dominant visual dynamic is vertical, from below looking upward, and from above looking downward, sometimes at as sharp an angle as 180 degrees. At the very beginning, in the playground and the L.A. Forum parking lot, police helicopters pass overhead, asserting what seems an ominous function that reminds viewers that this is an urban jungle where danger constantly threatens. These aerial watchdogs are gradually transformed to assume a more benign character, and before long the audience begins to see and understand the world from that aerial perspective. It looks down and observes life, tracking the characters as they go about their separate lives: Mack as he gets lost in the ghetto, Simon's tow-truck as it approaches the station, Claire as she broods on the departure of her only child for a summer at camp, Claire as she tends to the abandoned baby, and many more. Thus the images of the helicopters join with recurrent down-looking camera angles to pull the viewer into a peculiar experiential sense of an observant omnipresence that weaves in and out of the characters' lives. As viewers see the world of the film vertically, the possibility that there is something up there beyond that world and looking down on it seems all the more likely.

This is a perspective that the characters themselves come to understand and embrace only belatedly, and then only partially. Filmgoers, on the other hand, have from the very first scenes seen this world from above and beyond and therefore understand more fully. It is possible to say that viewers themselves get "the feel" of omniscience, though in their ordinary humanity they are a long way from it. Relatively speaking, they are far better off in knowledge and understanding than the characters in the movie, and they leave the theater with a fullness of perspective not available to the whole cast of characters in the film.

Editing also gives palpable shape to this metaphysical reality of vertical observation. In one oft-repeated device, the camera assumes the perspective of the helicopter and its searchlight, a telling metaphor in this context; it moves the story from one location to another, for example, when the searchlight's gaze moves from the gas station to the tough neighborhood where Simon's sister and her children live. The helicopter's movement does more than simply get the audience from one scene to another; these scene shifts also work to show a continuity of vision, or Presence, from one world to another. And because the sites it visits often stand in stark contrast to one another, the helicopter's view represents a continuity that expresses a dimension of care. The device at once shows the essential sameness of people everywhere and the fact that the observant Presence goes everywhere and does not seek a select kind of people to benefit. In one variation on this theme, Simon's nephew Otis watches a television report on the Lakers game. The camera zooms in to fill the frame with a black-and-white TV version of the game; when it pulls back, we find ourselves inside a color telecast of the game in Mack's family room, where his son Roberto watches the same report. This strategy emphasizes the stark socioeconomic contrast between the two boys while at the same time showing their fundamental similarity: people are people, boys are boys, and boys, regardless of social class, tend to watch basketball. Furthermore, this shift emphasizes that the Presence attends to all boys, both rich and poor.

In another instance, one scene ends as the camera pans the darkness in Dee's lonely apartment and moves in a seamless shift from that quarter-lit darkness to full darkness and then to the sunrise that fills Davis's dawn-drenched hospital room when he sees "the light." The same darkness has held them both, to be sure; but while Davis will momentarily embrace Light, by the end of the story it is Dee who finds connection and hope, and it is Davis who disappears into darkness. In yet another such instance, the camera catches and then follows Simon's gaze at a house plant in his apartment, and as the camera descends toward the base of the plant, it morphs into another plant in another setting where Jane, who will soon pair up with Simon, is sitting. In a last example, this time a wipe (one image "wipes" another from the screen), after Claire's lengthy sweet nostalgia in the parking lot following Roberto's departure, her mini-van drives left out of the frame as Davis's Ferrari moves in from the right to take its place. Soon he is mugged and shot, and the camera looks down on his body as he pees in his pants and vomits. This is indeed a radical sort of juxtaposition, but a juxtaposition that is constant in this film, reminding viewers of the constant mixed tangle of darkness and light. Here, though, is also a kind of knowledge, even omniscience, that jumps around the world it observes to focus viewers' attention here and there so all may appreciate the filmmakers' point about the reality of an omni-abiding Presence.

Even the film's music works toward the same effect, as it melds different musical themes. On the one hand, there is the raucous assault of heavy percussion that we first encounter as Mack gets lost deeper and deeper in the ghetto. His car stereo plays "Send lawyers, guns, and money, get me out of here," and he sings along with it — and half prays. Irregular staccato drums raise the tension of his predicament; they persist until the golden rescue light of Simon's truck arrives, and the ethereal lilting choral music plays faintly beneath the still-persistent percussion. Those two themes replay constantly throughout the film, leitmotifs that underscore competing metaphysical realities. Heavy driving percussion dominates early, as befits the dark tone of the early part of the film; but again and again, intruding on that ominous refrain is the light, airy, even angelic music. The tension replays and then resolves in the jogging sequence in which Claire finds the baby. As she runs, the music pounds away: low horns and strings give way to bass percussion, bringing the viewer to expect the worst. Then, as she hears the baby crying and ventures into the thicket, low strings and lilting harp music interweave. A still more abrupt — and complete — shift from one motif to the other takes place when Claire encounters the homeless man who delivers his oracular instruction to keep the baby: in this segment, after we hear the man's message, the ominous note disappears entirely, and the music turns to elation; a white screen ends the sequence, matching Claire's glad astonishment. The last musical comment comes in the triumphal finale, when the camera undertakes its glad flight through the Grand Canyon. Trumpets and soprano chorus dominate, pealing out the exultant mood of a loving reality that runs the universe.

At Home Together at the Canyon

All of Kasdan's cinematic strategies come together in the closing scenes of the finale. The first of these comes directly after — and contrasts sharply with — Mack's farewell to the solitary, embittered Davis. As opposed to the necessity of Mack's visiting Davis on his studio turf, which is typical of their lopsided friendship, Simon bothers to venture into Mack's snazzy world, just as Mack has earlier sought him out. Simon

341

does so to thank Mack for helping his sister find a safer place to live and, especially, for linking him up with Jane. It is evening and darkness has settled in, but it fills only the edges of the frame. Under the driveway floodlight (a reprise of their first late-night chat under the lights of the gas station), the new friends get ready to play basketball, recalling the first image in *Grand Canyon* and the first topic of conversation between the two at breakfast. This time it is a game of one-on-one, and it is an apt image for their emerging friendship. They have gone from talking and helping one another to now playing together (in this it also differs from the opening shots of Mack as Davis's guest at a Lakers game). Their two disparate worlds, contrasted in the opening scenes of the film, have now come together, a culmination of the film's movement toward reconciliation, trust, and harmony. And there is gratitude: for Simon, Jane is the "best thing that has happened to me in a long time"; for Mack, he's alive instead of being a murder statistic, as he might have been if not for Simon. And for Mack, we guess, Simon is a badly needed new friend, because it's difficult to imagine Mack remaining close to the vitriolic and cynical Davis. As Claire, in her sagacity and foresight, has earlier suggested, these two are likely to be friends for the rest of their lives. For all the darkness that abounds in the world, there are circles of light within the dark, as Mack and Simon have found sitting outside the gas station, in the diner, and now again in this driveway.

Simon's gesture of gratitude ends the film. The scene in the driveway cuts to a rental passenger van stopping somewhere in golden, almost incandescent light once again — this time at dusk. Seven people pile out of the van: Mack and Claire with their newly adopted baby (who wears the sacred Pittsburgh Pirates cap), Roberto, Simon, his new girlfriend, Jane, and finally Otis, whose frustration with the journey is clear but who is soon struck by something they all see. Surprise and awe visits each face, one by one, as the camera pauses on each with a warm full light, untouched by shadow of any kind. In the only words in this long sequence, Simon asks Mack what he thinks: with obvious understatement, Mack says that it's "not all bad," affirming finally, and for the first time aloud, that the mysterious Presence shaping and animating life is benign.

From this long frontal seven-shot, the camera slowly circles around and behind them in one continuous flowing crane shot, allowing filmgoers to see what the characters see. Before them lies the limitless grandeur of the Grand Canyon, and they stand before it in humble, exultant praise. At one point Claire spontaneously rises up on her toes and

The closing tableau of the film brings together almost all of the story's disparate characters into a new kind of family.

lifts her arms, saluting the ineffable beauty of the vast warm radiance of the canyon. The contrast to Simon's initial view of the indifference of the Grand Canyon, or Davis's cynicism near the end, could not be greater, and here the resplendent canyon becomes an apt visual emblem for the loving Creator who has both made it and brought them before it in wonder and adoration. Very different and long journeys have — very improbably — brought these seven people together, and they comprise a new family of sorts. For them, all life has come to show a markedly different face: no Darwinian indifference has brought them together but rather, as Claire has earlier declared, surprises and miracles. And now most of those in the group have the sense and vision to see those miracles, however momentary they may be.

Through Kasdan's cinematic ingenuity, the audience senses something of what these characters sense, this ubiquitous Presence that hovers over, pervades, and shapes human well-being. Surprises, angels, miracles — how else can we explain these peculiar intrusions and bondings? The clarity and felicity these characters share is no doubt only temporary, for darkness will come again to devour whom and what it can. Nonetheless, this closing tableau suggests a cautious, rightly chaste hopefulness that these souls are not alone, cast away in a world devoid of kindness and intimacy, but are the creatures of a mysterious and transcendent Presence that cares for human flourishing.

Kasdan Filmography

Films Directed by Lawrence Kasdan
Dreamcatcher (2003)*
Mumford (1999)*
French Kiss (1995)
Wyatt Earp (1994)*
Grand Canyon (1991)*
I Love You to Death (1990)
The Accidental Tourist (1988)*
Silverado (1985)*
The Big Chill (1983)*
Body Heat (1981)*

Films Written by Lawrence Kasdan
The Bodyguard (1992)
Star Wars: Episode VI, Return of the Jedi (1983)
Continental Divide (1981)
Raiders of the Lost Ark (1981)
Star Wars: Episode V, The Empire Strikes Back (1980)

* indicates that Kasdan also wrote the screenplay

CHAPTER 12

THE WAR OF THE ROSES

Meaning and Epiphany in *American Beauty*

The makers of *American Beauty* were not sure of how to open their story. The opening sequence was to have featured the film's middle-aged narrator, Lester Burnham (Kevin Spacey), flying over his neighborhood in the manner of Superman or an angel — or perhaps like Mack in *Grand Canyon*. But the theatrical release departs from this rather drastically, instead inserting an entirely unrelated scene that replays later in the narrative. The filmmakers follow that with Lester, but this is not a flying Lester. Instead, we see only the world below and hear Lester's laconic narration indicating that what we see is his neighborhood, his street, and his life. The airborne camera moves over the leafless trees and the streets and the houses containing hundreds of lives, all individual, different, and unknown — and all wrapped in mystery. Then he adds, calmly, matter-of-factly, "In less than a year I'll be dead."

One effect of this bird's-eye view is to make the familiar distant and strange, briefly yanking viewers out of their accustomed blinkered ways of perceiving the world and themselves. The result is a certain sense of wonder tinged with apprehension, for such moments of strangeness spook people into an acute, if fleeting, awareness of the particularity and finitude of their own mortal lives, the inescapable fact of their fragile aliveness and consciousness. The bird's-eye view and the voice-over together provide an enticing way to hook viewers' curiosity into the film but, more than that, to force them to contemplate the thematic core of the story: the necessity to "look closer," to behold with wonder the exquisite beauty of ordinary human life. In its central evocation of wonder, *American Beauty* shares much, thematically as well as visually, with another American classic about American normalcy, Thornton Wilder's *Our Town*.

American Beauty (1999)

Studio:	DreamWorks SKG
Producers:	Bruce Cohen, Dan Jinks
Screenwriter:	Alan Ball
Director:	Sam Mendes
Cinematographer:	Conrad L. Hall
Production Designer:	Naomi Shohan
Editors:	Tariq Anwar, Chris Greenbury

Cast

Kevin Spacey	Lester Burnham
Annette Bening	Carolyn Burnham
Thora Birch	Jane Burnham
Wes Bentley	Ricky Fitts
Mena Suvari	Angela Hayes
Peter Gallagher	Buddy Kane
Allison Janney	Barbara Fitts
Chris Cooper	Colonel Frank Fitts

Academy Awards

Best Picture:	Bruce Cohen, Dan Jinks
Best Actor:	Kevin Spacey
Best Director:	Sam Mendes
Best Cinematography:	Conrad L. Hall
Best Original Screenplay:	Alan Ball

Additional Academy Award Nominations

Actress:	Annette Bening
Film Editing:	Tariq Anwar
Original Score:	Thomas Newman

Like many other American films, *American Beauty* did better abroad than it did in the United States, winning more awards in major categories.

Whatever stimulus toward wonder and reflection this overhead survey of his world provides, Lester's announcement of his forthcoming death ups the dramatic stakes considerably. That is not, after all, the usual starting point or narrative perspective for storytelling, and a number of questions more or less smack the viewer in the face. First, there is the riddle of Lester's whereabouts: if this fellow is dead, from what place exactly, and from what state of being, is he telling this story? More than that, if he's already dead, why bother with whatever it is he wishes to tell about his last year of being alive? Most people are eager to know about the far side of death, what Shakespeare called "the undiscovered country" to which everyone is headed. There is also the question of how Lester has died — or will die — looming very large given the opening sequence of the theatrical release (this immediately precedes Lester's flyover and announcement of impending death). A videotape shows Lester's sulky teen-aged daughter, Jane (Thora Birch), discussing with her boyfriend the possibility of killing her father, whom she, with some justification, considers a pathetic sex-crazed geek because he has lately taken to fawning over her sexy best friend. The gist of these opening minutes is that, whoever this Lester is, neither his life nor his prospects look encouraging.

Mystery is layered on mystery, effectively setting the tone for everything that follows: what does follow, for the most part, is a depiction of exactly how mistaken a direction Lester's life has taken, how he comes to die, and then to live again. It is at once a hilarious and a dispiriting tale, a scathing, dead-serious satire of some very messed-up contemporary American notions of what makes for meaning and beauty in life. Yet, despite Lester's many tawdry — even criminal — delusions about these matters, especially about manhood and sex, by the very end he does arrive at a genuinely luminous place that takes everyone, himself and viewers alike, by surprise. At the brink of death, Lester has a glowing epiphany about his life that fills his dying moments, and the life hereafter, with wonder, joy, and soul-shaking gratitude. Delivered from his wrongheaded quests, Lester at last sees his very ordinary world as it truly is: resplendent and suffused with a radiant, implacable love that shows itself in the exquisite beauty of the very fabric of the created world.

A Rose of a Different Color

It takes us almost to the end of this long, eventful film to reach that destination. Lester tells his story mostly in the form of a heavy-duty satire

347

on middle-class, middle-aged confusion about what makes life meaning-ful and satisfying. Much of the bite of the satire comes from Lester's wry honesty about his very average existence as husband, father, and public-relations writer for a trade magazine. His narrative, told from the after-life, features the silliness and tawdriness of his humdrum mortal life, which he came to realize only in the last minutes before his death. At the same time, because he has lived those days, Lester's postmortem narra-tive remains sympathetic to that "stupid little life," as he summarizes it, deeming it all plausible and even inevitable given the cultural air he breathed. Judgment and sympathy converge in Lester's recognition of just how much his choices have resulted from living in a fundamentally wrong-headed, peremptory culture that misdirected whatever twitch he might have had toward a more meaningful existence.

Indeed, from the beginning until near the end, Lester's problem is that he has consigned himself, body and soul, to contemporary Amer-ica's glittering credo of salvation by pleasure, a devotion that the visual scheme of *American Beauty* captures extraordinarily well. Most of the film's moral satire targets the pervasive hedonistic selfism that finds the self's satisfaction, and the end of one's being, in the pleasure found in power, acquisitiveness, or sex. In all cases, the "me" prevails, leading to a perceptual myopia that demeans the glory of the rest of life. In Lester's particular, but rather typical, case, his blindness results from his mistaken notions about sexuality and sex. In this regard, poor Lester is no more than the usual willing devotee of the popular media's exalta-tion of pubescent male sexuality as a sensible route to personal whole-ness. Not until a few moments before his death, indeed in the very in-stant of fulfilling his driving fantasy, does Lester come to his senses once and for all, discovering that macho conquest counts for nothing in the world as it really is.

As Lester comes to know, and as the filmmakers make clear, it is no surprise that he is befuddled and buys into dreams of sexual conquest and orgasmic bliss. These at least promise to deliver him from the "death in life," meaning the utter blandness, in which he now lives. Immedi-ately after he observes that he will be dead by story's end, he adds that he was, of course, "in a way . . . dead already," so "sedated" and "coma-tose" had he become. At one time, long ago, he was happy, and his wife and daughter were happy with him; now those two think of him as "this gigantic loser." During the opening minutes, director Sam Mendes makes Lester's plight palpable by repeatedly filming him behind bars and grids, in cages of different kinds. When Lester looks out the front window at his wife, Carolyn (Annette Bening), who is trimming her roses and chatting with their gay neighbor, Lester peers out through a grid of the window panes. His work space at the office is a small cell-like cubicle in a huge room that forms a grid of such cubicles, like pods in an egg crate. Columns of figures on his computer screen repeat the image of bars. Clearly, in ways he himself does not realize, Lester is enclosed and bound, caged in a half-life of routine and boredom. So stultifying is his existence that the "highlight" of each day comes early, when he masturbates during his morning shower (another cage); and the chief pleasure of his weekends comes from yet another box, James Bond movie marathons on the TNT network. When he sits, he slumps; when he walks, he shambles; when he talks, he whines; and always his face is limp and hangdog. The portrait is subtle but thorough, and it is thoroughly convincing, thanks to the studied understatement of Kevin Spacey.

The sadness of Lester's circumstance lies in its irony: like millions of others, he has everything but nothing. From his ordinary name, Lester Burnham, onward, this pathetic fellow who is about to die is meant to be everyman in "everyburb." On the one hand, he lives in a picture-perfect world: a two-story white frame house enclosed by a white picket fence and American Beauty roses, all emblems of American material and domestic accomplishment. But the movie portrays this suburban utopia, on the other hand, as a realm of soul-numbing niceness and triviality; none of its charms keeps Lester or countless other suburbanites from unhappiness and a desperate scramble for significance, meaning, and satisfaction in their lives. This is the first note struck in the film, and it plays repeatedly throughout.

No better off than Lester is his vacuous spouse, an attractive and energetic woman who apparently adores Martha Stewart, given the look of her home and the regime she tries to impose on her family. Lately she has thrown herself into real estate sales, and each day she pumps herself into an entrepreneurial frenzy by listening to motivational tapes as she drives around in her Mercedes SUV. At home, in matching garden shoes and shears, she trims her picket-fenced yard with its red roses, which constitute for her a figurative incarnation of sorts. And that's not all she's trimmed: apparently she has done the same to her husband, since the last shred of romance and respect is long gone from what was once a satisfying and lively marriage. Her world certainly looks tidy enough in its idyllic, "house beautiful" domesticity: the lovely manse, "nutritious yet savory" evening meals eaten in the dining room with background Muzak, and tolerant, upbeat neighborliness with the ingratiating gay

The seemingly endless and impersonal cubicles at Lester's workplace reiterate the sense of containment and indifference that he feels at home.

couple next door. Altogether it is a fetching American millennial version of Pleasantville, or Eden.

Nothing suggests this ethos better than Carolyn's love of her bright red American Beauty roses, which represent a picture-perfect bourgeois success as they line the picket fence that encloses not only the yard, but, in still another of his cages, Lester as well. A lush bouquet of American Beauties appears in almost every interior shot of the Burnham home, stark and garish, against the predominant colorlessness of everything else, including Lester and their marriage. The exterior of the house is also white, except for its eerily bright red door. Roses are everywhere, but in the Burnhams' lives they are mostly a mask covering a bleak, unbeautiful reality. They have been pulled from their natural earth to adorn a meretricious vision of what makes for beauty. Carolyn's self-deluding vision argues that, as long as there can be roses, all is well.

The point is clear enough, though the audience does not feel bludgeoned by it, largely because the narrator is not, for all his wry humor, in a joking mood. The Burnhams' problem is that nearly all of their thinking and thirsting derive from contemporary media-driven American notions of success and contentment. Unbeknownst to them, they are thorough-going materialists philosophically, and devout consumers ethically, meaning that they expect to find contentment by acquiring all the rudiments of conventional American beauty. Before these they seem powerless. The sad fact is that Lester and his wife and daughter are helpless in the face of the prettified economic and sexual stereotypes, holy grails that they and their culture have designated for their salvation.

Clearly, these bogus routes — shiny and alluring outside but hollow and tawdry inside — prove hugely attractive and virtually irresistible, adorned as they are with all the glitter and hype that America's vast commercial enterprise can muster.

Even in their professions (Lester in public relations and Carolyn in real estate), the two serve the very idol that has co-opted their freedom. Everybody here wants something like happiness, a just and proper human appetite. But all of them, teenagers and adults alike, really have little idea of what happiness is or how to achieve it. Swept up in the commercial swoon of dot-com prosperity, they spend their days foundering in a withering cultural confusion that sorely distracts and depletes what spiritual resolve they have left. Groping and lurching around in a thick fog, they don't have a clue about the kind of rescue the film will eventually propound. Lester's own mournful story shows clearly just how awry this can go.

Boy Wonder

The soul-withering niceness of Lester's world might have gone on forever, save for two events. First, Lester learns from an unctuous young personnel manager at his company that he is about to be down-sized; second, and more important, he encounters his own pathetically masculine version of American beauty, another kind of rose, in a nubile blonde cheerleader who is his daughter's best friend. At his first glimpse of the girl, Lester's erotic imagination runs wild as he watches her dance routine during halftime of a high school basketball game and he fantasizes it into a striptease. The full extent of Lester's instantaneous fixation with young Angela (Mena Suvari) is artfully displayed in Mendes's comic surrealism: in Lester's then-and-there fantasy, the crowd and the other dancers disappear, and as she unzips her sweater, rose petals — red American Beauty rose petals — billow out and upward. When Lester suddenly awakens and snaps to attention, he is instantly fixated and obsessed with something, and only one thing, from the soles of his feet. If his wife's roses suggest the customary female delusion of domesticity as the "good life," Lester's roses signal a male version of the same: a preposterous fantasy of wholeness through sexual bliss, a carnal redemption proffered by this celestial bimbo, the savior nymph.

In some of the film's most vibrant visual wit, Mendes and Ball repeatedly identify roses and sexual fixation. When Lester lies awake at

American Beauty on DVD

The DreamWorks DVD edition of *American Beauty* is well rendered. The cinematography of the late Conrad Hall glows throughout, and the disk also includes a well-done "making of" documentary. Best of all, though, for those with a serious interest in film, there is director Sam Mendes's audio commentary (screenwriter Alan Ball is present as well, but he doesn't say much). Mendes ventures into the technical aspects of the film but does so without pretense or arcane minutiae. Better still is a feature of the commentary that examines Mendes's elaborate use of storyboards and his collaboration with Hall. And last, the disk presents the screenplay with corresponding film footage and storyboards. It also includes the standard theatrical trailers and biographies of cast and crew. Overall, the film's motto of "look closer" applies to the qualities of this DVD disk.

night next to the sleeping Carolyn and thinks of Angela, rose petals cascade from the ceiling. In another nighttime sequence, this one a dream, Lester journeys down the hallway to the steam-dense bathroom. The clouds swirl and fade, and Lester comes upon a large elevated bathtub in which Angela seductively reclines amid mounds of red rose petals. Director Mendes couches the scene in starkly religious terms, as he indicates in his commentary on the DVD edition of the film. His intent was to suggest, through setting and imagery, that Lester has entered the inner sanctum of a tabernacle, a holy of holies where the divine itself is housed. It is clear that Lester's imagination has at least beatified Angela, placed her on an altar, as if she were a goddess and he a lowly acolyte of devotion.

Unfortunately, Lester's dream of seduction and bliss does not go unnoticed. The teenage vamp, his angel of liberation (aptly named Angela), is herself lonely and bored, and she encourages his lascivious attentions. After Lester overhears Angela telling his daughter, Jane, that he would be especially cute if he got in shape, he starts jogging and lifting weights in order to lose his middle-aged gut and buff up his torso. Feeling his oats, he tells the personnel honcho at the office to stuff the job, and at the same time he extorts a fat severance deal by threatening to make public the sexual indiscretions of one of the company's officers. The loss of his job and his fixation on the teenager conspire to prod Lester into combating his flagging sense of "manhood." At home, this

In a quasi-religious sexual fantasy, Lester (Kevin Spacey) kneels at the altar of Angela (Mena Suvari), who is immersed in a raised rose petal-covered bathtub as light pours in from over her shoulder.

takes an ugly turn when he asserts a certain version of manhood by hurling a dinner plate against the dining room wall — to make the point that he would like some deference from his daughter and wife, especially the latter. The audience even feels like cheering his progress, for at least Lester is no longer numb and asleep; at least now he is twitching back to a semblance of living. After all, he has achieved a bit of justice, however cynically, in response to the ruthless greed and dishonesty of the corporate world. And his initial responses to the seductive cheerleader Angela play comically, since the audience does not yet foresee the depth and seriousness of Lester's resolve. We almost root for him, so accepting are we of his pitiful self and the woefully commonplace solution for what ails him. And Lester *is* sympathetic: at least he knows something is wrong, and he does try to find some facsimile of life, though his macho get-tough and get-laid nostrums, of course, are shallow and vain.

Indeed, much of the movie's satiric power, and its bracing moral fun, comes from its success in enticing viewers into identifying and sympathizing with Lester to the extent that they hope the poor boggled guy succeeds in seducing his teen angel of restoration. This sympathy is made easier because the girl herself is far from innocent as she parades around, and she cares not a whit for virtue of any kind. Quite in contrast to her name, Angela's endless babble is so painfully vulgar, full of obscene chatter about the details of her conquests, that it is difficult to conceive of a more resolutely earth-bound creature. Worse still, she seems to have embraced MTV's fanciful — and sanitized — vision of pubescent sex as the apogee of human fulfillment. Sympathy for Lester certainly comes more easily to men than to women, who inevitably, and rightly, have a very different take on Lester's newfound "life" of lust and domination. The extent to which males cheer for Lester's "progress" says more than enough about prevailing notions of maleness: boys will be boys, meaning lustful and predatory, and they can't do much about it, given their surfeit of hormones.

Nor are we helped to a clear moral perspective by Lester's own occasional voice-over commentary. He tends to give just the facts, conveying his state of mind at the time without comment or judgment; but writer Alan Ball has selected and arranged those facts to make his behavior seem at least understandable, if not sensible or moral. His dream is the story's controlling sensibility, and only his tone of sad, bemused wonder at human affairs — including, especially, his own — serves to suggest an alternative moral vision of what matters most in this world. But Lester does not seem to have a clue for most of the movie, and he persists in his delusion almost to the end.

All of Lester's testosterone bluster works at least for a while, odious daydream though it is. The truth, as it soon becomes ludicrously clear, is that his model for this foray into "living," much like Angela's, comes not from adulthood but from childhood, specifically from Lester's flawed recollection of the last time he was really happy, as an adolescent flipping hamburgers at a drive-in and enjoying a lot of marijuana and sex. Much the same counts as manhood now, and it is the very route the culture celebrates, more fervently than ever, as the path to wholeness. The common thinking about maleness holds that men must be boys in order to be men. Lester's recourse comes within whispering distance of juvenilizing male sexuality, the constant irrational sexual buzz of adolescence. And insofar as it does, it becomes, as reviewer Jay Carr suggests, a "false god" (*Boston Globe*, 9/17/99).

Just as Carolyn has her notions of beauty at home and work, and Angela has her carnal bravado, Lester opts for this badly muddled ideal in mistaking pubescence for maturity. It seems quite sensible then, satirically speaking, for Lester to get a job at the local fast-food joint and to buy a red 1970 Firebird, the very car he yearned for as a teenager, which he now parks at home nose out, smack in the middle of the driveway, pointedly leaving no room for his wife's upscale SUV. Some of these stunts are fueled by his new habit of smoking the expensive marijuana he is conveniently supplied, on credit, by the mysterious but clean-cut neighbor kid, Ricky Fitts (Wes Bentley).

Meanwhile, Lester's disaffected but entrepreneurial spouse has herself gone off the ranch: she has furtive power lunches and then power sex with an egomaniacal real-estate king (Peter Gallagher), who forthwith gets Carolyn into the power-leisure exercise of shooting handguns. "Nothing makes you feel more powerful," says he. And as if this were not enough, Lester's isolated and fearful daughter, the plain Jane (Thora Birch), becomes enamored of strange neighbor Ricky, an eighteen-year-old loner whose usual expression is a faint Zen-like smile. Spookier still is Ricky's father (Chris Cooper), a hard-nosed retired Marine colonel who has browbeaten his wife into catatonia, and who fulminates against homosexuality and moral decline in general while collecting Nazi paraphernalia.

The Boy Next Door

The only relief from all this benighted confusion and self-pursuit comes from the oddest of places — Ricky, who is certainly peculiar, especially by the standards of niceness and conventionality that prevail in this American Beauty neighborhood. His most striking oddity is his habit of videotaping virtually everything he sees, from neighbors and classmates to dead birds and paper bags blowing in the wind. The walls of his bedroom are crowded, shelf upon shelf, with the videotapes of his filming obsession. His father thinks the money for all his expensive video gear comes from his job with a caterer, when in truth the boy has acquired it by selling high-grade marijuana.

Jane likes Ricky because, as opposed to her confused and generally terrified self and the abusive mess of her friend Angela, he seems "so confident." In fact, Ricky has about him a serene imperturbability, even as he goes about his constant videotaping. He is tall and thin, with dark piercing eyes, and he wears a stocking cap pulled down over his head even in warm weather, which makes him an oddball in the trendy suburban high school they attend. Plus, he's an eighteen-year-old sophomore, and there are rumors about why he is that old. The truth is, as he matter-of-factly tells Jane, he was sent to a military school after his father caught him smoking marijuana; and he was expelled from there when he attacked an abusive classmate, after which he was placed in a mental hospital. Even now his father personally imposes periodic urinalysis to test Ricky for drugs (though Ricky subverts the test by substituting urine he gets from a friend who works in a clinic).

355

What Ricky does with all his videotape is stranger still, and this is where the movie breaks free of its own resolute churning of cliches about gender and American mores. It shows that, more importantly, Ricky supplies yet another rendition of beauty, one diametrically opposed to the renditions set forth by Carolyn, Lester, the gay Jim and Jim, Angela, or Ricky's own father (whose piece of Nazi flatware is his vision of aesthetic beauty). In Ricky's radically different vision of life, the emphasis falls on beauty itself, pure and very simple, free of its often grotesque American incrustations. He videotapes everything he sees because he wishes, as he puts it, to "remember," to not miss anything in all its iridescent gorgeousness. What he fears he might miss is "beauty," by which he means, as *American Beauty* gradually makes clear, all the "amazing" uncompromised glory of the created world, a beauty so intense and stunning that he can't take it all in, lest his heart "cave in" from the joy it incites.

For Ricky, what counts most is his deep relishing of the beauty in everything ordinary, all of which he assiduously tries to capture and memorialize on tape. He proudly replays for plain Jane the "most beautiful thing I've ever filmed," a white plastic bag being tossed by the wind on a gray winter day. For fifteen minutes he filmed it, and as we watch his video of it with Jane, as the white bag leaps and falls again and again against the backdrop of an enameled red brick wall, Ricky explains his fascination. His quiet intensity slowly gathers force until, by the end of his monologue, he is almost sobbing: "This bag was just dancing with me. Like a little kid, begging me to play with it. . . . That's the day I realized that there was this entire life behind things, and this incredible benevolent force that wanted me to know there was no reason to be afraid. Ever. . . . Sometimes there's so much beauty in the world I feel like I can't take it . . . and my heart is going to cave in."

True love casts out fear, the Bible says (1 John 4:18). And Ricky has seen through both matter and all the cultural dross of his time to grasp the radiant splendor of the created world, and what he sees is enough, for him, to warrant constant attention and praise. Ultimately, what sustains and shows through the beauty of it all, as he says, is God.

Part of what fascinates Ricky is the utter "amazing"-ness of the world, because everything is laden with meaning and revelation. Early in the film, as Ricky and Jane walk along a parkway in the distance, beneath a long line of trees whose naked branches glow against the molten dusk, he tells her that he once videotaped the body of a frozen homeless woman because death itself is momentous: "When you see something like that, it's like God is looking right at you, just for a second. And if you're careful, you can look right back." In that glimpse Ricky fathoms the innermost nature and purpose of the created world, God the Revelator; there is the possibility of knowledge and, from that knowledge, a loving relationship between people and Whoever-It-Is that made the world.

The scene arrangement in this movie makes clear that this path to identity and meaning is radically at odds with the usual routes to satisfaction, power, and significance that the film's chief characters — and contemporary culture as a whole — feverishly try to turn into salvation. The long sequence of Ricky and Jane, from their walk home to their viewing of the bag-in-the-wind video, is crosscut with shots of Carolyn's desperate first tryst with the real-estate king, Buddy Kane, and Lester's own plunge into adolescence. For Ricky, love suffuses the world pervasively, and that reality fosters in him a posture of radical wonder, awe, and gratitude for the splendor of it all. In Ricky, and at the core of *American Beauty* as a whole, lies the rudimentary assertion that what counts most in human life is pure, astonished amazement at the fact that anything at all should exist and, greater still, that anything and everything should display such beauty.

Beauty as Light

From there the plot becomes complicated, ending, as the voice-over repeatedly informs us, with Lester's last living day on earth. Ricky has fallen for Jane, again showing his ability to see beauty in the ordinary. His vision and camera continuously search for her face, even when conventionally seductive exhibitions, such as Angela's, try to grab his attention. And Jane falls for him, for the first time encountering depth and authenticity amid the florid hollowness of her suburban life. Among the supposed adults, Lester, in a hilarious sequence as a newly minted fast-food jockey, catches his wife lovey-dovey with the vapid real-estate agent at Mr. Smiley's drive-in window. And Colonel Fitts suffers more violent "fits." The first comes when he concludes — mistakenly, but not without clear evidence, as he sees it — that his son is having a homosexual relationship with Lester. He promptly proceeds to beat Ricky because of his own tortured hatred of homosexuals (which has become evident in one of the opening scenes). His son cowers in the face of his father's violence, but he gets his revenge when he goads his super-macho father by graphically confessing to having sex with Lester, which is not true. More jealous than angry, the desperate, yearning colonel then makes a sexual advance to Lester himself, only to be rebuffed; and he turns homicidal for fear that Lester will reveal his heretofore fiercely closeted secret.

How all this comes about seems, even to the departed Lester, strangely incidental, at least in light of the quiet epiphany that comes to him in his last living moments. In the midst of these events, the dewy Angela appears for a "sleep-over" with Jane. But after alienating both Jane and her new boyfriend, Ricky, Angela is alone in the house and turns her naively seductive charms on the new fitness buff, Lester. Then, in what is a deeply uncomfortable sequence, the teenage girl and the middle-aged man proceed to seduce each other. And it is only when the girl confesses at the last moment that, despite all her bravado and constant randy chatter, this is her "first time," that Lester comes to his senses — morally and metaphysically speaking. Suddenly Angela, Lester's would-be sexual angel, is transformed from what the shooting script calls "the mythically carnal creature of Lester's fantasies" into the posturing, deeply fearful and "nervous child" that she actually is. The sudden chilling glimpse of himself as a sexual predator of children sobers Lester into reality, perhaps for the first time ever. Instantly, as is the way with epiphanies, the aging lecher leaves behind his adolescent posturing and is finally transformed into an adult and a father.

In the middle of this sequence, to show the radical nature of Lester's turnabout, dialogue and voice-over fall silent, and his gestures take the place of words: Lester holds and comforts the half-naked girl in a blanket. Empathizing with her sudden sadness and embarrassment, he pats her back in a fatherly fashion, and then he feeds her. The machismo is gone, as are all the occluded mythic contortions that foster its delusions. In an instant, care has supplanted lust for Lester, and he immediately understands and embraces his own life and world, however belatedly, with immense gratitude. For the first time in the movie, and in his life, Lester clearly and fully sees himself, Angela, Jane, and his wife for the fragile and poor but wondrous creatures they are. In short, he comes upon the fullest moments of his earthly existence, which are literally his last; for he finally apprehends the irreplaceable glory that was there all along but that he never had the wit or soul to recognize. With his new vision of life, Lester has come to recognize and care about something apart from himself.

Sitting with Angela in the kitchen, but at a proper distance (i.e., on opposite sides of the room and no longer in the same shot), Lester asks her how Jane is. He needs to ask Angela because Jane will never tell him — and understandably so, given the kind of father he has been. He laughs with pleasure when he hears that Jane is happy and in love. Then Angela, acting for the first time like an actual human being, asks Lester how he is. At first mystified by the question, noting that it has been a very long time since anyone has bothered to ask him, he then replies, again smiling deeply, "I'm great." Even after Angela leaves for the bathroom, the solitary Lester lingers on that thought, "wondering why he should suddenly feel so content," as the screenplay puts it. In his amazement he repeats aloud to himself, "I'm great."

Alone, laughing to himself, he catches a glimpse of a picture on the counter across the room, and he moves over to gaze at it: it's a photo of Carolyn, Jane, and him at an earlier time, a picture that has appeared briefly at the beginning of the movie. He smiles like a man, as the directions in the screenplay put it, "who just now understands the punch line of a joke he heard long ago. . . ." And then, as he chants in quiet relish, "Man, oh man . . . Man, oh man oh man . . . ," the barrel of a pistol invades the right-hand side of the frame. The camera pans slightly to the left, placing the framed photo of the young family beside a large vase of roses. It fills the center of the frame, indicating that here at last is the real American beauty: the three of them together, appropriately enough, at an amusement park. The vase of red roses appears against a white wall, a visual scheme that recalls Ricky's luminous vision of the white plastic bag against a red wall. The camera continues to turn further left until we see nothing but the white tile wall. A gun fires, and a large blood splatter stains the white tile.

Two strange events conclude the film. First, the sound of the gunshot brings Jane and Ricky downstairs, where they find Lester dead, eyes wide open, slumped over the counter in a pool of crimson blood. Ricky crouches to look into Lester's face, much as he said he did when he found the homeless woman frozen to death, through whose death mask he thought he saw God looking back at him. Lester's face has on it a look of calm contentment, and for a full thirty-five seconds the camera switches between Lester's immobile stare and Ricky's searching gaze. Halfway through the sequence, having tilted his head to look more directly into Lester's eyes, Ricky grins, as if recognizing something in Lester's expression, and then mutters a hushed, amazed "Wow" to himself.

And then, in another strange occurrence, with the camera still fixed on Lester's face, we again hear his voice — again from his after-life perspective. In a slow, chant-like montage, Lester recalls all his life's moments that in hindsight burn with light and fire, their intrinsic beauty now revealed: as a boy, seeing shooting stars, falling yellow leaves, and his grandmother's papery hands; and as a man, seeing little Jane at Halloween and the young laughing wife at a carnival — all of these glowing and full. In the end, after all his living, what counts is not the blonde teen bimbo showered in red rose petals but the glory of the ordinary that was there all along. The hard irony of finally "getting it" in the last seconds of his physical life does not much bother the still-living soul that narrates the film. Lester admits that he could be angry about the violent, capricious death that befell him, "but it's hard to stay mad when there's so much beauty in the world." The beauty is so dazzling and abundant that Lester confesses, as Ricky has earlier, that sometimes "it's too much, [and] my heart fills up like a balloon that's about to burst." Instead, now that he is calm and knowing, joy "flows through me like rain, and I can't feel anything but gratitude for every single moment of my stupid little life." In the film's last words, he assures the audience that, while they may now deem him crazy, someday they too will know — "someday."

And Lester is not the only Burnham family member to finally "get it." Jane has earlier embraced this understanding through her association with Ricky: her assent follows her viewing of the blowing-bag video and hearing his confession, when she wordlessly places her hand on his. For her part, wife Carolyn also seems, at the very least, to glimpse that same thing when she arrives home and discovers Lester's body. She has been in a homicidal rage at Lester for discovering her affair with Buddy Kane, so much so that she seemed, moments ago, to be contemplating doing what Colonel Fitts has already done. On seeing her dead husband, she first thinks to conceal her own target pistol in a clothes hamper in the laundry room; but then, overcome by grief and in a gesture of exquisite tenderness, Carolyn turns away from the scene to embrace and sink into a rack of Lester's freshly ironed shirts. Lester's death is drastic therapy for her, but she too recognizes — belatedly, as did her husband — the value of the irreplaceable goodness of their ordinary family and the ordinary world.

And thus is resolved their long war of the roses, in which the competing glittery visions of American beauty have all proved hollow, even fatal. What they held so dear and staked their lives on is trumped by a true, radical notion of beauty that delivers, despite its unspectacular humility, all the ecstasy and meaning promised by the delusions of beauty for which they have recently expended their lives.

Looking Closer

In one way, then, *American Beauty* depicts, in the words of director Mendes, "imprisonment in the cages we all make for ourselves and our hoped-for escape," cages that prove woefully small and whose dense opacity precludes the smallest glimpse of the glowing reality in which we live and breathe. With passion and incisiveness, *American Beauty* satirizes contemporary America's pervasive selfism, which argues that acquisition — particularly sexual acquisition — is the quintessence of being, the purpose for which one lives and the means by which one knows one is alive. It is a dark portrait of American benightedness that dramatizes commercial culture's relentless pandering to just about everything material and buyable, especially with the allure, once again, of sex. Consequently, there is much in *American Beauty* that is unpleasant to contemplate, as is the case in a recent spate of movies on the male condition, such as *Fight Club* (1999), *Boiler Room* (2000), and *High Fidelity* (2000), which focus on contemporary male susceptibility to fear, voyeurism, lechery, greed, violence, and other corrosive human silliness. What distinguishes *American Beauty* from other films is the wit it uses to capture the shabbiness of this society's usual American beauty solutions for what afflicts the soul: for men, more machismo; for women, success outside of domesticity; and for both, plenty of sex. Along the way, it displays a familiar enough theme, the deep spiritual discontent that drives the incessant quest for meaning and connection, for which all this gender frenzy is but a poor diversion. All these characters are hungry, confused, empty, and alone, because individually they lack the smallest measure of intimacy, and nothing in their world besides glandular pursuit promises the least satisfaction. A happy place it is not.

Best of all, though, *American Beauty* charts a path through those genderized cages to genuine redemptive deliverance, a bracing and exultant vision of life and its purposes. Most of these characters fear what they take to be the flat, mundane ordinariness of the world, composed as it is of pervasive and tawdry commercial nothingness. That dread of the ordinary comes out repeatedly in the actions and words of perhaps the most desperate of all the characters, the teenager Angela, who often asserts that there is "nothing worse in life than being ordinary," a prospect for herself that she regards with utter terror. And one can hardly blame her, given the pervasive banality and narcissism of the sexualized culture in which she is trying to grow up. *American Beauty* flips these misguided assumptions about the ordinary upside down. Instead of confusion, boredom, and dis-ease, a few people come across the bedrock of "the Real," what Emerson called "the miraculous in the commonplace," the gift of an iridescent beauty in the God-created ordinary that offers relish, goodness, and hope — if only they could see it. Ultimately, glands and social conditioning, neither of which we can escape, do not define people so much as the soul's thirst for intimacy with the lovingkindness that created the exquisite show in the first place.

In stunning, succinct fashion, *American Beauty* lays out a simple taxonomy of the sacred, especially on the question of beauty, something that Christians are, surprisingly, not very good at. Writer Ball and director Mendes find the means to convey a cogent apprehension of the transcendent relationship between love and beauty and their compelling reality in human experience: it is Love that infuses the ordinary world with enormous stores of beauty. In the end, the quiet ecstasy afforded by the irreplaceable glory of ordinary living argues that we move — and at times even play and dance — within, as Ricky Fitts puts it, an "incredible benevolent force" that bestows that very radiance. Of that and of life, say these filmmakers, there is "no reason to be afraid."

*   *   *

Viewers, film critics, and public intellectuals of varying backgrounds have been somewhat hard-pressed to know what to make of *American Beauty*, especially its assertion of the divine blessedness of the ordinary. Some have missed the point altogether, objecting to the film's disparagement of the substance of American life. Or they are so put off, even outraged, by Lester's pursuit of the teenager Angela that, by the time he has his epiphany, a quarter step from completing his seduction, they are too fumed to notice his profound change of heart and vision. For those who do note the religious substance at the core of this movie, the usual response has been to label it Zen Buddhist, as writer Alan Ball himself has done. But we should point out that what ends up on the screen runs counter to central Buddhist teachings, which advise detachment from and rejection of the world. On the contrary, at the end of *American Beauty*, Lester moves to embrace and adore the profound goodness that resides in the radiance of ordinary life.

In its profound reverence for the beauty of creation, and especially in the redemptive grace that Ricky and then Lester ascribe to the beauty they encounter, *American Beauty* is soundly Judeo-Christian in its central assertion: from Eden onward, there is goodness in ordinary life, a profound and unfathomable gift of God that has soaked into the fabric of the world. The central claim of that religious tradition is that what suffuses this world is Love, the inmost character of God. What the characters in this movie detect is Love's embrace of the world, mediated and expressed in beauty, whose care is so radical that it casts out fear. This is a notion of *relationship,* of an intimacy with the creation that is not found in the impersonalism and emptiness of the Zen universe of cosmic indifference. The numinous reality that surrounds Lester, even in his death and throughout his postmortem voice-over, baldly declares the reality of the soul, the certainty of an afterlife, and the transcendent Love that sustains the whole rapturous show.

CHAPTER 13

THE SOUND OF THE COLOR OF LOVE

The Construction of Meaning
in Kieslowski's *Three Colors: Blue*

In Krzysztof Kieslowski's *Three Colors: Blue*, the big central mystery that drives the whole story comes full-blown early on, less than twelve minutes in; and it stays, haunting and unresolved — for both the protagonist and the audience — virtually all the way to the end. But getting to that end, where all comes clear, is a long and difficult journey for the bereft main character, Julie Vignon de Courcy (Juliette Binoche), a woman in her early thirties who has lost her only child and her husband, a celebrated composer, in an auto accident in which she herself has been badly injured. The story follows Julie's after-accident life of retreat and withdrawal, chronicling in minute detail its motives, contours, and events, particularly the simple question of what in the world will happen to Julie. So exclusive and sustained is *Blue's* narrative focus on Julie and her fate that there is hardly a shot without Julie; for all practical purposes, she seems to be *Blue's* only character.

Yet there is also the recurrence throughout of a starkly mysterious musical "presence," a persistent enveloping "force," both formidable and delicate, that repeatedly bursts, unbidden and unsought, onto Julie's consciousness. Remarkable random bursts of sonorous orchestral music come to her — unprompted, apparently out of nowhere, and for no discernible reason — overtaking and transfixing her attention like a storm wind. Five boldly declarative chords sound and are then, after a one-beat rest, followed by a plaintive contrapuntal oboe refrain that simply aches with yearning. This leitmotif, and the variations on it, "resound," as the screenplay puts it, over and over, ten times in all, haunting the young

364

widow's mental life and shaping her very fate.[1] These "visitations" beset and hound her, are discomforting and disturbing; for a long time they seem to have no clear purpose, and Julie wants no part of them. They simply erupt, intrusive and arresting, usually accompanied by waves of deep dark blue on the screen, which forms a distinctly visual aura to the enticing yet enigmatic music (the screen typically fades all the way to black for the duration of the music). Julie seems to have no choice but to confront these unwanted intrusions of sound that assail her mind and soul, pulling her entirely out of her mundane life, and she repeatedly tries to mute or obliterate them. Thus, though they are without material substance, these unwelcome intrusions become as decisive a player as any character. In their extremity and otherness, at once transfixing and beautiful, they have a marked kinship with the long tradition in the Christian West of quasi-mystical revelations of the divine presence.

And with them each time come the inevitable questions about their origin, nature, and meaning. To these riddles Kieslowski gradually constructs answers of sorts through the course of the film; but he withholds full disclosure of their meaning until one last climactic visitation in the very last minutes of the film. Indeed, much of the effectiveness of *Blue* derives from the fact that the mystery that visits the main character is also the viewer's mystery. Finally, in that last sequence, a long montage of images and music displays the meaning of that central musical mystery, one that is at once psychological, aesthetic, and profoundly religious. There it becomes fully clear, especially for the viewer, that what pursues Julie in these numinous blue "soundings" is a divine love that will not abandon her to the silent stone house of negation to which she has consigned herself. Instead, the insistent music now seems rapturous and beckons her to "follow," to again love and embrace the immense gift of life, fraught though it is with perils and sorrow. Ultimately, what the stricken protagonist has confronted within these aural-visual epiphanies is no less than the Spirit of God wresting her back from despair and numbness into hope and love. In short, the music affords her a glimpse of divine love — simultaneously fierce, beautiful, and encompassing — that illuminates a path back into the fullness of living and loving.

It is bravura moviemaking, especially to the extent to which Kieslowski makes his telling of Julie's story so fully cinematic. As far as words go, *Blue* is, in fact, almost a silent movie, at least in terms of

1. Krzysztof Kieslowski and Krzysztof Piesiewicz, *Three Colours Trilogy: Blue, White, Red*, trans. Danusia Stok (London: Faber, 1998), p. 10.

script. Nothing reveals that more than the contrast between the screen-play and what actually ended up on the screen. Kieslowski seems to have scraped away all unnecessary language, all the easy exposition that words provide, choosing instead to tell his tale with images, colors, sound, and, of course, the remarkable acting of Juliette Binoche. He does this extraordinarily well, making his film a virtually wordless visual-aural poem. Throughout the film he deftly uses consonant visual and aural schemes that move the narrative, assume much of the burden of meaning, and largely determine and deepen *Blue's* mood and the theme of divine pursuit. Each of the films in the *Three Colors* trilogy fo-cuses, obviously, on a single color; but neither of the other two (*Red* and *White*) is nearly as effective in using the tonalities and connotations of their subject color, and neither even begins to conjoin music and color in the way or to the extent that *Blue* does (the usual critical terms for this melding of means is *synaesthetic*).[2] Kieslowski soaks *Blue* in one shade or another of blue, finely and complexly modulating intensity and sources to suggest markedly different moods and meanings from the obvious one of sorrow and despair to its surprising opposites of delight and love. It is, in fact, this latter evocation that "decides" the film: the narrative of the film makes clear that blue is not only Julie's favorite color but a color that somehow bespeaks love itself in her private store-house of meaning. All the important elements of her "pre-accident" life are blue, and the color even suggests an inescapable abiding presence of divine love, to which Julie has steadfastly closed herself off in the after-math of the accident.

The color blue is scattered throughout the film. The street musi-cian whose melodies remind Julie of her husband's work stands before a mottled blue wall, and Julie swims in a luminescent blue swimming pool that on the one hand seems to betoken the depth of her sorrow but on the other suggests that even in the midst of her profound grief she is en-compassed by love. Julie may in fact be enveloped by divine love, even though she doesn't know it at the time. In any case, for Julie blue proves to be the color of love, and blue gives rise to the music of love — or per-haps it's the other way around. It is fitting, then, that the music that summons Julie back into life arrives in floods of blue. The music and color mysteriously conjoin to display in sight and sound a divine pres-ence that will not leave Julie alone until she re-enters a world that, as we

2. Paul Coates, "Kieslowski and the Antipolitics of Color: A Reading of the 'Three Colors' Trilogy," *Cinema Journal* 41 (Winter 2002): 48.

Three Colors: Blue (1993)

Studio:	Miramax
Producer:	Martin Karmitz
Screenwriters:	Agnieszka Holland, Slavomir Idziak,
	Krzysztof Piesiewicz, Krzysztof Kieslowski
Director:	Krzysztof Kieslowski
Cinematographer:	Slavomir Idziak
Production Designer:	Claude Lenoir
Editor:	Jacques Witta

Cast

Juliette Binoche	Julie
Benoît Régent	Olivier
Florence Pernel	Sandrine
Charlotte Véry	Lucille
Hélène Vincent	Journalist
Hugues Quester	Patrice
Emmanuelle Riva	Mother of Julie

Nominations and Awards

The first film in Kieslowski's *Three Colors* trilogy, *Blue* was barred from Academy Award consideration because of its "confused" nationality: it was shot in France but financed in Poland. In France it did win three major Cesars and was nominated for six others. It won the grand prize at the Venice Film Festival, including a best actress award for Binoche. Kieslowski's *Three Colors* project gained considerable notoriety as each successive film appeared, and for *Red* (1994), the last film in the series, Kieslowski received an Academy Award nomination for best director.

eventually conclude, she once so dearly loved. Ultimately, this artful melding of music and visual palette conveys one manner of disclosure by which God makes himself known. Even the mode of this theophany — God accommodating divine speech to address Julie's very particular need and understanding — says much about God's character, specifically about divine humility and passion in bothering to couch the divine presence in the musical and visual terms that are meaningful to Julie.

Unfortunately, most critics of the film tend to reduce these displays to the purely psychological, "the return of the repressed," as Annette Insdorf describes them.[3] The numinous manner of their occurrence and the effect they have on Julie plainly mark them as starkly religious in origin and substance. That is not to say that they are not also fully psychological; after all, the psychological and religious cannot be separated from one another. What follows is a lengthy and careful exposition in which I seek to track the intricate control with which Kieslowski has constructed his representation of divine love.

Accident

The opening moments of *Blue* are virtually silent, and are also steeped in blue, albeit of a more ominous sort. Mostly, there are only the ordinary sounds of life — automobiles and wind noise. What words there are prove inconsequential, all a prelude to the one-car accident that kills Julie's husband and young daughter. As the credits play, the camera watches a dark blue Peugeot sedan travel an expressway, pulling off once onto the shoulder to let a young girl run into the roadside woods to relieve herself. Here the camera cuts briefly to the car's undercarriage, where brake fluid slowly leaks. And for a while after that, a silver-blue candy wrapper flutters from the rear window of the speeding car; we briefly glimpse a bored young girl peering out of the back window of the car on a blue-gray world, a drab day that is cold, damp, and completely uninviting. The first identifiable person we see is a fresh-faced boy in his mid-teens sitting in a gray fog beside a deserted two-lane country road. While waiting for a ride, he amuses himself with a simple wooden toy by trying to catch on the top of a stick a wooden ball on a string. As he plays, the Peugeot we have already seen emerges from the morning fog, passes him, and seconds later — immediately after the boy succeeds in spearing the ball — we hear screeching tires and then the unmistakable clank and crunch of a vehicle crash. The boy turns his face, and in the near distance we see what he sees: the blue Peugeot wrapped around the single huge tree on the flat, empty horizon. The boys reacts, stands, drops his toy, and runs toward the accident. For a long twenty seconds, as the boy runs toward the crash, the camera

3. *Double Lives, Second Chances: The Cinema of Krzysztof Kieslowski* (New York: Hyperion, 1999), p. 143.

gazes at the distant wreckage, a blemish on the tranquility of the somber French countryside.

And then, abruptly, the scene switches to the aftermath. In extreme close-up, with everything else out of focus, the camera dwells on the down feather of a pillow as it flutters in response to someone's exhalations. One eye opens, and reflected in it is a white-coated physician who gently tells the owner of the eye that her husband has died in the wreck and, when asked about the child, confirms that she is dead as well. The woman's eyes close, she sobs, and she then buries her head in the pillow. In the next beat, the camera cuts, again abruptly, to the sudden loud breaking of a large plate glass window, a jolting sound that deftly reiterates the surprise and shock of the accident. The cascade of broken glass perfectly catches the effect of the accident on Julie's life, a potent emblem of sudden and utter breakage. The next shot shows that the person who shattered the window is actually Julie; she stands alone in her hospital gown and neck brace in a long windowed hallway, having just thrown a water pitcher through the window to divert the pharmacy nurse from her post. Once she has ducked into the pharmacy, Julie removes a pill bottle from a cabinet of drugs and empties its contents into her mouth. But she pauses before swallowing — eyes closed, her face immobile but pensive — and finally spits the pills back into her hand. When the nurse returns to the pharmacy, Julie hands the pills to her and, in her first real words in the film, quietly says, "I can't," and then apologizes for breaking the window.

Her loss is so great that she wishes she could kill herself, but some remnant of something in life, or in her own shattered self, keeps her from following through. As the story unfolds, what that something is slowly becomes clear. The hard finality of Julie's circumstance is poignantly emphasized when a male guest arrives with a tiny portable television he's brought so that Julie can watch her family's nationally televised funeral. The telecast dwells on two coffins, one large and one small, and as horns play a mournful strain from the dead composer's favorite composer (the fictional Van Den Budenmayer, a pseudonym for *Blue*'s composer, Zbigniew Preisner), the injured Julie places a finger on the smaller of the two coffins pictured on the television set. As Julie fights back sobs, a tear runs off her nose.

This is a spare, jolting opening — all the more because Kieslowski rejects histrionics or sensation. And it is virtually without the mediation of any words explaining what is going on; instead, Kieslowski trusts the events and images to convey the pure horror of a calamity that has shattered the warm center of Julie's world. Kieslowski emphasizes the enormous grief of these events in his choice of giving Julie's hospitalization period a reddish tint, either by means of the lighting or occasionally the use of a reddish filter. This coloration imparts warmth and intensity to Julie's sorrow; it runs, uninterrupted, for a full seven minutes, and then appears only rarely through the rest of the film, and then only in muted form. In this Kieslowski is consistent with the connotative uses to which he puts the color in the concluding film of the *Three Colors* trilogy, *Red* (1994), where red becomes the color of intense feeling.

The return from red to blue takes place in the last scene of Julie's hospital convalescence. The sun shines from above and behind a balconied wing of the hospital, and although pink dominates, new and different shades of blue begin to seep into Kieslowski's emotional palette. The building as a whole, and especially the walls where Julie sits, have a pinkish-red hue to them, while some objects, such as the large windows, are a mottled display of bright and dark blue — both equally dense. These are the first instances of blue since the opening accident sequence. The chaise longue on which Julie reclines with her eyes closed is a light cool blue, as is the background to her right, although the background to her left and the light on her face still retain the reddish hue. At this stage in Julie's history, colors seem to confront one another, dividing her world, working to suggest new conflict and perhaps, insofar as blue has reappeared — somewhat ominously, given its earlier associations — impending transition to more tragedy or some other mood. Instead, something altogether new and different breaks into the story.

Thus far the dominant sound in the film has been no sound, that is, protracted silence, especially now in the hospital in the accident's aftermath, the absence of consolation or hope. There has been no music at all, except for what is played at the televised funeral, music that is subdued in composition and performance, as befits the mood of a funeral. Then, for no apparent reason, patches of faint blue light begin to flicker and play on Julie's still battered face; as the blue light thickens to a haze, music bursts out, startling her to surprised alertness and then keeping her in rapt attention. As is typical of these musical visitations in the movie, light comes first, shining softly on Julie, and it is then followed by the enveloping music. It is not even clear whether Julie sees the light, though the audience certainly does. But these two different phenomena seem to be the warp and woof of the same force that regularly visits Julie through the course of the film. The dominant event of the scene is that, out of nowhere, "the full music drops on," to adapt a line from Emily

The convalescent Julie (Juliette Binoche) is startled by the music as it intrudes upon her as she tries to rest.

Dickinson, riveting Julie's mind and imagination.[4] Though perhaps less intense and melodramatic than the opening of Beethoven's Fifth Symphony, say, the music is nonetheless boldly declarative, at once enveloping and insistent, and it clearly transfixes Julie. In this sequence the blue light waxes and wanes in synchrony with the intensity of the music. In the brief pause after the opening notes of the full orchestra, the image on

---

4. The contours and gist of Julie's religious encounter with the music bear a striking similarity to Dickinson's own. The poem (#315) is one of Dickinson's better-known works.

> He fumbles at your Soul
> As Players at the Keys
> Before they drop full Music on —
> He stuns you by degrees —
> Prepares your brittle Nature
> For the Ethereal Blow
> By fainter Hammers — further heard —
> Then nearer — Then so slow
> Your Breath has time to straighten —
> Your Brain — to bubble Cool —
> Deals — one — imperial — thunderbolt —
> That scalps your naked Soul —
> When Winds take Forests in the Paws —
> The Universe — is still —

the screen (Julie's face) disappears altogether, but then it comes back again in the antiphonal refrain of an oboe.

During this musical invasion, the camera pulls back and then returns to close-up, in part to mirror the fluidity of the music and in part to make sure that viewers note the extent to which Julie is "swallowed up" by the urgent, unbidden music. The way the music comes and the extremity of its effects, as will happen repeatedly in the story, suggest that more is afoot here than the resurgence of a repressed psychological nostalgia. The expression on Julie's face is a mixture of mild astonishment, perplexity, and a faint note of belligerence. Her response, despite the fact that she is taken by the beauty of the music, is far from either warm or joyous. Not even the gentle longing of the oboe's response diminishes her steely apprehension. Here, though, everything has suddenly changed, for a new and unwanted horizon has burst into Julie's estimate of the world. It will take the whole rest of the story for Julie to recognize this "horizon" for what it is — in short, to allow herself to embrace the music, and to be embraced by it.

The oddness of the scene only deepens. Her gaze into the distance remains fixed, even after the music stops, and in the next instant someone off-camera says, "Bonjour." As Julie haltingly turns to look at the speaker, confused, the invasive music starts over again, emphatic and pressing, and this time Julie is more enveloped than before; the screen now fades to full black for six seconds while the music plays. For Julie, the transfixing and demanding music seems totalizing, summoning her entire consciousness into the spell of its solemn but insistent majesty. Indeed, in the replay, as the screen goes black, the suggestion is that Julie has somehow fully melded with the music. A remarkable line from T. S. Eliot's *The Four Quartets* captures the extremity of Julie's ravishment with the music: Eliot speaks of quasi-mystical moments, what he calls "distraction fits," in which "you are the music while the music lasts."[5]

---

5. The reference is to the third of the quartets, "The Dry Salvages," and it is worth quoting the section in which it occurs at length, for it provides another context for the sort of experience Julie undergoes (*The Complete Poems and Plays, 1909-1950* [New York: Harcourt, 1962], p. 136).

> For most of us, there is only the unattended
> Moment, the moment in and out of time,
> The distraction fit, lost in a shaft of sunlight,
> The wild thyme unseen, or the winter lightning
> Or the waterfall, or music heard so deeply
> That it is not heard at all, but you are the music
> While the music lasts.

The voice that has interrupted Julie's "distraction fit" belongs to a journalist of her acquaintance who has come to ask Julie a question for a story about her late husband. Julie is downright rude, forcefully showing that she resents the woman's intrusion. Typically, Kieslowski states the verbal conflict in visual terms: here he does so by placing between the two women a large pane of opaque ice-blue glass that resembles a room divider. Appropriately, matching her chilly hostility, Julie stands either in front of the blue pane itself or in its reflected blue light; the journalist is just beyond it in quite normal daylight. The latter's question is about whether her husband, before his untimely death, had finished a long-anticipated commission, "The Symphony for the Unification of Europe," a symphonic choral work whose hopeful intent was to celebrate the impending dissolution of historic nationalist barriers among the nations of Europe. Julie tells the journalist an outright lie: "It doesn't exist."

The truth is that the symphony is partially completed, and in the final third of the film Julie will labor, with the help of her late husband's assistant, Olivier, to complete the unfinished work. But her response to the journalist suggests that now, quite understandably, she wants nothing to do with hope, or even the merest suggestion that life has anything good within its bounds. When the journalist expresses her disappointment in Julie's rudeness, a new and uncharacteristic coldness, the full measure of Julie's anger at the loss of her family becomes clear for the first time. Her grief has moved to indignation at the newfound meanness of the world. "Haven't you heard? I had an accident. I lost my daughter and my husband." As Julie indignantly exits the room, the journalist asks if it is true that she wrote her husband's music, a suggestion that hangs in the air through the remainder of the movie and comes to the viewer's mind again toward the end, when Julie assumes the task of finishing the unfinished choral symphony.

Refusal

Soon after her release from the hospital, it becomes clear that Julie is determined to distance and insulate herself from everything most people would call life. These scenes, like those in the first segment, are largely silent, at least with respect to any verbal text that might spell out her thoughts and feelings. Again Kieslowski trusts simple, patient "watching" and — as is appropriate in a story about a composer's widow — listening. Julie gets out of a cab outside the high walls of a large country estate. Her face set in resolve, she strides across the stone courtyard to the elderly gardener, who is running a power trimmer on the hedges. When he shuts the machine off to greet Julie, she asks only whether he has done what she has instructed, specifically, emptying everything out of the "blue room"; but her comment does not indicate that the blue room had been her daughter's room (though the speech in the published screenplay included that detail). Here she doesn't say "Anna's room," but just the "blue room," and viewers are left to derive its significance on their own.[6] That the room has special meaning for Julie becomes clear, though, when the first thing she does, once inside the house, is head straight upstairs to that room. The door creaks open to reveal its empty blue-gray walls. It seems that she has quite consciously, even defiantly, designated this as her first "homecoming" task, just to get it over with. She knows only too well that this house no longer is any kind of home, and visiting it will prove very difficult. And again Kieslowski painstakingly documents Julie's reactions. The camera silently follows Julie as she enters and crosses the room, stopping before a glass-bead mobile, again blue, hanging from the ceiling with a large window's light playing brightly on the beads. She abruptly reaches up, grabs a strand of beads, and angrily yanks it off the mobile.

Leaving the empty blue room, Julie, in another conscious pursuit, hurriedly searches through stacks of large music folios spread on a table on the interior balcony of the large country home. Not able to find what she is looking for, she descends the stairs to a grand piano in the large room below; as she moves toward the piano, random piano notes sound in her head, a broken tune that resembles but is not the tune of her earlier musical "visitations." At the piano, with the music still sounding in her head, she finds a fragment of a score written on note paper, glances at it, and nods her head emphatically, as if to say, "Ah, this is it, this is what I have been looking for."

Her attention is broken by the sound of weeping from another part of the house, prompting her to fold the paper, leave it at the piano, and then locate the sound of the grief. In the pantry at the far end of the kitchen, her face buried in hanging aprons, Marie the maid weeps loudly. Julie asks why she's crying, and the maid's answer is telling: "Because you're not." The humble maid has pointed emphatically to what is distinctly odd in Julie's demeanor on returning to her home, the site of a good deal of whatever richness she has had in her life. There have been no tears and no apparent sorrow, only a kind of steely resolve to get through

---

6. Kieslowski and Piesiewicz, p. 15.

all this. In contrast to this avoidance of emotion, Marie says to Julie: "I keep thinking of them. I remember everything. How could I forget?" Forgetting is clearly what she thinks Julie is either doing or attempting to do. As the camera looks over Marie's shoulder during Julie's comforting embrace of her, the background again glows red, however briefly, recalling the sorrow Julie experienced in the days after the accident.

Shaken by this encounter and Marie's simple eloquence about the realities of loss, Julie again retreats upstairs, half-staggering, leaning against doorways, and finally squatting awkwardly on the entry stair of Anna's room, and she just sits there for a long time while a mysterious narrow horizontal shaft of faint blue light plays across her eyes and forehead. This time there is no music, only the blue light layering and deepening the silence. Throughout, she broods and ponders, no doubt about her circumstance in general and very likely, given what we've seen thus far and what soon follows, the wisdom of what seems to be her regimen of emotional abolition.

The extremity of that course becomes fully clear in the remaining scenes in this phase of the film. Immediately following her retreat to the upstairs, surrounded by the blue walls of the living room, Julie meets with the family lawyer and instructs him to sell everything — meaning absolutely everything, the house and all its contents — and to put the proceeds in her private numbered account, withdrawing money only to support her mother and the household servants. When he asks if he may inquire as to why she is choosing this route, she gives him a simple "no," accompanied by a broad, knowing smile. The camera tilts down to look at her hands, in which she fondles the handful of the blue beads that she earlier tore from the mobile in her daughter's room, and this explains the source of the faint blue light that was dancing on her face when she sat in the doorway contemplating her fate and future. Blue light reflected from the beads, that single remaining emblem of her past life with her daughter, lay across her vision (eyes) and mind (forehead) as she pondered the sense of her present course.

After meeting with the lawyer and dispatching the material world of her past, Julie goes right back to the music, namely, that sheet of manuscript that she left on the piano and the haunting mystery it has become. This marvelously constructed encounter, again entirely wordless, at once deftly dramatizes the central tension in *Blue* and, as a part of that, emphatically underscores the force of what's becoming clear as Julie's willed avoidance of life itself. More than any other scene in the film, this interlude at the piano dramatizes the profound ambivalence that roils Julie's soul.

The scene begins with the camera in radical close-up slowly moving through a line of individual hand-written musical notes; as the camera tracks the musical line, a piano strikes each note (the music plays in Julie's mind; she is not actually playing the notes). From the page the camera moves to glimpses of Julie standing by the piano reading the notes on the once-folded page until they end. Then, unexpectedly, though the written notes have ceased, the music continues, its momentum moving Julie toward a continuation and completion of the melody within her. As the music goes on playing in her imagination, she slowly and deliberately turns her head away from the page to look at her hand resting on the base of the rod that supports the raised lid of the grand piano. With the music still sounding, Julie slowly moves the rod down the skid allowing the lid to collapse; it crashes down on the piano *and* the music with a loud echoing boom. In the silence that follows, that blue light again plays faintly on Julie's face. She inhales deeply, closes her eyes, and rather than exhale as in a sigh, she purses her mouth and grits her teeth, apparently choosing to suppress whatever recollection or emotion the music has evoked. The music bids her to go again toward life, but she'll have nothing to do with it or what it signifies about life.

The meaning of the last cryptic gesture is amplified in the next scene, which finds Julie in a city — presumably Paris — getting out of her small red car, slamming the door, and running determinedly across the street, an expression of angry resolve on her face. She charges up an apartment building stairwell, rings the bell, and enters the apartment of her husband's copyist, the woman who transcribes edited scores into clean, revised ones. The camera slowly surveys the unfurled folio pages of music, all in black ink except for editorial corrections and, in one instance, a sizable addition in the broad strokes of a blue felt-tip marker, the same kind of pen, we come to know, that Julie habitually uses in editing her husband's work. As the two peruse the score together, the young woman comments that the music is very beautiful and calls Julie's attention to an example of that beauty in a choral section. As her fingers follow the passage, a choral section of the unfinished symphony bursts forth in a virtual shout. Julie grudgingly admits that the music is beautiful — "Oui" — but at the same time she begins to roll up the score, and as the film's music continues, at once urgent and jubilant, she exits the building.

With the rolled score in her hand, she approaches a large garbage truck making its collection rounds. As the music continues, undiminished and enveloping, she throws the score into the truck's large rear hopper and then simply watches as the enormous toothed jaws of the truck pierce the score and devour it along with the other garbage into its dark oblivion. The noise of the truck at first competes with the music, and then as it demolishes the score, drowns out the music completely. Indeed, our last view of Julie suggests that the destruction of the music was the purpose of her trip to the city, a desire that brings to completion her deliberate collapsing of the piano lid. There she had chosen to literally close down the music rather than let it continue to expand in her imagination and soul. And now, as Julie watches the garbage truck do its work, Kieslowski lights her in shadow and a curious, almost ghostly blanched light, making her face a striking mixture of melancholy and resolve. The scene ends with her breathing in deeply and then exhaling as if to suggest that still another parting is now accomplished and done with.

This gesture assumes all the more significance because Julie knows full well the meaning of the words the chorus sings, which seem to scream at her in particular. The words are not in French or a language recognizable to most viewers, unless they happen to know Greek; for reasons that are not entirely clear, Kieslowski chose not to provide a subtitled translation of this excerpt from the choral section of the "Unification Symphony," perhaps because it would have diluted the unfolding mystery of its power to haunt Julie. And it is no wonder, given Julie's current course of action, that she seeks to trash — quite literally — her husband's music; for the text that resounds so emphatically is from the New Testament, specifically from the thirteenth chapter of St. Paul's first letter to the church at Corinth, what is commonly known as his great hymn to love (see sidebar for text). It is certain that Julie wants nothing to do with either the music or what it speaks about, because her action is resolute and almost violent as she rebukes the music's emphatic demand to become part of its experience. This is something that, in her trauma, she wishes to exclude from her life, no matter what the cost; this is her renunciation of the music, of life, and — for those who know the words — of love itself and, presumably, God.

Two more scenes emphasize her choice to erase the past and refuse the present and future. Sitting on a naked mattress before a glowing fireplace at her country estate, Julie plunges her hand into her purse, and when she cannot find what she is looking for, impatiently dumps its contents onto the bed. Amid the purse's random contents she comes across a large candy sucker wrapped in blue foil of the kind that ruffled in the wind from the rear window of the car in the film's opening shots. In tight close-up, her hand moves slowly toward the candy, trembling, holding it reverently for a few seconds. Finally, the camera cuts to her

Chorus, from I Corinthians 13

If I speak with the tongues of men and angels,
but have not love,
I am a noisy gong or a clanging cymbal.

And if I have prophetic powers, and understand
all mysteries and all knowledge,
and if I have all faith, so as to remove mountains,
but have not love,
I am nothing.

Love is patient, and kind;
Love is not jealous or boastful;
it is not arrogant or rude.
Love does not insist on its own way;
it is not irritable or resentful;
it does not rejoice at wrong, but rejoices in the right.
Love bears all things, believes all things,
hopes all things, endures all things.

Love never ends;
as for prophecies, they will pass away;
as for tongues, they will cease;
as for knowledge, it will pass away....
So faith, hope, love abide, these three;
but the greatest of these is love.

The text above comes from the Revised Standard Version of the King James Bible, which the translated text in the liner notes of the sound track album of the film, *Trois Couleurs Blue* (Virgin Records, 1993), closely follows.

face to show Julie's head turning away, reeling, as if to say, "Oh, not again, not again, I thought I was done with this." She then unwraps the candy, which is also pale blue; bringing it to her mouth and indecisively holding it there, she tastes it rather tentatively, clearly uncertain what to do with this unwanted reminder of her daughter. But then, in a gesture that repeats the repudiations enacted in the previous scenes, she begins to chomp on it, initially chewing frantically but then swallowing it with her characteristic resolve until it disappears. She tosses the stick and wrapper into the fire.

Still chewing the remnants of the sucker, she recalls what had sent her rummaging through her purse in the first place: locating her address book for a phone number. A male voice answers when she dials, and Julie identifies herself and then asks straightaway whether the man on the other end loves her. He replies that he does, and she asks how long he has loved her. The answer, "Since I started working with Patrice" (her late husband), identifies the man as Olivier (Benoît Régent), the one who brought the small television to Julie in the hospital and who has been seen cleaning up Patrice's musical affairs in earlier short scenes. For example, prior to Julie's release from the hospital, he was shown going through the desk in Patrice's studio, putting much of its contents into a large blue folder; he seems to debate its fate, and once he even tries to deliver it to Julie. His reluctance to do that, it becomes clear, is because, included among Patrice's papers, there are photos of Patrice with another woman, who, from the looks of things, is his mistress. Olivier knows that this is not the time to reveal the photos to the new widow. "Do you think of me? Do you miss me?" she asks him over the phone. After a soft "Oui," she says, "Come, if you want," and then she adds, "right away." While Olivier's voice is quiet and diffident during this peculiar conversation, Julie's is rather business-like, even imperious.

When he arrives, soaked by a driving rainstorm, Julie invites him, somewhat perfunctorily, to make love. As they disrobe from opposite sides of the room, and Olivier approaches, Julie explains: "They took everything. Only the mattress is left." The statement explains the emptiness of the house on a literal level but also describes Julie's sense of her own life and perhaps why she is now resorting to a sexual intimacy that she has not thought out or prepared for emotionally. Indeed, it seems to be a very strange recourse for this woman who until now has sought to put aside any human contact that might entail emotion. And the suggestion that, having jettisoned the past, she is starting up with a new love is abruptly discounted the next morning. The love scene onscreen is cut short; indeed, in the middle of the first kiss, the scene jumps to the sleeping face of Olivier in the morning sun, with a cup of coffee next to his head. Julie proceeds to tell him that their night together was not a beginning but a farewell, done in part for herself — "I appreciate what you did for me" — but also to show him that she is like any other woman and not worth pining over: "But you see, I'm like any other woman. I sweat. I cough. . . . You won't miss me. You understand that now."

Before Olivier can think to respond, Julie stands to leave, telling him to "shut the door" when he leaves. He calls after her from a window, but she is already outside the gate, walking down the rain-soaked drive. She is dressed in blue jeans and her constant black sweater and a blazer, and all she carries is a large, light box bound with string. Walking toward the camera, she seems to begin to stagger, drifting toward the rough stone wall that surrounds the estate. At the brink of tears, she thrusts the back of her hand against the wall and runs it along its rough surface, abrading her knuckles until physical pain diverts her from the emotional anguish that besieges her as she leaves this place that held the precious lives to whom she now struggles to bid farewell.

Julie's homecoming to the estate has been a farewell that marks the beginning of her departure from everything that life has heretofore represented for her, especially the intense happiness she felt in the midst of that bygone existence. Everything she does, from destroying Patrice's music to devouring her daughter's sucker, moves toward a renunciation of the past and, as the next segment of the story suggests, of any sensible version of a whole or complete life. The extremity of her rejection of these things suggests the depth and pervasiveness of grief at her loss. If she cannot bring herself to suicide, she will then obliterate everything that ignites that onrush of sorrow, and for her, just about everything in her old life prompts waves of grief. So she empties her house as a means of ridding herself of her past, of all the goodness she has lost. How fully glad she was in that life Kieslowski once again chooses to express with the signature color of the film. Intense shades of blue cover almost the whole interior of the house. And when the music comes, either lilting or in its full symphonic heft, it comes in blue — that is, it's blue Julie sees when she hears the music. Blue is a central token and emblem of the deepest emotional rhythms and attachments of Julie's psyche and soul, a color that for her symbolizes intense full-blown joy in the goodness of life, a life that she clearly loved in all respects. The predominant use and signification of the color in *Blue* (though it is occasionally used to denote either sadness or coldness) is as the color of love, both personal and metaphysical; and as such it provides the key to understanding the film's full complexity and meaning.

Escape . . . Maybe

After leaving the country estate, Julie searches for an apartment in the city, one where there will be no children in the building and where she can do "nothing" for a living, "nothing at all," as she tells the apartment broker. For added measure, she goes back to using her maiden name, in effect trying to officially deny the reality and hold of marriage and motherhood. She takes immediate possession of a large upper-story corner apartment whose large living room has two walls of solid windows. Once inside, she rushes to the cardboard box she has carried with her from her now forsaken home and takes it into the center of the light-filled living room and hurriedly unties its knotted string. A faint look of pleasure gathers on her face as she gazes at its contents. A quiet clatter and then a strand of beads shows that it is the mobile Julie had found (and attacked) in Anna's bedroom. After hanging it from the ceiling, Julie ponders the mobile, the camera gazing at her through the bright blue beads as the music again mounts, this time more insistent and less broken. She slowly circles the mobile, stopping on the side away from the windows. With her face inches from the mobile, her hand reaches up to caress one of the beads. At this point in the musical score a somewhat harsh flute evokes Julie's internal conflict; she slowly pulls back her hand and, tremblingly folding it into a fist, she brings it tight against her mouth and, with her usual fierce determination, again struggles to resist the recollection and relish of the goodness now lost. With the blue light, the color of love, emanating through the mobile on her face, she bows her head as the light slowly darkens and the shot fades to black.

Once settled in the city, Julie seeks to slide into whole days of "nothing," by which she means a kind of mental and emotional blankness, a state of minimal or detached consciousness that permits only the slightest sensate pleasures. Efficiently but tellingly, Kieslowski sketches the routine of Julie's new emptied-out life. She daily sits in a café for her "usual" coffee and ice cream, listening to a homeless man play a flute as he stands against a mottled blue wall across the street. And she swims laps in a blue pool whose bright hue resembles the blue of the mobile. Or she lounges in a chair in her apartment, enjoying a cigarette. Or she sits on a park bench relishing the sun on her face. What she does try to avoid in this anonymous new existence is any meaningful human contact whatever. In this she is stalwart, as Kieslowski shows when in the middle of the night Julie is awakened by loud noises from the street. On the street below, three men are beating another man, kicking his fallen body.

Julie slowly circles the blue mobile she has hung in her new apartment; it is the only memento of her daughter that she has kept.

When he manages to escape them, he enters Julie's apartment house and pounds on successive doors in hopes that someone will give him refuge. When he pounds loudly on her door, Julie stands frightened and paralyzed, a faint bluish light again resting on her face, suggesting perhaps the slightest twitch toward engagement with a world beyond herself.

When the poor fellow finally leaves, Julie — apparently unable to shake either concern or curiosity — cautiously ventures into the hall, looking down the building's long central stairwell to see if he's still there, asking "Is anyone there?" a question that has large implications for the whole of Julie's own life. Meanwhile, wind from an open window blows the door to her apartment shut, locking her out of her sanctum for the night. So Julie sits on the stairs, silently observing what little activity takes place in the middle of the night. One floor down, she sees a young woman arrive home; before she enters her apartment, she scratches lightly on the door immediately next to her own. A somewhat older man comes out of his apartment and enters the young woman's apartment. Before entering, sensing someone's presence, he glances up and sees Julie. Seconds later the woman's door opens, and she peeks out to see Julie. But then everything is quiet and, hoping to get at least some rest, Julie leans her head against the vertical slats of the wooden railing. But when she closes her eyes, instead of sleep the music comes again, now much quieter and less insistent, a variation on the piano and choral music but this time sounding very much like the humming of a male chorus or a collection of low strings. But it's clearly the same music with the same note of demand. And while the music plays, random splotches of blue light dance in the frame, looking very much like the reflections from the mobile hanging in the center of her living room. What distinguishes this scene from earlier ones is that here Julie seems to allow herself to savor the music, which seems quiet and soothing now; she lets it wash over her, apparently finding some measure of comfort in it as she sits locked out of her room and alone through the long night. While it is still unbidden, it is not the alien assault that she has resented up until now.

Nonetheless, Julie proves stalwart in her effort to fend off people. Kieslowski's cut to the next scene is abrupt and jolting. Startled by the sound of her doorbell, Julie drops a house plant, a telling indication of how far she has removed herself from human interchange. She opens the door and immediately apologizes, thinking a neighbor has come to complain about the noise she's making moving things around in her apartment. Actually, the neighbor has come to ask her to sign a petition to evict the young woman Julie has observed from the stairwell, a woman the neighbor angrily labels a whore (it is apparently her husband Julie observed entering the young woman's apartment). Julie simply refuses, saying she does not want to get involved. The noninvolvement motif is reiterated in the next scene, where Julie sits in the sun on a park bench with her eyes closed, savoring the sunlight and listening to the homeless man's solitary flute. The primary visual focus in this sequence is the slow progress of a bent-over and very decrepit old woman who painstakingly makes her way toward a large bottle-recycling receptacle. Once there, she can barely reach up to the hole to deposit her bottle. This woman's journey is painfully slow, but Julie remains oblivious to it as she basks in the sun with her eyes closed. Her indifference to the plight of the elderly woman, whose persistence amid terrible difficulties presents an apt foil to Julie's willed passivity and insularity, contrasts markedly with the Julie who re-emerges by the end of the film (and it contrasts with the help given to the same old woman by Valentin [Irene Jacob], the heroine of *Red*, in the concluding film of the trilogy).

And Julie would remain that detached if she could. But as the remainder of the film makes abundantly clear, the world, or life, or herself, or God — or whatever — will not allow her to remain alone in her cocoon of renunciation. One event after another, especially the musical visitations, hound her back into life and to the hard burden of loving the very world she wishes so desperately to flee. Events and people, both past and present, join those persistent musical "eruptions" to beckon her back to the joys, albeit risky ones, for which human life was made in the first place.

First comes the young man who was at the roadside when their car crashed. While Julie is visiting her doctor for a post-accident checkup, the phone rings and the doctor indicates it is for her, explaining that this young man has been trying to reach her. Antoine (Yann Trégouët) says he wants to meet for an important reason, to which Julie responds, characteristically, "Nothing's important." He tells her that he has something of hers he'd like to return — "a necklace . . . with a cross on it."

Julie's response, with a look of alarm, is to reach for her neck to feel for the missing necklace. In an abrupt shift of scene, Kieslowski cuts to an extreme close-up of the cross dangling from the chain. For a long time Julie looks fondly and wordlessly at the cross until she quietly says, her voice tinged with sorrow, "I'd forgotten all about it," a comment that perhaps explains the whole cause and logic of her retreat. After all, the cross is preeminently an emblem that melds love and suffering, both of which Julie now seeks to avoid. The boy then invites her to ask about anything she wants to know concerning the accident, since he arrived at the scene only seconds after it happened. Julie responds with a quick and emphatic "no"; as she says it, that assertive music she first heard during her hospital convalescence resounds again as the scene fades to black for a full fifteen-second reprise. Here, however, the oboe refrain of the opening declaration noticeably slows, protracting its mood of sadness and longing. As before, there is the mood of profound longing for the good life of family. This time, though, the longing amplifies in clear response to the cross, particularly, it seems, to the specific meanings of love and devotion that the cross symbolizes. As such, the scene conjoins nicely with the "hymn to love" of the choral score. Here the emphatic and lengthy return of the music broadly underscores the significance of this cross for Julie — certainly personal but apparently also religious.

When the music stops, we are back in the café, where the young man asks Julie the meaning of her husband's last words, "Now try coughing." At that, Julie bows her head, and for a short time viewers cannot tell whether she is laughing or crying. When she finally raises her head, a laughing smile plays on her face, the first we've seen in this movie, and she then tells the boy about her husband's habit of repeating the punch lines of jokes. At the time of the accident, Patrice was telling a story about a woman's visit to the doctor; the punch line is what the boy heard repeated just before Patrice died. It suggests, first, that Patrice died laughing and, second, that it is possible to laugh even in the midst of one's own death, a lesson — or even a command — that Julie has thus far refused to acknowledge or follow in her own emotional death. When Julie finishes explaining the joke, she abruptly gets up to leave, as if the burden of her recollection of Patrice has been too painful. Rising, she tells the boy that he can keep the cross: "You returned it. It's yours." In effect, having already forgotten the cross, Julie refuses it when it is returned to her, either as a memento or as a matter of existential embrace, just as she shuns the fullness of life.

The camera cuts suddenly to a close-up of Julie's swimming, an arduous physical activity that is both diverting and tiring, and to which she turns when in turmoil. As usual, the pool is empty except for her; the facility is virtually without light, and the small amount of light is dim and very blue, the deep background fading to pitch blackness. Blue is above and below, in the water and out, and for Julie there is no escaping it. At the end of a lap she pauses and then pulls herself out of the pool. When her face rises out of the watery blueness into some semblance of natural light, an aggressive rendition of the orchestral music erupts, full of loud horns and percussion, foreboding in mood and rhythm. Again the music startles and assails her, so much so that she slides down into the pool to escape the sound, in effect trying to drown it out — and perhaps drown herself as well. The gesture works, for the sound is muffled as long as Julie stays submerged, which she does for fifteen seconds. The origins of the music are no clearer, and it shows no sign of leaving her alone.

The scene shifts again to show Julie walking an empty Paris street past the flute-playing street musician, who is now asleep on the sidewalk. Julie crouches over him to ask if he is okay. He awakens, raises his head, and smiles, and when he does Julie slides beneath his head the slender case that holds his instrument. His response is telling, an incisive comment on the human condition in general and specifically on Julie's relinquishing of the cross to the teenager: "You always gotta hold onto something." Julie doesn't understand his words, and she asks him to repeat them; but as if to affirm his wisdom, he lays his head on the case and promptly returns to his rest. But his words have spoken directly to Julie's refusal to hang on to anything at all, either human or divine.

Julie's insular world is again disturbed by a neighbor, Lucille (Charlotte Véry), the young woman about whom the eviction petition has been circulated. She comes by with a small bouquet of flowers to thank Julie for not signing the petition, thus allowing her to stay in the building. Somewhat to Julie's dismay, the young woman more or less barges in, looks around, and then notices the blue mobile hanging from the ceiling in the living room. She approaches the mobile and then explains that she had one just like it as a child: "I'd stand under it and stretch out my hand. I dreamt of jumping up and touching it." Julie is surprised and riveted by the account, clearly finding something true and resonant in Lucille's recollection. With rapt delight on her face, Lucille reaches out to nestle the beads in her palm; again her reaction startles Julie, especially since it is a repetition of her own emotional response when she hung the mobile in the new apartment. And just as hanging the mobile was Julie's first act upon moving into the apartment, Lucille's first act on entering is to appreciate and, in effect, embrace the mobile. Stranger still, Lucille's next words — "I forgot all about it" — repeat Julie's words (only the verb tense changes) on seeing the cross necklace, another touchstone of love within life. So when Lucille asks Julie where she got the mobile, the normally self-assured Julie is quite tongue-tied, her emotion-filled eyes fixed on Lucille. Julie can only manage to say that she found it and passively agree to Lucille's suggestion that it was perhaps a souvenir. Lucille continues her intrusion on Julie's insularity by inquiring about her being single ("You're not the type somebody dumps"). In spite of her efforts at withdrawal, in Lucille Julie meets another person who grasps the world as she does and disorients her resolve to be alone.

A further disruption to Julie's insularity in this part of the story occurs while she is having her daily coffee and ice cream at the corner café. Someone calls her name, and she looks up to see Olivier; he explains that he has been looking for her and, thanks to the coincidence of his cleaning lady's daughter having seen Julie in the neighborhood, he's found her. He confesses that he misses her, but at this declaration of emotion and connection, Julie turns her head and sighs, clearly exasperated with the sense of reality that the gentle Olivier presents to her. When she says nothing, Olivier says that she simply "ran away" and wonders if it was from him. Looking intently at Olivier, Julie quietly shakes her head in the negative, all but announcing her affection for him. Throughout the sequence, a mild, warm light from the window illumines one side of her face, while the other stays in shadow, aptly portraying the conflict she now feels. The camera then looks over Julie's shoulder as she watches a chauffeur-driven Mercedes stop on the street. A tall, elegantly dressed blonde woman emerges from it, along with the homeless flute player. The woman kisses him farewell, returns to the car, and the vehicle drives off, leaving the man behind to open his instrument case and start playing. Hearing the distinctive music, Olivier turns to see the flute player against his usual mottled-blue wall. With surprise, Olivier notes the similarity of the music to Patrice's unfinished symphony. With that tune playing in the background, Olivier leaves, telling Julie that the simple fact of seeing her will suffice for now and that he'll try not to bother her in the future.

After Olivier has left, Julie concludes the sequence by asking the flute player how he knows this music, to which he replies that he simply invents "lots of things. . . . I like to play." His mysterious speech and identity — plus the fact that he, too, knows music resembling Patrice's — suggests that there is more afoot here than meets the eye or ear (his presence resembles that of the mysterious silent figure who reappears regularly throughout Kieslowski's *Decalogue* [1988]). Perhaps it suggests that the sonorous mystical music Patrice composed was not "heard" just by him but by others, especially by those whose understanding of life diverges from the ordinary, as this man's clearly does. Strange as it may seem to Julie, it is this man's life's calling to play the music she has repudiated. His life could also be secure and without pain, given the affluent world from which we've seen him depart; instead, he embraces the music he hears and seeks to disseminate it, a choice Julie herself will finally embrace — but only after much resistance.

Julie faces a last disturbance of her insularity when she finds in her apartment a family of mice, a mother and a litter of tiny hairless babies. This is a problem: their scurrying and squeaking keep her awake at night, and Julie has always feared and disliked mice. She seems ready to kill them all with a broom, but she can't bring herself to do it after looking closely at the nest. It is clear, however, that she is alarmed by their presence; she even inquires about the possibility of moving to another apartment. Julie is bothered enough by the mice that she visits her mother in the nursing home solely to ask her mother, or so it seems, whether she (Julie) was afraid of mice as a child. This visit is complicated by the fact that her mother (Emmanuelle Riva) suffers from Alzheimer's, or some other dementia that has robbed her of her memory. When Julie arrives, her mother mistakenly identifies her as her own sister, Marie-France, Julie's aunt; and even after Julie corrects her, her mother does so again seconds later, remarking that she is not dead, as she has been told, and in fact appears to be so young.

Throughout this sequence, Julie's mother sits in a chair watching television, regularly returning her gaze to a documentary showing a very elderly man bungee jumping! Perhaps recalling that she is a mother, and also aware of her memory loss, she asks Julie if there's anything she wants to tell her about her family. When Julie says that they're all dead, the mother remembers that she had been told that. It's clear that Julie has come for some measure of comfort and understanding from her mother; she even tries at one point to beckon her with a simple, urgent "Mom." But, before long, her mother is calling her Marie-France again. Oddly, to this person who no longer knows her, Julie offers a satisfied and contented smile, perhaps realizing that the life she now hopes for is much like her mother's, disconnected from everyone and remembering only what suits her.

Perhaps it is for this reason that Julie offers her mother the film's longest explanation of her post-accident posture toward life. Lest there be any doubt, the explanation exposes Julie's deep fear, not of mice, but of the hurt that life can inflict when it takes away what one loves most: "Now I have only one thing left to do: nothing. I don't want any belongings, any memories. No friends, no love. Those are all traps." By the time Julie leaves her mother, she seems less afraid of the mice but frightened of something far more profound that is somehow connected with what she has suffered and with this new course of life she has just now spoken aloud in the starkest terms. During this long exchange between mother and daughter, in two different kinds of remove from life, the television plays continuously the ironic images of the elderly man and others who plunge into the fullness of life, despite conspicuous perils, on the end of a bungee cord.

How perturbed Julie is can be seen in the radical gesture that follows. She borrows a neighbor's cat and then releases the animal in her apartment to rid it of mice, a scene that is filmed in cool light and shadows. Immediately afterward, the camera cuts to Julie again in the pool; the blue color and lighting are now much lighter and cooler, reflecting the emotional distance she seeks from life. She swims her breaststroke somewhat frantically, and when she pulls up at the end of the pool, her new friend Lucille is kneeling at poolside. Julie gasps, "Why are you here?" Lucille replies that she has come out of concern: "I saw you from the bus. You were running like crazy." In wide-eyed amazement at her neighbor's compassion, Julie searches her face, and Lucille asks if Julie is crying. Julie responds that it's only pool water that makes it look like she's crying; but when Lucille reaches toward Julie, she begins to sob, confessing that she has let the cat loose on the mouse and its babies. Full of understanding, Lucille assures Julie that her response is normal, and she offers to go back to the apartment and clean up the messy remains of the cat's deadly work. Julie gives Lucille her keys.

This is a telling sequence that illuminates what the fear she has confessed to her mother is all about. The mice and the girls from the swim class (who have just jumped into the pool) remind Julie of what she has lost, but also of the goodness of life itself and what might still lie ahead for her in choosing to live. She is, in effect, assailed simultaneously from two directions: the deep sweetness of life that again beckons her and the overwhelming pain life can inflict when love is torn away. In apposite terms, the music tolls at this point because what Julies has encountered is love — both Lucille's gesture of compassion and caring and her own relish of love represented by the exuberance of the little girls.

Return

In the last phase of the film, this conflict resolves, gloriously, as Julie is decisively hauled back into living and love; and this resolution is precipitated by two unexpected and very odd occurrences. In the middle of the night, Julie's phone awakens her: it is Lucille asking Julie to come immediately, even though it's late at night, to a rather mysterious address. Julie reluctantly agrees, and she ventures down dark streets and alleys to eventually ask admission at a seedy doorway. It soon becomes clear that Lucille works as a performer in a sex club. Julie makes her way through the garish red light to Lucille's dressing room. Lucille anxiously explains that, while she was preparing to go on stage, she glanced at the audience and saw her father sitting in the front row. When the manager refused to make him leave, the distraught Lucille called Julie; but before she got there, Lucille's father had left to catch the last train to his rural home. Lucille says: "I didn't know who I could count on. I was desperate. I didn't know who to talk to."

Julie asks Lucille why she engages in this dubious work, to which the latter replies, with a note of defiance, "Because I like to. I think everyone likes to." Perhaps Lucille is referring to the kind of bondedness that sex can offer; and in a way, at this stage she has a deeper and more complex understanding of the nature and purposes of human life than Julie does. As if to prove it, Lucille returns to a subject that Julie would just as soon ignore: "Julie, you saved my life." Julie demurs, but Lucille asserts the truth of her statement: "I asked you to come and you came. Same thing." In this sequence we can see that, short of death, Julie can't for long remain detached from her essential humanity. Lucille's gratitude impresses Julie with the fact that, like it or not, life has her in its clutches and there is no running from it.

Julie's visit to Lucille at the sex club takes a decisive twist when Lucille happens to see Julie's face on a TV screen and calls her attention to it. What Julie now sees on television will yank her decisively to a full-blown re-engagement with living toward which the music has pushed her. Onscreen, Olivier is speaking to the journalist who came to interview Julie at the hospital. A series of still photos of Julie and Patrice play on the screen while Olivier explains that he has been asked by the European Council to finish the "Symphony for the Unification of Europe," which Patrice was working on at the time of his death. Olivier displays the manuscript scrolls containing Julie's corrections; he then removes an array of documents and photos from the blue packet that he took from Patrice's desk at the conservatory. The pictures slowly play across the screen: shots of Julie or Patrice alone, of Patrice and Julie together, and finally of Patrice and a young woman Julie has never seen before. It is clear from the pictures that Patrice and the young woman were romantically involved. Julie's eyes widen as she cranes her neck to take in the series of pictures, a look of mild alarm on her face.

On leaving the club, Julie immediately goes to the music copyist, even though it is now the middle of the night, to ask for the journalist's address and to demand to know how Olivier got a copy of the unfinished score. Julie was under the impression, of course, that she had thrown the last copy into the jaws of the garbage truck. In a truth that Julie should know — and probably once did — the young copyist explains that she knew Julie would destroy it, and she adds: "This music is so beautiful. You can't destroy things like that."

The next day, in a dramatic reversal of Olivier's earlier search for Julie, she goes in search of Olivier. He is driving off in his car just when Julie locates him. She runs after him, calling his name, and catches him at the far end of a parking lot, getting his attention by pounding on the back window of his old Volvo station wagon. She indignantly reports the rumor that he's going to finish Patrice's composition. He says, as he did on television, that he will perhaps try to finish it, but that success is by no means certain, for the task is very difficult indeed. To Julie's protests that this is unfair, he tells her straight out that he has agreed to try completing the work as a way to break through her withdrawal and insularity: "It was a way . . . to make you cry, make you run. The only way of making you say, 'I want' or 'I don't want.'" "You don't leave me any choice," says Olivier. Julie claims over and over that his choice is not fair — no doubt meaning to both the music and herself. Finally, though, she consents to look at what Olivier has done with the music, just to make sure that he has understood Patrice's intentions in the composition.

The scene shifts to Olivier's apartment in what is perhaps the pivotal scene in the film, the climactic moment when event and music combine to propel Julie to a new embrace of living. Julie first listens to Olivier's piano renditions of Patrice's score for the choral conclusion. Something is amiss in Olivier's rendition: it sounds discordant and harsh. Perplexed, Julie goes to Olivier's bookshelf and pulls out a conspicuously old book, though it is not clear what the book is. Famously secretive as a composer, Patrice had not told Olivier the source of his Greek chorus. Looking at the text over Julie's shoulder as she holds it, Olivier hums its apparent rhythm, moving closer to Julie as he does so. Julie at least knows the meaning of the Greek on the page, for it is the "love" hymn from 1 Corinthians, the same wild choral text that sounded when she confiscated what she thought was the only extant copy of the chorus and dumped it into the garbage truck.

It seems appropriate, then, that in the midst of St. Paul's emphatic love declaration, Julie recalls the televised pictures of her husband and the other woman. She abruptly asks Olivier, "Who was that girl?" He is astounded that she did not know that Patrice and the woman were, as Julie puts it, "together" — and for several years at that. In response to Julie's questions, he tells her where the woman lives, what she does for a living, and where they'd met. When Olivier asks, "What do you want to do?" Julie gives an immediate answer. Without the least pause, the music from Julie's convalescence again bursts out, immediate and direct, unsought and startling, louder and more insistent than ever.

As if the music has told her something, Julie promptly answers Olivier's question with a slight smile: "Meet her." Here apparently the music has singularly "spoken" to Julie, displaying a path of engagement, though she is not yet sure of its measure or shape. The scene is of strategic importance for the viewer because it is the first time that Julie seems to respond positively to the substance of the Greek text; on previous occasions she has sought to obliterate it and its power. Previously, these two strands of text and music have stayed apart, but now they begin to converge so that the text can inform and clarify the music. And for Julie it is perhaps revelation, because she is confronted not only by music and the exultant text but by matters in life that seem to demand attention and, more than that, her love. In fact, the joining of text to the previously wordless music explains to Julie what that music was all about in the first place. The music resounds, and Julie unhesitatingly and unflinchingly goes out to meet life again, and seemingly with relish. The many musical visitations have "sounded" that notion of love in Julie's soul through the whole long ordeal of her mourning, haunting her flight from life. Now, however, circumstances and the music itself have conspired to propel her again toward living. Her decision to meet the mystery woman is a long way from hiding in a solitude so complete that the ring of the doorbell startles her. From this moment to the end of the story, Julie acts with resolve to relish again what she can from life, although that is never without some measure of conflict.

Julie goes in pursuit of the mystery woman, locating and then shadowing her in the court building where she, Sandrine (Florence Pernel), works as a lawyer. Finally, Julie intercepts her in the women's restroom, and Sandrine is very obviously pregnant. Julie confronts her directly: "You were my husband's mistress? I didn't know, I just found out." "That's a shame," replies Sandrine. "Now you'll hate him. You'll hate me, too." "I don't know," says Julie, genuinely unsure of her future attitude. And, yes, she admits, the baby is Patrice's; she discovered the unintended pregnancy only after his death, but now she wishes to raise the child. Julie refuses Sandrine's offer to give her details of the affair. And Sandrine does not need to declare that Patrice loved her. Julie says, "I know he loved you," because the young woman wears a cross necklace identical to the one Julie lost in the accident. Julie already knows its apparent meaningfulness to Patrice: it is a symbol of care that speaks for itself, something he prized highly and intended to celebrate in his "Unification Symphony." Jolted by all of this, Julie heads for the door; but Sandrine poses a last question that goes unanswered, "Julie, will you hate me now?"

The answer to that comes in two dramatic gestures. First, though, there is Julie's inner struggle, which Kieslowski immediately conjures in an abrupt cut to Julie's dive into that blue-black pool. Then there is only long silence as Julie swims underwater for a very long half minute, so long that viewers wonder whether she has succeeded in drowning herself. Finally, though, she breaks the surface, coughing and sputtering, gasping for air. The sequence is a poignant visual corollary for the whole long process of Julie's slow recovery from grief. Indeed, it is closer to a rebirth for Julie, so thoroughly has she struggled to suppress her fundamental humanity. She has essentially gone underwater into an insular world of retreat and silence, muting but not quite extinguishing the resounding and resounding musical call she keeps getting to resume life. It is important to note that this is the only occasion when Julie swims that she does not hear the music, suggesting that she has indeed moved to the next stage of response to her vast personal tragedy. If she was submerging herself in the water to escape from life itself before, the next scenes suggest that she has now gone beyond the need to swim.

Julie goes to visit her mother once again, but this time she simply observes through the window as loud and percussive piano variations of the central theme play in her head. The same motif dominates, but now it becomes still more insistent, one individual note after another crashing and echoing, joining in accumulating force to a relentless momentum. Julie flees to Olivier's apartment, where she seems to reckon, once and for all, with the reality of the mistress.

Olivier opens the door to a distressed Julie and asks whether she has met Patrice's mistress. She gives no answer but asks Olivier whether the photos of Patrice and the mistress were in the packet he had offered her and she refused. She speculates, smiling impishly the whole time, that if she had taken them she would have either looked at them herself or would have simply destroyed them as she had everything else in her past life. If the latter had happened, she says, she would never have known about the mistress. Olivier agrees, but then Julie matter-of-factly demurs from this seemingly happier scenario: "Maybe it's better this way." This remark is cryptic, and the usual interpretation is that her new knowledge of the mistress diminishes her estimate of her husband and thus allows her to move on more readily to put her grief behind her.

But that is rather too easy an analysis, and it tends to trivialize the role of the music and the nature of Julie's grief, making it mostly a matter of romance. What Julie lost was not just the husband she loved but also her daughter and, more importantly, her relish for life itself and her sense that life was made for love. Julie's apparent deep satisfaction in having come across the knowledge of the liaison and the child who will be born from it seems to move her forward to the view that even from life's darkest surprises can emerge new life and hope. More than any diminishment of her husband's stature, the recognition of this truth about the irrepressible goodness of life — what the music has chanted — has occasioned her optimism that even difficult news can also somehow ultimately be good news.

The view that her new and harsher estimate of her marriage is the catalytic factor that returns her to life is also contradicted by Julie's next actions. First, she immediately begins to help Olivier complete the unfinished "Symphony for Unification." Indeed, that seems to be the primary purpose for going to his apartment, especially as the music crashes through her mind when she leaves her mother's nursing home. Her initial response to Olivier's announcement that he would try to finish the music had been that he should not do it, since it was Patrice's music and to place it in another's hands was somehow "unfair." Now, however, her attitude toward the task indicates a complete reversal. Before, her purpose in living, so to speak, was to shut down, destroy, or run from the music; but now, as she leaves her mother's residence, she flees to the music, ready to explore and complete its depths of love, both aesthetically and existentially. Having dispatched the matter of fate, or providence, in learning about the mistress, Julie asks Olivier to "show me what you've composed."

Olivier has laden the simple score with violins and a bit of bombast with much percussion. Julie suggests lightening the music by doing without the percussion. She then strips away the trumpets, leaving only the various registers of the strings, allowing the fluidity of the music to emerge. They experiment with a piano overlay, but then end with a flute. Through much of the discussion and revision, Kieslowski has allowed the camera to go out of focus, transforming Olivier's apartment into a blur of light and color, apparently to suggest the composers' entrance into a magical creative realm of inspiration and delight. The strangeness of the revision process is extended when the flute solo finally sounds through and over the orchestra, distinctly recalling the sound of the mysterious street musician who roosted outside Julie's café. When the camera returns to focus, Julie stands in the warm light of Olivier's apartment, a faint smile of pleasure on her face, intently relishing the music as it plays in her head. When it stops, Olivier asks what the finale will be, a question that applies as much to Julie's future course as it does to the music. She responds pointedly, "I don't know," but then remembers the musical remnant, the memento Patrice had given her, on which she had slammed the piano lid early on. Her comments emphasize "counterpoint" to the rather somber mood of the portions extended by Olivier; she tells him to "try weaving it back in," a statement that applies as much to her own effort to find some counterpoint to the tragedy in her own life.

With its abundant testament to the power of love, the "memento" now provides the course to completion, both for the symphonic suite and for Julie's own life. First, she asks if the house has sold and tells Olivier to tell the lawyer not to sell it. She then in effect consigns the fate of Patrice's music to Olivier, telling him to "handle" all of it, extracting his promise that he will show it to her. All of this she does with quiet assurance and pleasure, an attitude in great contrast to her former insular, numb soul that lived anonymously and disconnected in the heart of one of the world's great cities. Both the "memento" and the street musician's music seem to intervene here — coincidentally if not providentially — to clarify the music and the course of life Julie should pursue.

Her plans for the house become immediately clear. The scene shifts to the empty estate, where weeds dominate the courtyard; Julie helps the gardener remove shutters from the windows. A car drives in, and the person who emerges from it is, of all people, Patrice's pregnant mistress. Julie takes her on a quick tour of the house, which ends in the kitchen, where Julie asks the sex of the still-unborn child (it is a boy). Struggling slightly with her choice, she says, "I thought he should have his [Patrice's] name and his house. Here." Julie freely gives what had been priceless and inviolable to her to this woman for whom she could reasonably harbor hatred and jealousy; for with the birth of this child, Sandrine will now have what Julie herself so prized and loved. In a supreme gesture of generosity and love, her reaction is the opposite of what would be the expected and understandably "human" reaction. And in this act Julie answers the young woman's parting question from the restroom, "Will you hate me now?"

After Julie's announcement, the mistress starts to laugh and claims she "knew it" — knew what Julie was about to do. Unsmiling and unresponsive, Julie thinks this is none too funny, even inappropriate. But Sandrine explains that "Patrice told me a lot about you," something Julie is again not happy to hear. What Patrice told Sandrine, however, was "that you are good. That you are good and generous."

As if Julie's gesture of radical forgiveness and charity were not enough, what follows next indicates that she has indeed returned to the life she once embraced. The penultimate scene in the film shows Julie, with her characteristic blue felt-tip pen, working feverishly on what is apparently Olivier's attempt to finish the "Unification Symphony." Once again she resorts, as her last instruction on the page indicates, to the "flute solo." Once again, the visual and musical elements tell as much or more than the script does. For the first time in the film, Julie has discarded her black sweater and wears a blue blouse, suggesting that she has at last come to embrace that color — or, more likely, that blue has embraced her. She phones Olivier, who answers as he sits slumped and quiet at the piano in his darkened apartment. Julie tells him that she has finished the symphony and that he can pick it up tomorrow or that very evening if he is not too tired. Olivier tells her that he won't be picking it up at all, for he will not pass off her work as his own.

"This music can be mine," he tells her, "a little heavy and awkward, but mine. Or yours, but everyone would have to know."

After a long deliberative pause, she concedes that he is right and hangs up the phone. She turns away from the camera and for a long time sits with her head down, immobile, her back to the camera, until she reaches for the phone and again calls Olivier. She asks if he still has the mattress on which they once made love. He confesses that he does, and Julie asks if he still loves her; he tells her, directly and simply, "I love you." Between long pauses Julie asks if he is alone, and then she finally tells him, "I'm coming."

Before she leaves her apartment, though, she turns again to the score spread out on her work table and searches for a particular part of the chorus where the music and words speak of the supremacy of love. This is clearly a part that Julie wishes to hear again, as if to reinforce her course of action in going to Olivier, because it is essentially a return to the fullness of life — though it could be full of peril and the risk of loss. And while the music continues to resound, as it will unbroken through the rest of the film, the camera pulls back again to see Julie at the table as she gathers and rolls up the many pages of score. The camera rises toward the ceiling to where the blue mobile of glass beads enters the top of the frame. Though the room is dark, the beads glow bright and luminous, lambent, as if lit from the inside. The camera continues to rise until it looks through the shower of beads as Julie walks from the room on her way to Olivier. There could hardly be a more apt symbol of Julie's progress in the film. Earlier scenes had shown her looking at the mobile, either in anger or curious longing; now, as the camera looks down on her through the beads, she is surrounded and engulfed by the blue beads, that emblem of love, and it is Kieslowski's suggestion that the blue of the beads and everything that color symbolizes for Julie and for this film about love has come to bless her world.

Next there is a close-up of Julie, her eyes closed, her face at first still but then, as the camera pulls back slightly, moving with pleasure within Olivier's embrace. It seems throughout, as the music roars over the scene, that the music itself is as much her lover as Olivier; indeed Julie seems to be in both "realms" at once. And the viewer cannot really be sure of the source of what is here her full re-submission to the power and beauty of life, of which music and love-making are apt symbols. From the beginning of the sequence, Julie is seen amid a luminous bluish haze (the scene is actually shot through a large illuminated fish tank); Kieslowski is attempting to render visually the psycho-spiritual realm of music and carnality. Paul Coates goes so far as to suggest that the imagery in the sequence suggests a new birth for Julie: "It is as if they are enclosed in a combination of uterine waters and star-strewn heavens. St. Paul's words suggest their cradling within the divine."[7]

Again the music is crucial, both in mood and its literal content. The emphatic chorus is displaced by an eloquent, majestic soprano, whose voice and urgent articulation of the verbal text dominates and envelops the action, especially as Kieslowski moves the camera through complete darkness until it rests on the hand of an awakening young man reaching to shut off an alarm. In the faint morning light, shot in blue sepia, sits the young man from the accident who tried to return Julie's cross. From the alarm clock his hand reaches to caress the cross, and as he looks to his left, the camera tracks right into darkness, arriving at Julie's mother, who is either sleeping or dead as a nurse approaches; then it glimpses the sex club and the face of Lucille. This panorama concludes, appropriately enough, with ultrasound images of the baby in Sandrine's womb. And then it goes back to Julie again: she seems to listen to the music as a solitary tear drops down her right cheek. We have a lengthy view of the woman who can now properly grieve her lost family from the midst of her return to life and love. Through this long sequence Julie's face is sad and serious; but it is without her former resolve to avoid fear and sorrow, which now clearly pass through her. Here again the music speaks as loudly as the image: as the camera moves to the image of Julie, the choral refrain beseeching love stops and is followed by a sober but jubilant mixture of strings and male chorus (without words), followed by a full orchestra that fades, appropriately, to a solitary flute joining with the slow plucking of lute strings. Rhythm and meter all but announce "alleluia" over and over through the whole length of the credits as they play over a blue screen.

Refrain

In *Blue*, Julie suffers utter calamity, losing just about everything she has cared for. In the aftermath, unable to bring herself to the suicide that would extinguish the devastating pain of her grief, she resolutely seeks

7. Coates, p. 49.

397

Kieslowski on DVD

At long last a significant part of Kieslowski's early work will be widely available for an English-speaking audience. In August, 2004, Kino released on DVD a number of early feature films that have only sporadically been available on VHS: *Car* (1976), *Camera Buff* (1979), *No End* (1985), *Blind Chance* (1987). Earlier in 2004, Kino released on DVD *A Short Film About Love* (1988) and *A Short Film About Killing* (1998), films that Kieslowski developed from episodes in his *Decalogue* series for Polish television. The first of Kieslowski's international features, *The Double Life of Veronique* (1991), is available on VHS but the visual quality of it is very poor.

Kieslowski's late masterworks were slow to arrive as well, but they are now available in splendid transfer in special edition sets on DVD. In Spring of 2003 Miramax released Kieslowski's *Three Colors: The Exclusive Collection*. All the films had previously been available on tape and laser disk, but this edition comes with a feast of supplementary materials. The quality of the visual transfer is especially important in viewing Kieslowski because he so precisely modulates lighting and color. The same is true with sound: the story of *Three Colors: Blue* loses a good deal of its force if the soundtrack is muted or if the reproduction equipment is not up to the task of delivering it in its full magnitude. That is also true, though to a lesser extent, for *Three Colors: Red,* the final work in the trilogy, where the rhapsodic music of Preisner delivers substantial commentary on the events described. The variety of supplemental materials in the boxed set remains pretty constant throughout the set. Each of the disks features brief, fascinating "cinema lessons," with Kieslowski seated at his editing machine explaining why he has made particular choices. Each also has a substantial informative interview and scene commentary with Kieslowski's leading actresses, all of whom were clearly thrilled to work with Kieslowski. Producer Martin Karmitz also comments on different challenges in the making of *Three Colors* on each of the disks.

to detach herself from any part of life, past and present, that might produce any significant emotion, whether joy or sadness. She discards, with notable vehemence, all palpable remnants of her past life, including her country estate, the furniture, and her husband's unfinished symphony, on which she has at least collaborated. She goes to live obscurely and

Two of the disks contain three short student films from Kieslowski's student years. And all the disks contain an assortment of additional material, such as clips of Kieslowski on location. Finally, for the specific task of understanding each of the films, the disks include useful discussions of different aspects of Kieslowski's life and films. These mostly feature members of the production team and critics Annette Insdorf and Geoff Andrew. While limited in various ways, these are nonetheless provocative and illuminating. The greatest disappointment in the special edition is the audio commentary by Insdorf, who throughout seems film-school officious and, very often, dead wrong. Especially notable is her clear hostility to any sort of religious interpretation, going out of her way in *Red*, for example, to deprecate religious interpretations of the films. At one point she argues that while Kieslowski was "spiritual" he was not "religious," a claim that is not only semantically confusing but breathtaking in its provincialism.

In 2000, Image Entertainment and Facets Video released, at last, a DVD edition of *Decalogue* (1988), a ten-part series on the Ten Commandments made for Polish television. The video release made the series widely available for the first time in the United States. Before this, those who wanted to see any of the films had to journey to Europe or art museums in major American cities. Better still, in August 2003, Facets released its own special edition that includes a short introduction to the film by the always astute Roger Ebert, three short documentaries on Kieslowski, an extended interview from the early 1990s with Kieslowski, and a short printed interview with Krzysztof Piesiewicz, Kieslowski's screenwriting collaborator.

Kieslowski fans will also want to see a charming hour-long documentary on Kieslowski, entitled *I'm So and So . . .* (1995), produced and directed by Kieslowski's own collaborators. The film includes commentary on his early life, on early and late films, and ruminations on life in general. Best of all, it offers an extended look at the personality behind a remarkably compelling film oeuvre.

anonymously in Paris, allowing herself only the most minimal, unthinking pleasures, such as sunlight on her face or an afternoon coffee. Mostly, she strives to keep life distant and herself numb. The major portion of the film describes the process by which Julie returns to or, more aptly, is hauled back into life — with all its risks, sorrows, and joys. That process is rather more than the simple "reintegration into a world of unrepressed emotions" that Geoff Andrew sees in *Blue*.[8] Rather, Kieslowski couches Julie's return in more extreme terms: it is redemption instigated by the mysterious press and prodding of divine love, and the wonder of *Blue* lies in the fresh, arresting means Kieslowski improvises to convey the nature and fullness of that love.

The chief means he uses, at once the theme and setting for the protagonist's journey, is the pervasive blue that seems to soak just about every frame of the film. On its most obvious symbolic level, it is one of the colors of the French flag, whose three colors provide the thematic and literal source for Kieslowski's "trois couleurs" trilogy. The blue in the flag denotes liberty, which is what Julie sets out to find, a freedom wholly independent of ties to humanity and the usual course of experience. Blue is also the color of grief and sadness, which is the dark emotional region where Julie finds herself after the deaths of her husband and daughter. But it is also clear that the color bears for Julie an entirely different meaning and is of immense personal significance, suggesting at the very least the full intense beauty of life itself. The most important rooms in Julie's country house, such as her daughter's and the living room, are painted an intense blue; and one of the few items she keeps from her pre-accident life, taken from Anna's room, is a mobile of blue glass beads. And finally, in those frequent moments when light plays on Julie's face, it most often has a faint bluish tint. The same blue light accompanies light of another kind, the remnants of an unfinished symphony, when these loudly burst into the calculated unthinking and unfeeling detachment that is Julie's new un-life. To call Kieslowski's use of blue "multivalent" hardly approaches the measure of his accomplishment in modulating the expressive potential of a single color.

Of greater narrative importance are those resounding musical visions, again soaked in blue, that come out of nowhere to envelop, transfix, and assail Julie with the momentousness and utter rapture of living itself, the first coming when she is still convalescing in the hospital. These musical intrusions (or visitations) recur throughout, some of them seeming new and fresh, as if coming out of nowhere, and others seeming to derive from her husband's (and her own) unfinished work. But she stalwartly resists their majestic allure and power, and she goes so far as to destroy what she believes to be the last copies of the work-in-progress. Julie's response to the music's substance and mood suggests

8. *The 'Three Colours' Trilogy* (London: British Film Institute, 1998), p. 33.

her conviction that fully basking in the lush beauties of life, specifically the people closest to her, risks insurmountable pain when these are torn away. Eventually it becomes clear that the music mediates the very voice of God, a voice to which Julie eventually responds by returning to life and assuming the task of completing the unfinished symphony and, by implication, the perilous task of living and giving.

Kieslowski's final means of telling this story — and equally decisive for Julie's recovery — are the events themselves, the odd coincidences (or providences) that the mature Kieslowski increasingly deploys in his films. A teenage boy tracks Julie down to return the cross necklace she lost in the accident; a neighbor befriends her; a mouse in her apartment has babies; a homeless man plays a flute; she discovers that her husband had a long-term mistress, who is pregnant from their affair; and finally, a copy of music she thought she had destroyed turns up. These events, along with the recurring music, prod Julie to realize that she cannot run from life; what the music claims about life is real and inescapable; and finally, that she cannot "kill" that music, no matter how much she wishes she could. All of that seems to resound loud and clear in the joyous choral culmination of the unfinished work that she and Olivier labor to complete. With its choral text, from 1 Corinthians 13, the symphony resolves its tensions in hymnic praise of the center and rapture of life's venture. Like the color blue, that center envelops Julie and beckons — even demands — that she love life and people even though she may suffer many sorrows, which are often the high cost of bestowing that love. As the closing montage suggests, love of life and God go everywhere, as omnipresent as the blue that pervades the film, especially to the joy and sorrow that ever mysteriously tangle up and wrestle in the midst of living.

Krzysztof Kieslowski Filmography

Three Colors: Red (1994)
Three Colors: White (1994)
Three Colors: Blue (1993)
The Double Life of Veronique (1991)
The Decalogue (1988)
No End (1985)
Blind Chance (1982)
Railway Station (1980)
Talking Heads (1980)
Camera Buff (1979)
Seven Women of Different Ages (1978)
Night Porter's Point of View (1978)
I Don't Know (1977)
The Scar (1976)
Hospital (1976)
Curriculum Vitae (1975)
X-Ray (1974)
Bricklayer (1973)
Between Wroclaw and Zielona Gora (1972)
The Principles of Safety and Hygiene in a Copper Mine (1972)
Refrain (1972)
Factory (1971)
Before the Rally (1971)
Workers (1971)
I Was a Soldier (1970)
From the City of Lodz (1968)
Concert of Wishes (1967)
The Tram (1966)
The Office (1966)

[Since *No End* (1985), Krzysztof Kieslowski has cowritten all of the films he has directed with Krzysztof Piesiewicz.]